Rediscovering the Triune God

Rediscovering the Triune God
The Trinity in Contemporary Theology

Stanley J. Grenz

Fortress Press
Minneapolis

REDISCOVERING THE TRIUNE GOD
The Trinity in Contemporary Theology

Cover design: Kevin van der Leek
Interior design: Beth Wright

ISBN 0-8006-3654-6

The paper used in this publication meets the minimum requirements of American National Standard for Information Sciences — Permanence of Paper for Printed Library Materials, ANSI Z329.48-1984.

Manufactured in the U.S.A.
11   10   09   08   6   7   8   9   10   11   12   13

To Phil C. Zylla, D. Th.
in gratitude for over twenty years of friendship

Contents

Preface

For as long as I can remember I have been a trinitarian. Like most Christians who have been raised in the church, at an early age I came to accept as self-evident that God is three persons yet one divine being.

On one particular occasion during my seminary days, I was able to put my well-grounded knowledge of the doctrine of the Trinity to what at that time seemed to be an especially gratifying use. I was busily writing a theology paper on this particular Christian teaching when the doorbell rang. The caller, whom I invited in for a chat, introduced himself as an elder in the local Kingdom Hall. As our ensuing conversation quickly, yet seemingly inevitably, turned to the doctrine of the Trinity, I was ready. With my engagement with the relevant biblical texts and the historical development of this doctrine fresh in my mind, I easily put the evangelist for modern Arianism on the defensive. Flushed with evangelical fervor, I relished watching as the hapless Jehovah's Witness apologist attempted for forty-five minutes to mark a retreat from my living room, only to have me counter each of his steps toward the door with yet one more question that further demonstrated the unreasonableness of his claims about the undifferentiated oneness of the God of the Bible and the ontological inferiority of Jesus Christ to the one God.

Although my upbringing and seminary training had provided me with a degree of deftness in defending belief in the doctrine of the Trinity, it was not until I encountered the work of Wolfhart Pannenberg—first as his graduate student and later during a sabbatical year in Munich—that I began to see the deeper importance of this Christian confession for the theological enterprise. In seminary, I had been schooled in what had become the classical Western approach that presents the one God before moving to the divine triunity. Pannenberg, in contrast, argued that because the God disclosed in Jesus Christ is Father, Son, and Holy Spirit, the explication of Christian doctrine must begin with the three persons of the Trinity and only then explore the divine unity. Moreover, in contrast to the systematic theologies that I had read in seminary, which relegated the doctrine of the Trinity to a single chapter within a larger framework, Pannenberg sought to show how the triunity of God ought to inform all systematic theology.

Ever since I gained this new perspective from my work with Pannenberg, I have thought about the possibility of composing a sketch of the renaissance of trinitarian theology in the twentieth century, in which story he was such an important participant. This interest was given a needed boost by a conversation with Michael West of Fortress Press that occurred during the meeting of the American Academy of Religion in November 1998. Michael and I met to celebrate the completion of a little volume, the *Fortress Introduction to Contemporary Theologies,* which I had written with my former university philosophy professor, Ed. L. Miller. Near the end of the conversation, Michael inquired as to what projects I was thinking about launching. When I offered a verbal precis of a potential work charting the story of the "rebirth" of the doctrine of the Trinity in theology, he responded with keen enthusiasm. My being named a Luce Fellow in Theology for the academic year 1999–2000 meant, however, that this particular idea would need to simmer on the back burner while I gave priority to the Luce project, which was subsequently published as *The Social God and the Relational Self* (2001). In a sense, this delay was fortuitous. *Rediscovering the Triune God* follows quite naturally after *The Social God.* In fact, it constitutes a book-length expansion of the first chapter of that earlier work, in which I sought to set the theological context for the discussion of the *imago dei* within the renewal of trinitarian theology. More importantly, however, *Rediscovering the Triune God* forms a kind of "prequel" to the projected second volume in the planned series of contributions to theology, *The Matrix of Christian Theology,* of which *The Social God* was the initial installment.

The writing of *Rediscovering the Triune God* straddles a time of transition—or, should I say, upheaval—in my own life and career. When I began work on the project in fall 2001, I was happily engaged in my teaching role at Carey Theological College and Regent College in Vancouver, British

Columbia. The following summer, I was invited to become Distinguished Professor of Theology at Baylor University and Truett Seminary. Although the new assignment commenced that fall, the actual relocation to Waco, Texas, was to occur in August 2003. In late February and early March 2003, however, a constellation of events emerged that led my wife, Edna, and me to conclude that we were not being released to leave Vancouver, even though this decision would likely require that I relinquish the position at Baylor. Rather than a move to Texas, therefore, August 2003 brought a relocation within the Vancouver area and a return to Carey Theological College, where I resumed my duties as Pioneer McDonald Professor of Theology.

One constant during the upheaval surrounding the writing of *Rediscovering the Triune God* was access to the resources of the Regent-Carey Library, which I was privileged to enjoy, as well as able help in tracking down literature and footnote references provided by my teaching assistant, Jay Smith, pastor of the First Baptist Church in Bellingham, Washington, who over the past several years has become a cherished friend. To Jay and to the library staff I owe a debt of gratitude.

I have known Phil Zylla since September 1981, when we both entered the North American Baptist Seminary (NABS) community in Sioux Falls, South Dakota—he as an MDiv student and I as a budding young faculty member. Phil and I quickly became not only intellectual conversation partners, but also racquetball buddies and good friends. This friendship has grown over the years since his graduation from NABS. In his capacity as principal of ACTS (Associated Canadian Theological Schools) Seminaries in Langley, British Columbia, Phil arranged to have me be the recipient of the hospitality of the school during what was to be the time of transition from Vancouver to Waco. To this end, the school named me Distinguished Visiting Professor of Theology for the academic year 2002–2003. Insofar as much of *Rediscovering the Triune God* was written during the months of my honorary appointment at ACTS, I wish to thank the faculty of the cooperating seminaries for the kindness they extended to me and especially Professor Archie Spencer for his keen interest in engaging with me regarding the content of this volume.

Even more significant than his spearheading the provision of a transitional academic "home" at ACTS, however, was Phil's significant input into my life, when Edna and I were seeking to make sense of what we perceived to be the signs from God that we were not to leave Vancouver. Several years ago, Phil had challenged me to appoint a "discernment committee" to assist me in the process of determining which of the manifold variety of ministry opportunities that come my way I should accept, a role that at my bidding he had accepted. Quite naturally, therefore, Phil was the one to whom I found myself repeatedly turning for advice and counsel in my struggle not only to discern but also to affirm the Spirit's leading with regard to the pending move to Texas. By being "there" for me, walking with me, and serving as my spiritual director during those tumultuous days, he proved himself to be "the friend who sticks closer than a brother" (Prov. 18:24).

In gratitude for his friendship over the years but especially during those tumultuous weeks in early 2003, therefore, I dedicate this book to Phil Zylla.

Introduction:
The Trinitarian Theological Story

"Trinitarian thinking has proved to be one of the best-kept secrets in theology during the last half of the twentieth century," declared Ted Peters in 1993.[1] When viewed from our vantage point this side of the dawn of the new millennium, his statement appears to run exactly opposite to what is now the actual situation. Far from being a secret, the doctrine of the Trinity has become one of the most widely acknowledged Christian teachings, exploring the triunity of God has developed into one of the most popular theological pursuits, and trinitarian theology has emerged as one of the most widely touted theological labels, encompassing the efforts of thinkers representing nearly every ecclesiological tradition and theological persuasion. So great is the interest in trinitarian thought that a scant five years after Peters voiced his remark, David Cunningham opined wistfully that trinitarian theological studies had become so prevalent that "the phenomenon begins to look not so much like a renaissance as a bandwagon." Cunningham then went so far as to assert, "Once threatened by its relative scarcity in modern theology, the doctrine of the Trinity now seems more likely to be obscured by an overabundance of theologians clustered around it."[2]

Whenever the story of theology in the last hundred years is told, the rediscovery of the doctrine of the Trinity that sprouted and then came to full bloom during the eight decades following the First World War must be given center stage, and the rebirth of trinitarian theology must be presented as one of the most far-reaching theological developments of the century. With the passing of the twentieth century and the dawning of the new millennium quickly receding in our communal rearview mirror, we now stand at an opportune vantage point to narrate the intriguing story of

1

the renaissance of trinitarian theology that appears to be running its course.

The century had barely passed its midpoint when provisional sketches began finding their way into print. The most important of these studies was the midcentury report, *In This Name: The Doctrine of the Trinity in Contemporary Theology*, penned by the Yale Divinity School professor Claude Welch. Convinced that theological developments from the publication of Karl Barth's *Römerbrief* to his own day had signaled "a renewed and growing interest in the trinitarian conception," Welch viewed 1952 as an appropriate occasion to review what had transpired. More specifically, he set himself to the task of bringing together "in a single focus the widely divergent lines of thought represented in the contemporary theological scene, ranging from complete indifference or outright opposition to the notion of the Trinity, to explicit efforts to restore this doctrine to the central place in the theological scheme."[3]

During the half century since the appearance of Welch's treatise the situation has changed dramatically. The theological hostility to the doctrine of the Trinity that he found so prevalent in 1952 has waned, even as the desire to give it its due, which was only in its nascent phase in Welch's day, has flourished. Moreover, the discussion of the place and character of trinitarian theology, which already in the patristic era was international or ecumenical in scope, has increasingly given due regard to the awareness that the church finds itself in a thoroughly pluralistic context.[4] This realization has opened the door to a globalization of the discussion, as voices from Africa[5] and Asia[6] have joined with those from Europe and the Americas. These conversation partners have brought to the table ideas and models for understanding the divine triunity that draw from a communitarian focus that has largely disappeared from modern Western society but has remained a central dimension of cultures elsewhere in the world. Other scholars are pushing the "global" character of the discussion in a quite different direction. They seek to bring overlooked figures from the past into the contemporary conversation, believing that, both when they soar and when they stumble, past theological proposals can contribute to the contemporary reconstruction of trinitarian thought, to paraphrase Amy Plantinga Pauw's conclusion regarding the potential contribution of Jonathan Edwards.[7]

The situation today differs from that of Welch's day in another manner as well. By the end of the twentieth century, the interest in proposing new ways of conceiving of the triunity of God, which was so much a part of the situation in 1952, had largely lost its momentum. With the coming of the new millennium, many theologians began turning away from the task of trinitarian doctrinal formulation. Believing with Robert Jenson that the doctrine of the Trinity "is not a separate puzzle to be solved but the framework within which all theology's puzzles are to be solved,"[8] these thinkers launched into explorations as to how the insights of the renaissance of trinitarian thought might be applied to other theological topics and issues. For some, this has taken the form of drawing the implications of trinitarian theology into other foci of Christian doctrine, such as anthropology,[9] ecclesiology,[10] and the doctrine of creation.[11] Others are attempting to push trinitarian thinking into the realm of church practice,[12] whether with the hope of finding a way of dealing with particular issues, as is evident in the recent discussions among evangelicals of the implications of the doctrine of the Trinity for the role of women in the family and the church,[13] or with the intent of mining from the doctrine of the Trinity a crucial impulse for pastoral practice more generally.[14]

The task of sketching all the variegated dimensions of the resurgence in trinitarian thought surpasses what can be adequately accomplished within the confines of any single book. Therefore, what follows attempts a much more modest objective. My goal is to narrate the story of the renewed interest in the doctrine of the Trinity as it developed within the main trajectory of Christian theology during the eighty years from the publication of Barth's *Epistle to the Romans*, which many observers (including Welch) credit with providing the initial impetus for this theological renaissance, to the appearance of T. F. Torrance's magnum opus, *The Christian Doctrine of God*, which might be considered to be the last comprehensive trinitarian theological offering of the century.

To accomplish this task, I focus on a short list of eleven theologians who in my estimation have proven to be the most significant contributors to the renewal of trinitarian thought. Although these eleven are by no means the only voices in the discussion, each of them has made a lasting contribution to the flow of the conversation; each has produced a significant milestone in the scholarly treatment of the doctrine of the Trinity that has affected the current climate of trinitarian thought. Taken together these theologians have set the tone for the contemporary understanding of doctrine of the Trinity as a whole. In short, the figures discussed in the following chapters have emerged as not only representatives of but also trendsetters within the central current of trinitarian thinking in the twentieth century. Of course, a host of other thinkers have offered their own unique perspectives to the larger whole. Yet the other voices in the conversation generally find themselves repeatedly and routinely drawing from the work of one or several of the eleven theological trendsetters whose work is outlined in these pages.

The sketches of the thought of the theologians that comprise this study follow a similar, two-part pattern. Each section begins with a presentation of the theologian's trinitarian proposal. This, in turn, leads into a shorter summary of the critical response that the proposal evoked or the reception that it has enjoyed.

Although the book presents the work of eleven thinkers, it is not divided into eleven chapters. Hence, in what follows, I do not simply recount the work of eleven independent thinkers. Rather, to facilitate the goal of telling the story of the rediscovery of trinitarian theology, the volume is ordered topically. The narrative unfolds in four major chapters, each of which delineates a central theme of the story by grouping together the leading theologians who both contributed to and comprise variations on that particular theme. Indeed, despite the complexity of trinitarian studies in the twentieth century and the circuitous route that the rediscovery of the doctrine of the Trinity has followed, the story of the trinitarian renaissance can be told by means of a surprisingly short list of central themes.

Rather than launching directly into the post–World War I narrative, however, I first sketch the background to the story by providing an initial chapter that seeks to put the twentieth-century renaissance of trinitarian theology within the context of the larger story of which it is one installment. As the chapter title, "The Eclipse of Trinitarian Theology," indicates, I present this previous history, especially in the West, as leading to an unceremonious loss of interest in the doctrine of the Trinity, before sketching the role of Friedrich Schleiermacher as a harbinger of the rebirth of trinitarian theology and then summarizing G. W. F. Hegel's even more important context-determining contribution to the rediscovery of the doctrine that came to the fore in the twentieth century.

The main storyline begins in chapter 2 with the theme reflected in the chapter title: "Restoring the Trinitarian Center." Here I survey the two great German Karls—Karl Barth and Karl Rahner—who more than any other thinkers both launched the renewal and set the parameters for the trinitarian theology that would arise in the twentieth century. Chapter 3, "The Trinity as the Fullness of Divine History," highlights a second theme, one that was articulated above all by three thinkers—two Germans, Jürgen Moltmann and Wolfhart Pannenberg, and one American, Robert Jenson. These three explored the possibility that the divine self-disclosure and hence the identity of the triune God might be viewed as arising out of the interplay of the three trinitarian members within the flow of history, viewed as the story of God, rather than in the event of the divine self-disclosure in the Word of God, as Barth and Rahner had proposed. The nascent social trinitarianism and relational ontology evident in the work of the "theologians of history" became more explicit in the explorations of three other significant thinkers, Leonardo Boff, John Zizioulas, and Catherine Mowry LaCugna. Exploration of this theme is the focus of chapter 4, "The Triumph of Relationality." The story concludes by highlighting a final theme that became increasingly prevalent as the century drew to a close, namely, the renewed concern that the elevation of the three trinitarian persons and devising of an ontology of relationality not be allowed to overshadow the importance of the acknowledgment that God is eternally triune apart from the interplay of the three persons in history. To this end, I delineate under the title "The Return of the Immanent Trinity" the contributions of three thinkers who to varying degrees upheld the integrity of the eternal God who remains triune even apart from the ebb and flow of salvation history: Elizabeth Johnson, Hans Urs von Balthasar, and Thomas F. Torrance.

In his masterful treatment of the development of trinitarian theology in Christian history, published at the three-quarter mark of the twentieth century, Edmund Fortman concluded, "The doctrine of the Triune God has had an amazing history."[15] Our perspective as those who stand on this side of the dawning of the new millennium allows us to see that at no period in the history of Christian theology has the story been more amazing than during the twentieth century. Indeed, the eight decades from Barth's first book to Torrance's magnum opus witnessed a truly remarkable, monumental, and far-reaching development—the rediscovery of the triune God.

1

The Eclipse of Trinitarian Theology

In 1972, John P. Whalen and Jaroslav Pelikan bemoaned the deplorable state of Christian theology, a dire situation they found evidenced above all by the unfortunate status of the doctrine of the Trinity. "This monumental dogma," they declared, "seems to many even within the Church to be a museum piece, with little or no relevance to the crucial problems of contemporary life and thought."[1] In substantiating their case, Whalen and Pelikan contrasted the modern epoch with the patristic era, when debates about the status of and relationships among Father, Son, and Spirit were deemed crucial to the theological enterprise. According to Whalen and Pelikan, the formulation of the doctrine of the Trinity was "the most important theological achievement of the first five centuries of the Church."[2]

Even as Whalen and Pelikan were bemoaning the deplorable theological amnesia that in their estimation forms a central characteristic of the modern church, a revolution was quietly transpiring in many theological circles. A renaissance was underway in the very trinitarian theology that these two distinguished church historians found so lacking throughout much of the modern era. The goal of the following paragraphs is to set the stage for the exploration of this renaissance. To this end, I begin by sketching the historical movement that led initially toward, but then away from, the doctrine of the Trinity as the central enterprise of theology. I then turn attention to the manner in which two thinkers in the nineteenth century provided the immediate impetus for the renewal of trinitarian thought that emerged as perhaps the greatest contribution of theology in the twentieth century.

6

The Triumph and Defeat of Speculative Trinitarianism

Since Erasmus's discovery that 1 John 5:7 was a spurious addition to the biblical text, the overwhelming majority of theologians has concluded that the writers of scripture nowhere delineate a formal doctrine of the Trinity. Rather than arising out of the explicit teaching of the Bible, the understanding of God as triune emerged from what Edmund J. Fortman characterizes as "three centuries of gradual assimilation of the Biblical witness to God."[3] Yet once it came to full flower in the fourth century, the doctrine of the Trinity retained its status as forming the center of the orthodox doctrine of God, even in the face of recurring trials, until it was dethroned from this lofty position by impulses that stirred in the late Middle Ages and burst forth fully in the Enlightenment.

The Centrality of the Doctrine of the Trinity in Theological History

The history of the development of the doctrine of the Trinity in the patristic era has been recounted repeatedly. Therefore, it needs only a brief rehearsing here.

The crafting of the doctrine. The initial impetus in the direction of what became the church's teaching about God as triune was spawned by the theological puzzle posed by the early church's confession of the lordship of Jesus and the experience of the indwelling Holy Spirit, both of which developments emerged within the context of the nonnegotiable commitment to the one God of the Old Testament that the early believers inherited from Israel. The quest to bring these three strands together arose somewhat indirectly, following on the heels of two crucial theological decisions forged in the crucible of the Arian controversy.

The first dispute—regarding the relationship of Jesus to God—was ignited by Arius's attempt to protect the absolute uniqueness and transcendence of God by transposing into the temporal realm Origen's concept of the Father's generation (or begetting) of the Son as a movement within the divine life. In so doing, Arius suggested that the distinctions among the three persons are external to God, and hence that in the eternal divine nature God is one and in no way three.[4] At the First Ecumenical Council at Nicea in 325, the church unequivocally affirmed the full deity of Christ, a position summarized in the council's assertion that the Son is "begotten of the Father, of the substance of the Father, begotten not made, of one substance with the Father."[5] In this manner, the council set the christological foundation for the subsequent development of the doctrine of the Trinity.

A second theological debate, which emerged in the aftermath of Nicea, provided the corresponding pneumatological basis for the church's trinitarianism. This dispute also had its roots in Arius's teaching. Just as Arius had asserted that the Son was the first creature of the Father, his followers—including Macedonius, the bishop of Constantinople[6] for whom the controversy is often named—theorized that the Holy Spirit was the first creature of the Son.[7] The dispute reached its climax in 381, when the Council of Constantinople sided against the pneumatological Arians and, in a statement popularly known as the Nicene Creed, announced that the Holy Spirit is to be "worshiped and glorified together with the Father and the Son."[8]

The conciliar decisions affirmed the full deity of the Son and the Spirit along with the Father and thereby set the parameters for the future development of Christian teaching about God. Nevertheless, these documents did not stipulate *how* the three persons comprise one God. The task of devising a manner of talking about the triune God fell to the Cappadocian fathers—Basil, Gregory of Nyssa, and Gregory of Nazianzus—whose efforts birthed what became the classic formulation of the doctrine of the Trinity.[9] Their search for a middle ground between the error of positing three gods (tritheism) and the equally suspect idea that the three persons are merely modes of the revelation of the one God (Sabellianism),[10] led the Cappadocians to the ingenious idea that God is one *ousia* (being) but three *hypostases* (realities). Although the Cappadocian formulation provided the church with a fixed reference point, it did not bring the discussions of the doctrine of the Trinity to an end. Instead, it opened the door for an ensuing debate as to the exact way of construing the threeness and oneness of God, a debate that eventually led to a theological parting of ways between the Eastern and Western churches.

The breach between East and West. The theologians of the East sought to draw out the implications of the distinction posited by the Cappadocians between the words *ousia* and *hypostasis,* as well as their use of the latter term to refer to the concrete particularity of Father, Son, and Spirit.[11] As a result, Eastern thinkers tended to focus their gaze on the three members of the Trinity, rather than on the divine unity.[12] Moreover, they emphasized the role of the Father as the source of deity as well as the one from whom the Son is generated and from whom the Spirit proceeds in eternal movement. Finally, the Eastern theologians highlighted the specific operations of each of the trinitarian persons in the divine acts of creation, reconciliation, and consummation.

The linguistic, cultural, and theological temperaments that separated East and West[13] steered Western theologians toward a somewhat different path. Because their first language was Latin, they were not always fully cognizant of the nuances of the Greek linguistic formulations of their Eastern colleagues. Instead, they drew on Tertullian's Latin formula *tres personae, una substantia.* This way of speaking about the triune God served to complicate the discussion with Eastern theologians, because *substantia* was the usual Latin translation of *hypostasis*, not *ousia.* Furthermore, the Latin formulation disposed Western theologians to emphasize the one divine essence or substance, rather than the plurality or threeness of persons characteristic of the East, and to emphasize the joint working of the three, as the one God, in creation and salvation.

The classic statement of the Western understanding of the Trinity came in Augustine's influential work *De Trinitate.* Because humans are created in the image of God, Augustine declared, the human person displays "vestiges" of the Trinity and hence provides analogies of God's triunity.[14] In Augustine's estimation, the concept of love provides the key to understanding the Trinity. The human mind knows love in itself, he argued, and as a consequence knows God, for God is love. This leads to a knowledge of God's triunity, in that love implies a Trinity consisting of "he that loves, and that which is loved, and love."[15] Actually, Augustine offered a series of analogies, based on humans as the *imago dei,* that drew an understanding of the Trinity from the human self. Although he proposed that the closest of these is the mind that remembers, knows, and loves God,[16] the analogy that was most influential in later Western theology was the triad of *being, knowing,* and *willing,*[17] which in the depictions of subsequent thinkers often took the form of the mind, its self-knowledge, and its self-love.

Augustine's psychological analogy of the Trinity, with its focus on the oneness of God in contrast to the Eastern emphasis on the divine threeness and with its starting point in the divine essence revealed in the human psyche rather than the saving act of God in Christ, set the stage for the trinitarian theologizing prominent among subsequent Western theologians.[18] Furthermore, it sparked a heated controversy between the East and the West. In *De Trinitate*, Augustine went beyond the statement about the Holy Spirit that had been included in the creed devised at Constantinople. Although the creed affirmed that the Spirit is to be worshiped and glorified together with the Father and the Son, it declared simply that the Spirit proceeds from the Father.[19] Augustine, in contrast, taught that the Holy Spirit proceeds from the Son as well.[20]

Two centuries later, a regional Spanish synod (the third Council of Toledo in 589) incorporated Augustine's view into the Latin translation of the ancient creed, adding the word *filioque* ("and from the Son") to the description of the Spirit's procession.[21] Then in 809, a synod in Aachen, Germany, adopted the altered version as the official creed for the newly constituted Holy Roman Empire.[22] These developments eventually evoked a vigorous reaction from the Eastern church. In 867, the patriarch of Constantinople, Photius, leveled the charge of heresy against the West for assuming the prerogative of tampering with an ecumenical creed.[23] The two positions subsequently solidified, the East rejecting what to them was an unwarranted inclusion into the creed and the West defending the move. In the end, the differing outlooks toward the triune God that had separated East and West for centuries contributed to a theological parting of ways that climaxed in the Great Schism (1054), which divided Christendom into Orthodox and Roman Catholic communions.

The Trinity in the medieval West. The *filioque* controversy marked the last great ecumenical debate regarding the doctrine of the Trinity. After the schism of the eleventh century, other theological issues came to the fore, although the ecclesiastical breach did not terminate discussions of the doctrine, especially in the medieval West. Yet rather than offering new proposals as to how the doctrine might be understood, thinkers in the High Middle Ages tended to direct their efforts toward the task of rounding out the Augustinian legacy by responding to the intellectual questions that they sensed had been left unanswered by the great church father.[24] To this end, they focused their attention on what in the twentieth century came to be designated the "immanent Trinity." The medieval theorists were, in the words of John Loeschen, "caught up in the logical intricacies of understanding a doctrine they all believed: that God was at once One in the basic sense of the term, and at the same time Three in an equally profound sense of the term."[25]

Roger Olson and Christopher Hall offer this appraisal of the medieval discussion: "Overall and in general the high medieval era in Europe was not a time of great creativity with regard to trinitarian reflection, but it was a time when certain Christian thinkers returned to rigorous examination and construction of the doctrine of the Trinity using the tools of divine revelation and human reason."[26] Actually, the theological thinking of the Middle Ages was much more creative than contemporary Protestant commentators generally suggest. The creativity of the era is evidenced above all in the work of two theologians, Richard of St. Victor and Thomas Aquinas.[27]

In his treatise *De Trinitate,* the twelfth-century thinker Richard of St. Victor provided what has been hailed as one of the most learned expositions of the doctrine of the Trinity in the Middle Ages.[28] Like other medieval theologians, he grappled with the interface of faith and reason. Hence his goal in *De Trinitate* was to provide "necessary reasons" for, and lines of reasoning that explicate, what faith declares about God's triunity.[29]

Of particular interest is Richard's discussion of the necessary plurality of persons in the Godhead. To develop a rational demonstration of this aspect of Christian belief, Richard drew from, but then thoroughly recast, the analogy from love found in Augustine's work. The result was an example of what has come to be denoted as a "social" understanding of God as triune.[30] Richard's main line of reasoning begins with the idea of supreme goodness, which, he argued, must involve love. Because self-love cannot be true love, supreme love requires another, equal to the lover, who is the recipient of that love. Furthermore, because supreme love is received as well as given, it must be a shared love, in which each person loves and is loved by the other. Finally, because supreme love must desire that the love it experiences through giving and receiving be one that is shared with another, it is not merely mutual love between two but is a love that is fully present among three and only three.[31]

Richard is often hailed as the one medieval theologian who departed radically from Augustine's psychological approach by looking instead to persons-in-relation for the key to understanding the triune nature of God.[32] In keeping with this appraisal of Richard's contribution, Fortman declares that as a result of his work, "there will be two great trinitarian theories in the medieval theological world, the Augustinian that St. Thomas will systematize, and the theory of Richard of St. Victor, whose principal representative will be St. Bonaventure."[33]

Dwarfing both Richard and Bonaventure in importance as the leading theologian of the Middle Ages is, of course, Thomas Aquinas, whom

Fortman honors for producing "the finest metaphysical synthesis of trinitarian doctrine that had thus far appeared in West or East."[34] Olson and Hall characterize Aquinas's work on the Trinity as a "subtle, creative synthesis of the traditional Augustinian psychological model and the communal-social model of Richard."[35] Yet Aquinas expressed reservations about Richard's theological approach, insofar as it appeared to him to be built upon the erroneous assumption that God's triunity can be known by natural reason rather than solely through revelation.[36] Despite these misgivings, Aquinas's proposal also carried the burden of offering a reasoned engagement with the church's teaching, including the traditional understanding of God as triune.

The starting point for Aquinas's conception of the Trinity is the supposedly biblically based, ecclesiastical teaching regarding a double movement in God consisting of the generation of the Son and the procession of the Spirit. Aquinas set forth this double movement as the dynamic within a divine intellectual essence involving the acts of understanding and willing, which he saw as corresponding to the procession of the Word and of love.[37] In the first process, the divine intellect produces an image of itself that is consubstantial and coequal with itself; consequently, this process entails what Catherine Mowry LaCugna characterizes as a "likeness-producing act" and corresponds to the generation of the Son. In the second process, the divine will is directed toward the image conceived by the intellect resulting in love, which is likewise consubstantial and coequal with the other two; this "impulse-producing act," to cite LaCugna's characterization, corresponds to the breathing of the Spirit. Aquinas then asserted that these two processions produce four relations, which are constitutive of God's being in that they give rise to three persons. Thus the procession of the Word or "generation" entails the relations of fatherhood and sonship, leading to the first two persons of Father (the one who begets) and Son (the one who is begotten). The procession of love, in turn, entails the relations of spiration and procession, leading to the third person, the Holy Spirit (the one who is spirated by the other two, who are constituted by their relation to each other).[38]

The Waning of the Centrality of the Doctrine of the Trinity

In the eyes of many historians, Aquinas's proposal is the high water mark of reflection on the doctrine of the Trinity and hence of trinitarian theology as a whole. Typical of such appraisals is Fortman's declaration regarding Aquinas's significance as a theological innovator: "For the first time in trinitarian history there is a clear-cut differentiation of divine generation and divine procession in terms of the intimate life of the Triune God."[39]

Regardless of the extent to which we might want to laud Aquinas's greatness as a theological mind, his proposal not only stood at the apex of medieval trinitarian theology, but it also became the precursor of its demise. Some of his twentieth-century critics offered the controversial suggestion[40] that Aquinas contributed to the decline of trinitarian theology, insofar as his monumental theological treatise, the *Summa Theologica*, began with the doctrine of the one God and only later developed an understanding of God as triune.[41] Also fashionable in theological circles has been the equally contested claim[42] that the root of the decline of trinitarian theology predates Aquinas's approach to systematic theology by several centuries, for it is lodged in the entire Western model of the Trinity spawned by Augustine's elevation of the oneness of God as the basis for delineating the divine triunity. John Cobb provides a typical appraisal of the outworking of the Augustinian theological move and its inherent inferiority to its Eastern rival: "We must acknowledge that the doctrine of the trinity in the East is an integral part of its total theological understanding. The same cannot be said for the Western formulation stemming chiefly from Augustine. Here, the doctrine is an unneeded appendage to theology."[43] More recently, some theological historians have offered the even more radical conclusion that both the Eastern and the Western traditions must shoulder the blame for laying the foundation for the eventual demise of the doctrine.[44]

Whatever the relationship of the dissolution of trinitarian theology to the specific proposals voiced by Augustine and Aquinas—or by the whole college of patristic and medieval church theologians for that matter—the central role that the doctrine of the Trinity played in the theological agenda of the scholastics in the Middle Ages did, ironically, precipitate its decline. In part, this was due to the fact that despite its rich theoretical achievements, medieval trinitarian thought was simply too complex to relate easily to popular piety or religious experience.

The Reformation: from aversion to denial. Already in the Middle Ages, the theological subtleties that the scholastics introduced into the church's doctrine of the Trinity triggered what Robert S. Franks describes as an "aversion of simple piety."[45] For example, even though Aquinas's trinitarian thought informed many of the writings of Thomas à Kempis, in his widely read devotional handbook, *The Imitation of Christ,* the latter Thomas asked, "What will it avail thee to argue profoundly of the Trinity, if thou be void of humility, and are thereby displeasing to the Trinity?"[46]

Yet it was in the Reformation that the revolt against scholastic theology in the name of Christian piety first became pronounced. Such sentiments were clearly evident in some of Philipp Melanchthon's musings. On the basis of the dictum, "To know Christ is to know his benefits, not as the Schoolmen teach, to know His natures and the modes of His incarnation," Melanchthon asserted, "There is no reason why we should spend much labour over those supreme topics of God, His Unity and Trinity, the mysteries of creation and the modes of the Incarnation. I ask you what the scholastic theologians have achieved in so many ages by occupying themselves with these questions alone?"[47] In this seemingly wholesale dismissal of the medieval fixation on the immanent Trinity (which he subsequently revised to some degree), Melanchthon was simply following Martin Luther. One of the great Reformer's guiding principles was to speak of God primarily—if not exclusively—in relationship to us or in salvation history, that is, in God's *operationes ad extram.*[48]

In addition to the revulsion to speculation in the name of piety and hence in keeping with a focus on the economic Trinity, the decline of trinitarian theology in the Reformation was simply the result of a neglect necessitated by the sense of crisis in the midst of which the Reformers carried out their theological endeavors. They had more pressing theological issues to handle, such as the understanding of salvation, which was, in turn, related to the nature of authority in the church. In the estimation of Luther and others, the gospel itself was under attack, and this threat was not related to issues connected to the church's doctrine of the Trinity. In response to the speculative theology that had characterized medieval scholasticism, the Reformers seemed quite content to affirm the trinitarianism embodied in the ancient creeds, simply because they believed that the scriptures taught this doctrine. In recent years, the early Protestants have been criticized for failing to relate the doctrine of the Trinity effectively to the central principles of the Reformation.[49] Although this charge may have some basis, it must be noted that Luther's emphasis on God-for-us was in keeping with the central theme of his articulated theology, justification by faith.[50]

The demotion of the doctrine of the Trinity prepared the way not only for the evacuation of trinitarian theology from the center of church life but also for its eventual outright denial. The methodological foundation for such denial was laid, albeit inadvertently, by the biblicism of the Reformers themselves, especially Luther. The Reformers' adherence to the doctrine of the Trinity rested ultimately on their interpretation of the Bible and only secondarily upon church creeds or human reason. Although the major Protestant thinkers went on record in claiming that the ancient creeds had encapsulated the message of scripture regarding God's triunity, they opened the way for others to differ with them on the matter. Indeed, in the wake of the Reformation, a small but influential chorus arose that claimed that the doctrine of the Trinity is not the teaching of the Bible or is contrary to reason.

The outright denial of the church's teaching regarding the triune nature of God emerged already within the sixteenth century. Their application of the Reformation principle of *sola scriptura* led some thinkers to conclude that the ecclesiastical doctrine of the Trinity constituted a departure from the testimony of the biblical writings.

Perhaps the best known of the sixteenth-century antitrinitarians is Faustus Socinus. Socinus accepted scripture as the supreme authority in matters of faith but insisted that it be interpreted in accordance with reason and not in the context of the traditional creeds. On this basis, he argued that God was one in both essence and person. In his *Racovian Catechism*, which Fortman sees as "the best presentation of the Socinian rejection of the Trinity," Socinus reasons that if the divine essence is one in number, there cannot "be several divine persons in it, since a person is nothing else than an intelligent, indivisible essence."[51] Thus, although orthodox theology had always carefully distinguished between essence and person, Socinus equated the two and as a consequence asserted that God is a single person. The Socinian understanding later provided an important aspect of the theological basis for Unitarianism in England and America.

The Enlightenment: denial in the name of reason. In the Enlightenment, an even more thoroughgoing rejection of the doctrine of the Trinity arose from the elevation of reason as the final arbiter of truth, indicative of the emerging Age of Reason. Several thinkers, especially in late-seventeenth-century Britain, did harness the power of reason in defense of the orthodox doctrine, offering rational vindications of the Christian teaching regarding God's triunity.[52] Nevertheless, the spirit of the Enlightenment entailed a deep suspicion of ecclesiastical dogmas, including the doctrine of the Trinity, which ultimately could be established only by appeal to "external" authorities such as scripture or church tradition.

Their commitment to the centrality of reason in the human epistemological quest led many thinkers in the Age of Reason to embrace only those theological assertions that reason was able to discover and substantiate. Not only did Enlightenment thinkers elevate reason to being the instrument of religious thought, for some it comprised the very content of religion, insofar as it functioned as the criterion by means of which all theological assertions were to be judged.[53] At best, this approach netted only a bare minimum of theological postulates—above all, the existence of God, human freedom, and the immortality of the soul—that formed the heart of the new religion of reason, replacing the supposedly revealed religions associated with what was now deemed as humankind's superstitious, unenlightened past.

The elevation of reason attained its zenith but also suffered its demise in the work of Immanuel Kant.[54] By means of his "Copernican revolution" in philosophy, that is, the assertion that "scientific" knowledge is limited to the realm of experience shaped by the rational structures of the mind, Kant effectively closed the door to Enlightenment claims to knowledge of God through pure reason. Yet, in the manner that he reformulated and deepened the rejection of external authority characteristic of the Age of Reason, Kant also made traditional trinitarian discourse not only illegitimate but also superfluous. For all practical purposes, the doctrine of the Trinity had been banished from the theological realm. The upshot of the work of the Enlightenment and Kant was to render the doctrine little more than a religious ornament.

The Stirring of Interest in Trinitarian Theology

Kant's philosophical innovations set the stage for the theological programs of the nineteenth century. Even conservative Protestant theologians, who largely eschewed Kant's approach, were not untouched by his

influence. Although, in contrast to Kant, they affirmed the classical orthodox doctrine of the Trinity on the basis of scripture or tradition, conserv-
atives gave little actual place to the doctrine in their systematic
theologies.[55] Rather, they increasingly came to view God's triunity as a
mystery to be confessed but not as the center of Christian theology and
hence not as providing content and structure to the whole theological
enterprise. If a renewed interest in trinitarian theology was to arise, it
would need to emerge from other circles.

The Trinity as the "Coping Stone" of Christian Doctrine: Friedrich Schleiermacher

That Friedrich Schleiermacher (1768–1834) holds a prominent place in
the theology hall of fame (or infamy, in the opinion of some) is undis-
puted. He has been dubbed a "Prince of the Church,"[56] a "giant of Christian theology,"[57] "the most influential thinker since Calvin,"[58] "the father
of modern theology,"[59] and even "the founder of modern religious and
theological thought."[60]

The showering of accolades upon Schleiermacher continues unabated.
Nevertheless, it has become common parlance under the far-reaching
shadow of the scathing critiques by Karl Barth and Emil Brunner to
cite—among other theological "sins"—Schleiermacher's placement of the
doctrine of the Trinity at the end of his monumental *The Christian Faith*
as evidence of at best a lukewarm stance toward the classical orthodox
teaching.[61] For his part, Barth mused in a parenthetical note in his Göttingen lectures of 1923–1924 that he was not sure whether Schleiermacher's use of the doctrine of the Trinity "to crown the whole development
of the consciousness of grace" was "an instance of perplexity, genius, or
extreme systematizing power."[62] Similarly, Claude Welch censured
Schleiermacher for reducing the Trinity "to a doctrine of second rank."[63]
In his sympathetic characterization of Welch's critique, Ted Peters
explains:

> If we follow Schleiermacher too far and affirm with him that the doc-
> trine of the Trinity does not stand on a par with primary symbols
> such as God as Creator, the divinity of Christ, or the deity of the
> Spirit, then it is quite understandable why the Trinity becomes
> demoted to secondary importance. The assumption that the doctrine

is a synthesis of otherwise random convictions regarding a more fundamental monotheism renders the Trinity systematically superfluous. The triune nature of God is removed from the center of our faith affirmations.[64]

Several commentators, however, have argued recently that dismissals of Schleiermacher often come at the expense of a fair reading and clear grasp of the profundity of his theological perspective.[65] This revised perspective is long overdue. To reject wholesale Schleiermacher's treatment of the doctrine of the Trinity is to risk overlooking the crucial role he played not only in renewal of theology in the nineteenth century, but, more importantly, in the rekindling of interest in trinitarian theology in the twentieth.[66]

The move to intuition. Schleiermacher's outlook toward the doctrine of the Trinity must be placed within the overarching theological method that emerged out of his desire, which he shared with several other early-nineteenth-century theologians, to move beyond the post-Enlightenment impasse by inquiring as to the essence of religion and the special place religion holds in human life. In his widely hailed *On Religion: Speeches to Its Cultured Despisers* (1799), Schleiermacher set out to explicate the true nature of religion by taking his cue from both his own heritage in pietism and the new cultural phenomenon of Romanticism.[67] In keeping with these impulses, he asserted that the essence of religion does not lie primarily or immediately in such matters as rational proofs for the existence of God, supernaturally revealed dogmas, or ecclesiastical rituals. Rather, religion—which, according to Terrence Tice's description of Schleiermacher's stance, is a "fundamental, distinct, and integrative element of human life and culture"[68]—entails perceiving the integral relationship of God to the world but especially to humankind.[69] This perception, Schleiermacher claimed, comes about through "feeling."

Rather than a conscious sensation connected to some particular aspect of one's experience of the world, as the typical English translation suggests, in Schleiermacher's rendition "feeling" *(Gefühl)* connotes a deep awareness lying on the prereflective plane of consciousness beneath and before explicit thought or sensation. This perception consists of "the immediate consciousness of the universal being of all finite things in and through the infinite, of all temporal things in and through the eternal,"[70] or, to cite his well-known subsequent formulation, the sense of "absolute dependence."[71] It is, according to Paul Tillich's helpful characterization, "the impact of the universe upon us in the depths of our being which transcends subject and object."[72] This feeling, which Schleiermacher connected to "piety," is the primal act of the human spirit (albeit an act of receptivity),[73] and hence it is both fundamental to, and universal in, human experience. Because feeling cannot be reduced to some other aspect of human nature, such as reason or conscience, which give rise to science and morality,[74] religion—which is the outworking of feeling—is essential to a full understanding of humanness.

In this Romantic emphasis on the intuitive dimension of human existence in the form of a fundamental human feeling, Schleiermacher initially found the clue to reconstructing theology. He asserted that experience (that is, the feeling of absolute dependence), rather than supposedly revealed or ecclesiastical pronouncements about God, was theology's primary source. Hence, in his *Speeches,* he declared that true religion is "an immediate relation to the living God, as distinct from submission to doctrinal or credal propositions about God."[75] In the broadest and most general sense, therefore, theology is simply reflection on human experience of God, that is, on religion or piety. Because piety always expresses itself in some concrete form of religious life in and through some religious community, that is, because all religion takes some "positive" form,[76] reflection on religion is always reflection on a particular form of religious expression. Consequently, *Christian* theology is connected to the particularly Christian conception of piety. To cite Schleiermacher's own words, "Christian doctrines are accounts of the Christian religious affections set forth in speech."[77]

The reconstruction of the doctrine of God. Martin Redeker reflected the opinion of many when he wrote, "It has justly been said . . . that, aside from Calvin's *Institutes,* there has been no system in Protestant theology which, *qua* system, has attained the status of Schleiermacher's *The Christian Faith.*"[78] In his magnum opus originally published in 1821–1822 and revised in 1830–1831, Schleiermacher carried out the systematic-theological program that drew from the conception of religion set forth in his *Speeches.*

According to Schleiermacher, the uniqueness of Christianity lies in the Christian experience of God-consciousness and self-consciousness as formed and fulfilled in and through the salvation that comes in Jesus

Christ: "the distinctive essence of Christianity consists in the fact that in it all religious emotions are related to the redemption wrought by Jesus of Nazareth."[79] The task of Christian theology, in turn, is to set forth a coherent articulation of the dogmatic propositions that emerge out of logically ordered reflection on the religious experience of Christians as it is mediated in and through Jesus Christ and his redemptive work.[80]

The whole of the treatment of theology that resulted from this methodological move might be characterized as a reconstruction of the doctrine of God as it arises from the feeling of absolute dependence on God that characterizes pious Christian people leading to the centrality of the divine causation. In this manner, Schleiermacher shifted the focus of theology away from the speculative task of seeking to probe the being of God or *aseitas dei*. He replaced the attempt to determine truths about God in the eternal, transcendent divine essence with the goal of describing God on the basis of the Christian experience of God through Christ. This is evident in Schleiermacher's reformulation of the traditional discussion of the divine attributes: "All attributes which we ascribe to God are to be taken as denoting not something special in God, but only something special in the manner in which the feeling of absolute dependence is to be related to Him."[81] Drawing from the feeling of absolute dependence as the touchstone for such God-talk led Schleiermacher to ascribe absolute causality to God,[82] that is, to speak of God as the all-determining reality, the ultimate cause of everything, the one who acts but cannot be acted upon.

In the first part of *The Christian Faith,* Schleiermacher gave place to the attributes that express the general relationship between God and the world. Yet he deemed as even more important the theological assertions that are explicitly bound up with the Christian experience of redemption from sin. The explication of this aspect of the Christian religious feeling comprises the bulk of *The Christian Faith,* which quite naturally focuses on the christological and pneumatological assertions that arise from the consciousness of grace. The discussion climaxes with Schleiermacher's articulation of the divine love and the divine wisdom, which in turn opens the way for his short engagement with the doctrine of the Trinity, with which the work concludes.

The crucial role of the doctrine of the Trinity. Schleiermacher approaches God's triunity circumspectly. He confesses that he is unable to provide an adequate construction of the doctrine,[83] largely because the Trinity is "not an immediate utterance concerning the Christian self-consciousness but only a combination of several such utterances."[84] Hence he suggests that our access to this doctrine arises only indirectly, via Christology and pneumatology. As Samuel Powell explains: "Since Jesus Christ and the Holy Spirit are the principles of the knowledge of God, the doctrine of God cannot be completed until they have been treated. Further, since the knowledge of God rests exclusively on revelation, the Christian doctrine of God is identical with the doctrine of the Trinity."[85] For Schleiermacher, therefore, affirmation of the triunity of God is the product of synthetic construction. Rather than being part of the primary witness of the Christian faith, it is the product of the attempt to pull together the various elements of Christian experience.

Contrary to the assessment of many of his critics, therefore, by placing the treatment of the doctrine of the Trinity at the end of *The Christian Faith*, Schleiermacher is not suggesting that this teaching is unimportant. Although the declaration of God's triunity does not arise immediately from Christian experience, it is nevertheless crucial in that it provides coherence to what may otherwise be seen as disparate conceptions of the God who is manifest in the world, in the redemptive work of Christ, and in the presence of the Spirit in the church. Thus, for Schleiermacher, the doctrine of the Trinity gathers into a single whole what may be asserted on the basis of the various aspects of the Christian God-consciousness. Tillich helpfully characterizes this aspect of Schleiermacher's trinitarian perspective:

> The doctrine of the trinity is the fullest expression of man's relation to God. Each of the *personae* . . . is a representation of a certain way in which God is related to man and the world. . . . The doctrine of the trinity stands at the end as the competed doctrine of God, after all particular relations—such as those dealing with sin and forgiveness, creation and death and eternal life, the presence of the Spirit in the church and in the individual Christian, etc.—have been positively described from the religious consciousness of Christians. After this has been done, the lines can be drawn up to the divine as such, which yields to us trinitarian statements.[86]

Hence the short discussion of the doctrine of the Trinity does not comprise an appendix to *The Christian Faith*. Rather, it marks the conclusion of the entire systematic-theological treatise, insofar as the doctrine emerges as the logical culmination of Schleiermacher's doctrine of God.

The role of the doctrine of the Trinity in Schleiermacher's theological reflection does not end here, however. He appears to put the doctrine to an even deeper use. The postulate of God's triunity provides the basis for the christological and pneumatological construction that forms the heart of *The Christian Faith*. Gerhard Spiegler explains: "Schleiermacher recognizes quite clearly that it is the original purpose or function of the doctrine of the Trinity to support the doctrines of Christ and of the Spirit. Or as we might also put it now, it is its function to account speculatively, that is, in terms of possibility for the actuality of God's relationship to man and the world. This doctrine . . . is meant to be explanatory of what is encountered as actual."[87] In short, the doctrine of the Trinity forms "the coping-stone of Christian doctrine," to cite Schleiermacher's own evaluation of its importance.[88]

While granting to the doctrine of the Trinity this crucial status, Schleiermacher wants to avoid any semblance of viewing it as speculation regarding God in the divine eternity apart from God's relationship to the world. Franks aptly points out this concern: "Schleiermacher would have us be satisfied with the Trinity of Revelation, rather than try to penetrate behind it into the eternal Being of God."[89] Perhaps the way to make sense of Schleiermacher's agenda is to see it as an extension of Luther's understanding of theology as the explication of the revealed God-for-us rather than speculation about the hidden God-in-eternity. Indeed, Schleiermacher concluded his discussion of the doctrine of the Trinity in the first edition of *The Christian Faith* by musing as to what the outcome would be if not only "the philosophical presentation of the doctrine of the Trinity, older as well as more recent," but also "the repeatedly appearing . . . distinction between the hidden and the revealed God were subjected to a thorough critique."[90]

At first glance, this might suggest that Schleiermacher is solely interested in what in the twentieth century scholars came to designate the "economic Trinity." Yet to limit his interest to this is to misconceive Schleiermacher's intention, for his goal goes beyond merely talking about the economic Trinity. Insofar as he refuses to separate the being of God in eternity from the being of God in redemption (that is, "the union of the Divine Essence with human nature both in the personality of Christ and in the common spirit of the Church," as he described the latter[91]), he is refusing to differentiate between the immanent Trinity and the economic Trinity. In fact, just such a separation is precisely what Schleiermacher found problematic in the orthodox doctrine of the Trinity, with its emphasis on the eternal being of God described apart from God's work in redemption:

> what has become the ecclesiastical manner of teaching asserts that the threeness is something in the deity that is completely internal and originally distinct, as well as independent of the various operations of the deity; [it asserts] that the deity would have been Father, Son and Holy Spirit in itself, from eternity, even if God had never created, never united himself with a single human being, and never had come to dwell within the community of faith.[92]

Viewed from this perspective, Schleiermacher's cautious treatment of the doctrine of the Trinity is again reminiscent of Luther's distinction between the revealed God and the hidden God. In fact, we might suggest that Schleiermacher is attempting to take the Reformer's point to its logical, orthodox trinitarian conclusion, insofar as Schleiermacher posits a complete coincidence of the revealed God ("the Divine Essence considered as thus united to human nature") and the hidden God ("the Divine Essence in itself").[93] For this reason, Robert R. Williams is surely on track when he asserts that Schleiermacher's thesis not only "establishes that the Redeemer is identical with God himself and therefore immanent in God's being," but "it does so in such a way that the actual historical divine self-disclosure in incarnation is the foundation of this ontological immanence, and not merely a speculatively derived deduction or inference concerning God's inner life." Borrowing from Claude Welch's categories, Williams then suggests that Schleiermacher actually proposed a third alternative, a focus on an essential Trinity lying between the economic Trinity and the immanent Trinity.[94]

The use of such designations is, of course, anachronistic. Nevertheless, they suggest the manner in which Schleiermacher contributed to the modern renaissance of trinitarian theology. He may well have been the first modern theologian to perceive the crucial role that the threefoldness of God in the divine historical self-disclosure (what later came to be termed "the economic Trinity") must play in any attempt to recast the doctrine of the Trinity in a manner that avoids the dangers of the speculative approach. By making the doctrine of the Trinity the "coping stone" of theology, that is, by demonstrating that the assertion of the triunity of God can only come as the conclusion of our declarations regarding the incarnation of the divine Son in Jesus of Nazareth and the presence of the divine Spirit in the church, Schleiermacher introduced historicity into the eternal divine life.[95] In this sense, Franks appears to have been proved right when he claimed in 1953, "The modern way of looking at both the Incarnation and the Trinity depends upon the general revolution in theology introduced by Schleiermacher, which was as great as the philosophical revolution initiated by Kant."[96]

Despite its importance, Schleiermacher's trinitarianism comes up short at one crucial point. Perhaps contrary to his own intention, treating the doctrine of the Trinity solely at the end of the discussion inevitably makes for a Christology and a pneumatology that are insufficiently trinitarian, insofar as they are by necessity not developed within their proper trinitarian context. This opens the door to the question as to whether God is truly internally relational. The possibility that the eternal God may be viewed apart from the relationality of the trinitarian persons, in turn, can all too easily undermine the very christologically oriented theological program that Schleiermacher set out to develop.[97] Unless God is seen to be internally relational from all eternity, relationality—including the relationality between the divine and the human that is evident in Christ's redemptive work and the Spirit's presence within the church—loses its transcendent ground. The loss of the grounding of relationality in God is what, in turn, leads to the reduction of theology to anthropology, with which Schleiermacher has repeatedly been tagged. Although Spiegler's critique of Schleiermacher may be overdrawn, he summarizes this point well: "We can say that it is only when God is said to be capable of relatedness that predications concerning the relatedness of God and man, as asserted in Christology and pneumatology, can become theological predications and are not forced to remain merely anthropological descriptions."[98] It is just this potential difficulty in Schleiermacher's program that lends credence to Karl Barth's hyperbolic, yet ultimately perceptive, wholesale dismissal of his predecessor's work: "One can *not* speak of God simply by speaking of man in a loud voice."[99]

The Trinity as the Dynamic of Absolute Spirit: Georg W. F. Hegel

Despite Schleiermacher's significant contribution, the anthropocentric danger latent in his theology eliminated him from contention as the premier nineteenth-century hero of the story of the renewal of trinitarian theology. In most accounts of the narrative, the place of honor is occupied by Schleiermacher's colleague and protagonist at the University of Berlin, Georg W. F. Hegel (1770–1831). Yet Hegel attained status as a theological hero somewhat indirectly. Unlike Schleiermacher, he is generally viewed primarily not as a theologian but as a philosopher, and his claim to theological fame emerged through his very un-Schleiermacherian efforts to effect an integration of the Christian doctrine of God as triune with speculative philosophy. Hence Hegel became the most important exemplar of a seemingly ironic characteristic of nineteenth-century intellectual history: Philosophers, and not theologians, played the preeminent role in keeping alive the idea of the Trinity in the wake of its undoing in the Enlightenment.[100]

Reality and thought as dynamic movement. Theologian Robert S. Franks lauds Hegel for offering "the most completely rounded philosophical system of modern times."[101] At the heart of this "award-winning" philosophical program was Hegel's attempt to delineate the movement inherent in pure thought, for in his estimation, thought is dynamic; it "moves." It is commonplace to encapsulate Hegel's understanding by suggesting that he viewed the dynamic of thought as an ongoing movement through the three stages of thesis, antithesis, synthesis (a perspective that Hegel likely inherited from Fichte[102] or Schelling[103]). His own understanding of the logical flow of thought, however, was somewhat more complex.

Hegel's proposal regarding the dynamic of thought gives a much more prominent place to the act of negation than the typical description of the so-called Hegelian dialectic implies.[104] So central is the element of negativity or negation that he speaks of "the simple point of negative self-relation" as "the innermost source of all activity, of living and spiritual self-movement, the dialectic soul, which all truth has in it and through which it alone is truth."[105] Hegel conceives of thought as moving through a kind of double negation, occurring first in the negation that posits the opposite (or antithesis) and second in the negating of the opposition (that is, in the synthesis). Horst Althaus pinpoints the significance of the innovation Hegel offered in his work on logic: "That A (preserved in B) = non-A, and that the infinite should become the infinite through the power of the negative, is something that before Hegel perhaps only Heraclitus could have claimed with equal boldness. What was new about the self-confessedly abstruse treatment characteristic of Hegel's book was that such a formula and all its implications would henceforth belong amongst the indubitable first principles of logic itself."[106]

Hegel was convinced that the dynamic of double-negation, or differentiation and reconciliation, did not merely describe the movement of abstract thought, but that the logic operative in thought is present in reality as a whole, which he understood as the world process. As he tersely stated it, "What is rational is actual and what is actual is rational."[107] It was the intimate connection between thought and life that gave importance to the dynamic that he determined characterized thought itself. Hence, as Althaus explains regarding Hegel's perspective, "Logic is the reason immanent in all things themselves."[108] Therefore, in Hegel's estimation, reason is not something that is externally brought to life, but emerges out of experience, and above all, from experience as a whole.[109] Even more significant, however, is a further step that Hegel took. He asserted that this pattern is rooted in a spiritual dynamic that lies behind (or beyond) the world and that reveals or even actualizes itself in the world process.

Hegel's designation for the dynamic present in both thought and reality, and that brings reality into a unified whole, was *Geist*, a term that combines the concept of rationality reflected in the English word "mind" with the dimension of the supramaterial bound up with the idea of "spirit." What allows for the dialectic movement of *Geist* is the power of "overreaching" that it possesses.[110] Emil Fackenheim aptly describes the working of this power: "Spirit, first, tolerates the other-than-Spirit *beside* itself. Secondly, it can and does overcome this side-by-sidedness, by absorbing the other-than-Spirit. Thirdly . . . it reconstitutes the other in its otherness even while absorbing it."[111]

Hegel asserted that *Geist* takes on objective form and comes to full awareness of itself through the historical process, the stages of which the movement of Spirit—like the dynamic of thought—creates as it passes through them. Above all, the different epochs in human history form the stages through which *Geist* passes en route to self-discovery.[112] Consequently, the history of human culture not only involves the human spirit encountering its own conscious life,[113] but also *Geist* coming to know itself. One crucial aspect of this process is the development of religion, which, in turn, reaches its fullness in modern Protestant Christianity.[114] For Hegel, Christianity sets forth in the form of representation the coming into being of the Absolute Spirit, or God, coming to self-consciousness through the activity of the human spirit.

Geist *and the Trinity.* Unlike the Enlightenment philosophical theologians who looked to nature to find the footprints of a God deemed to be

its transcendent Designer, Hegel found the self-revealing and self-actual-
izing God in the ongoing process present at the heart of both rational
thought and reality. In fact, Hegel's intent was to speak about the self-disclosure of the living God, rather than merely about dialectical movement
as an abstract principle of logic. Hans Küng explains the connection: "God
himself contains antithesis within himself, and he himself reconciles this
antithesis. He is the dialectic. This is the God, proceeding through polar-
ity toward reconciliation, whom Hegel intends to describe—not in
abstract propositions, but in a living process, focussing not on an abstract,
dead divine essence, but on the concrete, living act that God himself is."[115]

Hegel's desire to link God and thought was connected to a larger program, namely, the task of reaching not only an *entente cordiale* but a full
reconciliation between theology and philosophy. As he himself noted at
the conclusion of his lectures on the philosophy of religion in 1824, his
goal was "to reconcile reason with religion in its manifold forms, and to
recognize them as at least necessary."[116]

A reconciliation of the two is possible, in Hegel's estimation, because
philosophy and religion express the same content—God—but do so in
different ways. More specifically, as he points out in his 1827 lectures on
philosophy of religion, religion and philosophy share the same "object,"
namely, "the eternal truth, God and nothing but God and the explication
of God." As a result, ultimately "religion and philosophy coincide in
one."[117] For its part, religion speaks about God by means of images
(Vorstellungen). Philosophy, in turn, uses concepts *(Begriffe)*. For Hegel the
chief aim of philosophy is to conceptualize what is given in religion as
images.[118] As Powell explains, "The reconciliation Hegel proposed con-
sisted in a transition from representational thinking to conceptual
thinking, a transition that involves transcending the non-essential representational form, retrieving the truth contained in the representations,
and restating that truth in conceptual terms."[119]

Central to the reconciliation task as Hegel conceived it was the Christian conviction regarding the triunity of God. In his estimation, the content of the doctrine of the Trinity was not merely a religious teaching but
also lay at the heart of the philosophical understanding of all reality. In
fact, Hegel believed that the Christian conception of God as triune was
crucial for understanding the dynamic entailed in the philosophical conception of God as "Spirit" *(Geist)*. In fact, he went so far as to assert that
"Spirit" remains an empty word if God is not conceived in a trinitarian

manner. As he stated the point in his 1824 lectures on the philosophy of religion, "the definition of God by the church as a Trinity . . . is the concrete determination and nature of God as spirit" so that "spirit is an empty word if it is not grasped in this determination." In this context, Hegel offered what has become a widely influential understanding of the doctrine of the Trinity: "God is thus grasped as what he is for himself within himself; God [the Father] makes himself an object for himself (the Son); then, in this object, God remains the undivided essence within this differentiation of himself within himself, and in the differentiation of himself loves himself, i.e., remains identical with himself—this is God as Spirit."[120] In so doing, Hegel suggested that the divine triad may be viewed in one sense as referring to the relationships within the triune God, in which God is seen as the Absolute-itself, its being-other, and its unity with itself.[121] Thereby he gave place to what later became known as the immanent Trinity.

As this description of the divine triunity indicates, like other thinkers in the Western tradition, in delineating the concept of the Trinity, Hegel elevated the idea of love. To this end, reminiscent of his forebears, he identified love and spirit. In his estimation love—similar to spirit—embraces differentiation and unity (or reconciliation) simultaneously. Differentiation is inherent in the presence of love's subject (lover) and love's object (beloved), and reconciliation emerges in love's subject being found in the union with the beloved insofar as love is the supreme surrender of oneself in the other (or being outside oneself in the other).[122] Borrowing the traditional language of the doctrine of the Trinity, we might say that for Hegel, God apart from the world is an inherently complete dynamic of love in which the Son is separated from the Father only to be reunited in the Spirit.

Yet Hegel offered an important twist on the "immanent" Trinity. For him, the Christian idea of an eternal or ontological Trinity is not to be viewed as referring to an actual divine being existing as three persons apart from the world, but as a representational way of speaking about the dynamic of thought in an abstract manner. The "immanent" Trinity represents the dialectical movement of differentiation and reconciliation that the philosopher explores under the rubric of the science of logic.[123] John Burbidge offers this characterization of Hegel's perspective: "God before creation is the self-determining universal that, like the self-contained process of conceiving, eternally differentiates (or particularizes) the Son from the Father while yet negating that negation to give God concrete individuality or singularity as spirit."[124]

For Hegel, *Geist* cannot be left merely on the level of pure abstraction, however. As Charles Taylor explains, "In Hegel's philosophy, the timeless truth itself unfolds necessarily in history. Historical events are not an irrelevant by-play, at best illustrating or dramatizing universal truth, but the inescapable medium in which these truths realize and manifest themselves."[125] The abstract God—the "immanent" Trinity—comprises only the first logical moment in the divine dynamic. Because *Geist* is integrally related to the world process, the "immanent" Trinity must give way to what we might call the economic Trinity, to the Trinity in history that comprises the self-revelation and self-actualization of God.

In this historical process, Hegel saw three moments, analogous to the three persons in the Christian concept of the Trinity.[126] The first involves abstract Being and hence God in God's essential reality. The second marks the entrance of abstract *Geist* into existence through the creation of the world, as God enters into relation with what is other. According to Hegel, this "objectively existent spirit" (the world) is characterized by being "the Son" (that which "knows itself to be essential Being"), on the one hand, and on the other hand by alienation and abandonment (evil). The third moment is *Geist* passing into self-consciousness, which occurs above all in human history and in the endeavors of the human spirit. In his *Philosophy of Mind*, Hegel articulated the connection between the divine self-knowledge and human knowledge of God in the following manner: "God is only God so far as he knows himself; his self-knowledge is, further, a self-consciousness in man, and man's knowledge *of* God which proceeds to man's self-knowledge *in* God."[127] This third moment marks the completion of the dynamic of differentiation and reconciliation, and hence the fullness of *Geist* or Absolute Spirit.

In Hegel's understanding, Jesus is crucial to this process, because in him the idea of the unity of God and humankind has been made explicit in history. In the incarnation, the universal philosophical truth of the divine-human unity has been actualized in a particular historical individual. Because history is the actual unfolding of reality, this event has significance not only for creation but for God as well. In Christ, God has actually passed from abstract idea into historical particularity, and as a result "the pure or non-actual Spirit of bare thought has become actual."[128]

This truth, Hegel adds, is most clearly expressed in the crucifixion, an event that speaks about God taking on radical finitude, the highest form of which is death, and thus about the death of the abstract God. Hegel wrote: "The death of the mediator is death not merely of his *natural* aspect, of his particular self-existence: what dies is not merely the outer encasement, which, being stripped of essential Being is *eo ipso* dead, but also the abstraction of the Divine Being."[129] At the same time, the crucifixion constitutes the reconciliation of creation with God and thereby marks the reconciliation within God. As Hegel put it in his 1824 lectures on the philosophy of religion, "Through death God has reconciled the world and reconciles himself eternally with himself."[130]

Rather than marking the end of the narrative, in the Christian story Christ's death sets the stage for the resurrection. In Hegel's understanding, this event marks the advent of the universal or Absolute Spirit and of the Kingdom of the Spirit, which is not only the goal of history but also constitutes God's full historical realization.

Geist *and the God of Christian theology.* Franks claims to have found "a natural affinity between Hegel's philosophical triad and the Christian Trinity as psychologically illustrated by Augustine and Aquinas."[131] Other commentators have not been so quick to include Hegel within the orthodox fold.

At the heart of the theological queasiness that the Hegelian pill produces in the stomachs of many of his critics is the suspicion that in the end he has co-opted theological language for what to him is an overriding philosophical program. Without a doubt, Hegel gives a certain priority to philosophy. Charles Taylor aptly encapsulates the higher epistemological status the Hegelian synthesis affords to the philosophical aspect of the human intellectual endeavor: "The believing worshiper senses that the *Vorstellung* of God puts him in contact with the absolute. This is the 'testimony of the spirit' which tells him that this content is spirit. But with philosophy this obscure sense is replaced by the certainty of reason."[132] But does the primacy of philosophy in the Hegelian synthesis mean that the sovereignty of theology is undermined and that Hegel has jettisoned the biblically focused, ecclesiastical doctrine of the Trinity for a speculative philosophical clone? Claude Welch is convinced that this is precisely the outcome. In his estimation, "Hegel's doctrine of the Trinity is a philosophical truth, resting entirely on general philosophical premises. The truth of that doctrine can be established and elaborated in complete independence of religion. Indeed, it can be understood and *known* to be true *only* by the speculative reason through the analysis of the nature of logic and concrete actuality."[133]

Other critics are less thoroughgoing in their chastisement of Hegel. Burbidge, for example, acknowledges the problem but suggests that in the end the philosophical component of the Hegelian synthesis needs the theological at least as much as the latter is dependent on the former: "To be sure, Christian doctrine is not expressed in such logical terms. It needs to be conceived philosophically before the inherent pattern is visible. But the relation is not one-sided. For philosophy also benefits from this encounter. Were it not for the fact that Christian doctrine represents as true of the cosmic order the same pattern that emerged in the processes of pure thought, Hegel could not have assumed that what is rational is actual and what is actual is rational." Burbidge then adds, "He must believe Christian doctrine; else his philosophy becomes illusion—nothing but a Kantian categorical framework which says nothing about the world in itself."[134] Fackenheim comes to a similar conclusion: "Without the Christian dimension of modern life his own philosophy could not have reached its all-comprehensive goals; without the Christian dimension Reason could not be complete in the modern world."[135] Indeed, Hegel himself appears to authenticate this appraisal, when he writes, "Religion can exist without philosophy. But philosophy cannot exist without religion; rather, it is much more the case that it encloses religion within itself."[136]

Whatever ought to be said about the relationship between theology and philosophy in Hegel's program, we dare not minimize the influence his innovative proposal has had for subsequent trinitarian theology. Powell was surely correct when he quipped, "Looking back, it is clear that the fact that there is any contemporary interest in the doctrine of the Trinity at all owes a great deal to Hegel."[137]

Yet Hegel's legacy does not only lie in his role in kick-starting the renewal of trinitarian thought. Of crucial significance is his stance with regard to what subsequently came to be known as the problem of the relationship between the immanent Trinity and the economic Trinity. According to Walter Kasper, for Hegel the distinction between them is "in the last analysis an abstract one; considered concretely and in themselves, the two coincide."[138] By refusing to drive a wedge between these two dimensions of the Christian conception of the triune God, Hegel effectively set one crucial parameter for the ensuing conversation. In their attempts to revive the doctrine of the Trinity, theologians working in Hegel's wake would need to take seriously the close connection that he posited—in a manner that surpassed even Schleiermacher—between the Trinity and the unfolding historical process. They would need to think not only of the God of history, but, more importantly, of the history of God.[139]

It did not become immediately evident as to whether the introduction of historicity into the conception of God evident in the work of Hegel—and Schleiermacher for that matter—merely resulted in a deepening of the eclipse of the doctrine of the Trinity or actually served to open the way for trinitarian thought to eclipse its Enlightenment rival. Rather than leaving us in the nineteenth century, the hunt for the definitive answer to this question catapults us into the twentieth. Only in the discussion that was ignited after the First World War and that consumed a cadre of theologians during the ensuing seventy-five years do we observe the far-reaching outworking of the parameters of trinitarian thinking that were set in the early 1800s. For that reason, the main body of the story of the renewal of trinitarian theology begins some ninety years after the death of Hegel in 1831. It commences with the work of Karl Barth.

2

Restoring the Trinitarian Center

The nineteenth century provided the initial foundation for a renaissance of trinitarian thought in the twentieth. Although Friedrich Schleiermacher laid important theological groundwork for such a renewal and called for others to engage in what he saw as an uncompleted task, nineteenth-century theologians did not generally capitalize on this aspect of his work. The significant impulse toward a trinitarian revival came instead from philosophy, above all from Georg W. F. Hegel's innovative proposal. The twentieth century, however, witnessed the reversal of this trend. With the waning of idealism, interest in trinitarian thought among philosophers evaporated, even while it mushroomed among theologians.

The shift in leadership in trinitarian thinking from the realm of philosophy to theology did not diminish the importance of Hegel. At least initially, most trinitarian theological programs followed the pathway that he had charted. Hence Samuel Powell concludes, "If we ask about any philosophical dimension to twentieth-century Trinitarian thought, we find that theologians who are most concerned to rehabilitate the doctrine . . . are beholden in one way or another to Hegel and are among the modern inheritors of his legacy."[1] Of the various theologians who followed in Hegel's train, none are more often named with him as setting the parameters for the trinitarian thought that developed in the twentieth century than the Protestant theologian Karl Barth (1886–1968) and his younger Roman Catholic counterpart Karl Rahner (1904–1984).[2]

Theology and the Self-Revealing God:
Karl Barth

The consensus of historians of theology is that Karl Barth stands unchallenged as the leading theologian of the 1900s. Throughout the century, his towering frame casts its shadow across the theological landscape. Gary Dorrien asserts regarding Barth's prominence, "As the preeminent theologian of his century, Karl Barth was the single figure that all other twentieth-century theologians had to deal with, if not define themselves against."[3] Some commentators have even gone so far as to declare Barth to be a "modern church father" and to place his name on the list of the most illustrious theologians the church has ever produced.[4] As the twentieth century gave way to the twenty-first, rather than diminishing in luster, Barth's star burned even brighter.[5] This is evidenced by the explosion of scholarly treatments of his work that emerged in the years just prior to or immediately after the celebration of the new millennium,[6] including a lively debate as to whether Barth is best understood within the context of the Enlightenment,[7] ought to be rethought in the light of the postmodern situation,[8] or somehow belongs to both.[9] John Webster would not be accused of overstatement in declaring not only that "Barth is the most important Protestant theologian since Schleiermacher" but also that "the extraordinary descriptive depth of his depiction of the Christian faith puts him in the company of a handful of thinkers in the classical Christian tradition."[10]

Barth was by no means the first theologian in the wake of Schleiermacher and Hegel to pay attention to the doctrine of the Trinity. On the contrary, the turn of the twentieth century found a group of thinkers on both sides of the North Atlantic busily attempting to work out the theological implications of the Hegelian elevation of the divine subjectivity. Yet Barth's efforts have predominated, almost to the point of consigning the work of his immediate predecessors to the dustbin of theological history. In the story of trinitarian theology, Barth must be afforded the place at the head of the train of those responsible for the twentieth-century renaissance because he, more than any of his contemporaries, offered a thoroughgoing trinitarian perspective on the method and content of theology. Thus in 1989 Robert Jenson declared regarding Barth's role, "It can fairly be said that the chief ecumenical enterprise of current theology is rediscovery and development of the doctrine of the Trinity. It can also fairly be said that Barth initiated the enterprise."[11]

The Revelation of the Triune God

Claude Welch cites two major impulses at work after World War I which, because they demanded a reconsideration of the classical Christian understanding of God, led "inevitably" to the reappearance of the doctrine of the Trinity on the theological agenda: the revival of the category of revelation and the desire to reassess human nature. Renewed interest in the foundational role of revelation led directly to a consideration of the God who is disclosed in revelation. The route through anthropology was less direct. As theologians came to repudiate late-nineteenth-century optimism and to gain a renewed awareness of the depth of sin, they naturally questioned anew the nature of redemption, which led to christological inquiry as to the character of Jesus' salvific work and culminated in the theological themes of God's nature and the role of the doctrine of the Trinity in the theological system.[12] In both of these major areas of interest, the theologian whose efforts launched trinitarian theology in the new manner was Karl Barth.

Despite the efforts of some to provide compendia to the *Church Dogmatics*,[13] the sheer size of Barth's literary output defies any attempt to capture in a neat summary his theological proposal, whether in its entirety or merely in a particular dimension. Nevertheless, the two themes—revelation and Christology—almost always surface in treatments of Barth's thought.[14] Taken together, they likewise form the center of Barth's contribution to the trinitarian renaissance.

The theological beginning point: the self-revealing God. The motivation for the crucial attention that Barth gave to the doctrine of the Trinity emerged from his convictions regarding revelation as the basis of his entire theological agenda. His goal was to launch theology anew in the face of the claim of the nineteenth-century left-wing Hegelian thinker Ludwig Feuerbach (1804–1872) that all God-talk was simply talk about humankind, that is, that theology was ultimately anthropology. Barth castigated his liberal predecessors for falling prey to an anthropologizing tendency that rendered theology unable either to appeal to, or to speak about, a transcendent God beyond the realm of the human. Barth argued that theology arises ultimately out of a prior act of God that humans cannot initiate but can only receive: revelation.[15]

Throughout his writings, Barth declared that revelation is an event. Revelation happens. Moreover, revelation is something that God does. Although Barth acknowledged that humans are involved, he retained the focus on the priority of the transcendent God in the revelatory act. God remains the Subject in every aspect of revelation. In this manner, Barth sought to preserve the "from above" character of revelation and hence the divine initiative in human knowledge of God,[16] thereby overcoming Feuerbach's critique that all theological language is ultimately anthropological. To this end, Barth devoted his energies to the task of developing a theology that is integrally linked to and arises immediately out of the divine self-disclosure. In fact, the central goal that characterized his theological endeavors following his turn away from liberalism was that of grounding theology in "the objectively real Self-speaking of God in revelation," to cite Bruce McCormack's description.[17] Hence Trevor Hart offers this judgment: "From the first edition of *The Epistle of the Romans* (1919) onward, a singular concern may be identified in Barth's writing on the theme of revelation: namely, to give an account of the reality of this event in which the proper (and vital) distinction between God and the world is maintained."[18]

Barth's concern to develop a Word-focused theology found its methodological exposition in what is perhaps his most widely read treatise, the inaugural half-volume of the *Church Dogmatics* bearing the expressive title, *The Doctrine of the Word of God*. Barth's point of departure lies in his crucial assertion that the proper location of theology is in the life and activity of the church. Moreover, because the church is under direct divine command to engage in this activity, its principal task is proclamation, which Barth sees, in keeping with the Reformation heritage, as involving primarily word (that is, preaching) but also sacrament.[19] The judge and criterion for all proclamation can only be God's own pronouncements— God's own disclosure—that is, the Word of God. Theology, in turn, "guides the talk of the church"; it seeks to foster the agreement of the church's declarations about God with the "being" of the church, which is Jesus Christ.[20] In short, theology measures the church's proclamation by the Word of God.[21] Hence Barth concluded that all the questions of dogmatics ultimately focus on the single query as to "whether the words, the phrases, the sequences of thought, the logical construction of Christian preaching have or have not the quality of serving the Word of God and becoming transparent for it."[22]

Because the Word of God is the criterion for all theological reflection, the doctrine of the Word of God functions as prolegomenon in Barth's

Church Dogmatics. Following the lead of many Protestant theologians, he places epistemological weight on this section of the dogmatic endeavor (together with the discussion of the knowledge of God in volume II), for he describes the prolegomenon as "the attempt to give an explicit account of the particular way of knowledge taken in dogmatics, or . . . of the particular point from which we are to look, think and judge in dogmatics."[23] Barth, however, is not interested in offering a general theory of human knowledge in the form of a philosophical epistemology. For him, the proper epistemological stance for theology can only be the Word of God, which, he argues, constitutes the sole criterion of dogmatics. Moreover, because the Word of God is always spoken to specific persons, the epistemological question can only be: How can the particular persons to whom the Word is concretely spoken know it? And Barth's response is again simply "the Word": "our answer must be that they can do so when the ability is given to them by the Word itself."[24] For this reason, Barth adamantly declares, "The possibility of knowledge of God's Word lies in God's Word and nowhere else."[25]

Barth's concept of the Word of God is one of his most innovative theological proposals.[26] He speaks of the Word of God preached, written, and revealed—or as proclamation, Bible, and revelation—which, rather than being three different forms of the Word of God, constitute the one Word in its threefold form.[27] This leads to Barth's fuller description of the task of dogmatics as that of "measuring Church proclamation as man's word by the second form of the Word of God, that is, Holy Scripture, in so far as this itself is in turn witness to its third and original form, revelation."[28] The central task of his theological prolegomenon, in turn, is that of expounding the Word of God as revealed, written, and preached, a task that consumes the second half of the first half-volume of his *Church Dogmatics* as well as the lengthy second half-volume.[29]

Barth carefully maintains a dynamic, over against a merely static, understanding of the concept of the Word of God. For him, the Word of God is not simply proclamation and scripture but the dynamic of God's revelation in proclamation and scripture.[30] Furthermore, the Word of God is *divine* acting. It is God's speech, of course. But when God speaks something happens; God's speaking produces a change. Because of its connection to God's own being and act, the Word of God is efficacious, and hence God is revealed as the Lord in the divine speaking. The Word of

God is likewise free. In volume II of his *Church Dogmatics,* which comprises *The Doctrine of God,* Barth bases the freedom of the Word of God on an innovative description of the classical concept of aseity, namely, the idea that God is not dependent on anything but is the source of God's own internal and external freedom.[31] Because it is free, the Word of God emerges out of God's sovereign decision; the Word of God is connected to God's unlimited intervention, which is never completely enclosed within history but always remains free. Above all, the Word of God is Jesus Christ, who is both the speaker and the message.

The trinitarian character of the Word. The question of the means by which church proclamation is to be compared to scripture leads Barth to the theological underpinnings of his prolegomenon. In his estimation, the only true analogy to the Word of God is the doctrine of the triunity of God, for the names of the divine persons can be substituted for revelation, scripture, and proclamation and vice versa, and the same basic determinations and mutual relationships are evident in both triads.[32] In Barth's prolegomenon, therefore, the doctrine of the Trinity arises immediately from the idea of proclamation. Gary Dorrien offers a succinct statement of the connection Barth posits between the two: "The Word becomes present as preaching in the same way that the Holy Spirit makes God present to us. That is, just as the Holy Spirit proceeds from the Father and the Son, the Word as preaching proceeds from revelation and scripture. . . . Just as the Father and Son are made present only through the movement of the Spirit, the Word as revelation and scripture are made present 'in, with, and under' preaching and only through preaching."[33]

Yet what more directly occasions Barth's introduction of God's triunity is his discussion of the concept under which even proclamation must be ordered—revelation—for this concept emerges immediately from the task of clarifying how church proclamation is to be measured by scripture. Because revelation cannot be treated as a general concept but only in the concrete, Christian dogmatics involves "dealing with the concept of the revelation of the God who according to Scripture and proclamation is the Father of Jesus Christ, is Jesus Christ Himself, and is the Spirit of this Father and this Son."[34]

For Barth, at the core of the scriptural witness is the assertion that "God reveals Himself as the Lord," which is simultaneously the form and content of revelation.[35] Revelation, therefore, is revelation of the divine lordship, and thereby it is the revelation of God.[36] Consequently, the first theological question is: Who is the God who reveals himself? a question that cannot be separated from two others: How does it come about that this God reveals himself? and What is the result of this revelation in the person to whom it happens? thereby forming a triunity of queries that leads naturally to a triunity as the answer. Barth encapsulates his initial response to these three questions in his often quoted dictum, "*God* reveals Himself. He reveals Himself *through Himself.* He reveals *Himself.*" By this, Barth means that the same God is the revealing God, the event of revelation, and the effect of revelation on the human recipient. Or to paraphrase another of Barth's well-known postulates, God is the Revealer, the Revelation, and the Revealedness in unimpaired unity but also in unimpaired distinction.[37]

More significant theologically than the actual wording of his trinitarian formulation is Barth's observation that the inseparability of these three questions places the discussion of God's triunity at the center of the prolegomenon rather than postponing it for the doctrine of God. To cite Barth's own words, "If we really want to understand revelation in terms of its subject, that is, God, then the first thing we have to realise is that this subject, God, the Revealer, is identical with His act in revelation and also identical with its effect. It is from this fact, which in the first instance we are merely indicating, that we learn we must begin the doctrine of revelation with the doctrine of the triune God."[38]

As this quotation suggests, the concept of revelation leads to a conception of the Trinity that includes both differentiation among the three and full equality of the three in their unity. Barth's initial unfolding of God's triunity out of the biblical witness to God's self-disclosure emerges as a kind of theological exegesis of the biblical idea of revelation as the self-unveiling, imparted to humans, of the God who by nature cannot be unveiled and therefore remains veiled (Father) even in this act of unveiling (Son) in which humans participate (Spirit).[39] The three parts of this statement lead Barth to the idea of the self-revealing God who is Lord in a threefold manner: in the act of self-revealing (sonship), in being inscrutable apart from this free act (fatherhood), and in the effect of this act (spirithood). Furthermore, in the dynamic of revelation, God is subject, act, and effect,[40] or subject, predicate, and object. But for revelation to occur, the subject of revelation must be repeated in the predicate and the object, so that revelation and revealing are equal to the revealer.[41] In this manner, the concept of revelation as the self-disclosure of what is otherwise hidden suggests an ordered triad that forms the threeness of the one God. God is the one Lord in threefold repetition. Barth offers the following illuminating explication:

> applying our ternary of revealer, revelation and being revealed, we can also say quite confidently that there is a source, an authorship, a ground of revelation, a revealer of himself just as distinct from revelation itself as revelation implies absolutely something new in relation to the mystery of the revealer which is set aside in revelation as such. As a second in distinction from the first there is thus revelation itself as the event of making manifest what was previously hidden. And as the result of the first two there is then a third, a being revealed, the reality which is the purpose of the revealer and therefore at the same time the point or goal of the revelation.[42]

In short, for Barth, revelation is what Eberhard Jüngel describes as "God's self-interpretation," an event that presupposes a self-distinction within God. The doctrine of the Trinity, in turn, becomes—to cite Jüngel's terse characterization of Barth's position—"the interpretation of the self-interpretation of God."[43]

The Triune God of Revelation

In their preface to the revised translation of the first half-volume of Barth's *Church Dogmatics*, G. W. Bromiley and T. F. Torrance declare, "In introducing his translation of this work Professor G. T. Thomson claimed that it was 'undoubtedly the greatest treatise on the Trinity since the Reformation,' but when it is studied in connexion with volume two on the doctrine of God, the claim may well be made that it is the greatest treatise of the kind since the *De Trinitate* of St. Augustine."[44] Although they might be speaking hyperbolically, his editors rightly underscore the importance of both the method and content of Barth's delineation of the doctrine of the Trinity for the renaissance of trinitarian theology. Ted Peters offers a more circumspect statement that captures what has become nearly a consensus as to the scope of Barth's influence:

> The major contributors to the contemporary rethinking of the doctrine of the Trinity either extend principles already proffered by Barth or else follow lines of thought that parallel his *Church Dogmatics*. Most specifically, they rely upon the priority of revelation-analysis

and Barth's belief that the historical event of Jesus Christ belongs to the becoming of God proper.[45]

At the heart of Barth's contribution, therefore, is his depiction of the triune God of revelation.

The Trinity revealed in the Word. Barth's programmatic exposé on the doctrine of the Trinity comprises the first topic of the discussion of the Word of God and hence of the revelation attested in scripture, which revelation is the source and norm of the church's proclamation. He views the doctrine of the Trinity as providing the answer to the question about the *subject* presupposed in the concept of revelation (whereas, as he points out in the second half-volume, the doctrine of the incarnation of the Word of God in Jesus Christ delineates the event indicated in the concept, and the doctrine of the outpouring of the Holy Spirit speaks to the effect and goal of the revelatory event[46]). According to Barth, scripture attests to "the revelation of the God who, as the Lord, is the Father from whom it proceeds, the Son who fulfils it objectively (for us), and the Holy Spirit who fulfils it subjectively (in us)."[47] Hence, in revelation, "the Father represents, as it were, the divine *Who,* the Son the divine *What,* and the Holy Spirit the divine *How.*"[48]

The quotation above suggests what was noted earlier, namely, that central to Barth's delineation of the doctrine of the Trinity is his claim that the biblical witness may be summarized by the declaration that "God reveals Himself as the Lord," which statement can be interpreted in three different senses corresponding to the three members of the Trinity.[49] By lordship Barth is not meaning to speak about God exercising power over humankind. Rather, drawing from the personalism of thinkers such as Martin Buber, Barth speaks of the divine power as the act of God in history in making his power known to humankind by coming to humans as an I to a Thou. This occurs in the event of revelation.[50] At the heart of the historical divine self-disclosure is, of course, Jesus Christ, who in scripture is called Lord.

Upon the foundation of the divine self-disclosure in Christ with its trinitarian structure, Barth builds his revelational delineation of the doctrine of the Trinity. He proceeds from the close connection he posits between God and the revelatory act, so that what can be said about God from the perspective of revelation corresponds to an inner reality within the eternal God. Or as he states it, "We have to take revelation with such utter seriousness that in it as God's act we must directly see God's being too." Later, in introducing his explication of the doctrine of God under the rubric of the declaration "God is" in the second volume of his *Church Dogmatics*, Barth reiterates the point: "our first and decisive transcription of the statement that God is, must be that God is who He is in the act of His revelation."[51]

Barth, therefore, refuses to allow any separation between God's self-disclosure and the eternal divine being, that is, between who God is in revelation and who God is in eternity. He is convinced that were God-in-eternity not one with God-in-revelation, the God who encounters humans in revelation would not truly be God, for the real God would remain hidden behind the revealed God. This would amount to a type of Sabellianism, in which God's historical self-disclosure does not serve to reveal but to conceal God, so that in revelation we encounter only an appearance of God.[52] Perhaps Jüngel has offered the most penetrating understanding of this aspect of Barth's theology. He writes, "God's being *ad extra corresponds* essentially to his being *ad intra* in which it has its basis and prototype. . . . *As interpreter* of himself, God corresponds to his own being. But because God as his own interpreter (even in his external works) *is* himself, and since in this event as such we are also dealing with the *being* of God, then the highest and final statement which can be made about the being of God is: God corresponds to himself."[53]

At the same time, Barth finds equally abhorrent any collapsing of God into the divine self-disclosure. Collapsing God into the event of God's historical self-disclosure would rob God of eternal and hence independent existence, thereby impinging on the divine freedom. For Barth, therefore, the event of revelation always arises as the result of God's freedom.

Although God is identical with the act of revelation, God is not reducible to that act. Rather, revelation exhibits what is antecedent in the eternal life of the Trinity, which transcends the act of revelation and stands as the eternal prototype of revelation.[54] Lying behind the revelatory event is a divine self-revelation within the eternal God, a Word of revelation uttered by God eternally, by means of which God possesses self-knowledge.[55] As Barth states it, "Primarily and originally the Word of God is undoubtedly the Word that God speaks by and to Himself in eternal concealment."[56] The Word of God directed toward humankind, in turn, is a historical enactment of the revelational dynamic that occurs in eternity. In this manner, Barth distinguishes between God-in-eternity and God's self-revelatory act in time, even while adamantly seeking to hold together God in eternity and God in temporal revelation, or what is now commonly called the "immanent Trinity" and the "economic Trinity."

En route to developing his revelatory trinitarianism, Barth revisits a question that has generated theological controversy throughout the history of the church: How ought the three trinitarian members to be conceived? His response to this question builds from his claim that God can have only one personality,[57] a conclusion he grounds in the revelation event itself: If Jesus Christ were another personality different from the Father, he could not be the Father's *self*-revelation. This consideration leads Barth to reject the term *person* as a reference to the trinitarian members, because to modern ears the word inevitably implies "personality." Nor in his estimation is God a threefold subject, for this would constitute tritheism.[58] Hence Barth links God's personhood or subjectivity with the divine substance or *ousia* rather than with the three *hypostases*. For this reason, he replaces the traditional language of *person* to refer to the three members of the Trinity with his controversial designation "modes of Being" *(Seinsweise)*.[59] In his estimation, Father, Son, and Holy Spirit are the three ways of being in which God eternally subsists in absolute unity, yet whose distinctions form the precondition for God's revelation in Jesus Christ and for God's spiritual presence within the life of the church.

Barth develops his revelational delineation of the doctrine of the Trinity by means of an exposé of each of the three trinitarian members in order: the Father, the Son, and the Holy Spirit. Following a stylized method, he begins each discussion by returning to his orientation point, the divine self-disclosure in Christ, and then draws his theological conclusions—by means of an exposition of appropriate phrases from what has come to be known as the Nicene Creed—as to what must be regarded as true about each within the dynamic of the eternal God.

It comes as no surprise that Barth first addresses the topic of God the Father. He begins with the biblical witness to Jesus' disclosure of the God from whom he distinguished himself as the Son of the Father. Through Christ's death and resurrection—through Good Friday and Easter—this God comes to be known as the one who as Lord of death and life is Lord of human existence. Hence the Father is the Creator, a designation that according to Barth means that God is our Father. Barth quickly adds, however, that being "Father" belongs to the being of God even apart from creation, for God is the Father of Jesus Christ, who is the Son. From this observation Barth concludes that the trinitarian name *Father* "denotes the mode of being of God in which He is the Author of His other modes of being."[60]

At the heart of Barth's revelational doctrine of the Trinity is his exposition of God the Son. This discussion arises out of a second aspect of the biblical testimony to Jesus' revelation of God the Father, namely, the witness that Jesus also spoke about his unity with the Father. This aspect of revelation, which Barth sees as Jesus' disclosure of himself in contrast to his disclosure of God as his Father, leads to the confession of Jesus' deity as the Son and as Lord. Scripture bears witness to Jesus as the one who reveals the Father and who reconciles sinful humankind to the Father. Barth finds in both of these aspects of Jesus' work indication of his deity as the Son distinct from the Father.

According to Barth, Jesus' deity is necessitated by the dynamic of revelation itself. He argues that if Jesus "were only a creature He could not reveal God, for the creature certainly cannot take God's place and work in His place. If He reveals God, then irrespective of His creaturehood He Himself has to be God."[61] In Jesus' work of revealing the Father, Barth finds a second lordship that is quite different from the revelation of God as Creator that he had noted in conjunction with the Father. The lordship evident in Jesus consists of a revelation in the midst of human darkness and rebellion, a revelation of the divine word of reconciliation spoken to sinful, guilty humans. According to Barth, this requires that we speak of a second mode of the divine being separate from the first, that is, the Son. Barth summarizes his argument in this manner: "For as we have to say that reconciliation or revelation is not creation or a continuation of creation but rather an inconceivably new work above and beyond creation, so we have also to say that the Son is not the Father but that here, in this work, the one God, though not without the Father, is the Son or Word of the Father." Furthermore, because reconciliation presupposes and hence follows from creation insofar as it is the reconciliation of fallen creatures, these two moments lead to a particular ordering in our conception of the divine reality: "the Reconciler . . . follows the Creator."[62]

Once again Barth then moves from revelation to eternity. He notes that Jesus does not first become God's Son or Word in the event of revelation, but that he reveals himself in that event as the one who he is apart from this event. For this reason, Barth is adamant that rather than being limited to the event of revelation, Jesus' sonship or wordness—like fatherhood—belongs to the reality of the eternal God. Hence, on the basis of his claim that "revelation has eternal content and eternal validity," he declares, "Down to the very depths of deity, not as something penultimate but as the ultimate thing that is to be said about God, God is God the Son as He is God the Father."[63] Against the tendency he sees in modern theology to restrict theological discourse to what can be said about God "for us," Barth applies his basic methodological principle to the discussion regarding God the Son: "He is the Son or Word of God for us because He is so antecedently in Himself."[64] Barth develops this assertion by looking at the christological descriptions of Jesus Christ as Son and as Word.

Although he admits that theology is not able to fathom the depths of what is ultimately mystery, Barth is certain that the key to understanding the biblical figure of Jesus as Son, which befits most clearly the understanding of God's action in Christ as reconciliation, lies in viewing the father-son relation as having its "original and proper reality" in God, rather than in creatures. In expounding the declaration in the ancient creed that the Son is "begotten, not made," Barth concludes that what can be said is that the begetting that characterizes God denotes "the bringing forth of God from God" and that this is superior to the act of creation, which represents "the bringing forth of the creature by God." Barth then expands the thought:

> In the superiority of bringing forth from God in God over bringing forth by God, in the superiority of the freedom in which God posits His own reality over the freedom in which He posits a reality distinct from himself, in the superiority of the love in which He is an object to Himself over the love in which the object is something that exists by His will in distinction from Himself—in this superiority lies the significance of the "begotten, not made."[65]

Like the figure of Jesus as the Son, Barth sees the description of Jesus Christ as the Word of God, which he links more closely to the understanding of God's action in Christ as revelation, as also speaking of a second mode of being in God distinct from, but one in essence with, the first mode of being. The analogy Barth offers in this case is that of a word spoken, which is distinct from the speaker, yet as the word of the speaker is not different in essence from what the speaker is.[66] In the case of God, the unity Barth sees between God and the Word is based on an important epistemological-ontological assumption that runs through his entire theology, the unity between human knowledge of God and the divine self-knowledge: "The Word of God in which God gives Himself to be known by us is none other than that in which God knows Himself."[67] As in the case of the confession of Jesus as the Son, Barth admits the mysterious dimension to the declaration that Jesus is the Word of God, insofar as the relation between the Word and God is beyond our speech actions as creatures: "We know no word which, though distinct from a speaker, still contains and reproduces the whole essence of the speaker."[68] For this reason, Barth prefers the designation "Son" to that of "Word" in referring to Jesus' deity.

Finally, Barth turns his attention to the question as to how people come to confess, "Jesus is Lord." Or, as he put the query, "How does *homo peccator* become *capax verbi divini?*"[69] Consideration of this question introduces the subjective side of revelation, which for Barth leads to the Holy Spirit. By being God present to creatures, the Spirit makes the human reception of revelation possible, so that—to cite Barth's own words— "God himself becomes present to man not just externally, not just from above, but also from within, from below, subjectively."[70] To this end, the Spirit is the Lord, who acts as the Redeemer in setting humans free and constituting them as children of God.

As an orthodox Christian, Barth is convinced that this Spirit is fully God. Scripture, says Barth, testifies that "the Holy Spirit is no less and no other than God Himself, distinct from Him whom Jesus calls His Father, distinct also from Jesus Himself, yet no less than the Father, and no less than Jesus, God Himself, altogether God."[71] Stated in terms of the revelatory event, the subjective element in revelation is of the essence of God. Furthermore, because God is in essence what God is in revelation, "within the deepest depths of deity . . . God is God the Spirit as He is God the Father and God the Son."[72] To explicate this point, Barth develops an Augustinian or Western model of the Trinity with its focus on the idea of the Spirit as the concretization of what is shared between the Father and the Son. Hence, Barth declares that the Spirit is the "togetherness" or the "act of communion" of the Father and the Son; he is the "common factor in the mode of being of God the Father and that of God the Son," which is above all the "reciprocal love of the Father and the Son." Again, the

Spirit is "the act in which the Father is the Father of the Son or the Speaker of the Word and the Son is the Son of the Father or the Word of the Speaker."[73]

Barth, therefore, is an adamant defender of the appropriateness of the presence of the *filioque* in the creed. He argues for this position on the basis of the principle that has informed his delineation of the doctrine of the Trinity at every point, the connection between God in revelation (the economic Trinity) and God in eternity (the immanent Trinity). Or, as he states the axiom in this context, "statements about the divine modes of being antecedently in themselves cannot be different in content from those that are to be made about their reality in revelation."[74] On the basis of this dictum, he asserts that because in revelation and hence in his *opus ad extram* the Spirit is to be understood as the Spirit of both the Father and the Son—regarding which Barth finds nearly universal agreement—the Spirit must be the Spirit of both the Father and the Son in all eternity as well. Perhaps even more forceful is a second argument. In Barth's estimation, the identity of the Spirit as the eternal communion between the Father and the Son provides the eternal, intradivine basis for the communion between God and humankind that the Spirit produces in time. Hence, if in eternity the Spirit is only the Spirit of the Father, the communion between God and humankind lacks objective ground and content; it remains a temporal truth with no eternal basis or guarantee in the communion within God. It is a temporal reality without an eternal content.[75]

With this in view and on the basis of all that he has said to this point about the dynamic of the immanent Trinity, Barth offers a grand summarization of the Western version of the doctrine of the Trinity that provides a fitting climax to the first half-volume of *The Doctrine of the Word of God*: "As God is in Himself Father from all eternity, He begets Himself as the Son from all eternity. As He is the Son from all eternity, He is begotten of Himself as the Father from all eternity. In this eternal begetting of Himself and being begotten of Himself, He posits Himself a third time as the Holy Spirit, that is, as the love which unites Him in Himself."[76]

The Trinity and human knowledge of God. As the above summary suggests, throughout his delineation of the doctrine of the Trinity in his prolegomenon, Barth follows a particular theological method, which proceeds from revelation to the eternal God, that is, from what has come to be termed the economic Trinity to the immanent Trinity. Barth is convinced that human knowledge of God as the triune one arises from revelation, not merely in the form of specific statements about God in the Bible, but also from the structure of revelation itself. Moreover, the three central moments of revelation—creation, reconciliation, and redemption—lead to a consideration of God the Father, God the Son, and God the Spirit (even though Barth clearly acknowledges on the basis of the idea of *perichoresis* that all three persons are involved in each aspect of what is ultimately the work of the one God). In short, the economic Trinity serves as Barth's noetic starting point, but the immanent Trinity retains ontic priority.

What is evident in the theological method of *The Doctrine of the Word of God* is given further explication in Barth's discussion of the knowledge of God that comprises the first topic in volume II of his *Church Dogmatics*.

Mentioning the second volume, *The Doctrine of God*, raises the contested issue regarding a supposed significant turn in Barth's thinking at some point early in the writing of the *Church Dogmatics*. Perhaps the most widely held view, which many commentators attribute—rightly or wrongly—to Hans Urs von Balthasar, speculates that in addition to his turn away from liberalism Barth's thinking underwent one more significant shift, triggered by his study of Anselm—a turn from dialectic to analogy,[77] from "the Word" to "Jesus Christ," or from a strictly existentialist theology of the Word[78] to a christocentric theology.[79] This thesis, however, has come under intense scrutiny in recent years. Bruce McCormack, to cite one especially insightful critic, offers a revised paradigm that interprets the development in Barth's thinking as occurring in four stages with a crucial shift emerging in the wake of a lecture Barth heard by Pierre Maury in June 1936, and hence after revising the first volume of the *Church Dogmatics*. McCormack theorizes that Barth replaced the idea of the election of individuals as the effect of a revelation-event in the present with a focus on the election of Christ as Mediator (and of individuals in Christ). This resulted in a shift from a pneumatocentric to a christocentric orientation, that is, "from a concentration on the present actualization of revelation to a concentration on the *Deus dixit* in the strict sense."[80]

Crucial for Barth's trinitarianism is McCormack's further claim that the modification in Barth's doctrine of election carried implications for his treatment of the being of God as well.[81] This is supposedly evidenced by his declaration in volume II of the *Church Dogmatics*, "God is who He is in the act of His revelation."[82] Although Barth's statement may appear simply to echo the methodological axiom that drove his delineation of the doctrine of the Trinity in the *Church Dogmatics* I/1, in *The Doctrine of God* he seems to be offering a thoroughgoing ontological, and not merely an epistemological, statement. He is not only saying that the being of God is made known to humans in revelation, but also that, insofar as God's being is being-in-act (or perhaps more accurately stated, being-in-the-free-act-of-love[83]), God's own being is in some sense established in that particular act.[84] Moreover, McCormack points out that the act of revelation in Barth's purview is not a series of revelation-events in which God gives himself to be known to humans here and now, but *the* act of revelation that took place then and there and therefore in which all subsequent revelation-events are grounded. Hence, by the time of the writing of *The Doctrine of God*, Barth had supposedly come to conclude that the being of God is not to be understood in terms of the categories of event, act, and life in general, but in a most concrete and unique event. To cite his words, *"Actus purus* is not sufficient as a description of God. To it there must be added at least '*et singularis.*'"[85] Thus, Jüngel concludes regarding his theological mentor, "Barth's theology embodies a decisive turn in the direction of the particular, specific, and concrete, in order to make the universal into something concrete and specific as well."[86]

The foregoing summary of Barth's delineation of the doctrine of the Trinity in the first half-volume of the *Church Dogmatics* suggests that McCormack may—for the sake of presenting what is largely a valid corrective to the understanding of the development of Barth's thought—have exaggerated the shift in Barth's thinking. Nevertheless, McCormack is surely correct in highlighting the particular themes of Barth's doctrine of God evident in the *Church Dogmatics* II/1, for these provide an informative augmentation of certain aspects of the theological perspective evident already in *The Doctrine of the Word of God*.

Perhaps the most significant development is Barth's expansion and clarification in *The Doctrine of God* of his thesis that human knowledge of God is ultimately possible, because it is an outworking of the triune God's eternal knowledge of himself. Lying behind this thesis is a postulate, reminiscent of Hegel, that is central to Barth's entire understanding of the dynamic of revelation: "God is known by God and by God alone."[87] Moreover, and again evidencing similarity to Hegel's proposal, Barth declares that God's self-knowledge is a trinitarian event: "first of all and in the heart of the truth in which we know God, God knows Himself; the Father knows the Son and the Son the Father in the unity of the Holy Spirit."[88] In our knowledge of God we become participants in this intra-trinitarian act as the external expression of the dynamic within the divine life. Consequently, for Barth human knowledge of God entails a reflection in the temporal realm of what is present in the eternal: "Our knowledge of God is derived and secondary. It is effected by grace in the creaturely sphere in consequence of the fact that first of all, in itself and without us, it is actual in the divine sphere."[89]

The relation that Barth—perhaps following a path somewhat reminiscent of that traversed by Hegel—posits between the divine self-knowing and human knowledge of God finds its most significant outworking in human thought and speech. According to Barth, human thinking and speaking possess no innate capacity for describing or bearing adequate witness to God. Nevertheless, human attempts to conceive of and to speak about God succeed insofar as God "truly claims" human thinking and speaking.[90] In this gracious act of God, human concepts and words bear analogous, or partial, correspondence to and agreement with their divine object. Within the limits of the human sphere and despite the unsuitability of speech about God, such declarations may be deemed correct and true. In this divinely produced miracle, Barth asserts, "we come to participate in the veracity of His revelation, and . . . our words become true descriptions of Himself."[91]

In the subsequent volumes of the uncompleted *Church Dogmatics*, Barth's intention was to trace out what is implicit in both *The Doctrine of the Word of God* and *The Doctrine of God*. His goal was to treat, in turn, the doctrines of creation (volume III), reconciliation (the uncompleted volume IV), and redemption (the projected volume V). At each point, Barth's theological reflections give evidence to his conception of the trinitarian pattern of God's relationship to the world delineated already in *Church Dogmatics* I/1. This entails a movement "from primordial ground, to gracious encounter, to consummate effect," to cite Johnson's apt description.[92] And this relationship, like revelation itself, is possible because God is antecedently triune. As Barth declares regarding "the One who reveals Himself according to the witness of Scripture" in *The Doctrine of the Word of God*, "this Lord can be our God, He can meet us and unite Himself to us, because He is God in His three modes of being as Father,

Son and Spirit, because creation, reconciliation and redemption, the whole being, speech and action in which He wills to be our God, have their basis and prototype in His own essence, in His own being as God."[93]

Revelational Trinitarianism and the Future of Trinitarian Theology

Barth is widely noted for his unwavering commitment to the priority of Jesus Christ in all dimensions of theological reflection, but especially in revelation and hence in the knowledge of God. John Webster rightly notes that "as his thought developed, Barth became increasingly confident that no answer to the question of God's relation to humanity can be considered satisfactory which abstracts from the axiomatic reality of God's self-presence in Jesus Christ."[94] Yet Barth's chief significance in the story of trinitarian theology does not rest in his purported revelational christocentrism. In this aspect Barth was merely standing within a long tradition of Christian teaching that upheld the primacy of God's act in Christ as the basis for human knowledge of God. Rather, his central contribution lay in the close connection he posited between the idea of revelation and the triunity of God. Barth set in motion a revelation-oriented approach to the doctrine of the Trinity that came to characterize much subsequent trinitarian thinking. Hegel had seen in God's three-in-one nature as espoused by the doctrine of the Trinity the reflection of the structure or pattern of both thought and the world process. Barth, in turn, saw in God's triunity the structure present within the revelatory act of the one God in Christ.

By treating the Trinity in connection with revelation, Barth underscored his contention that the doctrine arises from an exclusively revelational (as opposed to a philosophical) basis, thereby avoiding the speculative approach to the doctrine characteristic of so much of the Western theological heritage.[95] Yet not all theologians since Barth have lauded the specific way in which he went about the task of recasting the doctrine of the Trinity.

Some have taken issue with Barth's methodological trinitarianism for its utilization of God's triunity to provide the "essential grammar" of the divine engagement with humankind, especially in revelation.[96] These critics fear that this robs God of personhood, for it reduces the triune God of the Bible to the grammatical form of revelation. Furthermore, in the eyes of his critics Barth's proposal ends up in the same anthropocentric caldron as the liberal theologies he sought to overcome, for it suggests that the triune God ultimately exists for the sake of revelation and hence for the sake of human knowledge of God.

A second set of criticisms has arisen from Barth's focus on the one divine subject that he inherited from the Western theological tradition as a whole, but especially from Hegel.[97] Wolfhart Pannenberg, to cite an especially perceptive example, sees in Barth a model of the Trinity that is structurally identical with Hegel's idea of the self-conscious Absolute. But by viewing the doctrine as "an exposition of the subjectivity of God in his revelation," Pannenberg adds, Barth leaves "no room for a plurality of persons in the one God but only for different modes of being in the one divine subjectivity."[98]

Some, including as careful a scholar as Catherine Mowry LaCugna,[99] have found in this aspect of Barth's doctrine of God vestiges of a latent, if not an overt, modalism. One basis for painting Barth with a modalist brush is his preference for the designation "modes of being" *(Seinsweise)* rather than "persons" to refer to the three trinitarian members.[100] This, together with Barth's focus on Jesus Christ, leads critics such as S. Paul Schilling to see in his position a christomonistic modalism. Schilling writes, "It is difficult to harmonize the dominance of Christology in Barth with the claims of a fully trinitarian view of God. He definitely espouses a modalistic trinitarianism, but it is questionable whether he preserves the uniqueness of the Father and the Holy Spirit or their full equality with the Son."[101]

The charge of modalism arises as well out of Barth's answer to the perennial theological question as to how to bring together God's oneness and threeness. Although he seeks to remain at every point thoroughly trinitarian, Barth tends to come down on the side of giving priority to the divine oneness. In his insistence that "personality" and hence personal characteristics be predicated of the one divine essence rather than of the three trinitarian persons,[102] he appears to grant logical, and perhaps even ontological, precedence to the divine *ousia* over the *hypostases*. As sympathetic a commentator as George Hunsinger acknowledges this: "Note that Barth does not see the divine *ousia* as a function of the *perichoresis*, as do some recent theologies, but rather the reverse. . . . Although there is no *ousia* without the *hypostases*, and no *hypostases* without the *perichoresis*, the divine *ousia* is, in Barth's judgment, logically prior and determinative."[103]

Barth's position on this matter drew the fire of those who worry that he is in effect creating a God who is a fourth above the three persons.

Barth's supporters have not been unable to deflect such criticisms. Rowan Williams, for example, demurs that Barth's entire account runs counter to positing God as a "neutral fourth" behind the three persons.[104] Attempts to exonerate Barth tend to appeal to his concept of reiteration, which in turn arises out of his repeated claim that God is eternally and antecedently who God is in revelation, together with his description of the divine freedom as involving God's prerogative to become what God is not, without ceasing to be God—"to differentiate Himself from Himself, to become unlike Himself and yet to remain the same," to cite Barth's words[105]—and hence to become God in a second form or "a second time in a different way."[106] Thus, rather than positing a God beyond the Trinity, Barth concludes from the event of revelation that God subsists in the relationality between the Father and the Son in the Holy Spirit. After surveying several of the more common bases for the variety of modalistic characterizations of Barth, Hunsinger goes so far as to say, "modalism can be charged against Barth only out of ignorance, incompetence, or (willful) misunderstanding."[107]

Jürgen Moltmann introduced a third line of attack. He chastises Barth's theology for being insufficiently eschatological,[108] for being too wedded to the idea of the eternal present in time, which commitment prohibits him from viewing theology from the perspective of God's eschatological future. As an example of his tendency, Moltmann cites Barth's little theological primer from the 1940s, in which he wrote, "Christ's coming again . . . is described in the New Testament as *the* revelation. He will be revealed, not only to the Church but to everyone, as the Person He is. . . . In full clarity and publicity the 'it is finished' will come to light. . . . What is the future bringing? Not once more a turning-point in history, but the revelation of that which *is*. It is the future, but the future of that which the Church *remembers*, of that which has already taken place once and for all."[109] David Mueller sums up the criticism in a single, terse sentence: "Barth's mode of thinking is retrospective rather than prospective."[110]

The query as to whether Barth is sufficiently eschatological in orientation leads to a final question: Is Barth's theology sufficiently trinitarian? This question may be posed in two related ways.

The query must be raised first with regard to the structure of the *Church Dogmatics* as a whole. Some commentators find in Barth's magnum opus an undergirding trinitarian structure. Graham Ward, to cite one example, is convinced that "the doctrine of the Word of God provides the dogmatic basis for the three-fold doctrine of God as seen in Creation, Reconciliation and Redemption."[111] Barth himself, however, denied that the doctrine of the Trinity provided his structuring motif. In commenting about his "dogmatic method" in the waning pages of the second half-volume of *The Doctrine of the Word of God*, he declares forthrightly that he intended to structure his dogmatics according to the concept of revelation, and not according to God's triunity: "we did not derive our differentiation of the four *Loci* from the doctrine of the Trinity. We derived the doctrine of the Trinity itself from the same source as that from which is now derived the differentiation of the *Loci*, viz., the work and activity of God in His revelation."[112] On this basis, Barth claims that "the impression can and must be destroyed that at every point we have to do with a system of trinitarian doctrine," and he takes great pains to distance himself from those of his immediate predecessors "who with more or less inward justification and consistency have constructed their dogmatics according to a trinitarian plan."[113]

In the light of declarations such as these, Jenson's cautious statement appears to be superior to any suggestion that a supposedly trinitarian structuring of the dogmatic enterprise constitutes Barth's lasting contribution: "It is . . . from Barth that twentieth-century theology has learned that the doctrine of Trinity [*sic*] has explanatory and interpretative *use* for the whole of theology; it is by him that the current vigorous revival of trinitarian reflection was enabled."[114] In any case, Barth may be forgiven for writing in reaction to what he saw as the errors of his predecessors. Nevertheless, doing so seems to have left him with a theological proposal that is less trinitarian than might have been expected from the one who is commonly hailed as inaugurating a renaissance of trinitarian theology. The importance of the doctrine of the Trinity as the hallmark of the uniquely Christian conception of God (as Barth himself declares) coupled with its role as *giving* structure to ancient creeds and theological treatises suggest that, Barth's hesitation notwithstanding, Christian theologians do well in drawing their structural motif from this central doctrine.[115]

This observation leads to the second aspect of the question as to whether Barth's theology is sufficiently trinitarian. As the quotation cited above indicates, Barth's rejection of the doctrine of the Trinity as the structuring motif for his dogmatics is based on his conviction that revelation deserves theological priority. Despite the important role that the concept of revelation has played since the Middle Ages in providing the prolegomenon to systematic theology, the question must be raised regarding the advisability of developing a revelational theology. Alan Torrance chastises Barth (albeit mildly) for finding the root of the doctrine of the Trinity in God's lordship in revelation rather than in worship. He asks rhetorically, "If worship can be described as the gift of participating by the Spirit in the Son's communion with the Father and if it denotes the very *telos* of human existence and communion with God, might Barth not have framed his trinitarian discussion and the root of the doctrine of triunity in these terms?" Although "worship" may not be the best replacement for revelation as the starting point for theology, Torrance is surely on the right track in looking toward the eschatological *telos* for the key to unlocking the theological treasure chest.

To conclude: Barth was surely correct in arguing that theology arises ultimately out of a prior act of God that humans cannot initiate but can only receive. The question remains, however, as to whether "revelation," at least in the manner that Barth cast it, is the best beginning point for theological engagement with the nature of God's action toward creation in general and humankind in particular. The task of discovering what might lie at the heart of a trinitarian theology that not only takes Barth's insight seriously but also is thoroughly eschatological in orientation requires that we traverse further the theological journey of the twentieth century.

Theology and the Temporal Presence of the Eternal God: Karl Rahner

Karl Barth's work stood at the genesis of a renaissance in trinitarian theology that lasted throughout the twentieth century. In many respects, his revelational approach set the stage for the subsequent discussion. Above all, the close connection between God-in-revelation and God-in-eternity that lies at the heart of Barth's proposal ignited a lively conversation regarding the relation between God as disclosed in the economy of salvation and God within the eternal divine life, that is, between what is now often termed the economic Trinity and the immanent Trinity. Yet the theologian most often associated with this terminology and the one most generally viewed as casting the discussion in terms of this question is the "Father of the Catholic Church in the twentieth century,"[116] Karl Rahner.

At first glance, it may seem strange to link Barth and Rahner. Barth was a Protestant; Rahner a Roman Catholic. Barth rejected without compromise the concept of an *analogia entis;* Rahner stood within the heritage of Aquinas and the neo-Thomists. Barth viewed the Word of God as the prolegomenon for theology; Rahner followed an anthropological approach[117] that began with human existence and "experiential knowledge."[118] Barth saw little place for philosophy in the theological endeavor; Rahner viewed philosophy as a crucial aspect of what many Roman Catholic thinkers call fundamental theology. Barth sounded an unequivocal "No!" to any suggestion that humans possess an innate ability to know God; Rahner argued that the phenomenon of human transcendence signaled not only that humans have the capacity to receive divine revelation but also that they possess a kind of implicit knowledge of God.

Despite radical differences such as these, the theologies of the two bear striking resemblances. Both were convinced that theology must serve proclamation. Rahner's words might just as easily have come from Barth's pen, when he declared that "when viewed as a whole," theology "has no other task than to investigate the question of how the gospel can be preached in a way that awakens, and claims the allegiance of faith."[119] In their theological reflections, both elevated Jesus Christ and thus Christology. Again, Rahner's response, when asked to pinpoint the center of his theology, might just as easily have been voiced by Barth: "That can't be anything else but God as mystery and Jesus Christ, the crucified and risen one, as the historical event in which this God turns irreversibly toward us in self-communication."[120] Above all, both Barth and Rahner were committed to a renewal of trinitarian thought; both sought to recast the doctrine of the Trinity in a manner that could open new vistas for theological engagement in the modern world; and in certain aspects the recasting of theology that each advocated evidenced genuine affinity to that proposed by the other.

Rahner did not elevate the doctrine of the Trinity to the center of his theological proposal in the obvious manner that Barth did. Nor is he always cited for his work in trinitarian studies. In fact, in some theological circles he is better known for his concept of anonymous Christianity. Nevertheless, the doctrine of the Trinity plays a crucial role in his theology (although this is sometimes overlooked in presentations of his thought[121]). Harvey Egan goes so far as to claim that the Trinity ranks with the incarnation and grace as the three mysteries into which Rahner "compresses all Christianity,"[122] and William Dych asserts that this doctrine formed "the common thread which unifies all the various elements in Rahner's theology."[123]

Rahner has been hailed by Yves Congar for providing "the most original contemporary contribution to the theology of the Trinity."[124] Yet the reason that Rahner is often ranked with Barth in importance for casting the direction of the twentieth-century discussion has less to do with any general trinitarian theological proposal he might be seen as offering than with his articulation and consistent use of a methodological principle that informed the subsequent flow of trinitarian theology. J. A. DiNoia elevates this dictum as "the central axiom of Rahner's theology of the Trinity,"[125] and since the late 1980s it has come to be known as "Rahner's Rule."[126] In its basic form, Rahner's Rule declares, "The 'economic' Trinity is the 'immanent' Trinity and the 'immanent' Trinity is the 'economic' Trinity."[127] Writing in 1982, Walter Kasper indicated the broad influence this postulate had already achieved a scant fifteen years after Rahner formulated it: "What K. Rahner sets down as a basic principle reflects a broad consensus among the theologians of the various churches."[128] So standard has his terminological and methodological proposal become that it routinely appears in theological works without its source being cited. Thus, Rahner's perspective appears in an implicit, albeit unacknowledged, manner in Paul Fiddes's characterization of the theological method of the early church: "The early Christians moved back in thought from the 'economic' Trinity to the 'immanent' Trinity, or from the activity of God in ordering the household *(oikonomia)* of the world to the being of God within God's own self."[129]

The Theological Context for Rahner's Rule

Rahner elucidated the often-repeated formulation of "Rahner's Rule" in an essay composed in 1967 and originally published as a section entitled "Der dreifaltige Gott als transzendenter Urgrund der Heilsgeschichte" ("The Triune God as the Transcendental Ground of Salvation History") within volume 2 of a multivolume series delineating a salvation-historical theology,[130] written by several theologians prominent at the Second

Vatican Council.[131] Rahner's essay subsequently appeared in English as a short, programmatic book, *The Trinity* (1970). He himself admitted, however, that he was not the first to develop the principle associated with his name, and he expressed ignorance as to when and by whom the axiom was first formulated.[132] Kasper suggests that the idea was present already in Schleiermacher but was anticipated in a manner "less open to misunderstanding" by F. A. Staudenmaier, a theologian of the Tübingen school, who in a debate with Hegel spoke of the "vanity of the distinction between Trinity of being and Trinity of revelation."[133] Furthermore, although there is some debate as to the extent to which Barth may be in agreement with Rahner's actual formulation of the axiom,[134] theologians routinely find overtones of the idea in Barth as well. Kasper, for example, declares, "Barth had already written a comparable statement." He then cites as evidence the declaration in Barth's *Church Dogmatics* I/1: "The Reality of God in His revelation is not to be bracketed with an 'only,' as though somewhere behind his revelation there stood another reality of God, but the reality of God which meets us in revelation is His reality in all the depths of eternity."[135] Regardless of its genesis, by stating the precept succinctly and explicitly, Rahner gave it what has become its "classic," widely cited form and injected it into the renewed discussion about the Trinity.

Rahner's Rule has become standard currency in treatises on the Trinity in recent years, and therefore belongs to the story of trinitarian thought in the twentieth century. Nevertheless, it must be understood primarily—or at least initially—within the context of Rahner's own thought.

Transcendental mystery and the incarnation of the Logos. Like Barth, Rahner was a prolific author. Unlike Barth, his preferred mode of theological exposition was the essay,[136] rather than the extended treatise on dogmatics. The set of lectures and essays that comprises the bulk of Rahner's literary output, published as *Theological Investigations*, extends to sixteen volumes in the German edition. His use of the essay as his chief literary genre lends a somewhat haphazard cast to his thinking. Nevertheless, Rahner did display a systematic side, as is evident in the two books he penned dealing with philosophical or fundamental theology. Furthermore, although his theological proposal is scattered throughout his writings, its main lines are presented in the one-volume treatise, *Foundations of Christian Faith,*[137] written near the end of his life. In an interview that took place soon after its publication, Rahner offered a crisp summary of the purpose and theme of the book:

> I really only want to tell the reader something very simple. Human persons in every age, always and everywhere, whether they realize it and reflect upon it or not, are in relationship with the unutterable mystery of human life that we call God. Looking at Jesus Christ the crucified and risen one, we can have the hope that now in our present lives, and finally after death, we will meet God as our own fulfilment.[138]

As his terse synopsis indicates, Rahner—at least according to the standard reading of his work[139]—sees the central theological task to be that of indicating the significance of a suprahistorical orientation in humans toward a reality that transcends the world. His goal is to show that this human experience, the awareness of the presence of the self as subject in every act of knowing, is intelligible only in the light of the transcendent, holy mystery Christians call "God" and that God, in turn, is known in this experience of the self. For this reason, Rahner, together with several other Roman Catholic thinkers including his theological mentors, has been described as a "transcendental Thomist."[140] Anne Carr explains that he "unites the transcendental questioning of Kant with the theology of Aquinas, showing human transcendence of the world toward the infinite horizon, God."[141] To Kant and Aquinas, however, ought to be added the name of Heidegger, with whom Rahner studied in Freiburg from 1934 to 1936.

To accomplish his stated goal, Rahner develops what he called "transcendental reflection," an approach that begins with experience, albeit—as J. A. DiNoia notes—not with "observation and generalizations arising from sense-perception" but with "a reflexive analysis of the structures of knowledge itself."[142] This method ultimately nets the conclusion that according to Joseph Donceel was to become the trademark of Rahner's fundamental theology, the conviction that "because of the dynamism of our human intellect, we implicitly affirm the existence of God in every judgment and free activity."[143] Rather than being alien to human nature, therefore, God is the necessary condition for human subjectivity, insofar as in the act of cognition humans reach out beyond themselves and their finite world toward an infinite horizon of meaning, thereby showing that they already implicitly know "being as such" (that is, God). In keeping with this idea, in the second of his two early philosophical treatises, *Hearer of the Word*, first published in 1941, Rahner describes humans as "the beings who inquire about being in our every thought and action, who, while we inquire about being, and despite its basic hiddenness, have always already affirmed that we know it enough to inquire about it."[144] Furthermore, in that transcendental openness, humans are supernaturally "elevated by God," and as a consequence in some rudimentary sense they can experience God and can be the recipients of God's gracious self-communication. Thus, at the conclusion of *Hearer of the Word*, Rahner summarizes his entire anthropology by offering a definition of the human person: "We are the beings of receptive spirituality, who stand in freedom before the free God of a possible revelation, which, if it comes, happens in our history through the word. We are the ones who, in our history, listen for the word of the free God. Only thus are we what we should be."[145]

Although this "transcendental revelation" entails an implicit knowledge of God, Rahner argues, it always remains unthematic and even preconscious. It is lacking specific information about God that can be formulated conceptually. Instead, it simply reaches out toward an infinite, indefinable, ineffable "holy mystery."[146] God is present in the human transcendental experience, but as a question: as the "question of meaning"[147] or as the "'Whither' of transcendence."[148] For this reason, transcendental revelation must be augmented by "categorical" or "real" revelation, that is, by the specific revelation in history through events, words, and symbols, which discloses the God's "inner reality" and "personal and free relationship to spiritual creatures."[149] Although such revelation is present throughout history and across cultures, it is especially found in what Rahner describes as "public, official, particular and ecclesially constituted revelation,"[150] that is, the prophetic revelation found primarily in the Old and New Testaments, but above all in Jesus Christ as the incarnate Logos.

On the basis of Jesus' own self-consciousness coupled with his resurrection, Rahner concludes that Jesus is the absolute savior, an assertion that leads, in turn, to Jesus' ontological deity, insofar as only God in self-communicating grace can save absolutely. Far more than a mere "message" from God, the salvation toward which human transcendence strives involves the full acceptance of one's own humanity as well as the humanity of others. It entails embracing one's existence "in patient silence (or better in faith, hope and love)," acknowledging it "as the mystery which lies hidden in the mystery of eternal love and which bears life in the womb of death."[151] As the event of absolute salvation, Jesus is God present in a man; he is truly Immanuel, "God with us."

The affirmation of the incarnation leads Rahner to the mystery of the hypostatic union, that is, to the crucial christological question: How can infinite deity and finite humanity unite in the person of Jesus? Rahner believes he has uncovered a clue. As noted already, his transcendental method leads to the realization that humans are not merely closed in upon themselves and upon nature but transcendentally open to God. According to Rahner, the doctrine of the incarnation, in turn, teaches that God intends that human God-openness provide the potential for divine self-expression. Hence God created humankind to be the "cipher of God," the symbol and vehicle of God's self-expressive presence, that is, of the "self-expression of God becoming other."[152] To state the point tersely, "When God wants to be what is not God, man comes to be."[153] Consequently, rather than constituting a contradiction of either true humanity or true deity, the incarnation marks the ultimate fulfillment of both. In this act, Rahner argues, God's desire to express himself outwardly through what is not God came to fruition, and the human search for an absolute savior and human radical openness toward God attained its goal.

The temporal self-communication of the eternal triune God. Rahner's transcendental theology begins and ends with the interconnectedness of the divine and the human. In his estimation, the central mystery of the Christian faith is the reality of "God with us" in the divine self-communication to human creatures. This entails not only God's presence in human history as Logos in the incarnation but also God's presence in grace as Spirit in divinizing the human person in the innermost center of individual existence.[154] For Rahner, these two, together with the act of seeing God as forever mystery even in the beatific vision, comprise the three central facets of the one mystery of the Christian faith, the mystery of the Trinity. Hence he concluded his essay, "The Concept of Mystery in Catholic Theology," which first appeared in 1959, by declaring, "There are these three mysteries in Christianity, no more and no fewer, and the three mysteries affirm the same thing: that God has imparted himself to us through Jesus Christ in his Spirit as he is in himself, so that the inexpressible nameless mystery which reigns in us and over us should be in itself the immediate blessedness of the spirit which knows, and transforms itself into love."[155]

According to Rahner, the three mysteries find their unity as moments of the one act of divine self-communication, which itself has a trinitarian cast: "The absolute self-communication of God to the world, as the mystery which has drawn nigh, is Father as the absolutely primordial and underivative; it is Son, as the principle which itself acts and necessarily must act in history in view of this free self-communication; it is Holy Spirit, as that which is given, and accepted by us."[156] Elevating the divine self-communication as the central motif of his trinitarian theology leads Rahner to an understanding of the Trinity reminiscent of Barth's. In his 1960 essay "Remarks on the Dogmatic Treatise 'De Trinitate,'" Rahner declares in a somewhat Barthian fashion,

> this *self*-communication of God to us has, according to the testimony of revelation in the Scripture, a threefold aspect. It is a self-communication in which that which is imparted remains the sovereign and incomprehensible, and which even as something received continues to be unoriginated and not at the disposal or within the grasp of anyone. It is a self-communication in which the God who reveals himself "is there," as self-expressive truth and as free directive power acting in history. And it is a self-communication in which the God who imparts himself brings about the acceptance of his gift, in such a way that the acceptance does not reduce the communication to the level of merely created things.[157]

Furthermore, his use of the theme of the divine self-communication as the primary trinitarian motif leads Rahner to echo Barth's concern that the understanding of the doctrine of the Trinity arise out of revelation itself and that Christian theology not be beholden to categories borrowed from either philosophy or human experience, which are then subsequently applied to God. More specifically, he steadfastly opposed the kind of social trinitarianism that viewed Father, Son, and Spirit as three different consciousnesses. Although in 1960 he did not see this problem as so acute that it required that the word "person" itself be replaced by "some less ambiguous word" after the manner of Barth's proposal,[158] Rahner later appears to have changed his mind. In a lecture delivered in 1977, "Oneness and Threefoldness of God in Discussion with Islam," he admitted that the term carries ecclesiastical weight and therefore is in some sense binding for the Catholic theologian. But he quickly added that the modern notion of "person" leads to inevitable misunderstanding, for it suggests that the members of the Trinity are "three reciprocally related centres of mental action."[159] Convinced that in such a situation the kerygmatic task of the church requires that the theologian suggest viable alternatives,[160] Rahner offered what he deemed as two "very brief and awkwardly expressed suggestions," namely, that of speaking about three "hypostases in God" or about "three modes of subsistence of the one God in his one sole nature."[161] The second of these may well be a slight modification of the term he offered in *The Trinity*, namely, "distinct manners of subsisting."[162]

Rahner's focus on the mystery of God with us and hence on the temporal sphere as the location of the divine self-communication indicates the extent to which he approaches the doctrine of the Trinity from the perspective of the "economic Trinity," that is, from God's threefold activity in salvation. Thus, after outlining the triune character of the divine self-communication (cited above), he adds, "Since this 'as' which is used in relation to us really speaks of the self-communication of God *in himself,* this trinity appertains to God in himself—it signifies a distinction in God himself."[163] This point finds echo in *The Trinity*, in which he declares, "We may confidently look for an access into the doctrine of the Trinity in Jesus and in his Spirit, as we experience them through faith in salvation history. For in these two persons the immanent Trinity itself *is* already given."[164]

In approaching the immanent Trinity from the perspective of the economic Trinity, Rahner consciously places himself at odds with the Neoscholastic tradition in which he had been trained[165] but that in his estimation had resulted in the doctrine of the Trinity becoming irrelevant to Christian faith in general and to theology in particular.[166] According to Rahner, the Neoscholastics, who were the bearers of the "manualist" tradition in which each theological locus is treated as a different "treatise," had so separated the divine unity from the divine threeness that the former could be treated without reference to the latter, and the doctrine of the Trinity as a whole could be developed without recourse to the revelation of the three trinitarian members in salvation history. Moreover, the Neoscholastics, who stood at the end of a long process that began with

Augustine and was augmented by Aquinas, had separated God's threefold activity in history (the economic Trinity) from the threefoldness of God in eternity (the immanent Trinity). As a result they speculated on the inter-trinitarian relations completely apart from any reference to the salvation-historical activity of the three persons. In response, Rahner asserts categorically, "No adequate distinction can be made between the doctrine of the Trinity and the doctrine of the economy of salvation."[167]

Rahner, therefore, is convinced that the mystery of the economic Trinity is the mystery of the immanent Trinity, and this because of the connection between God-for-us and God-in-eternity: "God has given himself so fully in his absolute self-communication to the creature, that the 'immanent' Trinity becomes the Trinity of the 'economy of salvation,' and hence in turn the Trinity of salvation which we experience *is* the immanent Trinity. This means that the Trinity of God's relationship to us *is* the reality of God as he is *in* himself: a trinity of persons."[168] The task of trinitarian theology, in turn, becomes that of inquiring as to why the divine self-communication must take place in the manner Scripture presents it—that is, why the Son must appear historically in the flesh and why the Spirit must bring about our acceptance of God's self-communication—while remaining *one* divine self-communication.[169]

Rahner substantiates the connection between the immanent Trinity and the economic Trinity by appeal to Christian teachings regarding both the incarnation and the reception of grace,[170] although he places the greater weight on the former. In his estimation, the incarnation comprises the point in salvation history at which the unity of the immanent Trinity and the economic Trinity is most evident. In Jesus Christ the Logos, the second person of the Trinity, actually became a human person, with the consequence that the Logos in salvation history and the eternal Logos are identical.

According to Rahner, this identity means that only the Logos could have become incarnate in Jesus. Here again, Rahner stands against tendencies evident in his Neoscholastic heritage. He believes that by elevating the principle of the unity of the divine activities in the world and in so doing failing to be sufficiently trinitarian in their account of the divine work "for us and for our salvation," Catholic theology (following Aquinas himself[171]) had come to the erroneous conclusion that any of the trinitarian members could have been the subject of the incarnation.[172] According to Rahner, this idea replaces the Christian story of the incarnation of the

Logos with talk about a generic God becoming human.[173] Moreover, it means that the incarnation reveals nothing about the Logos himself.[174] It separates God-in-eternity from salvation history. It renders the incarnation superfluous to God's inner being, which would then remain unaffected by it. And it eliminates any genuine divine self-communication to humans within history.[175] So crucial is this, Rahner asserts, that to postulate that any of the three trinitarian persons could have become incarnate is to "throw the whole of theology into confusion." He then explains:

> There would be no longer any real and intrinsic connexion between the mission of a divine person and the immanent life of the Trinity. Our sonship in grace would have absolutely nothing to do with the sonship of the Son, since it would have been absolutely the same if it could have been based on any other incarnate person of the Godhead. There would be no way of finding out, from what God is to us, what he is in himself as the Trinity.[176]

Against the position of Neoscholastic theology, Rahner claims that the three members of the Trinity are distinct from each other precisely as persons or hypostases, and hence that these two words refer to each of the three in a unique manner. As a consequence, trinitarian thought seeks to determine what it means to say that the one who is incarnate in Jesus Christ is the Son (and the one at work in sanctification is the Spirit), as well as to indicate the significance of the role Jesus plays in salvation history for the place of the Son in the divine life.

The connection Rahner posits between the eternal Logos and the Logos incarnate opens the way to solving another potential problem that his axiom raises: the apparent contradiction between his conception of God and the traditional doctrine of the divine immutability. Equating the economic Trinity with the immanent Trinity seems to suggest that God changes in and through his relations with history. To deal with this potential problem, Rahner draws from the incarnation a distinction between God changing within the divine being and God changing in another, that is, between internal and external divine change. According to Rahner, "God can become something. He who is not subject to change in himself can *himself* be subject to change *in something else*."[177] This is possible because God created the human creature in such a way so as to be the "grammar of God's possible self-expression" and thus as a proper vehicle for God's own becoming-in-self-expression.[178] Rahner, therefore, concludes that in assuming human nature through the incarnation God "becomes" while remaining immutable.

Although Rahner's Rule posits a strong link between the immanent Trinity and the economic Trinity, in one respect Rahner also carefully distinguishes the two. He maintains the priority of the former as constituting the transcendent basis for the latter. Hence Rahner concludes that the triune God is able to share truth and love with what is not divine in the act of self-communication, because God is antecedently constituted by relations of truth and love within the one eternal divine reality: "There is real difference in God as he is in himself between one and the same God insofar as he is—at once and necessarily—the unoriginate who mediates himself to himself (Father), the one who is in truth uttered for himself (Son), and the one who is received and accepted in love for himself (Spirit)—and insofar as, *as a result of this,* he is the one who can freely communicate himself."[179]

Yet, despite Rahner's willingness to retain a kind of ontological priority for the immanent Trinity, the main direction of his work is toward the task of maintaining the closest possible connection between the immanent Trinity and the economic Trinity. For him, they are not understood as two distinct realities (with the result that the immanent Trinity can take precedence over the economic Trinity) but as constituting one triune God who is wholly present, as he eternally is, in his self-communication to us. In positing this, Rahner's doctrine of the Trinity becomes not merely the central aspect of the doctrine of God, but also, by extension, the central postulate regarding the mystery of God and the world. Rahner's trinitarianism led him to develop a conception that viewed God as the one who "gives himself away to this world" and "has his own fate in and with this world." In a lecture delivered in 1981 under the title "The Specific Character of the Christian Concept of God," he declared, "Only when . . . within a concept of God that makes a radical distinction between God and the world, God himself is still the very core of the world's reality and the world is truly the fate of God himself, only then is the concept of God attained that is really Christian."[180]

Rahner's Rule and the Future of Trinitarian Theology

As the foregoing discussion indicates, Rahner's articulation of what is now commonly termed Rahner's Rule arose within the context of his interest in returning salvation history to its rightful place in theological reflection. In a day when Catholic theologians were neglecting the trinitarian structure of the divine activity in salvation in favor of speculation regarding the inner dynamic of God apart from the world, Rahner hoped to shift the starting point for theology to God's interaction with humans in the economy of salvation, which always comes by means of the work of one or another of the three trinitarian members. Because the eternal God reveals the true divine self to humans through the redemptive process, he argued, the experience of God in the divine self-communication entails a genuine experience of the eternal God. For this reason, Rahner added, God is "actually internally just the way we experience the divine in relation to us, namely, as Father, Son, and Spirit."[181] Or, stated in other words, from the way that God gives himself to us in salvation history—namely, as Father, as Son, and as Holy Spirit—we know that the eternal God is in fact triune self-giving.[182] Thus, Rahner enjoined a theological method that begins with the manner in which the triune God relates to the world—as Father, as Son, and as Holy Spirit—and not from a prior understanding of God as a unity.[183]

Despite Rahner's own circumspect intentions, since 1967 theologians have debated not only the implications but even the meaning of Rahner's Rule. LaCugna appears close to Rahner himself in declaring, "The identity of 'economic' and 'immanent' Trinity means that God truly and completely gives God's self to the creature without remainder, and what is given in the economy of salvation *is* God as such."[184] Kasper, in contrast, attempts to overcome some of the difficulties he sees in Rahner's proposal, especially the possibility that it implies that "the eternal Trinity first came into existence in and through history," by restating the axiom: "in the economic self-communication the intra-trinitarian self-communication is present in the world in a new way, namely, under the veil of historical words, signs and actions, and ultimately in the figure of the man Jesus of Nazareth."[185] Peters goes even further in offering a radical interpretation of the dictum. In his engagement with Jüngel, he describes Rahner's Rule as implying that "the relationality God experiences through Christ's saving relationship to the world is constitutive of trinitarian relations proper. God's relations *ad extra* become God's relations *ad intra*."[186]

As these various restatements suggest, Rahner ignited an intense conversation about the relationship between the economic Trinity and the immanent Trinity. Some participants in this debate, such as Jüngel, concluded that Rahner's Rule "should be given unqualified agreement."[187] Others, however, were more cautious. The most vexing criticism voiced against Rahner's perspective has been the suspicion that he has linked the immanent Trinity too closely with the economic Trinity, perhaps even to the point of collapsing the former into the latter.

One aspect of this singular critique is the link Rahner posits between the missions of the Son and the Spirit in the world and the processions within the eternal divine dynamic. Rahner has been criticized for explicating this relationship by using the language of "self-expression" and "self-possession." Indeed, in a manner reminiscent of Hegel, Rahner develops a trinitarian depiction of being, which in the case of God means that "the Father is himself by the very fact that he opposes to himself the image which is of the same essence as himself, as the person who is other than himself; and so he possesses himself."[188] Stated simply, Rahner is suggesting that the divine life may be characterized as the Father expressing himself in the Son in order to possess himself in the Spirit. DiNoia points out, however, that any depiction of the dynamic of the triune God that draws from the concepts of self-expression and self-possession runs the risk of introducing an element of necessity into the divine action in the world, for it suggests that "the Trinity really could not be fully itself independently of the orders of creation and redemption." DiNoia then concludes, "Rahner's trinitarian theology risked a pattern of explanation in which the free actions of creation, incarnation, and grace could be seen as necessary extensions of God's inner self-expression and self-possession."[189]

John Thompson is likewise concerned about the problem of introducing necessity into the divine acting in the world. He believes that to fail to distinguish the immanent Trinity from the economic Trinity is to fall into the error of "making God dependent on his historical manifestation."[190] Thompson worries that by failing to distinguish between "the free mystery of grace in the economy and the *necessary* mystery of the Trinity per se," Rahner (albeit perhaps not by intention) "risks making God's actions *ad extra* a necessity of his being rather than a freely willed decision." Thompson, in contrast, is convinced that "neither an inner necessity of being nor an outward compulsion, but only his will to be our God, obliges God to act."[191]

Although his critics may have put their collective finger on an unfortunate implication of Rahner's Rule, Rahner himself clearly did not move in this direction, at least not fully or intentionally. In a manner somewhat similar to Barth, he grounded God's external self-expression in a prior act within the eternal divine life: "It is because God 'must' express himself inwardly that he can also utter himself outwardly; the finite, created utterance *ad extra* is a continuation of the immanent constitution of 'image and likeness'—a free continuation, because its object is finite—and takes place in fact 'through' the Logos."[192] Similarly, in his discussion of the divine processions, he writes, "The unoriginated God (called 'Father') has from eternity the opportunity of an historical self-expression and likewise the opportunity of establishing himself as himself at the innermost centre of the intellectual creature as the latter's dynamism and goal. These two eternal possibilities (which are pure actuality) are God, are to be distinguished from each other, and are to be distinguished by this distinction also from the unoriginated God."[193] LaCugna, therefore, may well have been correct in concluding, "Rahner's principle . . . ensures a commensurability between mission and procession. The mission of the Son, precisely to be the Son who discloses the Father, must be grounded in the 'intradivine' procession of the Son who is eternally begotten of the Father."[194]

The perceived difficulties in Rahner's theological proposal have led many theologians to add qualifiers to Rahner's Rule. Congar has voiced what has become the most typical cautionary revision. Citing as Rahner's axiom, "The economic Trinity is the immanent Trinity and vice versa," Congar suggests that the first half of the statement is "beyond dispute." But he proposes that the "vice versa" be dropped, so as to preserve the distinction between "the free mystery of the economy and the necessary mystery of the Tri-unity of God."[195]

Despite such revisions, as Congar's unequivocal affirmation of the first aspect of Rahner's Rule indicates, thinkers working in Rahner's wake are conscious of the essential connection between the doctrine of God and soteriology. Moreover, trinitarian thinkers since Rahner seek to give utmost seriousness to the epistemological link between the economic Trinity and the immanent Trinity. Yet, the question remains as to whether an epistemological connection does not also imply an ontological link, and thereby perhaps inevitably submerges the immanent Trinity into the economic Trinity. Writing in 1973, Helmut Thielicke cautions against just such a wholesale equating of the two (although the target of his attack is largely Schleiermacher, and he omits any reference to Rahner). While agreeing that the economic Trinity comprises the noetic principle in theology, he quickly adds, "The only question is whether God is absorbed into the revelation event, whether he does not just enter into history but becomes history, whether he not only sets up the relation to the world and man but is this relation." Thielicke advises that the crucial response entails "making a clear distinction between the noetic and ontic aspects" by which he intends the economic Trinity and the immanent Trinity, "and not allowing them uncritically to merge into one another."[196]

Whether Rahner's Rule intends the kind of uncritical merging of the two that Thielicke deplores is doubtful, despite the close connection Rahner adamantly posits between the immanent Trinity and the economic Trinity. LaCugna is convinced that rather than being guilty of this theological error, Rahner in fact intended the axiom to be viewed as offering a methodological, and not an ontological, insight. In her estimation, Rahner intends to declare that "the order of theological knowledge must adhere to the historical form of God's self-communication in Christ and the Spirit. Knowledge of God takes place through Christ and the Holy Spirit, according to the order (*taxis*) of the divine missions."[197] It seems, then, that Rahner—like Barth—retained the classical belief that God's eternal being is ultimately independent of historical events. If this is the case, then the question that lies at the heart of Rahner's Rule is, to cite LaCugna's characterization, "Can we affirm that God as God is altogether present in the economy of salvation history, and at the same time that God also exceeds and outstrips the human capacity to receive or explain this self-communication?"[198]

Many theologians working in the wake of Rahner have followed the more circumspect interpretation of the axiom such as that articulated by LaCugna. Others, however, have taken the principle in more radical directions. Peters pinpoints what in the opinion of many of these thinkers comprises the difficulty that theologians working this side of the advent of Rahner's Rule must address. He writes, "The problem with classical formulations is that when God is described as eternal it is assumed that the immanent Trinity is somehow fixed and immutable before entering history through the incarnation." What would happen, however, if this classical assumption were cast aside? What would emerge if theologians were—to cite Peters's description—"to reconceive the relationship between time and eternity so that what happens in the history of salvation becomes constitutive of the content of eternal life"?[199]

By preserving the distinction between the economic Trinity and the immanent Trinity, as tenuous as that distinction for them may have been, the two pioneers of the twentieth-century trinitarian renaissance—Barth and Rahner—did not themselves follow this more radical path. They left to other theologians the task of drawing out the more thoroughgoing implication of Rahner's Rule, namely, the idea that God finds his identity in the interplay of the three members of the Trinity within the temporal events of the economy of salvation. In the case of some thinkers, this interplay led to an additional step beyond Barth and Rahner. These theologians sought to strip the doctrine of the Trinity of the Hegelian vestiges that Barth and Rahner maintained, especially the characterization of God as the one divine subject.[200] Against the pioneers of the trinitarian renaissance, they boldly declared that the three members of the Trinity are not merely the three modes of being or ways of subsisting of the one, personal God, but are three persons—even three conscious subjects—who comprise in turn the one indivisible God.[201] To these thinkers we must now turn.

3

The Trinity as the Fullness of History

The consensus of historians is that Karl Barth set the tone for the twentieth-century renaissance of trinitarian theology. Ted Peters goes so far as to declare categorically, "The major contributors to the contemporary rethinking of the doctrine of the Trinity either extend principles already proffered by Barth or else follow lines of thought that parallel his *Church Dogmatics*." In fact, for Peters the work of the leading voices in the trinitarian renaissance marks the blossoming of "Barthian shoots."[1] Barth's importance is, of course, unequaled. In the wake of Hegel's insight that both thought and world process evidence a trinitarian structure, he declared that such a structure inheres in the revelatory act of the one God in Christ, for in the divine self-disclosure God is subject, act, and event. In the move to revelation, Barth was by no means a voice crying in the wilderness. Karl Rahner joined the refrain by asserting that the divine activity in salvation, which forms theology's starting point, displays a trinitarian structure, for God's saving interaction with humans always occurs through the work of one or another of the three trinitarian members.

The work of the two Karls injected the interplay of the themes of revelation and salvation history into the burgeoning trinitarian theology, as thinkers took up the challenge of characterizing the connection between God-in-revelation or God-in-salvation (the economic Trinity) and God-in-eternity (the immanent Trinity). In the ensuing conversation, some voices averred that Barth and Rahner had gone astray by conceptualizing the distinction between revelation and eternity in spatial terms, that is, by suggesting that revelation with its trinitarian structure discloses a divine reality that transcends the historical realm and comes to it, as it were, from "above." As an alternative, these progenies of the two Karls raised the possibility of an alternative manner of understanding the relationship: by appeal to a temporal—rather than a spatial—metaphor. They proposed that the interconnection of the three trinitarian persons in salvation, and hence in revelation, be understood as the dynamic of the triune God who dwells in an eternity located at the end of, rather than above, time. In their estimation, history is the story of the three trinitarian persons, and as a consequence the triune God emerges as the God of history.

A variety of theologians took up the theme of God as the fullness of (divine) history, including Roman Catholic thinkers such as Bruno Forte[2] and Protestants like Ted Peters.[3] Yet a trio of voices formed the centerpiece of the chorus: Jürgen Moltmann (b. 1926), Wolfhart Pannenberg (b. 1928), and Robert Jenson (b. 1930). Although they differ on the details, these Protestant thinkers share the desire to conceptualize the doctrine of the Trinity by looking at the work of the three trinitarian persons in history. Furthermore, Moltmann, Pannenberg, and Jenson are convinced that the turn toward history facilitates what in their estimation is a necessary move away from the focus on the one divine subject to which they believe Barth and Rahner remained captive.

The Trinity as the Divine Engagement with the World: Jürgen Moltmann

Jürgen Moltmann is undoubtedly the most decorated theologian since Barth, at least in North American circles. The accolade-articulation process began as early as 1973, when Douglas Meeks prophesied, "It is difficult to imagine any theology in the near future which could function without being consciously or unconsciously influenced by Jürgen Moltmann's 'theology of hope.' . . . Perhaps it will be said in the future that he has initiated a new theological era."[4] In 1996, two years after Moltmann retired from a celebrated career first as a pastor and then as a university professor, Thorward Lorenzen asserted that Moltmann "is one of the most read, most productive, and most relevant Christian theologians at work today. Next to Karl Barth he is internationally the best-known Reformed theologian in our century." Lorenzen then underscored Moltmann's global influence: "He has influenced the life of the church and its witness . . . throughout the world."[5] This statement echoed a judgment

Richard Bauckham had voiced a decade earlier: "Jürgen Moltmann has probably had more influence worldwide than any other Protestant dogmatic theologian alive today."[6] On the heels of the publication of the final installment in Moltmann's six-volume series of "contributions to theology," *Experiences in Theology*,[7] Geiko Müller-Fahrenholz summed up the significance of Moltmann's distinguished career. He extolled his former teacher as "the most important German-speaking Protestant theologian since the Second World War."[8]

Like Pannenberg, Moltmann looks to history for the center of his theological approach. Müller-Fahrenholz goes so far as to declare that history is *the* theme of Moltmann's theology.[9] Despite this similarity, his writings differ markedly from Pannenberg's in several respects. Above all, Moltmann has not given the sustained attention to a philosophically attuned and metaphysically concerned engagement[10] with the concept of history and its relation to the triune God that has been indicative of his German colleague.

Moltmann takes philosophical concerns seriously, of course, but his chief interest lies elsewhere. His intellectual efforts are directed more toward developing a trinitarian perspective that can serve the church's mission in the contemporary world. Although by no means bereft of critical interaction with the great theological voices of the day, Moltmann's writings—in the words of Müller-Fahrenholz—"reflect the problems which have left their stamp on the second half of the twentieth century."[11] Moltmann himself acknowledges the practical orientation of his theological work. In response to a series of essays published in 2000 dealing with his theology, he declared, "I am not so concerned with correct but more with concrete doctrine; and thus not concerned with pure theory but with practical theory."[12] Thus he sees the task of theology less as providing an interpretation of the world than as transforming it in the light of its ultimate transformation by God. To this end, he seeks to overcome the destructive separation between theology and Christian practice by providing a "critical theory of God" that will have direct social application. Looking back over Moltmann's career, Laurence Wood lauded this characteristic of his work: "Jürgen Moltmann has been a global pacesetter *par excellence* in modeling how theology can speak prophetically and therapeutically to a dysfunctional world."[13]

As his commentators have pointed out, Moltmann's overriding desire is to engage with contemporary life. Yet he does so from a thoroughgoing theological perspective. Bauckham summarizes Moltmann's stance in this manner: "Theology is in the service of the church's mission as, from its starting-point in the cross and resurrection of Jesus, it relates to the world for the sake of the future of the world."[14] Although Moltmann does focus on the cross and resurrection, especially in his first major works, he views these two events within a wider context, the entire history of God. Hence he tackles the questions raised by the church's context from the perspective of the triune God who is active in the world. Furthermore, for Moltmann, God's triunity is integrally connected to the divine engagement with the world, which forms a history centering on Jesus Christ.

The History of the Trinitarian Persons

In Moltmann's estimation, the genesis of trinitarian theology lies in history, above all, in the history of Jesus the Son,[15] but more particularly, in the history of his relationship to the one he called "Abba" that occurred within the context of the promissory history of Israel. This perspective casts Moltmann's trinitarian theology as a kind of historicizing of Barth's contention that the Christ-event is constitutive for the divine life in all eternity. Moreover, this approach leads Moltmann to view the doctrine of the Trinity less as a statement about the eternal nature of God apart from the world than as a retelling of the history of God viewed as the history of the communal relationships of the three divine persons. This dynamic comprises the history of God's love, liberation, and reconciliation of all creation,[16] for it brings about the inclusion of the world within the life of the triune God.

Like Pannenberg, Moltmann believes that launching trinitarian theology with the history of God results in the givenness of the three persons, so that God's oneness, rather than threeness, becomes the question with which theologians must grapple.[17] And like Pannenberg, he sees the unity of God emerging from the eschatological future.

History and the ontology of the future. Moltmann takes up the task of developing the conceptual framework for his perspective on the relationship of the triune God to history in his first major treatise,[18] *Theology of Hope.*[19] It is here that his work most resembles that of Pannenberg, as Moltmann sets forth his version of the eschatological ontology that they share.

Like his former colleague at the University of Mainz, Moltmann draws insight from the Hebrew conception of the historical character of reality mediated to him by the great German biblical scholars of the day, especially Gerhard von Rad. But the two theologians take the insight from their mentors in different directions.[20] For Pannenberg revelation is located in the "history of traditions," that is, in the events of history understood within their historical context climaxing in the definitive eschatological event. Moltmann, in contrast, retains Barth's focus on the Word as the locus of divine revelation. In this sense, he stands closer to Barth than Pannenberg does.

Yet on the basis of his acceptance of federal or covenant theology, Moltmann shifts the character of the revelatory Word to "promissory history."[21] In his estimation, history is the outworking of the faithfulness of the covenanting God who announces and then fulfills his promises. Thus, rather than viewing revelation as "epiphany" (that is, the unveiling of what exists eternally in the heavenly realm), as Greek philosophical theology purported, Moltmann concludes that according to the biblical viewpoint the divine presence occurs in the form of promise directed toward the future.[22] He points out that the promissory character of the Hebrew perception of the world gave rise to the concept of history as the linear movement toward the future,[23] together with the prophetic call for righteousness in the light of God's faithfulness and coming kingdom. The disciples of Jesus, in turn, came to see him as an event of divine promise. Consequently, they proclaimed his death and resurrection as God's promise of a general resurrection of the dead and a future kingdom of righteousness,[24] for which the Holy Spirit was the "earnest."

For Moltmann, then, revelation is not a supernatural incursion into history from a heavenly realm above. Instead, it is a promissory Word about a totally new reality lying in the future that, although not inherent in the present, can nevertheless be anticipated in the here and now. Rather than revelation arising out of history, therefore, history is the predicate of revelation, and in this sense the Word creates history. This biblical starting point leads Moltmann to conclude that the heart of Christianity is the hopeful anticipation—emerging from the promissory event of the resurrection of Jesus—of the coming of the kingdom of God, which comprises the eschatological fulfillment of the divinely promised freedom and community of humans, together with the liberation of creation from bondage to decay. Although it lies in the future, this kingdom of glory is nevertheless present, insofar as it affects the here and now. Specifically, "it works upon the present by awaking hopes and establishing resistance."[25]

The dynamic of promise and fulfillment leading to an eschatological hope forms the biblical basis for Moltmann's eschatological understanding of God. Like Pannenberg, he posits an insoluble link between God's being and the future kingdom of glory in which God will be fully manifest in the world. Consequently, in Moltmann's estimation, "God is not 'beyond us' or 'in us,' but ahead of us in the horizons of the future opened to us in his promises," so that "the 'future' must be considered as the mode of God's being."[26]

Moltmann developed his theological understanding in critical conversation with the revisionist Marxist philosopher Ernst Bloch. In his work *The Principle of Hope*,[27] Bloch sets forth an ontology of "not-yet-being," at the heart of which is the idea of an as-yet-unrealized utopia that exerts power over the present and past. Hence, in Bloch's view, the future is "ontologically prior" to the present. Rather than being determined by the present, the future determines the present. Furthermore, the future does not arise out of the present but comes to it, drawing the present forward into totally new forms of reality. In short, the future is not *becoming*, it is *coming*.

Drawing impulses from Bloch's ontology, Moltmann postulates that the future penetrates into the here and now, releasing events that propel the present into its future. These proleptic, anticipatory events are divine acts, for in them God is present in suffering and power. The greatest of these occurrences are connected to Jesus Christ, especially his cross and resurrection, together with the sending of the Holy Spirit. Moltmann, therefore, conceives of God's presence in the world in a trinitarian manner, for the divine presence is nothing else than the history of the three persons of the Trinity, which history comprises the history of God.

The trinitarian history of Jesus. Moltmann's first major theological treatise provides an important conceptual backdrop for his overall project. Yet the first significant expression of his innovative trinitarian theology comes in his subsequent book, *The Crucified God*[28] with its exposition of the cross as a trinitarian event.[29] Even here, the main focus is not the doctrine of the Trinity, for the book arises to a large measure out of the question of theodicy. In fact, Warren McWilliams considers this volume to be Moltmann's "primary contribution to the theodicy issue."[30] In *The Crucified God*, Moltmann does not treat evil as a reality that God resolves through the cross but as what God, in love, meets by voluntarily suffering with suffering creation.[31] Moltmann understands this divine suffering as a trinitarian event.

Crucial for the development of Moltmann's trinitarian theology is a thesis that has emerged as one of his central contributions to contemporary theology. He asserts that the cross not only effects human reconciliation but also marks the triune God's act of self-constitution within history. As he declares in *Experiences in Theology,* written nearly three decades after the publication of *The Crucified God,* "Christ's death on the cross is an inner-trinitarian event before it assumes significance for the redemption of the world."[32]

According to Moltmann, the basis of the Trinity lies in the separation-in-unity that the triune God experienced in this event. As Jesus surrendered himself on the cross to suffer the God-forsakenness entailed in his abandonment by his Father, the Father likewise suffered the anguish of being separated from the Son that was involved in his surrendering his Son to suffering and death. Yet at the point of their widest separation, the Father and the Son were united in a deep "communion of will,"[33] for they shared a common love for the godforsaken, suffering world. In so doing, they entered a new unity in the Spirit. Moltmann summarizes the point: "In the cross, Father and Son are most deeply separated in forsakenness and at the same time are most inwardly one in their surrender. What proceeds from this event between Father and Son is the Spirit."[34]

The trinitarian character of the cross carries a far-reaching theological implication. In Moltmann's estimation, this historical event shows that, contrary to classical theism, God is not immutable. Insofar as the historical event of the cross constitutes God's eternal being, God not only affects the world but is also affected by the world and above all by humankind. As the one who is able freely to take on the suffering of those who suffer, the very heart of God is touched by the world. In fact, the cross marks the entrance of human history with all its pain and evil into God's own life: "The concrete 'history of God' in the death of Jesus on the cross on Golgatha . . . contains within itself all the depths and abysses of human history," insofar as "all human history . . . is taken up into this 'history of God,' i.e., into the trinity, and integrated into the future of 'the history of God.'"[35]

In articulating this point, Moltmann is not merely repackaging the theodicy endemic to process theology.[36] At the heart of his proposal is the idea that the cross is ultimately an event within the divine history. By viewing the cross primarily as an experience between the Father and the Son, he places the manner in which God is affected by the world within the trinitarian relationships, rather than viewing them merely as the interplay between the world and God. Moltmann's position likewise differs from the various pessimistic proposals that see the cross as God's great contradiction to the present world. In this historical event, Moltmann avers, God not only takes into the history of the trinitarian relationships the contradiction of human history, God also overcomes that contradiction.[37] Bauckham summarizes Moltmann's point: "God does not offer hope for the world simply by contradicting its negativity. Rather, his love embraces the world in all its negativity, suffers the contradiction and overcomes it."[38]

The perichoretic life of the trinitarian persons. Moltmann engages with aspects of trinitarian theology in most of his subsequent books, including the third programmatic volume, *The Church in the Power of the Spirit.*[39] Yet the most complete explication of his doctrine of the Trinity comes in *The Trinity and the Kingdom*, which comprises the first installment of a six-volume series of "contributions to theology."

In his mature trinitarian theology, Moltmann (like Pannenberg) rejects what he sees as the erroneous fixation on the divine subject evident in Barth's trinitarian theology as well as the unfortunate appeal to impersonal philosophical terms (for example, *ousia* and *substance*) characteristic of the patristic era.[40] Moltmann demurs that Barth's starting point in the lordship of God led him to view God as one personal subject in three modes of being. Moltmann even suggests that Barth's attempt to launch his trinitarian theology with the divine lordship had the potential to entangle him in the mistake that characterized his great nemesis, Friedrich Schleiermacher, namely, the assumption that the fundamental Christian experience is the experience of the one God.[41] Moltmann, in contrast, avers that already in the New Testament, this experience is presented as trinitarian. Consequently, he bases his break with Barth (and the patristic writers) on the trinitarian character of the history of Jesus: "The history in which Jesus is manifested as 'the Son' is not consummated and fulfilled by a single subject. The history of Christ is already related in trinitarian terms in the New Testament itself."[42] For Moltmann, then, and in contrast to Barth, Jesus Christ is the locus of divine revelation, because his history, as narrated in the Gospels and as occurring in the context of the history of Israel, stands at the heart of the history of the triune life of God.[43]

On the basis of his observation that the biblical depiction of the divine action that centers on Christ reveals three persons at work rather than one, Moltmann contends that trinitarian theology must begin with the fellowship of a plurality of persons, understood as three centers of conscious activity; only then can the question of their unity be raised.[44] His commitment to this theological approach leads Moltmann to characterize his as a "social doctrine of the Trinity."[45] So consistent is he regarding this point that Peters concludes that Moltmann's proposal is "perhaps the biggest step yet away from the substantialist unity of God toward a relational unity in which the divine threeness is given priority."[46]

In *The Trinity and the Kingdom,* Moltmann extends the discussion begun in his earlier writings to include the various stages of the histories of both the Son and the Spirit at work in the world bringing about the glorification of the Father. To this end, he includes with the cross both the resurrection of Jesus and the sending of the Spirit. He claims that these events give evidence to the fact that the kingdom of God emerges as one trinitarian member hands on to the next person the task of effecting the divine program. Hence, rather than being the only active subject in the kingdom-inaugurating process, the Father is actually dependent upon the sending, surrender, and glorification of the Son as well as on the completed work of the Spirit.

As the focus of activity is passed from one person to the next, the "history" of God comes to be marked by shifting patterns of relationship among the three trinitarian members. The climax of this process is the eschaton (the ultimate future), at which point the divine activity arrives at its goal, the kingdom of God. Whereas his earlier focus on the cross appears to elevate this particular event in the past as a crucial location of the unity of the triune God, in *The Trinity and the Kingdom* (and in keeping with the ontology presented in *Theology of Hope*) he clarifies that the complete divine unity belongs to the eschatological future. When through the work of the Son and the Spirit the history of salvation comes to its eschatological goal, Moltmann argues, the immanent Trinity reaches completion: "When everything is 'in God' and 'God is all in all,' then the economic Trinity is raised into and transcended in the immanent Trinity."[47] As a result, Moltmann concludes, the cross of the Son and the joy of love in glorification through the Spirit mark the inner life of the triune God from eternity to eternity.[48]

Furthermore, the changing focus of the activity of the three trinitarian persons in the history of salvation leads Moltmann to suggest that the history of God is marked by shifts in the pattern of the ordering of the three persons.[49] Of these, the final and hence the ultimately most important is not the traditional ordering of Father–Son–Spirit that characterizes the sending of the second and third persons into the world but the eschatological flow of Spirit–Son–Father. In this eschatological series, Moltmann proposes that the Spirit is the subject whose activity leads to the glorification of the Father and the Son. The result is a trinitarian pneumatology that seeks to give full place to the Spirit as a divine person coequal to the Father and the Son. Hence Moltmann declares that as the glorifying and unifying God, "the Spirit is not an energy proceeding from the Father or from the Son; it is a subject from whose activity the Son and the Father receive their glory and their union, as well as their glorification through the whole creation, and their world as their eternal home."[50]

His search for a way of encapsulating the divine unity without recourse to the language of substance or appeal to the single divine subject brings Moltmann to the formulations in the Fourth Gospel that speak of each of the three trinitarian persons as being *in* each of the others. He sees this biblical theme reflected, in turn, in the patristic idea of *perichoresis,* at the heart of which is the "intimate indwelling and complete interpenetration of the persons in one another."[51] With respect to the unity of the three persons in the one God, he adds that *perichoresis* "denotes that trinitarian unity which goes out beyond the doctrine of persons and their relations: by virtue of their eternal love, the divine persons exist so intimately with one another, for one another and in one another that they constitute themselves in their unique, incomparable and complete unity."[52] In short, "the trinitarian persons form their unity by themselves in the circulation of the divine life."[53]

Moltmann extols *perichoresis* as the way to describe the divine community of persons as being thoroughly egalitarian and nonhierarchical. In his estimation, the idea that the unity of the triune God lies in "that triadic inter-subjectivity which we call perichoresis"[54] frees theology from elevating one of the three persons as the source of the divine unity, whether the Father whose monarchy is the seal of the unity (as proposed by Eastern tradition) or the Spirit who constitutes the bond of unity (as evident in Augustine's model). Furthermore, it facilitates a move away from the erroneous focus on "monotheism" characteristic of much of traditional theology and toward what Moltmann calls the "open Trinity."

Trinitarian eschatological panentheism.[55] The "open Trinity" comprises what may be the most significant aspect of Moltmann's relational trinitarianism. Drawing inspiration from the famous fifteenth-century Rublev icon upon which Moltmann repeatedly gazed as he composed his theological treatises, he asserts that, rather than being limited to the divine life, the relationality among the three trinitarian persons seeks the inclusion of creation. Hence to say that God is an "open Trinity" is to contend that God's relationality invites creaturely participation.

Moltmann announces this theme in *The Church in the Power of the Spirit*, in which he quotes approvingly Adrienne von Speyr's terse declaration, "The relationship of the divine persons to one another is so wide that it has room for the whole world."[56] In *The Trinity and the Kingdom*, Moltmann reiterates the point in summary fashion: "We understand the scriptures as the testimony to the history of the Trinity's relations of fellowship, which are open to men and women, and open to the world."[57] With this in view, Moltmann's goal becomes nothing short of the construction of a trinitarian history of God that encompasses, in the words of Richard Bauckham, "the uniting of all things with God and in God."[58] In this history, the Father sends the Son and the Spirit into the world with the purpose of gathering all creation into unity with and in himself. And according to Moltmann, without this history of God with humankind and creation, God is not truly God.[59]

Already in *The Crucified God*, Moltmann intimates that he would find the basis for the "open Trinity" in the divine love that is expressed in the cross. He declares, "If one conceives of the Trinity as an event of love in the suffering and the death of Jesus—and that is something which faith must do—then the Trinity is no self-contained group in heaven, but an eschatological process open for men on earth, which stems from the cross of Christ."[60] In his subsequent writings, Moltmann indicates that his innovative use of the traditional concept of the divine love is connected to another novel idea, namely, his understanding of creation as an act of self-limitation that began already within the divine life, a proposal that he terms "trinitarian panentheism."[61] "In order to create a world 'outside' himself," Moltmann explains, "the infinite God must have made room beforehand for a finitude in himself."[62] God "created" within the infinite divine reality a finite "space" (and "time"[63]) for the world by "withdrawing" from that space (and time).

In *Experiences of Theology*, Moltmann suggests that this understanding of the nature of God's creating act is closely connected to the divine *perichoresis*. He envisions the eternal dance of the three persons not only as a movement of each in the others but also as each offering the others "room for movement."[64] This making space for the others in oneself or making oneself inhabitable for the others, in turn, is similar to the act of God making space for a creation that can both indwell God and be indwelt by God. Yet Moltmann is careful to differentiate between the use of *perichoresis* to refer to the divine dance and its reference to the mutual indwelling of God and creation. Whereas in the former it links "others of the same kind," its use in the latter connects "others of different kinds."[65] He finds the basis for this differentiation in the Johannine language that speaks of the Father and the Son being in each other as well as in Jesus' prayer that his disciples might be "in us."[66] But the differentiation is also evident in the two different patristic uses of the term, for *perichoresis* denotes the interpenetration of the divine and the human in the incarnate Jesus as well as the link connecting the three trinitarian persons.

In the second installment of the six-volume series, *God in Creation*, Moltmann draws into the divine act of creation the dialectic of God's presence and absence, intimated in *Theology of Hope* and *The Crucified God*. The act of divine withdrawal that makes room for creation marks it as "Godforsaken" space. The glorious truth of Christianity, Moltmann adds, is that to redeem the godforsaken world, God enters this godless "space." This divine act involves suffering. Nevertheless, through such suffering God brings the world into God's own being: "By entering into the Godforsakenness of sin and death (which is Nothingness), God overcomes it and makes it part of his eternal life."[67] As a consequence, the trinitarian history of the cross entails the central act of suffering and death through which God not only effects the reconciliation of the world but is also constituted as the triune one.

The Trinity and human society. Moltmann's attempt to replace classical Christian monotheism with a social doctrine of the Trinity is not limited to the level of abstract theory. Rather, he is convinced that it leads to an entirely new outlook, one that Müller-Fahrenholz characterizes as "thinking in terms of relationships of equal importance and equal value."[68] This new trinitarian thinking, in turn, carries implications for human social and political interaction.

Moltmann is convinced that societies reflect their fundamental theological outlook—their basic understanding of God or the gods—in the way that they organize themselves. More particularly, whenever the doctrine of the Trinity disintegrates into "abstract monotheism," this erroneous "political and clerical monotheism"[69] is used to support civil and ecclesiastical totalitarianism. He elaborates: "The notion of a divine monarchy in heaven and on earth, for its part, generally provides the justification for earthly domination—religious, moral, patriarchal or political domination—and makes it a hierarchy, a 'holy rule.'"[70]

The future kingdom of glory, Moltmann avers, is not the universal monarchy of the Lord of creation, but a harmonious fellowship of liberated creation with God. This kingdom is God's "Sabbath"; it is the eschatological moment in which "the resting God begins to 'experience' the beings he has created." "The God who rests in the face of his creation," Moltmann adds, "does not dominate the world on this day; he 'feels' the world; he allows himself to be affected, to be touched by each of his creatures. He adopts the community of creation as his own milieu."[71] On that day, humans will enjoy a relationship with God, in which they will neither be "servants" nor "children," but "friends," and in this friendship "the distance enjoined by sovereignty ceases to exist."[72] In Moltmann's estimation, the concept of the *perichoresis* of the three trinitarian persons, which produces a doctrine of God that is characterized by mutuality rather than lordship,[73] provides the foundation for such a vision of the kingdom of glory, because it opens the way for a "cosmic *perichoresis*," for "a mutual indwelling of the world in God and God in the world."[74]

The History of God and the Immanent God

The reception of Moltmann's trinitarian theology, including his idea that the doctrine of the Trinity should serve as the "critical principle" for theology in its mission of transforming the world, has been nothing short of phenomenal. Many theologians standing in his wake have seen in his proposed "open Trinity" not only an innovative way of facilitating the inclusion of creation into the perichoretic dance of the trinitarian persons, but also as providing the occasion for bringing trinitarian theology and social anthropology together. The political theology he articulated embodied

Moltmann's own steps in this direction. But equally important has been the influence he has exercised on others who have trod even further the trail he blazed. This aspect of Moltmann's trinitarian theology has been appropriated by liberation theologians such as Leonardo Boff[75] and, although less uncritically, a variety of feminist thinkers including Elizabeth Johnson.[76] Yet Moltmann's proposal has also engendered sharp critique.

A worry articulated by a variety of Protestant[77] and Roman Catholic[78] readers, especially in response to *The Crucified God*,[79] is that Moltmann's social trinitarianism has elevated the three persons to the detriment of the divine unity and therefore that it borders on tritheism. Peters offers a nuanced version of this concern. He concludes that Moltmann's "continued emphasis on three discrete subjects or centers of activity makes it difficult to conceive of a principle of unity that is comparable to that of the plurality. It appears that we end up with a divine nominalism."[80]

A more telling apprehension arises out of Moltmann's bold thesis that the history of Jesus occurs within the triune life itself. Gerald O'Collins summarizes the vexation: "Many fear that Moltmann's insistence on the crucifixion and resurrection as an inter-trinitarian event (with a rupture in the divine life and the Father 'ceasing' to be the Father) may be confusing the intradivine life with the story of human salvation even to the point of 'imprisoning' God in the world's becoming."[81] Similarly, John Thompson writes regarding Moltmann's proposal, "The difficulty with this view is that it ties God to his relationship to the world and makes the world a contributory factor to the ultimate nature of God. God is therefore not Father, Son, and Holy Spirit without this relationship and reciprocity between himself and the world."[82]

Taken together, these various criticisms raise once again the question of the immanent Trinity and the economic Trinity. At first glance, his handling of this issue surfaces as the Achilles' heel of Moltmann's theology. Beginning with *The Crucified God*, with its bold thesis that the cross is an event in the trinitarian history of God, his program gives evidence to being a thoroughgoing appropriation of Rahner's Rule. Bauckham notes regarding Moltmann's proposal, "The doctrine of the Trinity is thus not an extrapolation from the history of Jesus and the Spirit: it actually *is* the history of Jesus and the Spirit in its theological interpretation."[83] Samuel Powell, in turn, draws out the implication: "Moltmann has made it plausible to erase the customary distinction between the internal and the external in God, between (to use the traditional terms) the eternal processions of the persons and their historical missions."[84] In short, insofar as the histories of Jesus and the Spirit not only belong to but actually constitute the history of the triune God, and insofar as the history of God constitutes God's being, Moltmann seems to countenance no distinction whatsoever between the immanent Trinity and the economic Trinity. On the contrary, the immanent Trinity appears to collapse into the economic Trinity, out of which it arises.

In *The Trinity and the Kingdom,* Moltmann accepts the challenge of describing the relationship between the immanent Trinity and the economic Trinity. He freely admits that his attempt to take the cross seriously as the basis for our understanding of God led him to follow Rahner's Rule to the limit: "In order to grasp the death of the Son in its significance for God himself, I found myself bound to surrender the traditional distinction between the immanent and the economic Trinity, according to which the cross comes to stand only in the economy of salvation, but not within the immanent Trinity."[85] His chief objection to the commonly acknowledged distinction is that it all too readily results in the positing of two different trinities, rather than being understood as referring to "the same triune God as he is in his saving revelation and as he is in himself."[86]

Moltmann tackles head-on the idea that a distinction between the immanent Trinity and the economic Trinity is necessary to preserve the freedom of God. He avers that with respect to God, the choice of either liberty or necessity is a false dichotomy. Because compassionate involvement with the world is the expression of God's overflowing love, in God "necessity" and "freedom" are transcended by God's own nature, which is love.[87] On this basis, Moltmann assigns the historicity of God to God's free and gracious choice from eternity "to go outside of himself" in what Moltmann characterizes as "seeking love."[88] In this way, he appeals to the divine love as the link that holds the immanent Trinity and the economic Trinity together, and in so doing he avoids pitting freedom against necessity.

The fear of dividing the immanent Trinity from the economic Trinity does not prohibit Moltmann from speaking of some type of distinction between the two. In his estimation, the chief place where such a differentiation emerges is in the doxological life of the church, which Moltmann appears willing to grant comprises to some extent an alternative, yet legitimate, pathway to theological knowledge. Hence, he declares, "the 'economic Trinity' is the object of kerygmatic and practical theology; the 'immanent Trinity' the context of doxological theology."[89] Even here Moltmann retains the epistemological priority of the former, insofar as knowledge of the economic Trinity must precede knowledge of the immanent Trinity. Yet he adds that doxology ultimately takes us beyond the worship of God for the salvation we have received to the worship of God "for himself." Moltmann summarizes: "all the terms of doxology crystallize out of the experience of salvation. But they grow up out of the conclusion drawn from this experience about the transcendent conditions which make the experience possible," thereby arriving "at that experience's transcendent ground."[90] In this manner, he holds out the possibility of a doxological discourse about the triune God as the transcendent ground of salvation, even though God in doxology is none other than God in the history of salvation.[91]

An even stronger sense that the immanent Trinity cannot be collapsed into the economic Trinity arises out of Moltmann's eschatological ontology, for by advocating the ontological primacy of the future, he has, in effect, provided the basis for such a distinction. He points in this direction whenever he waxes eloquent about the eschatological horizon. For example, at the end of his discussion of the doxological Trinity, he declares, "When everything is 'in God' and 'God is all in all,' then the economic Trinity is raised into and transcended in the immanent Trinity. What remains is the eternal praise of the triune God in his glory."[92] Thus, for all his insistence that "the economic Trinity not only reveals the immanent Trinity; it also has a retroactive effect on it,"[93] in the end Moltmann elevates the God who is all-in-all in the eschatological horizon and who thereby stands in some sense as judge over the world and the historical process.

Despite considerations such as these, sufficient ambiguity lies within Moltmann's innovative proposal to lend support to the charge that he has tied the immanent Trinity too closely to the historical process. Powell, to cite one critical voice, concludes not only that Moltmann "has compromised God's independence from the world," but also that he has "in spite of his protests, drifted over into idealistic territory in this, its most controversial tenet."[94]

Like Pannenberg, Moltmann does indeed accept the Hegelian idea that reality is in a sense historical and therefore that it is appropriate to

speak about the history of God. At the same time, Moltmann (like Pannenberg) finds Hegel's trinitarian theological proposal with its focus on
the one divine subject—and consequently Barth's as well—too modalistic.[95] His replacement of the one God with the three trinitarian persons as
the subjects of history facilitates Moltmann in standing apart from the
idealism of Hegel at this crucial point while retaining Hegel's focus on
history. Moreover, Moltmann's commitment to the futurist ontology that
he finds at the heart of the biblical view of history as well as in the philosophy of Ernst Bloch may serve to exonerate him from the charge that he
has reduced the triune God to the historical process.

The Triune God as the Truth of History: Wolfhart Pannenberg

In the eyes of many commentators, no theologian in the last fifty years has
displayed a greater intellectual breadth than Wolfhart Pannenberg. In
many circles, he is known chiefly for his engagement with the question of
the relationship between theology and science.[96] In fact, Jacqui Stewart
cites "the intellectual seriousness with which he treats the natural and
social sciences" as a feature that distinguishes him "from other major theologians of the second half of the twentieth century."[97] Yet Pannenberg's
interest in this question forms only a part of a larger theological agenda,
one that is universal in scope. He is unique among twentieth-century theologians in the manner in which he pursues this quest for the universality
of theology, for he seeks to show that the subject of theology—namely,
God, understood as the all-determining power—is the ground of, and
even provides the unity of, all reality.[98] Hence Mark Worthing asserts that
no contemporary theologian has made theology's claim to universality
"more strongly, explored its methodological foundations more thoroughly,
or pursued its implications more consistently" than Pannenberg.[99] John
Cobb, in turn, lauds him as "the one twentieth-century theologian" who
has "successfully renewed the nineteenth-century project," insofar as his
"conversation partners are social scientists and physicists as well as historians and philosophers. His own expertise ranges over the whole of theological scholarship. His analytic and speculative gifts are truly
extraordinary."[100] Finally, Peters credits Pannenberg with offering "one of
the most sophisticated and complex theological visions of the last half of
the twentieth century."[101]

At the heart of Pannenberg's project is the concern to articulate within the contemporary context a coherent statement of Christian truth, as it centers on the self-disclosure of the triune God.[102] Moreover, in his estimation, the locus of the divine revelation is history. As a consequence, of the three voices who took seriously the move to history that Barth and Rahner bequeathed to trinitarian theology, Pannenberg has offered the most sustained systematic and philosophically oriented development of the idea that the Trinity is the fullness of the historical process.[103]

History and the Task of Trinitarian Theology

In one of his early essays, based on a lecture he first delivered in 1959, Pannenberg articulated what would emerge as a central, fundamental methodological principle of his entire theological program. "History," he declared in the opening sentence of the address, "is the most comprehensive horizon of Christian theology. All theological questions and answers are meaningful only within the framework of the history which God has with humanity, and through humanity with his whole creation—the history moving toward a future still hidden from the world but already revealed in Jesus Christ."[104] In commenting on the importance of this essay as a seminal statement for the future of theology, Frank Tupper explains that Pannenberg's "new direction was more than a *return* to history, it was a decisive *turn* toward an eschatological theology of history."[105]

Like Barth's, Pannenberg's theology emerges out of the concept of revelation. Unlike Barth, he does not view the Word of God as the fundamental locus of revelation. Like Barth, Pannenberg introduces his magnum opus, the three-volume *Systematic Theology*,[106] with a prolegomenon that centers on revelation. Unlike Barth's, Pannenberg's discussion does not elevate the Word of God as synonymous with revelation. Rather, in keeping with the agenda he spelled out in his 1959 essay, he connects revelation to history—more particularly the history of God—in which he then finds what he deems as the appropriate place for the concept of the Word of God. Therefore, this theme, revelation as history (which encapsulates the "discovery" of the cadre of scholars in Heidelberg in the 1950s who came to be known as the "Pannenberg circle"), and not the Barthian idea of the Word of God, provides the ultimate methodological basis for the definitive expression of Pannenberg's trinitarian theology.[107]

The public character of theology. Pannenberg's orientation toward history rather than the narrower concept of the Word of God as providing the basis for his trinitarian theological proposal is closely connected to his understanding of the task of theology. For him, theology is a public discipline connected to the quest for truth. Truth, in turn, is eschatological in focus and historical in character.

Pannenberg's elevation of the public character of theology arises out of his desire to combat what he perceives to be a widespread privatization of religious belief in general and of theology in particular. In his estimation, the roots of the contemporary theological malaise lie in misguided attempts to overcome the challenge of the Enlightenment.[108] He points out that prior to the Age of Reason the historical events that were deemed foundational to the faith were accepted on the basis of what was claimed to be the authoritative witness of God, mediated either by the teaching office of the church (the Roman Catholic view) or by the Bible as the product of divine inspiration (the Reformation position).[109] The Enlightenment, however, replaced the idea of an authoritative testimony to historical knowledge with the enterprise of reconstructing past events by means of critical tools borrowed from the newer empirical science. By introducing an uncertainty regarding the historicity of biblical events, the new program of historical criticism called into question the historical basis for faith. Some theologians sought to remedy the potential difficulties that arise when faith is deemed to be dependent on historical research by moving the foundation for faith away from historical events to the subjective experience of conversion. For, unlike the vacillations of historical research, religious experience appears to provide its own certainty. In Pannenberg's estimation, this modern approach gave birth to two distinct yet equally erroneous alternatives. Radical pietists (of whom Rudolf Bultmann is an example) simply eliminate the historical content of the Christian tradition as irrelevant. Conservative pietists continue to maintain the historical character of Christianity but ground the plausibility of the historical aspects of the faith, such as Jesus' resurrection, in the conversion experience.

In Pannenberg's estimation, the way forward for theology requires an alternative to these two approaches. To facilitate this goal, he draws from Martin Luther's thesis that by nature faith cannot be derived from itself but *extra se,* beyond itself in Christ.[110] Pannenberg declares that for faith to be trust in God and not trust in itself, it must have a historical foundation, specifically, the historical revelation of God. Although the revelation that grounds faith remains contestable, Pannenberg adds, only intellectual argument, and not a nonrational decision of faith, can meet the philo-sophical and historical challenges to the Christian claim to knowledge of God.

Pannenberg's goal, therefore, is to place Christian faith on firm intel-lectual footing once again. To this end, he sets forth an approach that resembles the classical understanding of theology as a public discipline related to the quest for universal truth. Yet in contrast to traditional theol-ogy, he does not link truth to the unchanging essences lying behind the flow of time. Rather, in keeping with what he sees as the biblical teaching that the deity of God is unquestionably open to all only at the end of his-tory,[111] he declares that truth is essentially historical and ultimately escha-tological.[112] Truth is what shows itself throughout the movement of time climaxing in the end event but is anticipated in the present. Because truth can never be fully known until the eschaton, all human knowledge, including theological knowledge, is provisional, and all truth claims remain contestable. Pannenberg rejects, however, the seemingly inevitable conclusion that the provisionality of truth necessitates a retreat into a pri-vatized ghetto of individual or familial piety. Rather, he argues that the link between the theological task and the quest for ultimate truth (that is, the truth of God) results in theology's being a public endeavor, the pur-pose of which is to give a "rational account of the truth of faith."[113]

In a manner somewhat similar to the classical tradition, Pannenberg asserts that God is the all-inclusive object of theology and hence that the whole of systematic theology is essentially the doctrine of God.[114] More-over, he acknowledges the commonly held "semantic minimum" regarding the term "God" that views God as "the power on which all finite reality depends"[115] or "the power of the future" in the sense of "the power deter-mining the future of all that is present."[116] Pannenberg interprets this premise to mean that the deity of God is connected to the demonstration of God's lordship over creation[117] and that the idea of God, if it corre-sponds to an actual reality, must be able to shed light not only on human existence but also on the experience of the world as a whole. According to Pannenberg, therefore, the overarching task of theology is to show the power of the Christian conception of God to illumine all human knowl-edge.[118] The connection he draws between God's deity and lordship over creation implies as well that only the final salvation of God's creatures can ultimately confirm the assertion that God exists, and therefore that the entire process of history climaxing in the consummation constitutes "a

self-demonstration of God's existence."[119] As a result, history and eschatology emerge as the focus of theology, understood as the explication of
the divine self-demonstration in history.

The starting point for theology. Pannenberg's elevation of history as the
central theme in the prolegomenon to his trinitarian theological proposal
is related as well to his understanding of the proper starting point for the
theological enterprise. Because of the provisionality of truth, the unfolding of Christian theology cannot assume the reality of God. As a result,
theology must "win" its starting point, rather than simply launching into
the doctrine of God. The field on which this occurs is history, or, more
specifically, the history of religious traditions.

Pannenberg inaugurates the task of winning theology's starting point
with the observation that humans are in a sense naturally religious,[120]
insofar as the structure of the human person and of communal life is per-
vaded by a religious component. He connects this dimension of the human
situation to the contemporary anthropological concept of exocentrism, that
is, the idea that each human must ground personal identity outside oneself (the foundation for which Pannenberg finds in Luther's understanding of faith), as well as to Erik Erikson's well-known concept of basic
trust. Religious awareness, Pannenberg explains, arises out of the rudimentary consciousness of the difference between "I" and "world" found
already in the act of trust, which is then augmented by one's presence in
the family. As a person experiences finitude and temporality in everyday
life, an intuition of the infinite develops. At this point in the argument,
however, Pannenberg moves away from the psychologically oriented
approach that characterizes the philosophical and theological traditions
from Descartes to Schleiermacher. He notes that the intuition of the infinite does not itself comprise explicit knowledge of God. Such knowledge
emerges only within the context of religious traditions. Participation in
such a tradition facilitates a person in seeing that the immediate experience or basic intuition of the infinite entailed an "unthematized knowledge" of God. The history of religious traditions, therefore, is the stage
upon which conflicting religious attempts to express the unity of the
world are struggling for supremacy. Pannenberg is confident that the theological vision that best illumines the experience of all reality will in the end
prevail and thereby demonstrate its truth value.

This forms the context in which Israel's religious history becomes significant, for it gave birth to monotheism, which facilitated the envisioning

of the world as a unity. In addition, it produced the idea that Israelite history, including its future, is the history of the appearance of God, a perspective that Pannenberg sees as opening the way for understanding revelation as the coming into appearance of the divine reality even in the midst of the unresolved conflict of religious truth claims. Finally, in the history of Israel the mythical orientation to the past was taken up into the orientation toward history, and the eschatological future and God came to be seen as encompassing all dimensions of life, so that at least from the perspective of the eschatological completion of the process of history, the division into holy and profane was overcome.

Above all, Pannenberg looks to the history of Israel for the theological understanding of revelation. In fact, he finds in the biblical trajectory the development of a multifaceted concept of revelation, climaxing in the connection between revelation and eschatology that arose in the apocalyptic movement and in early Christianity, as revelation came to be seen as the explication of what was now hidden in the eternal God.[37] In his estimation, this multifaceted biblical understanding undermines the view that the divine self-disclosure comes only in the form of "Word." Even though "the Word of God" has God for its author, he avers, with the exception of John 1 its content is not immediately identical with God. Instead, the divine self-disclosure must be thought of as mediated through God's action, and hence revelation is basically indirect in nature. Moreover, the knowledge of God mediated by historical manifestations is found only at the end of the series of experiences that reveal God's deity. Only the future completion of world history in the coming of the kingdom of God will reveal completely the divine glory. Nevertheless, provisional, anticipatory revelations of the still-hidden end-event are found throughout history. This happens especially in Jesus' appearance and work, for in him the central aspect of the Jewish expectation—the coming kingdom—came to be operative, so that the person and history of Jesus comprise the anticipatory revelation of the deity of God. Because of Jesus' proleptic, revelational significance, Pannenberg concludes, Jesus' life forms the ultimate basis for the Christian doctrine of God.[121]

The Triune God of History

In a 1981 autobiographical essay for the *Christian Century*, Pannenberg signaled a significant turn in his own theological development. He announced that the doctrine of the Trinity would play the central role in his systematic theology, and that the result would be a theology that is "more thoroughly trinitarian than any example I know of."[122] Pannenberg's goal throughout the three volumes of the *Systematic Theology* is to construct this "more thoroughly trinitarian" theology. Yet his contribution to trinitarian thought is most clearly delineated in the two chapters in the first volume of his magnum opus that specifically delineate the doctrine of the triune God.

The priority of the three persons in the one God of revelation. In contrast to the tendency among modern theologians to treat the doctrine of God in general or the Trinity in particular as the concluding topic of systematic theology, Pannenberg places this discussion immediately after the prolegomenon. He is not thereby offering a concession to the classical theological tradition but is emphasizing the central role of this doctrine for dogmatics, insofar as the entire systematic presentation is in fact an unfolding of the Christian conception of God. He is also highlighting a basic methodological principle of his theological endeavor, namely, the axiom—which he shares with Barth—that the doctrine of God is the delineation of the divine self-disclosure in Jesus Christ and therefore that this doctrine explicates in a special way what is already implicit in the concept of revelation.

The placement of the doctrine of the Trinity immediately after the discussion of revelation and prior to the delineation of God's unity and attributes carries an additional theological significance. Against the majority of classical and modern theologians, who view the divine oneness as connected to a general understanding of God and only then proceed to the discussion of the Trinity, Pannenberg is claiming that the threeness of the Christian God is what arises out of God's self-revelation and therefore that the divine threeness must be developed before attention can be turned to the unity of God found in the divine attributes.

This ordering of the doctrine of God reflects Pannenberg's desire to take Rahner's Rule seriously and thereby to offer what he sees as a fruitful response to the question of the immanent Trinity and the economic Trinity.[123] The link he forges between these two concepts emerges from his understanding of theology as the explication of what is implicit in God's own self-disclosure. Consequently, he (like Moltmann) follows Barth in seeking to ground the doctrine of the Trinity in God's self-revelation in Christ, that is, in the economy of salvation. More particularly, Pannenberg develops the doctrine of the Trinity on the basis of the way that the Father, the Son, and the Spirit come into appearance and relate to one another in the event of revelation as presented in the life and message of Jesus, as well as in his death and resurrection.[124] Only then does Pannenberg move to the discussion of the unity of God found in the divine attributes. In this manner, he seeks to develop an understanding of God in which the immanent Trinity flows from the economic Trinity.[125]

The ordering of the doctrine of God serves another theological purpose as well. Pannenberg finds problematic the attempt to derive the plurality of the trinitarian persons from the concept of God as one being, indicative of traditional theology but also evident in both Hegel and Barth. In Pannenberg's estimation, this approach inevitably leads either to modalism or to subordination, for it necessarily posits a God who is ultimately a single subject, rather than three persons.[126] To overcome this difficulty, he proposes that the doctrine of the Trinity be grounded in revelation, that is, in the economy of salvation understood as the manner in which the Father, Son, and Spirit come to appearance and relate to one another in history. Only then can the theological presentation move to the question as to how the three can be seen as one God, a question that is answered, Pannenberg adds, by means of a delineation of the divine attributes as they are evident in the revelation of God as Father, Son, and Spirit.[127]

Like Barth, Pannenberg constructs his doctrine of God—and hence the doctrine of the Trinity—from the divine self-disclosure in Jesus Christ. But more forcefully than Barth, he does so because he is convinced that the historical path to the development of the Christian doctrine of God took its beginning point from the message and history of Jesus together with the apostolic proclamation. In fact, he suggests that Barth did not derive the doctrine of the Trinity from the revelation in Jesus, but from the idea of revelation or from revelation as a formal concept.[128] Central to Pannenberg's proposal, therefore, is his elevation of Jesus' relationship to the Father, especially as it is expressed in Jesus' message about the kingdom of God, which connected the concept of the fatherly care of the Creator to the eschatological theme of the coming of God's rulership. This message together with Jesus' life, death, and resurrection, in turn, provide the basis for the theological understanding both of Jesus as the Son and of the Spirit as a third divine person who is different from, yet bound to, the Father and the Son.[129] As a result, in Pannenberg's theological presentation, the doctrine of the Trinity ultimately becomes the interpretation of the relationship of Jesus to the Father and to the Spirit. In this manner, the unthematized infinite comes to be named by the purposeful activity of the three trinitarian persons in the world.

Central to Pannenberg's development of the doctrine of the Trinity is the concept of self-differentiation.[130] In traditional theology, this term refers to the bringing forth of the second and third trinitarian persons through the first person, which in Pannenberg's estimation unfortunately results in a prioritizing of the Father. To overcome this deficiency, he reinterprets "self-differentiation" by drawing from Hegel's proposal regarding the correlative character of the idea of person, which connects personhood to the act of giving oneself to one's counterpart and thereby gaining one's identity in relationship to the other.[131] Because the one who differentiates oneself from another is dependent on the other for one's personal identity, Pannenberg adds, dependence is an integral part of self-differentiation.

Applying this concept to the trinitarian persons enables Pannenberg to postulate that the mutual self-differentiation of Father, Son, and Spirit constitutes the concrete form of the trinitarian relations.[132] He notes that Jesus differentiated himself from the Father by subordinating himself to the Father's will and thereby giving place to the Father's claim to deity. In so doing, Jesus is the Son, a status confirmed and established retroactively by the event of his resurrection. Moreover, following Barth's lead, Pannenberg asserts that the relationship of Jesus to his Father is not merely a temporal reality but belongs to God's eternity.

In developing the corresponding delineation of the self-differentiation of the Father from the Son and of these two persons from the Spirit, Pannenberg draws from an additional seminal idea that Roger E. Olson has labeled "Pannenberg's Principle."[133] This axiom declares that "God's being is his rule,"[134] to cite Pannenberg's terse statement, that is, that God's being, which is likewise God's deity, is linked to divine rulership over the world. Although Pannenberg credits Barth with the idea, he also finds it in embryonic form in the writings of Athanasius. Appealing to Athanasius's argument against the Arians that the Father could not be the Father without the Son and to New Testament declarations that the Father has entrusted everything to the Son (for example, Matt. 28:18; Luke 10:22; John 5:23), he concludes that the Father's deity is dependent on his relationship to the Son, for in sending the Son he entrusted his kingdom and with it his deity to the Son and the Son's fulfillment of his task in the world.[135]

In articulating his point, Pannenberg sets forth what Peters calls a "startling argument":[136] "By handing over lordship to the Son the Father makes his kingship dependent on whether the Son glorifies him and fulfils his lordship by fulfilling his mission. The self-distinction of the Father from the Son is not just that he begets the Son but that he hands over all things to him, so that his kingdom and his own deity are now dependent upon the Son."[137] But for Pannenberg the mutual dependency that characterizes the Father and the Son (and by extension the Spirit) is not limited to the economy of salvation, for it is present within the eternal divine dynamic as well. He adds, "Hence, lordship goes hand in hand with the deity of God. It has its place already in the intratrinitarian life of God, in the reciprocity of the relation between the Son, who freely subjects himself to the lordship of the Father, and the Father, who hands over his lordship to the Son."[138]

For the biblical basis of the dependency of the Father and the Son on the Spirit and thus the self-differentiation of each of these two from the third member of the Trinity, Pannenberg looks to the Johannine statements about the Spirit's glorifying of the Son. In Pannenberg's estimation this act constitutes the Spirit as a special person next to the Father and the Son:

> As Jesus glorifies the Father and not himself, and precisely in so doing shows himself to be the Son of the Father, so the Spirit glorifies not himself but the Son, and in him the Father. Precisely by not speaking of himself (John 16:13) but bearing witness to Jesus (15:26) and reminding us of his teaching (14:26), he shows himself to be the Spirit of truth (16:13). Distinct from the Father and the Son, he thus belongs to both.[139]

In this way, Pannenberg draws a connection between the biblical idea of glorification and the self-differentiation of the Son and the Spirit. This link, in turn, fosters an understanding of the Trinity that sees the deity of each trinitarian person as a dependent,[140] or a received divinity, in that each of the three trinitarian persons receives divinity as a person-in-relationship with the other two.[141] By introducing into the eternal divine dynamic the concept of dependent relationality on the basis of the character of the relationships of the trinitarian persons in history, Pannenberg provides a way to forge a strong tie between the economic Trinity and the immanent Trinity.

The unity of the triune God of revelation. From the threeness of the persons Pannenberg moves to the question of the divine unity. Before setting forth his own perspective, however, he distances himself from the widely traversed pathways to the oneness of God. Hence he rejects the psychological approach, with its focus on God as the divine subject, that he finds prevalent in the Western tradition from Augustine to Barth. Pannenberg demurs that this model harbors a subtle modalism that insulates a supposedly immutable God from the vaccinations of time and history.[142] It likewise contravenes the concept of mutual self-differentiation, which implies that the three trinitarian persons are independent centers of action and not merely different ways in which the one divine subject exists. Nor can the divine unity be gained by reducing the three trinitarian persons to relations of origin in the one Godhead, as is reflected in the traditional terms *generation* and *procession.*

More promising for Pannenberg is the idea of *perichoresis,*[143] although he notes that the concept was never intended to account for the unity of the divine essence (the use to which Moltmann puts it) but presupposes that unity on the basis of the origin of the Son and the Spirit in the Father. Above all, Pannenberg draws from the traditional appeal to the monarchy of the Father, albeit under the rubric of Pannenberg's Principle. Because the deity of the Father is linked to the coming of God's future reign, which arises through the sending of Jesus into the world and the work of the Spirit who realizes the kingdom in the world, the Father is dependent on the other two trinitarian persons. Therefore, the monarchy of the Father is not the presupposition but the result of the mutual activity of the three persons both in their eternal communion and in history. In this manner, the history of the world becomes the history of God, and God is the trinitarian God of history.[144]

On this basis, Pannenberg concludes that the question of the unity of the triune God cannot be answered from the perspective of God's essence viewed apart from the mutual relations of the three persons disclosed in their work in the world; it cannot be delineated without recourse to the economy of salvation. Moreover, the unity of God in the threeness of the persons provides the basis of the unity of the immanent Trinity and the economic Trinity, and the unity of the divine life lies in the activity of the three persons on behalf of one another rather than merely in the idea of *perichoresis* (contra Moltmann[145]).

In proposing this approach, Pannenberg is attempting to overcome the tendency in theology since the Middle Ages to conceive of God as a currently existing being in accordance with the philosophical category of substance, but at the cost of rendering the divine essence devoid of relationality. Pannenberg, in contrast, asserts that the task of trinitarian theology is to set forth an understanding of the divine being in which the category of relation is not deemed to be external to God, but one that demonstrates how it is that God is relational not only in the divine activity in the world but in the eternal divine life as well. In short, Pannenberg proposes that the divine essence be seen ultimately as "the epitome of the personal relations among Father, Son, and Spirit,"[146] which unfold throughout the course of the history of the world.

In his *Systematic Theology*, Pannenberg follows two strategies for accomplishing this task. His more immediate approach is to show the unity of the three trinitarian persons by exploring the being and attributes of God. The all-encompassing theological project, in turn, entails demonstrating the unity of the immanent Trinity and the economic Trinity, which emerges through the divine activity in history.

To accomplish the narrower goal, Pannenberg reverses the traditional method in theology that assumes that knowledge of the existence and essence of the one God arises from the divine work of creation whereas the trinitarian differentiations are only knowable through special revelation. Pannenberg notes that since the fourth century the unity, and not the threeness, of God has been the central problem within the doctrine of the Trinity. In his estimation, the solution to this problem lies in viewing the divine attributes as arising out of the activity of God in the world, for God's essence (the divine "whatness") is bound up with God's existence (the divine "thereness"), and this existence is found only in the trinitarian persons. To serve this purpose, Pannenberg draws from the idea of doxological language (that is, statements that express adoration on the basis of God's works) that he developed in his essay "Analogy and Doxology." On the basis of his observation that biblical adoration intends to speak about what God is from eternity to eternity, he concludes that the activity of

God in the world (the economic Trinity) provides the basis for speaking—doxologically, not analogically—about the immanent Trinity.

En route to his solution, Pannenberg replaces the traditional conception of God as reason and will (that is, mind)—which in agreement with Feuerbach he rejects as a mere projection—with the biblical idea of spirit, interpreted by means of the metaphor of *field*. He asserts that the divine unity has the character of a field, that is, of a power that is incomprehensible yet manifest in a personal way as the three trinitarian persons. Moreover, in contrast to the traditional approach, which views the activity of God in a particular phase of the economy of salvation as the work of one trinitarian person in isolation, Pannenberg brings the relationality of the three persons into the divine activity in history. The result is an understanding of the divine unity that views it as bound up with the work of the three persons in the world (the economic Trinity), which work—and hence which unity—is completed only eschatologically and is linked to the relations found in the eternal life of the trinitarian persons (the immanent Trinity). In short, doxological speech opens the way to knowledge of the eternal God because of the eschatological unity of the economic Trinity and the immanent Trinity.

Pannenberg begins his elucidation of the unity and attributes of the triune God by returning to the sense of God as the infinite that emerged in conjunction with his theological starting point, developing it now, however, as the regulating principle of his entire conception of the divine attributes.[147] He argues that the unthematized infinite standing against one's own finitude comes to be named by means of the purposeful activity of the trinitarian persons in the world, resulting in the establishment of a reciprocal relationship between the concept of the "true infinite" and the Trinity, as F. LeRon Shults points out.[148] The process, however, is only completed eschatologically. Moreover, through this process climaxing in the eschatological future, God's essence—God's internal unity of life—manifests itself. The God thereby revealed is the infinite spiritual essence, understood not statically as mind but relationally as the dynamic field, that is, as the one who comprehends everything finite without blurring the distinction between the infinite and the finite.

The discussion of the divine unity comes to a climax in a somewhat parallel explication of love as the characteristic of the divine action in which the various attributes find their concrete reality. Pannenberg asserts that the conception of God as love unifies the various other attributes, for these may be viewed either as forms of the appearance of love in action or as being carried up into the movement of God's love. This love constitutes the essence of the eternal trinitarian life, for through the Father's relation to the Son, which is connected to the going forth of the Son from the Father, the divine Spirit as creative power comes to be concretized, an assertion that Pannenberg sees as cohering with the conclusion that "spirit" constitutes the common essence of the Godhead but also comes forth in the Holy Spirit as an independent hypostasis. Moreover, divine love takes into itself the tension between the infinite and the finite without laying aside their differences, for in love God affirms creation in its boundedness and thereby overcomes the separation of the world while retaining its difference from the divine being.

In this manner, the divine love emerges as Pannenberg's answer to the problem of the unity of the divine essence with God's existence and attributes, as well as the unity of the immanent Trinity with the economic Trinity. Yet the explication of the role of the trinitarian persons in the history of the relationship of the loving God to the world comprises the entire *Systematic Theology*, with the result that the love of God comes to its goal, and the doctrine of God to its conclusion, only with the eschatological completion of the world.

The God of History and the Immanent Trinity

In Tupper's estimation, Pannenberg's turn to history marked a theological watershed. The essay "Redemptive Event and History," according to Tupper, "signaled the end of the theological epoch that had literally dominated Protestant theology since the publication of Barth's *Römerbrief* in 1919."[149] Although this comment, written in 1973, may have been both premature and overdrawn, Tupper has not stood alone in his positive assessment of Pannenberg's importance in general and his contribution to the development of trinitarian theology in particular. For example, Ted Peters's sketch of "Trinity talk in the last half of the twentieth century," published in 1993, climaxes with an overview of Pannenberg, whom he lauds as "navigating at the point where the flow of trinitarian discussion is currently cresting."[150] Likewise, Timothy Bradshaw calls Pannenberg's proposal "a refreshing new trinitarian theology," and then concludes, "His work can only be regarded as a *tour de force*."[151]

Repeatedly, Pannenberg has been linked with Moltmann in pioneering the way forward. Yet since their days together on the faculty at Mainz, the two have carried on a lively debate that has not only highlighted the emphases they hold in common but also revealed the crucial distinctions that divide them. In *Theology of Hope*, to cite one example, Moltmann criticizes Pannenberg's approach as being too closely connected to "Greek cosmic theology" with its idea of truth as epiphany, in which "the Old Testament God of promise threatens to become a *theos epiphanes,* whose epiphany will be represented by the totality of reality in its completed form."[152] Regardless of the accuracy of Moltmann's charge, which has found echo in a variety of related criticisms of Pannenberg's position, this statement indicates that already in the beginning stages of their careers the two former colleagues were heading in similar yet distinct directions. This is especially evident in the manner in which they develop the eschatological perspective they share. Christoph Schwöbel offers a concise summary of this central difference: "Whereas for Moltmann the predominance of the eschatological perspective is grounded in the '*future of truth*' as it is revealed in the divine promise which is constitutive for the experience of reality as history, the eschatological perspective establishes for Pannenberg the *totality* of reality as history and the comprehensive horizon of meaning which, in turn, necessitates a conception of the future demonstration of truth."[153] As Schwöbel's characterization suggests, Pannenberg's futurity, unlike Moltmann's, arises out of a commitment to the intellectual task as the quest for the unity of truth and hence for the universality of theology, noted earlier in this section.

Pannenberg's orientation toward truth as an intellectual endeavor has been the focus of many of the criticisms leveled against his program, especially those associated with his purported rationalism. This is evident in Paul Molnar's suggestion that Pannenberg's focus on the quest for coherence and universality involves an unintended intellectual subjectivism. He explains: "Instead of saying that the thought that God is truth is and remains grounded in *God alone*, Pannenberg argues that this truth is grounded in the *perception* of the coherence and unity of all that is true. Theology shifts away from God (and the need for faith) to our perceptions and then discovers God as the locus of this presupposed unity."[154] Similarly, J. A. Colombo fears that the kind of history that lies at the center of Pannenberg's theological proposal is too intellectual in orientation:

"The 'history of the transmission of traditions' is itself an abstraction in which Pannenberg comes dangerously close to constructing history as the history of Ideas."[155] This rationalism, Colombo adds in a manner reminiscent of Moltmann and Johannes Metz, prevents Pannenberg from giving place to the "interruptive character of Christian faith in history and society,"[156] and hence to theology's subversive character and praxis orientation.

More germane to Pannenberg's own intention in developing a trinitarian theology are questions that focus on his attempt to navigate the waters between faith and reason. On the basis of such strategies as his use of the philosophical idea of the Infinite, many critics interpret Pannenberg as establishing the basis for the universality of theological truth-claims from the perspective of reason before turning to the explication of the contents of the faith given in revelation. Questioners such as Schwöbel wonder if a better approach would be to view this universality as an implication of the Christian revelation itself.[157]

The specific features of Pannenberg's delineation of the doctrine of the Trinity have also raised many eyebrows. Although he disavows the addition of the *filioque* clause in the ecumenical creed and rejects the psychological model of the Trinity, Pannenberg retains the Augustinian understanding of the Spirit as the love binding the Father and the Son, and as the concretization of the divine essence. Paul Fiddes speaks for many when he concludes that as a result Pannenberg "seems to lose the otherness of the Spirit."[158] In addition, his use of the metaphor of "field" to speak about God in general and the Spirit in particular has not won a large following to date. And like Moltmann, he has been charged with tritheism because of his suggestion that the three trinitarian persons comprise "living realizations of separate centers of action," perhaps even "centers of consciousness."[159]

The area of Pannenberg's trinitarian theology that has triggered the most intense discussion, however, has been the manner in which he connects the triune God with history, especially the future consummation of history.[160] Molnar voices a concern shared by many critics, when in comparing Pannenberg to Barth he writes, "While Pannenberg also insists that only God can reveal God, his method incorporates our philosophical knowledge into revelation in such a way that God becomes dependent upon the processes of history."[161]

Although a constellation of issues surround what Tupper has hailed as Pannenberg's "bold new 'eschatological theology of history,'"[162] they converge on his idea of the ontological priority of the future and the attendant retroactive significance of the eschatological consummation of history for the deity of the triune God and hence for the unity of the immanent Trinity with the economic Trinity.[163] John Thompson encapsulates the central question posed by Pannenberg's critics: "Is a reading back of an eternal Trinity from the end constituted by the rule of God through Jesus and the Spirit in the world a valid approach to the immanent Trinity? It does unite the immanent and economic Trinity but does it not at the same time make the rule of God in history in some measure constitutive of his being?"[164] In response, several observers have raised the possibility that this question fails to grasp what is entailed in Pannenberg's (and Moltmann's) future-oriented ontology.[165] Whether or not such is the case, Thompson's query leads to the central issue at stake in Pannenberg's trinitarian theology: the implications of his recasting of Rahner's Rule.[166]

As was indicated in the previous chapter, Rahner set forth the axiom that bears his name primarily to emphasize the soteriological significance of the doctrine of the Trinity in the context of a Neoscholastic theology that elevated speculation about the inner divine life at the expense of interest in the work of the three trinitarian persons in salvation. Pannenberg, however, puts the axiom to a quite different, albeit related, use and thereby sets forth a radical recasting of it. His revision of the axiom is evident in the description he offers in his *Systematic Theology*: Rahner's Rule "means that the doctrine of the Trinity does not merely begin with the revelation of God in Jesus Christ and then work back to a trinity in the eternal essence of God, but that it must constantly link the trinity in the eternal essence of God to his historical revelation, since revelation cannot be viewed as extraneous to his deity."[167] Pannenberg's exegesis of Rahner's Rule indicates not only that he goes beyond Barth in suggesting that the act of self-disclosure is somehow essential to God's being, but more importantly that he views his trinitarian theology as a historicizing of the axiom. The result is a proposal that varies greatly from the traditional approach.

Traditional trinitarian theology tends to view revelation as opening a window on an otherwise concealed interior divine life. This understanding is closely connected to a spatial conceptualization of the relationship of God to the world. Viewed from this perspective, the eternal identities of the trinitarian persons are deemed to be determined by their nontemporal relationships. The Father is unbegotten, the Son is begotten, and the Spirit is spirated. The relationships of the trinitarian persons in salvation history, in turn, are seen as secondary to these eternal relationships. Hence they are either irrelevant to the formation of the eternal identities of the three persons or relevant only insofar as they provide a partial glimpse into the eternal relationships within the divine life. Pannenberg demurs from this traditional view. He argues that the historical missions of Jesus and the Holy Spirit as sent into the world by the Father are constitutive of not only the eternal character of the three persons but also of their very deity. To cite Powell's description of Pannenberg's position, "The Trinitarian persons are what they are because of their mutual relations in salvation history."[168] Moreover, because the Father's deity is connected to his reign and as a result the Father also stands in relationship to the economy of salvation, the historical missions of the Son and the Spirit, which climax in the eschatological consummation, comprise the coming to be of the lordship of the triune God in history.[169] In this sense, the economic Trinity may be said to be the self-actualization of the triune God in the world.[170]

Yet Pannenberg's point is lost if he is read in accordance with the assumption that God is moving through history on a trajectory that begins in the past and culminates in the future, as if history were the stage for God's becoming. He is not a process theologian. Rather, his theology of history is much closer to idealism.[171] Thus, he writes, "Refuted herewith is the idea of a divine becoming in history, as though the trinitarian God were the result of history and achieved reality only with its eschatological consummation."[172] What, then, is the significance of the eschatological consummation? Pannenberg adds, it "is only the locus of the decision that the trinitarian God is always the true God from eternity to eternity. The dependence of his existence on the eschatological consummation of the kingdom changes nothing in this regard. It is simply necessary to take into account the constitutive significance of this consummation for the eternity of God."[173]

In this manner, Pannenberg's intellectual-focused program, which sees history as the arena in which the decision regarding God's being occurs, leads almost inevitably to his controversial axiom of the ontological priority of the future. But this principle, in turn, is closely connected to a particular view of eternity, namely, that eternity is both the fullness of time in its simultaneity and the meaning of history. Pannenberg's interpretation of the relationship between eternity and history parallels his use of the concept of infinity.[174] He argues that it is impossible to imagine the parts of time without presupposing time as an undivided whole that forms the background or context for the particular moments or pieces of time. Because this intuition of time as a whole points to God's eternality[175] as the Infinite in relationship to which the finite temporal parts find their reality, God may be said to be the "field" in which creation and history exist.[176] Similarly, Pannenberg points out that the meaning of history is profoundly future, for only at the end of history does this meaning (as well as the connection of each event with it) emerge in its fullness and undebatable clarity. In this sense, the end of history transcends each moment, as that glorious fullness toward which all history is moving.[177] God, Pannenberg concludes, functions as the whole that constitutes the meaning of the finite events of history in their interconnectedness.

Pannenberg's ultimate goal, then, is not to collapse the immanent Trinity into the economic Trinity or to submerge God into the world. On the contrary, he desires to maintain God's independence from the world. To this end, he proposes that the independent God not be conceptualized as standing "above" but "in front of" the world. This reconceptualization leads to the conclusion that from the perspective of the fullness of the future, the God of history (the economic Trinity) is the immanent Trinity.

The Triune God of the Historical Narrative: Robert W. Jenson

The list of contributors to the contemporary renaissance in trinitarian studies includes some of the most respected persons who over the past several years have been inducted into the theological hall of fame. Yet few have offered a more thoroughgoing trinitarian theology than Robert Jenson, who until recently was overshadowed by the tall theological stature of Moltmann and Pannenberg.

Discussions of God as triune are sprinkled throughout several of his writings.[178] Nevertheless, Jenson's claim to fame as a trinitarian theologian is based on his explicit exposition of trinitarian theology in two books, the publication of which spans a fifteen-year gap, *The Triune Identity* (1982)[179] and, more importantly, the initial volume of his *Systematic Theology* (1997).[180] The appearance of the first of these led Carl Braaten to hail Jenson as the "first American theologian to write a systematic construction of the Trinity."[181] The publication of the second title catapulted Jenson into the spotlight. Thus Kendall Soulen has acclaimed him as "perhaps the major trinitarian theologian writing in English today,"[182] and Mark C. Mattes lauds the two-volume *Systematic Theology* as "a brilliant, robust, and enduring 'critically orthodox' theology that presents the faith of the historic creeds in dialogue with the concerns of modernity and postmodernity," characterized by "a vigorous trinitarianism."[183]

During the early stages of his career (in the 1960s), Jenson's efforts centered on the attempt to engage theology with analytic and linguistic philosophy.[184] In a manner somewhat similar to Pannenberg and Moltmann, he proposed that the linguistic problem brought to the fore by the death of God movement might be overcome by appeal to an eschatological conception of the divine reality, which seeks to get beyond the alternatives of "God is" and "God is not" by means of discourse about God as "not yet."[185] This goal launched Jenson on what might be seen as his lifelong pursuit, namely, the reformulation of the doctrine of God, or the search for a truly Christian doctrine of God,[186] along the lines of what he later termed "revisionary metaphysics."[187] His interest in trinitarian theology emerged largely as an extension of this overarching theological program, albeit one that increasingly has come to be developed within the context of his growing sense of the centrality of the trinitarian tradition of the one church for the theological enterprise. In keeping with Jenson's deepened sense of the importance of ecumenical theological endeavors, Carl Braaten notes that he has "always been a Barthian with a sharp Lutheran cutting edge, but increasingly less so the more he has engaged the thought of Catholic (Joseph Ratzinger and Hans Urs von Balthasar) and Orthodox (John Zizioulas and Vladimir Lossky) theologians."[188]

The Narrative of the Radically Temporal, Eschatological God

According to James J. Buckley, "The character of Jenson's theology is inseparable . . . from the identity and character of the triune God, who is the beginning and middle and telos of human and cosmic life." Buckley then adds, "Jenson's theology is centrally about the identification of this God."[189] Indeed, Jenson has repeatedly sounded the theme of the Trinity as the divine identity. In his 1979 essay, "The Triunity of Truth," he declares, "The foundational theological task . . . is the *identification* of God," and therefore, "The function of the doctrine of Trinity is to identify which God we mean when in the Christian church we talk of God."[190] Moreover, as the title itself indicates, the chief goal of Jenson's book, *The Triune Identity,* is to identify the God of the Christian faith, whose "proper name," he argues, is "Father, Son, and Holy Spirit," and hence to explicate the doctrine of the Trinity, which he views as the "final truth of God's own reality,"[191] as the one event with three identities.[192]

Above all, however, Jenson's fundamental trinitarianism comes to the fore in his two-volume *Systematic Theology.* The division of his magnum opus into two parts, *The Triune God* (volume 1) and *The Works of God* (volume 2), indicates the extent to which he takes seriously Pannenberg's claim that the entire systematic unfolding of Christian theology is ultimately the delineation of the doctrine of God as triune. Although the two volumes must be read as a unit, Jenson's major contribution to the renaissance of trinitarian theology occurs in the first installment, which even as persistent a critic as Paul Molnar finds reason to laud: "Unlike many contemporary theologies of the Trinity, Professor Jenson's presentation sets out to make room for Christ's active mediation of himself to us today and does so with a renewed emphasis on the Holy Spirit that deliberately does not separate the Holy Spirit from Jesus himself or the Father."[193]

Jenson encapsulates his approach to theology and sets the methodological tone for its systematic unfolding in his magnum opus by repeating a theme near the beginning of volume 1 that he has sounded throughout his career. He writes, "the phrase 'Father, Son, and Holy Spirit' is a very compressed telling of the total narrative by which Scripture identifies God and a personal name for the God so specified; in it, name and narrative description not only appear together . . . but are identical."[194] As this declaration indicates, crucial to Jenson's project is his attempt to hold together the idea that God is identified *by* the events of the narrative of Israel and Christ with the realization that God is identified *with* these events.[195] Jenson's strategy for doing so is evident in the central dimensions of his proposal; for him theology arises out of the divine self-disclosure that displays a narrative, radically temporal, and eschatological character.

The narrative character of God's self-disclosure. Crucial to Jenson's strategy for holding together God's identification *by* and *with* salvation history is a focus on narrative (albeit not completely along the lines of Hans Frei and Paul Ricoeur[196]). Buckley goes so far as to assert that "narrative" and "drama" were ingredients of Jenson's theology before the rise of the contemporary interest in these categories.[197]

In Jenson's estimation, the task of theology includes identifying the God of the biblical narrative or drama as the triune one. In his 1991 essay, "Does God Have Time?" he succinctly encapsulates the crucial connection between the biblical narrative and the identification of God as the triune one. Simply stated, "the Bible tells a story about God" that "presents us with three agents of its action."[198] Then, in his 1990 plenary address to the Research Institute in Systematic Theology at King's College in London, he responded to the assigned topic, "What Is the Point of Trinitarian Theology?" by noting the connection between the biblical narrative and theological truth: "The function of trinitarian theology is to maintain against all compunctions that the biblical story of God and us is true of and for God himself."[199]

Jenson sounds the narrative note early in volume 1 of his *Systematic Theology*. He declares forthrightly, "The God to be interpreted in this work is the God identified by the biblical narrative."[200] What follows throughout the subsequent unfolding of the doctrine of the Trinity is an interesting interplay between classical theological reflection, in which Jenson draws from the greatest theological minds of the Christian tradition from the patristic thinkers to Barth, and the biblical narrative itself, especially the narrative of Jesus as Israel's Messiah. Lying behind Jenson's commitment to this approach is his appropriation of the shift to narrative that he sees as characterizing much of twentieth-century theology. Convinced that "narrative is Scripture's encompassing genre,"[201] Jenson concludes that the various biblical documents are to be read as "witness to the continuing action of one and the same agent," namely, the one God. This leads to a canonical reading of scripture, or what Jenson elsewhere denotes as "spiritual exegesis,"[202] which in turn is in keeping with what he sees as "the purpose for which the church assembled this book in the first place," namely, "to be in its entirety and all its parts witness to Jesus' resurrection."[203]

His introduction of Jesus' resurrection at this point indicates that for Jenson this event lies at the heart of the biblical narrative. In contrast to the widely followed approach that looks to the cross as the high point, Jenson argues for the centrality of the resurrection. In fact, he goes so far as to indicate that the fundamental witness of scripture (and hence of the church) is that God is ultimately identified by the resurrection of Jesus.[204]

In short, God is the one who is revealed in the resurrection of Jesus, and this God is triune.

As a consequence of his commitment to the narrative approach, Jenson's theological delineation becomes at its heart the task of identifying a plurality of what he calls the "characters of the drama of God."[205] Although the center of the trinitarian drama is the resurrection, he nevertheless swims against the Neomarcionite tendency of the church by indicating that the drama of the triune God did not first emerge in the New Testament but was present already in the story of God disclosed in the Old Testament.[206]

In his move to narrative, Jenson finds himself at odds with the dominant traditions of the Western and Eastern churches, and yet in continuity with impulses from each. Being a Barthian at heart, as Braaten has noted, Jenson draws extensively from his theological mentor. Nevertheless, he also chides this modern giant of the Western tradition for the binitarianism that seems to be inherent in his I-Thou approach to the doctrine of the Trinity.[207] It is, however, Jenson's relationship to Orthodoxy that is of greater interest. He drinks deeply at the Eastern well, drawing heavily and creatively from the Cappadocians as well as from less well-known scholars such as Gregory Palamas. Yet Jenson finds the Eastern tradition at odds with the narrative focus that drives his own theology, and he maintains that its insufficient regard for the biblical narrative leads to an incipient modalism. This perspective comes to the fore most sharply in his critique of Palamas: "It is one thing to say that abstract deity is itself always the same quality, as the Cappadocians did; it is quite another to say that deity taken as *God himself* is a static essence. Ironically, enough, Orthodoxy is here driven to a bluntly modalist doctrine: God himself is above the biblical narrative, which applies only to his activities."[208]

The radically temporal character of God's self-disclosure. Perhaps Jenson's central contribution to contemporary trinitarian theology is his understanding of *how* God is related to the biblical narrative. He is convinced that the narrative of the triune God is radically temporal, and this commitment to the temporal character of God's self-disclosure marks a second central aspect of Jenson's trinitarian theology.

As Jenson himself points out, his entire argument depends on a conceptual move that repeatedly comes to the fore in his work, the move "from the biblical God's self-identification *by* events in time to his identification *with* those events."[209] Jenson offers this telling appraisal of the importance of such a move: "Were God identified by Israel's Exodus or Jesus' Resurrection, without being identified *with* them, the identification would be a revelation ontologically other than God himself. The revealing events would be our clues *to* God, but would not *be* God." He then adds, "It is precisely this distinction between the god and its revelation that the biblical critique of religion attacks."[210] This perspective gives rise to the task Jenson sets before himself in the first volume of his *Systematic Theology*: "The God to be interpreted in this work is the *triune* God. For the doctrine of Trinity is but a conceptually developed and sustained insistence that God himself is identified by and with the particular plotted sequence of events that make the narrative of Israel and her Christ."[211]

What Jenson announces, he subsequently pursues. This is especially evident in his discussion of the significance of the history of Jesus for the eternal Trinity. Jenson is not content to overcome the theological puzzle of the incarnation by appealing to the tried-and-true method of positing an eternal divine being, the Logos, who for a time takes on humanity in the incarnation. Thus he expresses dissatisfaction with the Antiochene tendency to distinguish "the suffering Jesus from the Son"[212] as well as with the post-Chalcedonian tendency to identify the eternal Logos as "the 'synthetic' agent of the whole gospel narrative."[213] Instead, reminiscent of Pannenberg's work but in an even more thoroughgoing manner, he seeks to offer a consistent gloss on the insight of Nicea that Jesus is truly God. In his estimation, Nicene trinitarianism "identifies one who underwent gestation, birth, growth, a human career, rejection, torture and execution as 'true God.'"[214] Later he repeats the point in an equally cryptic manner: "Our divine savior is not an extra metaphysical entity, whether the unincarnate *Logos* of the Antiochenes or 'the Christ' of more feeble sorts of modern theology. He is Mary's child, the hanged man of Golgotha."[215]

Crucial to Jenson's trinitarian Christology is his claim that "the second identity of God is directly the human person of the Gospels, in that he is the one who stands to the Father in the relation of being eternally begotten by him."[216] To pull off this great christological feat, Jenson offers what emerges as one of the key insights of his entire proposal. He appeals to the social character of both deity and humanity: "That Christ has the divine nature means that he is one of the three whose mutuality is the divine life, who live the history that God is. That Christ has human nature means that he is one of the many whose mutuality is human life, who live the history that humanity is."[217]

The eschatological character of God's self-disclosure. "The biblical God is not eternally himself in that he persistently instantiates a beginning in which he already is all he ever will be," Jenson declares. Rather, "he is eternally himself in that he unrestrictedly anticipates an end in which he will be all he ever could be."[218] As this statement indicates, reminiscent of Pannenberg, Jenson develops the narrative of the radically temporal God in a manner that takes seriously the eschatological orientation of the divine drama.

In Jenson's estimation (and in contrast to Pannenberg), this understanding emerges directly out of the narrative character of theology. He notes that the "order of a good story is an ordering by the outcome of the narrated events."[219] For him, this "ordering outcome" actually provides a liberating dimension, for it frees each present from being simply the consequence of what has preceded it: "A story is constituted by the outcome of the narrated events. Within the sequence of events a specific opening future liberates each successive specious present from mere predictability, from being only the result of what has gone before, and just so opens each such present to its own content, given precisely as what it does not yet encompass."[220] Although his prose is somewhat obscure, the implication he then draws is unmistakably clear: the God of the Bible "is not salvific because he defends against the future but because he poses it."[221]

Above all, Jenson looks to the Spirit for the eschatological dimension of the story of the triune God. He summarizes the resultant eschatological pneumatocentric trinitarianism in the terse declaration, "Of course, we have already many times noted and said where in fact the Spirit stands: at the End of all God's ways because he *is* the End of all God's ways."[222] Consequently, just as the "divine beginning at which the relations of origin focus" comprises "the Father's Archimedean standpoint," Jenson cites the divine goal, "at which relations of *fulfillment* focus," as "the Spirit's Archimedean standpoint."[223]

From Biblical Narrative to Grand Fugue

In 1987, Ted Peters surmised that Jenson was charting a course "that will take him further than Barth in freeing the Christian Trinity from classical monotheistic metaphysics."[224] In the eyes of many commentators, Jenson's

Systematic Theology fulfills Peters's prophecy. In his review of the first volume, Philip Cary goes so far as to exclaim, "Reading Jenson is like no other experience in the world."[225]

Such accolades are not without warrant. By postulating an understanding of the divine self-disclosure as narrative, temporal, and eschatological, Jenson has set forth a unique proposal for conceptualizing the ontology of God that carries far-reaching implications for the relationship between time and eternity.[226] More specifically, he has sought to provide a way of freeing theology from its dependency on the classical concept of an atemporal divine eternity, by viewing God's life, as disclosed in the biblical narrative, as having a timelike structure, which, in turn, makes time as we know it possible, for "we inhabit the story that is the story of God."[227] According to Jenson, in the biblical understanding, the divine eternity embraces time; it consists of faithfulness through time, climaxing in the eschatological future, which for him—as for Moltmann and Pannenberg—retains an ontological priority.

Despite the recognition that Jenson's contribution has won, his theology is not without its detractors. In fact, Cary suggests that Jenson himself anticipates "without dismay" that "his radical diagnoses . . . and his idiosyncratic solutions . . . are unlikely to be widely accepted."[228]

If Jenson anticipated being controversial, then his expectations have been rewarded, for he has repeatedly found himself to be a partisan in theological battles. Perhaps few of these theological altercations have been as acrimonious as the heated controversy regarding language for God that raged within the Evangelical Lutheran Church in America (ELCA) in the early 1990s. In the midst of this dispute, feminist theologians railed against Jenson's defense of the traditional language of God as Father, which he articulated without apology in several of his earlier writings and seemingly assumed in volume 1 of his *Systematic Theology*. To cite one example, in a short essay in *Dialog*, the Lutheran-focused journal that Jenson himself had founded, Mary M. Solberg summarily rejected his arguments as "inconsistent, incomplete, and authoritarian."[229]

Jenson's close linking of the resurrected body of Christ with the church has likewise raised the ire of many readers.[230] Christoph Schwöbel fears that his thesis seems to minimize the significance of the general Reformation emphasis on the church as the "creature of the divine word."[231] The Roman Catholic scholar Susan Wood, in turn, senses that his position risks making the church an illegitimate "prolongation of the incarnation."[232] Moreover, Jenson's thesis appears to contradict such contemporary impulses as the resurrection of Jesus into the transcendent reality of the future kingdom of God, the exaltation of the risen Jesus as the Lord of the cosmos, and the sending of the Spirit to be Christ's presence in the church.

Likewise significant for his trinitarian theological proposal is Wolfhart Pannenberg's queasiness at Jenson's idea that God—and not just the Father, Son, and Spirit—is "person." In Pannenberg's estimation, Jenson's position risks making God a fourth person, in addition to the three members of the Trinity.[233] Pannenberg also chides Jenson for rejecting the idea derived from Augustine and Plotinus that eternity is the "simultaneous presence of time as a whole"[234] in favor of a more linear characterization.

Yet the dimension of Jenson's proposal that has most persistently distressed his critics is his radical application of Rahner's Rule. Douglas Farrow notes that, like Pannenberg and Moltmann, in whose company Jenson places himself, "he too embraces Rahner's Rule in the stronger sense rather than the weaker, arguing that only thus can we complete the liberation of Christian theology from its captivity to the timelessness or apathy axiom of Hellenic theology."[235] Although Jenson does not engage explicitly with Rahner's Rule in the *Systematic Theology*, in *The Triune Identity* he clearly expresses his desire to take the axiom seriously, while simultaneously maintaining divine freedom. Similar to Moltmann and Pannenberg, he proposes to accomplish this task by means of an eschatological orientation. He argues that God "*is* himself only eschatologically," and therefore that the immanent Trinity is the "eschatological reality" of the economic Trinity.[236] In his *Systematic Theology*, with its move toward a more explicitly narrative approach, Jenson seeks to accomplish his goal by a somewhat different yet parallel strategy. Here he appeals to the "by and with" character of the relationship between God and the narrative of history. By noting where the two poles lead when taken separately, Buckley indicates why this maneuver is crucial for Jenson's program:

> To simply say that God identified himself and is identified "by" the narrative of Israel and her Christ may make us wonder whether this is who God "really" is. Is God's character in the biblical story who God really is, or is God's character a role he abandons once the play is over? We could also ask the opposite question. If God is identified

"with" those events, does God have an "identity" beyond or besides the events?[237]

Critics wonder, however, if Jenson's radical application of Rahner's Rule has undercut the divine freedom that he has sought to maintain and in the process has lost the immanent Trinity. Even as friendly a reader as J. Augustine DiNoia asks, "Do the Father, Son and Holy Spirit enjoy a life independent of their engagement with us in creation and redemption?"[238] Molnar is less circumspect in framing the critique. In his review of the first volume of the *Systematic Theology*, he relentlessly accuses Jenson of advancing "a Hegelian notion of God's involvement with history," with the result that he has allowed history "to determine God's eternal existence" or to constitute "God's eternal being," thereby compromising God's freedom and confusing the immanent Trinity with the economic Trinity.[239] Jeremy Ive also worries that Jenson has purchased too much from Hegel. From his study of Jenson's work, he concludes, "By identifying the Persons of the Trinity as elements *within* the historical process rather than constitutive *of* it, there is a danger of reducing the Trinity *to* the historical process, as Hegel has done."[240]

In the face of his critics, Jenson remains firm in his refusal to leave behind the biblical narrative in the quest to speak about the triune God. He is convinced that so doing would mean losing God's very identity. Cary cites this reticence as his great contribution to trinitarian theology:

> Perhaps Jenson's most provocative contributions stem from his persistent refusal of metaphors of depth, which the Christian tradition has usually filled in with content drawn from the philosophical tradition. If God simply is the three divine characters (dramatis personae) revealed in Israel's story, then we do not find him behind or beneath the story (in timeless eternity or the depth of our consciousness) but only in it. The God of the Gospel is the One who raised Jesus from the dead. Hence the story of Jesus's life, death and resurrection belongs to the being of God, and Jenson treats it as a constitutive part of the doctrine of God.[241]

In upholding this perspective, Jenson stands firmly within the contemporary turn to history, which he shares with Moltmann and Pannenberg. Yet in his *Systematic Theology*, he appears unwilling to leave the matter there. Rather, following a similar move in Jonathan Edwards, whom he lauds as "America's theologian,"[242] and true to his own eschatological orientation, Jenson finds that the cognitive delineation of his topic—even in its historicist version—must eventually give way to the aesthetic. "God is *beauty*," Jenson announces. Hence "to be God is to be enjoyable."[243] Then reminiscent of his theological mentor, Karl Barth, who acknowledged a theological indebtedness to Mozart, Jenson invokes a musical form more generally associated with another great German composer, J. S. Bach. Having already extolled the roominess of God,[244] Jenson concludes the first volume of his *Systematic Theology* by noting the final limit of his theological reflections. He writes, "We close the doctrine of God with this evocation of God's being, beyond which there is no more to say: God is a great fugue. There is nothing so capacious as a fugue."[245] In the second volume, Jenson continues the musical metaphor, as "harmony" and "fugue" become the language he uses to describe both the *perichoresis* of three trinitarian persons and the place they make for humans within the divine conversation,[246] until it forms the capstone of his entire explication. "The point of identity, infinitely approachable and infinitely to be approached, the enlivening *telos* of the kingdom's own life," Jenson declares in his closing lines, "is perfect harmony between the conversation of the redeemed and the conversation that God is. In the conversation God is, meaning and melody are one. The end is music."[247]

By invoking the aesthetic, Jenson offers what appears to be a "surprise" ending to his *Systematic Theology*. In so doing, he raises the distinct possibility that the turn to history has run its course, leading ultimately away from history as such to history as the aesthetic.

4

The Triumph of Relationality

In the eyes of many observers, Robert Jenson's proposal marks a monumental shift in the dominant theological metaphor in trinitarian thought. Douglas Farrow, to cite one example, notes, "Where space once mediated ontologically between God and humanity, time and history (and narrative?) now generally serve that purpose." Farrow, however, proceeded to question the appropriateness not only of the older metaphor, but of the perspective that had superseded it as well. "Is God's infinity or transcendence really 'temporal rather than spatial'?" he asked. "Or should we regard *both* attempts to articulate the divine transcendence as misguided?"[1]

Farrow's query evidences that in recent years some thinkers have grown dissatisfied with the proposals offered by their theological mentors. To date, this discontent has not produced anything close to a consensus as to what approach, if any, might go beyond the focus on the divine historicity that characterized the work of Pannenberg, Moltmann, and Jenson. Yet a degree of unanimity regarding one aspect of trinitarian theology has emerged, an aspect shared by proponents and critics of the turn toward the temporal metaphor. In 1998, David Cunningham pinpointed the area of agreement. Regarding the current state of trinitarian theology, he observed, "Although contemporary trinitarian theologians vary enormously in the degree to which they are willing to renounce their allegiance to a metaphysics of substance, they seem to agree that more stress should be placed on the claim that God is *relational*."[2]

By the end of the twentieth century, the concept of relationality had indeed moved to center stage. In fact, the assumption that the most promising beginning point for a viable trinitarian theology lies in the constellation of relationships among the three trinitarian persons had become so widely accepted that it attained a kind of quasi-orthodox status. Although the two Karls set the stage for this development (as with other developments in the renaissance of trinitarian theology), the triumph of relationality was more directly abetted by Moltmann, Pannenberg, and Jenson, whose work left an indelible mark on subsequent theological thought. A host of thinkers standing in their wake have taken seriously their operative methodological principle, namely, that the doctrine of God cannot be constructed from the givenness of the one divine substance but should move from the three persons to the divine unity. This methodological commitment has been largely responsible for elevating relationality to the lofty place it has attained in trinitarian theology.

Despite the seminal character of the proposals offered by the thinkers surveyed in chapter 3, they were not the only trailblazers of the future. Rather, in the waning years of the twentieth century, additional insights emerged from the work of theologians who were pursuing alternative avenues of thought. Nor did all those who followed the pathway that Moltmann, Pannenberg, and Jenson had charted necessarily conclude that these thinkers had spoken the last word on the matter. Instead, a variety of suggestions arose as to how the relationality of the three trinitarian persons ought to be understood, and a wealth of ideas emerged as to the manner in which the divine relationality builds the unity of the one God who is three persons.

The Trinity as the Paradigm for Human Community: Leonardo Boff

In her introduction to *Trinity in Process: A Relational Theology of God*, a book of essays in which leading process thinkers engage with the doctrine of the Trinity, Marjorie Hewitt Suchocki elevates God's triunity as providing a model for human community. After asserting that "the deepest image of God in human society is attained not by an individual alone, nor by societies made up of like-minded and like-looking individuals alone, but only through a society that becomes community through its embrace of irreducible differences," Suchocki concludes, "The model of a trinitarian God, irreducibly diverse yet one, suggests a world community of irreducibly diverse communities, each of which is itself richly created in and through the irreducible diversity of its members."[3]

Several theologians have explored the connection between God's trinity and human community with a view toward replacing the metaphysics of substance with a relational ontology. Notable among them is Joseph Bracken, who draws from process thought to chart an understanding of the triune God as "an interpersonal process." In keeping with the process metaphysic with its focus on becoming, he describes God as "a community of three divine persons who are constantly growing in knowledge and love of one another and who are thus themselves in process even as they constitute the divine community as a specifically social process."[4]

Yet the thinker who stands out for his attempt to delineate the doctrine of the Trinity in a manner that carries explicit implications for human society—and hence is noted for venturing boldly in the direction toward which thinkers such as Suchocki point—is the Brazilian Roman Catholic lay theologian and former Franciscan Leonardo Boff. In attempting this intellectual feat, Boff provides an alternative to the historical focus that tended to predominate in the work of Moltmann, Pannenberg, and Jenson. Building on Moltmann's elevation of the concept of *perichoresis*, Boff looks to the connection between the community of the three persons and the ideal human community for insight into the ultimately ineffable mystery of the triune God.

The doctrine of the Trinity is not a theme that routinely finds its way into Boff's writings. Especially noteworthy is the absence of any such engagement in what is likely his most widely read book, his 1972 treatise on Christology, *Jesus Christ Liberator*.[5] Although Boff sprinkled references to the Trinity in several of his subsequent publications, his stature as a contributor to the trinitarian renaissance is based primarily on his 1986 work, *Trinity and Society*,[6] a nontechnical synopsis of which was published in 1988 and appeared in English twelve years later as *Holy Trinity, Perfect Community*.[7]

Boff's *Trinity and Society* was originally published as an installment in the "Theology and Liberation Series." At its inception, this program was purported to be "the most ambitious and creative theological project in the history of the Americas,"[8] for it claimed the involvement of over one hundred Latin American thinkers and had as its goal the application of liberation theology—as a "new way of doing theology"—to "the full spectrum of Christian faith." In keeping with the intent of the series, *Trinity and Society* is not directed solely to one particular, local situation but is explicitly addressed to the universal church.[9] The result is a statement of liberation trinitarian theology that since its appearance in the mid-1980s has enjoyed global appeal. Hence John W. Cooper speaks for many reviewers of Boff's work[10] when he declares that *Trinity and Society* "represents a fine example of systematic theology done by a first-rate liberation theologian," and then adds, "It is not just a promotion of liberation theology, but a generally informative and enlightening historical introduction to the doctrine of the Trinity."[11]

The Communal Trinity

Several years before composing his book-length treatment, Boff offered a foretaste of the communal-oriented approach to the doctrine of the Trinity that would characterize his explication in *Trinity and Society*:

> The God of Jesus Christ, recognized by the faith of the apostles and accepted by the Christian community, is a Trinity: Father, Son, and Holy Spirit. The ultimate principle of the world and of history is not a solitary being, then, but God the Family—God-Communion. From all eternity, Yahweh is a bond of loving relations, an unfathomable Mystery—the unoriginated Origin of all—called "Father." This Mother and Father emerges from the depths of the divine mystery in an act of self-communication and self-revelation. within the Godhead itself, and this emergence is the second person of God: "God the Son." Now Parent and Child—"Father and Son"—join in an embrace of love and in doing so express and give origin to the Holy Spirit, who is the Oneness of the first and second persons. This Trinity has not remained enclosed but has communicated itself, making human life its temple. The Trinity dwells in us and our history, divinizing each of us.[12]

This succinct yet thorough statement of trinitarian theology, tucked away in Boff's book *Faith on the Edge: Religion and Marginalized Existence*, contains in embryonic form the central features of his entire proposal.

The theological starting point for trinitarian theology. Boff emerged in the early 1970s as one of the early voices advocating what at that time was a fledgling theological movement found largely within the Roman Catholic Church in Latin America. His perspective as a liberation theologian has given shape to Boff's understanding of the nature of theology in all his writings, including *Trinity and Society*.

· Like other liberation theologians, Boff views theology as a "second moment" in the Christian life, to cite Otto Maduro's characterization.[13] Seen from this perspective, theology entails human reflection on the divine mystery encountered in the concrete situations of human existence, an encounter that elicits doxology and proclamation. As a "second moment," therefore, theology may be described as "devout reasoning."[14] Applying this understanding of the nature of theology to statements regarding the doctrine of the Trinity leads Boff to differentiate between the assertion "God is Father, Son, and Holy Spirit," which he views as a faith declaration, and the contention "God is one nature and three Persons," which in his estimation is an explication of faith.[15] Boff finds theology's "second moment" status evident as well in the historical development of doctrine during the patristic era, for theological reflection on the nature of Christ and the Spirit that led to the doctrinal formulations regarding God's triunity followed the profession of faith in the Trinity that occurred in both liturgy and sacramental practice.[16]

For Boff, the theological enterprise is likewise ultimately communal or ecclesial. It is one dimension of the church's attempt to respond to the challenges it faces at any particular juncture of history. Consequentially, he sees theology (and doctrine) as closely linked to human experience. Boff acknowledges the revelational grounding of the doctrine of the Trinity, which he carefully asserts is not primarily a construction designed to answer human problems but "the revelation of God as God is."[17] Nevertheless, his basic approach to the Trinity emerges from his interest in speaking to the contemporary social context, especially in Latin America, which—as a liberation theologian—he sees as characterized by oppression, together with a desire for liberation. He offers the following illuminating declaration:

> For those who have faith, the trinitarian communion between the divine Three, the union between them in love and vital interpenetration, can serve as a source of inspiration, as a utopian goal that generates models of successively diminishing differences. This is one of the reasons why I am taking the concept of perichoresis as the structural axis of these thoughts. It speaks to the oppressed in their quest and struggle for integral liberation. The community of Father, Son and Holy Spirit becomes the prototype of the human community dreamed of by those who wish to improve society and build it in such a way as to make it into the image and likeness of the Trinity.[18]

As this statement suggests, Boff believes that the Trinity and the ideal human community stand in a reciprocal relationship. In his estimation, "Human society is a pointer on the road to the mystery of the Trinity, while the mystery of the Trinity, as we know it from revelation, is a pointer toward social life and its archetype."[19] A decade prior to composing his treatise on the Trinity, Boff offered a hint as to what would characterize a human community that truly reflects the Trinity. In his book *Liberating Grace*, he declares that such a society "lives by truth, keeps seeking more truth, finds its nourishment in love, and works constantly for social relations based on greater love and brotherhood."[20] Then in *Trinity and Society*, he draws from the desire for liberation to suggest the kind of society—especially the kind of ecclesial community—that can serve as "the sacrament of the Trinity."[21] This kind of a community would give practical expression to liberation "in participation by the many, at all levels of social life, in the advancement of human dignity, in creating the maximum of opportunity for everyone."[22] Moreover, Boff's ideal community "furthers communion with God," and it "helps to form an understanding of divine filiation and of being brothers and sisters throughout the world."[23] In short, Boff is convinced that the doctrine of the Trinity provides insight as to the type of society that accords with God's plan, because the Trinity serves as a model for a just, egalitarian social organization in which differences are respected and place is given to personal and group expression.[24]

Reminiscent of Moltmann, Boff finds the communal ideal undercut by the atrinitarian monotheistic faith prevalent in the modern era, a situation that requires a return to the triune God of Christianity.[25] Moreover, in his estimation, both capitalism and socialism are found wanting when judged in the light of the model of the Trinity.[26] Nevertheless, Boff remains hopeful. He is convinced that the communion that characterizes the triune God not only provides the communal paradigm but also an ongoing source of inspiration for those who, like him, are fighting against tyranny and oppression.[27]

In keeping with trinitarian thinkers from Barth to Moltmann but drawing more explicitly from Irenaeus's metaphor of the two hands of the Father, Boff suggests that the actual development of the doctrine of the Trinity must begin with the divine self-disclosure in Jesus, together with the coming of the Spirit.[28] In this sense, Boff's theology might be characterized as an experientially based, christo-pneumatocentric trinitarianism. Already in *Liberating Grace*, he gave evidence that this would be the case. Boff declared, "Viewed in terms of the history of salvation, the Trinity is not a speculative curiosity. It is an explication of the Christian experience under the banner of Jesus Christ. For Jesus is the incarnate Son who made room for such a revelation of the Trinity and its attendant experience."[29] Boff repeated this combination of themes in the follow-up volume to his *Jesus Christ Liberator*, entitled *Passion of Christ, Passion of the World* and published in 1977: "Jesus' project of liberation sprang from a profound encounter with a God whom he experienced as, yes, the absolute meaning of all history, the God of the 'reign of God'—but whom he experienced as a Father, too, a Father of infinite goodness and limitless love for all human beings."[30]

Equally important methodologically in Boff's actual explication of the doctrine is the history of reflection in the church,[31] what he calls "the great theological inheritance we have received from the past and from recent investigations."[32] The legacy of church tradition as honored by the Roman Catholic magisterium mediates to him the parameters of trinitarian orthodoxy,[33] whereas newer trinitarian proposals offer him impulses for his own creative reflections.

Yet what occasions Boff's rethinking of the doctrine of the Trinity most directly is a third component of theological reflection, the context of contemporary culture. Boff cites the modern context above all for elevating categories, such as history, process, and freedom, that he believes theologians must take seriously. He notes as well that modern thought has led to a deeper understanding of the concept of person, as well as to a rejection of the static metaphysic of representation in favor of the more dynamic notion of participation. In Boff's estimation, these developments in the contemporary intellectual climate carry far-reaching implications for the articulation of the doctrine of the Trinity.

The "structural axis" of trinitarian theology. As Boff indicates in the lengthy paragraph cited above, his explication of the doctrine of the Trinity is facilitated by what he sees as its "structural axis," namely, the Greek concept of *perichoresis*. In elevating this term to central stage, he is following in the footsteps of his theological mentors, especially Jürgen Moltmann, whose approach Boff acknowledges as providing the stimulus to his own proposal.[34]

The appeal to *perichoresis* arises in the context of Boff's engagement with what he understands to be the central issue for trinitarian theology. He concurs with thinkers such as Moltmann that trinitarian reflection properly begins with the conviction that the eternal God is three persons and then moves to the question of the divine unity.[35] For the basis of the unity of the three, Boff looks beyond the traditional starting points—the Eastern appeal to the Father as the source and origin of the divinity of the other two persons, as well as the Western tendency to begin with the single divine nature shared by the three persons. Instead, he begins with the eternal communion of the three divine persons as revealed in scripture but especially in the historical actions of Jesus and the Holy Spirit. The divine unity, in turn, emerges out of the "eternal co-relatedness, the self-surrender of each Person to the others."[36]

Boff sees *perichoresis* as helpful in expressing this perspective, because the term signifies that "each Person contains the other two, each one penetrates the others and is penetrated by them, one lives in the other and vice-versa."[37] Hidden within this succinct description of the concept is a twofold meaning inherent in the Greek word, the static idea of one thing dwelling in another and the active notion of the interweaving of one with the others. Boff is convinced that *perichoresis* offers the best way of denoting the communion inherent in God, for it refers to "a permanent process of active reciprocity," and this "process of communing" forms the very nature of the three trinitarian persons.[38]

Despite his appropriation of the concept of *perichoresis*, which today is often associated with the Eastern theological tradition, as well as his attempt to position himself among those who eschew the mistakes of both East and West, Boff's trinitarian proposal is decidedly Western. His preference for the West over the East is especially evident in his repeated descriptions of the Spirit as emerging from the Father and the Son, rather than solely from the Father. Hence, Boff declares, "The distinction— Father and Son—makes possible a relationship of communion, understanding, love, mutual bestowal. What emerges from this is their union and reciprocal giving: the Holy Spirit."[39] Consequently, he can conclude, "The Father will always be the Father of the Son; the Son will always be of the same nature as the Father and in infinite communion with him. The Spirit is from always and for always the gift of the Father and the Son."[40]

His preference for the Western model is not surprising, given the centrality of liberation in Boff's work. Simply stated, the Western approach to the doctrine of the Trinity fits better with this focus than the Eastern does. Paul Fiddes offers a helpful explanation:

> There is something attractive about this stress upon a fellowship of equality among the persons, so very unlike our own inequalities in human society. Rather than persons being derived from each other as in the Eastern model, there is reciprocity, three persons simultaneous in origin. It is no wonder that, in the present day, theologians concerned with the liberation of people from oppressive governments, or with the liberation of women from inequality and discrimination in society, have turned to this Western model of the Trinity in preference to one based on the monarchy of the Father.[41]

Despite what appears to be a preference for the Western trinitarian tradition, Boff is clearly interested in providing a depiction of the divine trinity that can bridge the divide between East and West.[42] In fact, a kind of "third" perspective standing between the two traditional approaches seems to arise quite naturally out of his "structural axis." As Boff uses it, the concept of *perichoresis* suggests that all three of the trinitarian persons "are what they are because of their intrinsic, essential communion" so that "each Person receives everything from the others and at the same time gives everything to the others."[43] This means that each of the three emerges from the other two. Hence, the Spirit does indeed come forth from the Father and the Son *(filioque)*. But a corresponding twofold origin must also be posited regarding the Son. The Son is not begotten from the Father alone, but from the Father and the Spirit *(spirituque)*, for "the Father begets the Son in the maternal-virginal womb of the Holy Spirit."[44] Boff's preference for the revelational rather than the causal motif implicates the Father in this dynamic of reciprocity as well, for "the Son reveals the Father in the light of the Holy Spirit."[45] As a consequence—and this comprises one of the most crucial insights that Boff offers—rather than speaking about binary relations, such as Father—Son or Father/Son—Spirit, he argues that trinitarian theology must always posit triadic relations, relations involving all three trinitarian persons.

Perichoresis not only leads to a relational model of the Trinity but also facilitates a move beyond an older understanding that viewed God and the world as two opposed realities. Following the lead of the theologians of history but especially Moltmann, Boff maintains that rather than being a reality totally distinct from God, the world is the receptacle for

God's self-communication, and hence it belongs to the history of the tri-une God. Consequently, Boff asserts that reflection on the doctrine of the Trinity leads to a realization that *perichoresis* cannot be limited to the intra-trinitarian relations but denotes the relationship between God and the world as well.

The ultimate theme of trinitarian theology. In 1970, Boff completed work on a doctor of theology degree with Karl Rahner in Munich, Germany. Fourteen years later, he lauded his *Doktorvater* as "the most intelligent and creative theologian" of the twentieth century.[46] It comes as no surprise, therefore, that Boff's treatise on the Trinity finds a place for Rahner's Rule.

Although Boff acknowledges the principle articulated by his *Doktor-vater*, he applies it circumspectly and carefully. In his estimation, the axiom simply means that "the way God comes to meet human beings is the way in which God subsists."[47] As his definition of the axiom suggests, Boff appears willing to go only partway with Rahner. He readily acknowl-edges that the economic Trinity is the immanent Trinity, but he is reticent to run Rahner's Rule in the other direction. His commitment to the apophatic theological tradition—to the realization that "what the Trinity is in itself is beyond our reach, hidden in unfathomable mystery"[48]—requires that he avoid any hint that the economic Trinity exhausts the being of the eternal God. As Boff puts it, "The economic Trinity is the immanent Trinity, but not the whole of the immanent Trinity." Hence, "not the whole of the immanent Trinity is the economic Trinity."[49] In short, despite Boff's commitment to what appears to be a radical political agenda, he shies away from the radical theological end to which Molt-mann and others press Rahner's Rule.

Boff's careful appropriation of the axiom named for his teacher leads him to posit an immanent Trinity "above" the economic Trinity and to ele-vate the former as the ultimate theme of trinitarian theology. In fact, he forthrightly ascribes an ontological priority to the immanent Trinity. In his estimation, God appears in the economy of salvation as Father, Son, and Spirit, because God is in fact three-personed. Boff's clear and emphatic statement to this effect should be quoted in full:

> God's revelation to us is of the actual being of God. So if God appears to us as a Trinity, this is because God's actual being is a Trin-ity. And God is a Trinity (Father, Son, Holy Spirit) not just for us, but in itself. If God appears to us as source mystery and unoriginated ori-

gin (so absolute transcendence), and so as Father, this is because God is Father. If God is revealed to us as enlightening Word and Truth, and so as Son or eternal Logos, this is because God is Truth. If God is communicated to us as Love and Power for the purposes of carrying out God's final plan, and so as Holy Spirit, this is because God is Holy Spirit. The reality of the Trinity makes the manifestation of the divine in history be trinitarian, and the truly trinitarian manifestation of God makes us understand that God is in fact a Trinity of Persons: Father, Son, Holy Spirit.[50]

Despite his reticence to equate the immanent Trinity with the economic Trinity, Boff seems to draw without qualification from the divine self-disclosure as Father, Son, and Spirit to speak about the eternal reality of the triune God. The immanent Trinity may not be exhausted by the economic Trinity, but the economic Trinity remains the "gateway" to the immanent Trinity. Because he is convinced that "what happens on earth corresponds exactly to what exists in heaven,"[51] Boff readily looks to the earthly work of the incarnate Son and the Holy Spirit for "glimpses of life inside the Trinity."[52] Above all, Boff is certain that the perichoretic relationality of the three persons that is evident in salvation history reveals that the three trinitarian persons "are simultaneous in origin and co-exist eternally in communion and interpenetration."[53]

Boff's assurance that the economic Trinity reveals true, albeit incomplete, knowledge of the eternal dynamic within the triune God leads him to diverge in another manner from the path that Moltmann had charted. Although Boff shares with Moltmann the idea that the appeal to *perichoresis* leads to what his mentor termed an "open Trinity," he pushes the concept in a manner that would likely make his Protestant colleague uncomfortable. Not only is the second person of the Trinity incarnate in Jesus of Nazareth, the third person is in some sense "incarnate" in Mary.

Although Boff gives repeated expression to his heightened Mariology[54] throughout *Trinity and Society,* his most explicit exploration of the theological perspective that drives it emerges in his discussion of the mission of the Spirit. In response to the question, "If the Spirit was sent by the Father together with the Son, to whom specifically was it sent?" Boff appeals to the annunciation to Mary in the Lucan narrative (Luke 1:35) to conclude, "The words of the text permit us to deduce a mission proper to the Holy Spirit, that is, a personal (hypostatic) self-communication to the Virgin Mary."[55] In Boff's estimation, this pneumatological move parallels closely the christological act in the incarnation: "The Holy Spirit, coming down on Mary, 'pneumatized' her, taking on human form in her, in the same manner as the Son who, in a personal and unmistakable manner, set up his tent amongst us in the figure of Jesus of Nazareth."[56] The result is a kind of incarnation of the Spirit in Mary: "Mary, then, without metaphor or figure, is the true, physical temple of the Holy Spirit, in a way analogous to Jesus as the dwelling place of the eternal Son."[57]

According to Boff, the mission of the Spirit who came upon Mary has a wider, communal purpose. The Spirit's presence floods out from Mary to include others: "all the just, especially women"; the church, "of which Mary is the first and most perfect member"; and finally "humanity on its journey toward the Kingdom, a journey through change and liberation processes that make creation progressively more like its ultimate goal of communion in the Trinity."[58] In Boff's estimation, therefore, Jesus and Mary serve as the "two hands" of the triune God in the task of irreversibly inserting humanity into the mystery of the Trinity.[59] Through them, the perichoretic relationship between the open Trinity and creation has been effected.

The sending of the Spirit to Mary carries an additional theological implication, one that links the eternal God with human sexual differentiation. In keeping with patristic thought, Boff acknowledges that the humanity of Jesus has a feminine dimension that was divinized in the incarnation.[60] Yet Boff fears that the incarnation divinized maleness explicitly but femaleness only implicitly, a situation that in his estimation suggests a parallel explicit divinization of femaleness (and an implicit divinization of maleness) by means of the connection between the Holy Spirit and Mary. Consequently, Boff elevates Jesus and Mary together as representing the whole of humanity as well as "the eschatological event of the full divinization of men and women in the Kingdom of God."[61] Moreover, although Boff recognizes that the implicit divinization of Jesus' feminine side means that the incarnate Son reveals the "maternal face of God,"[62] he suggests that this dimension is more directly shown through the sending of the Holy Spirit to the woman Mary.[63]

Ultimately, therefore, for Boff the divine self-disclosure through the Son (in Jesus) and through the Holy Spirit (in Mary) reveals the one who is the "Maternal Father and the Paternal Mother."[64] Consequently, the vision of the immanent Trinity as communion and coexistence, and hence as both masculine and feminine, that emerges from the work of the two hands of God in the world (that is, from the economic Trinity) leads to a more complete and integrating experience of God.[65] This experience is truly liberating, because it honors irreducible differences even while bringing them together into a unity, after the pattern of the immanent Trinity, who is the final paradigm for creaturely life.

The Immanent Trinity and the Ideal Society

"Among Latin American liberation theologians," Otto Maduro writes, "Leonardo Boff has been the first to retrieve the feminine and maternal dimension of God revealed in the Bible and the history of the church, to analyze and critique the sexist and patriarchal character of most Christian theologies, and to propose, in explicit solidarity with feminist theologies, a trans-sexist theology of God as Maternal Father and Paternal Mother."[66] Actually, the theological task of bringing maleness and femaleness into the very life of the triune God (while maintaining that God is beyond maleness and femaleness) is not merely an attempt to take feminist concerns seriously. It forms a crucial aspect in Boff's overarching program of linking the doctrine of the Trinity to the human social ideal. As Maduro points out, in Boff's theology, "God as Trinity is . . . a paradigm of how human relations should be reshaped (including relations toward the oppressed, among the genders, within the church) as loving, egalitarian, cooperative, and dialogical."[67]

Reviewers across the theological spectrum have found helpful impulses in his attempt to delineate a trinitarian theology that has implications for human society.[68] Moreover, his thoroughgoing use of the concept of *perichoresis* has found echo in the work of other thinkers.[69] Yet many of Boff's readers also express reservations about specific aspects of his program as it is developed in *Trinity and Society*.

It comes as no surprise that many critics find themselves put off by Boff's heightened Mariology. Actually Boff readily admits that he has gone beyond official Roman Catholic Church teaching here. He seeks to clarify the matter by explaining that his intention is merely to offer a theological hypothesis based on an attempt to correlate the biblical narrative with related truths of the faith.[70] Yet the symmetry he posits between the incarnation of the Son in Jesus of Nazareth and a supposed incarnation of the Spirit in Mary not only produces a Mariology that goes beyond the teaching of his church but also suggests an adoptionist Christology that appears to stand outside the historic teaching of the church as a whole. Unfortunately, Boff's theological hypothesis plays such a crucial role in his trinitarian theology that it cannot be easily extracted without causing irreparable damage to the whole.

In addition to his questionable Mariology, some reviewers of Boff's work find him susceptible to, if not actually guilty of, tritheism.[71] Boff, however, consciously seeks to avoid this error, and he finds in the idea of *perichoresis* the means to this end. He explains: "The error of tritheism was in affirming *just* the existence of three divine Persons, without their reciprocal inter-relatedness, the Three being juxtaposed and separated as though they were three natures or substances."[72] So impressed is Shirley Guthrie with Boff's proposal at this point that he lauds him for providing a more promising solution to this difficulty than that offered by others: "Boff does an even better job than Moltmann of developing a trinitarian theology centered in the doctrine of *perichoresis* that is not vulnerable to the charge of tritheism."[73] In spite of Boff's efforts, many critics remain unconvinced. In fact, David Cunningham goes so far as to question the very idea of appealing to *perichoresis*, at least as it is often understood today, to portray the divine unity. In his estimation, the tendency of contemporary trinitarian thinkers to define the term in the active sense, that is, as designating the idea of interpenetration, is problematic, insofar as it is difficult "to imagine a scene of 'threefold interpenetration' that does not involve three *actors* or *agents*."[74]

Some reviewers of Boff's work are unconvinced by his attempts to draw a connection between particular doctrines of God and the supposedly corresponding political structures, together with his claim that a trinitarian conception of God promotes democratic social orders. Critics point to historical and contemporary societies that stand as counterexamples to Boff's contention that monotheism and monarchy go hand in hand. They also question whether any supposedly general correlation proves the kind of causal connection between theological vision and social ordering that Boff (following Moltmann) posits.

Some antagonists take the matter a step further. Not only is the connection tenuous, they declare, but the argument itself evidences the typically modern assumption that Christians owe some degree of ultimate allegiance to the nation-state and consequently have an ongoing interest in improving its structure. Cunningham, for example, applauds Boff (and Moltmann) for pointing out that the loss of trinitarian theology has consequences for the state. Yet he notes that these theologians fail to see that the loss does not support only absolutist states, but all states, regardless of their actual social structuring.[75] Cunningham is convinced that the doctrine of the Trinity calls into question the claim that Christians owe allegiance to the nation-state, *whatever* its form may be.[76] Furthermore, he wonders how Boff could have missed this point, given the "alternative politics" that the presence in Latin America of Base Christian Communities provides.[77]

The overarching question, however, has yet to be addressed: Has Boff accomplished his lofty goal of connecting the triune divine reality and the human social ideal? Some detractors remain unconvinced. Ted Peters, to cite one especially negative voice, concludes, "Although Boff wants to work with a correlation between a divine society and a human society on a nonhierarchical basis, the divine society of which he speaks is in fact a monarchy; and because this monarchy is shrouded in eternal mystery apart from the time in which we live, no genuine correlation with human society can be made."[78]

More devastating than Peters's debatable charge that Boff is working with a hierarchical model of God is the suggestion, implicit in Peters's critique, that his commitment to the apophatic approach has doomed his project from the beginning. In paving the way for his sweeping critique of Boff's project cited in the previous paragraph, Peters claims that "his emphasis on the eternity of the immanent Trinity causes Boff to shrink from the implications of Rahner's Rule."[79] By extension, Peters is suggesting that his unwillingness to appropriate fully Rahner's Rule prohibits Boff from drawing sufficient insight for the ideal human society from the divine prototype. In short, although Boff's work illustrates the commitment to relationality that came to characterize trinitarian theology in the late twentieth century, it demonstrates the difficulty inherent in any attempt to ground the human ideal by means of an appeal to the immanent Trinity, while rejecting the "vice versa" character of Rahner's Rule.

The Trinity and the Relationality of Being: John Zizioulas

The shift toward the focus on the relationality of the three persons that came to typify much of trinitarian theology in the waning years of the twentieth century reopened questions that remained less bothersome so long as the theological starting point lay with the single divine substance. Proponents of the relational approach find themselves confronted anew with the task of understanding and speaking about the threeness of the one God, as well as making sense of the relationality that is deemed to lie at the heart of the one God. Perhaps the most crucial challenge that plagues theologians who advocate a shift to a relational model of the Trinity is that of preventing themselves from slipping into an insipid tritheism. In his attempt to avoid this trap, Leonardo Boff follows Barth and Rahner in rejecting the idea that the Father, Son, and Spirit are persons in the sense of being three centers of consciousness, although he is willing to grant that each is "a centre of interiority and freedom."[80] In advancing this perspective, Boff consciously breaks ranks with many of those who build from the idea of the divine relationality, including his mentor, Jürgen Moltmann. Boff's defection highlights an issue that divided the participants in the late-twentieth-century renaissance of social trinitarianism[81] and separated many of them from their turn-of-the-twentieth-century predecessors.

The earlier turn to the social Trinity had its roots in Hegel. As was noted in chapter 1, Hegel's work introduced into the theological caldron the question as to how the divine subjectivity might be understood. Some post-Hegelian theologians sought to deal with this issue by attempting a retrieval of the Augustinian approach, which looks to human personhood as the window into the divine triunity. Others, in contrast, set out to solve the riddle of the divine subjectivity by returning to the social conception of the Trinity that traces its pedigree to the Cappadocian fathers but was injected into the Western tradition more directly though the work of the twelfth-century thinker, Richard of St. Victor.

In keeping with Hegel's elevation of subjectivity, proponents of the turn-of-the-twentieth-century reformulation of the social Trinity spoke boldly of the three trinitarian members as fully persons in the modern sense of the term, which views the person as a self or an ego.[82] In so doing, they accepted Hegel's focus on subjectivity, but applied the descriptor to the three trinitarian persons rather than to the one divine Subject, as Hegel had done. In the process, these thinkers—anticipating the work of Moltmann, Pannenberg, and Jenson—moved the locus of the divine personhood away from what they considered to be the problematic Western preference for the one God and toward the three trinitarian members.

Wilfred Richmond, for example, spoke of the divine unity as "a unity of Persons" and then concluded, "God *is* a fellowship, a communion of Persons."[83] A. M. Fairbairn concurred, claiming that if the divine essence is love, God "must be by nature social."[84] Similarly, J. R. Illingworth concluded that the doctrine of the Trinity "enables us to think of God, as if the term be guarded from any tritheistic connotation, a social being, or society."[85] Moreover, with the notable exception of George A. Gordon,[86] pre–World War I social trinitarians typically claimed that they were building from, and perhaps even clarifying, what the church fathers meant by *hypostasis* and *prosopon*.[87] Despite these attempts to build from Hegel's revival of trinitarian thought in accordance with the modern concept of the subject and to drink anew from the patristic well, in the years prior to World War I many thinkers remained unconvinced that the final word on the topic had been spoken.[88]

As the twentieth century unfolded, theologians sympathetic to social conceptions of the Trinity came to wonder if the problems encountered by their forebears were due less to the doctrine of the Trinity itself than to the modern, post-Hegelian subjectivist cast into which it had been set. Moreover, some concluded that the doctrine of the Trinity is not intended to suggest that God is three persons who have relations, but three subsistent relations that are in fact persons. Hence, Nicholas Lash declared that in contrast to humans, who "*have* relationships, God *is* the relations that he has." Lash then concluded, "God, we might say, is relationship without remainder, which we, most certainly, are not."[89] Although Lash himself questions the continued use of the term *person* to refer to the three trinitarian members,[90] the turn to relationality meant that the stage was set for a revised social trinitarianism. Once again the legacy of the Cappadocians came to be appropriated, insofar as the Cappadocians' preference for the language of "relation" over that of "substance" led many thinkers to consider anew the possibility that these patristic theological innovators might in fact offer the way forward.

Being as Communion and the Cappadocian Legacy

Turn-of-the-twentieth-century social trinitarians drew from the Cappadocians largely in accordance with Western theological interests and mainly for the purpose of resolving theological difficulties arising out of the encounter of Western theology with modern conceptions of personhood.

Their late-twentieth-century heirs retained their predecessors' hope that the light they obtain can illumine contemporary Western philosophical and theological difficulties. Yet they generally borrowed from the Greek fathers in a manner more self-consciously mediated through the Eastern tradition. No Orthodox thinker has been more important to this newer appropriation of insights from the Eastern church than the Greek theologian and metropolitan of Pergamon, John D. Zizioulas, whom in 1996 David A. Fisher hailed as the leading contemporary embodiment of the Byzantine intellectual tradition[91] and Yves Congar lauded fourteen years earlier as "one of the most original and profound theologians of our age."[92]

Zizioulas's place within the story of the renaissance of trinitarian theology is largely connected to his influential book *Being as Communion: Studies in Personhood and the Church* (1985),[93] which appeared while he was on the faculty of the University of Glasgow.[94] To this work should be added an important essay on anthropology published in 1975[95] and a handful of more recently written pieces sprinkled in various scholarly journals[96] and edited collections of essays by a variety of authors.[97]

Being as Communion is not a treatment of the doctrine of the Trinity per se. Its theme is ecclesiology or, more specifically, eucharistic ecclesiology, which in Zizioulas's estimation is closely connected to a Christian ontology of personal relatedness that he believes can provide the *telos* of the human quest for ontological freedom. Moreover, the primary context into which Zizioulas speaks is the debate within Orthodox circles regarding the principle espoused by the twentieth-century theologian Nicholas Afanasiev, that "wherever the eucharist is, there is the Church."[98] Zizioulas's goal is drawn from the concept of relationship to correct and extend Afanasiev's ecclesiological insight. Rather than an institution, Zizioulas argues, the church is a mode of existence; it is the manifestation of the relationship, or communion, of humans with God.[99] Despite its intra-Orthodox character, *Being as Communion* is also directed toward the ongoing breach between East and West. Zizioulas's stated hope is that his work might contribute to an integration between the two theological traditions by fostering a "neopatristic synthesis" that brings both closer to their common roots.[100]

The major thesis of Zizioulas's trinitarian ontology—from which the title of the book is derived—has become so influential that "being as communion" now ranks as a methodological axiom on the order of Rahner's Rule. In the eyes of relational theologians, his introduction of communion as an overarching metaphysical category has provided an ontology of personhood by means of which the mystery of the triune God can be named, explored, and—at least to a limited extent—understood. Consequently, Zizioulas might be credited with supplying an additional axiom to the renaissance of trinitarian theology, one that could bear the designation "the Zizioulas Dictum."

The Cappadocian philosophical "revolution." In typical Orthodox fashion Zizioulas looks to the doctrine of the Trinity as the starting point for his constructive theological reflection. He is convinced that the mystery of the church "is deeply bound . . . to the very being of God,"[101] and this because the sole model "for the proper relation between communion and otherness" is the trinitarian God.[102] In developing his perspective, Zizioulas elevates the Greek fathers, especially the Cappadocians, for their role in the story of the church's understanding of the Trinity. The exalted opinion of these theologians evident in the opening chapter of *Being as Communion* is spelled out more explicitly in an essay, "The Doctrine of the Trinity: The Significance of the Cappadocian Contribution," that Zizioulas presented at a conference on trinitarian theology held at King's College, London, in 1990.

Zizioulas is convinced that the Cappadocians, among whose ranks he includes not only the standard names—Basil, Gregory of Nazianzus, and Gregory of Nyssa—but also Amphilochius of Iconium, mark a watershed in Christian trinitarian theology and in the process launched a revolution in Greek philosophical history. In his estimation, their "theological and philosophical originality" not only "sealed the entire history of Christian thought" but also ignited "a radical reorientation of classical Greek humanism." In fact, he goes so far as to assert that the implications of the Cappadocians' theological proposal affected "the entire culture of late antiquity to such an extent that the whole of Byzantine and European thought would remain incomprehensible without a knowledge of this contribution."[103] The importance of the Cappadocians consists primarily in the ontology of personhood they inaugurated, which resulted in the elevation of the principle of freedom and facilitated a philosophical understanding that struck a balance between the one (that is, nature) and the many (that is, persons).[104]

According to Zizioulas's account, the Cappadocian revolution in Greek philosophy bequeathed to history the concept of the person.[105] To explicate their monumental accomplishment, he places their work within the development of ancient thought. Both the Greeks and the Romans explored the possibility of personal identity in the form of the capacity to act in a free and unique manner, as is evident by the use to which they put the Greek concept of *prosopon* (the mask worn by actors in Greek theatrical performances) and the Latin term *persona* (the role a Roman would adopt in social or legal relationships). Despite these forays along the road to personal freedom, both the Greeks and the Romans agreed that each individual life is ultimately determined by ontological necessity and hence that "other powers, not the quality of personhood, laid claim to the ontological content of human existence."[106] Moreover, the Greek (and Roman) philosophers viewed being a person—that is, being identified by unique attributes and being in relation with others—as something additional to one's essential nature (that is, one's *ousia* or *hypostasis*). Personhood was viewed as added to a concrete entity, as is evident in the link between the Greek term *prosopon* and the theatrical mask. In the midst of this philosophical situation, Zizioulas declares, the Cappadocians burst on the scene, providing the conceptual "lift" needed to move the philosophical anthropology of the ancients toward an ontology of personhood.

Zizioulas notes that the Cappadocians' far-reaching bestowal of ontological priority on personhood did not arise out of explicit philosophical reflection. Rather, it emerged from their engagement with the fierce theological controversy within the church of their day, which focused on the question as to the language that could express the fullness of Christian teaching about the God revealed in Jesus Christ. The Cappadocians entered the fray and set out to overcome the modalism, tritheism, and subordinationism that beset the various proposals bandied about by their contemporaries.

In response to the claim of the Sabellians that the trinitarian members are merely roles assumed by the one God (modalism), the Cappadocians asserted the full ontological integrity of the three persons of the Trinity. To do so, Zizioulas explains, they identified the Greek term *hypostasis*, which hitherto had been a synonym of *ousia*, with *prosopon*, a concept with which *hypostasis* had enjoyed no previous connection in Greek philosophy. By connecting *hypostasis* with *prosopon*, Zizioulas concludes, the Cappadocians transformed "person" into the constitutive element of a being,[107] and the concept of being itself became relational. As Zizioulas states it, "*To be* and *to be in relation* become identical."[108]

The Cappadocian innovation emerged likewise in the context of the orthodox response to the ontological subordinationism inherent in an extreme form of Arianism known as Eunomianism. In reflecting on the church's teaching about the generation of the Son and the procession of the Spirit, Eunomius raised the question as to the implications of the causative role of the Father. On the basis of his conclusion that being "ungenerate" or "unbegotten" must belong to the divine *ousia*, he surmised that the Son must be of a different *ousia* from the Father, in that sonship consists in being begotten. This meant, however, that the Son as well as the Spirit are ontologically subordinate to the Father. In arguing against this position, the orthodox thinkers distinguished between substance and person in God. Thus, they asserted that the delineation "unbegotten" refers to the personhood *(hypostasis)* of the Father and not to the divine substance *(ousia)*. Furthermore, they declared that each of the three persons is defined through a property (for example, unbegottenness, begottenness, spiration) that is not shared with the other two. This understanding of the Trinity led the Cappadocians to the philosophical insight that a person is identified by means of each one's uniqueness rather than through a common "nature" or "substance."

Zizioulas also cites the Cappadocians for the manner in which they avoided the error of tritheism. To accomplish this goal, they linked *ousia* with *physis*, which they understood as a general metaphysical category that can be applied to more than one person. This provided the Cappadocians with the philosophical basis for distinguishing between the one divine *ousia* and the three *hypostases*. Although to illustrate this distinction they drew an analogy from the one human nature or substance that is shared by concrete human beings, they also pointed out that the interplay of the one and the many in humankind differs categorically from the interplay within the triune God. The key to the difference, they determined, lies in the temporality of human existence in contrast to the eternality of God. Humans share human nature, which preexists and is logically prior to them. The divine nature, in contrast, does not precede the three trinitarian persons; therefore, rather than sharing a preexisting divine nature, the three coincide with that nature. Furthermore, the Cappadocians pointed out that in contrast to humans, the one and the many coincide in God, for the three trinitarian persons are united in such an unbreakable communion that none of the three can be conceived apart from the others. Hence, their elevation of a fundamental relationality among the trinitarian persons undercut any suggestion that Father, Son, and Spirit are to be viewed as autonomous individuals.

Regarding this aspect of the Cappadocian innovation, Zizioulas writes, "The mystery of the one God in three persons points to a way of being which precludes individualism and separation (or self-sufficiency and self-existence) as a criterion of Multiplicity. The 'one' not only does not precede—logically or otherwise—the 'many,' but, on the contrary, requires the 'many' from the very start in order to exist."[109] In this manner, the Cappadocians freed divine existence "from the servitude of personhood to substance, a servitude that applies only to created existence." "Being," Zizioulas concludes, "is simultaneously relational and hypostatic," and this because the divine eternality means that "the three persons are not faced with a given substance, but exist freely."[110] In short, Zizioulas's account pinpoints the Cappadocians as forming the headwaters of an innovative philosophical anthropology. By joining an ontological term (*hypostasis*) to a sociological concept (*prosopon*) they sparked a revolution in ontology. As John G. F. Wilks explains, "The notion of personhood as something more than merely an individual entered and altered ontological definitions. Simply to possess divine (or human) substance was not proof of personhood: something totally different to the substance also needs to be recognized. This is the ability to be in relation."[111]

The ontology of persons-in-communion and the triune God. Zizioulas notes that the Greek fathers' conception of God in general and the Trinity in particular emerged out of their experience of what he calls "ecclesial community." Because this experience had the character of "ecclesial being," the patristic theologians concluded that being means communion and, by extension, that humans could only speak about God through the relational language of communion.[112] In this manner, the Cappadocians discovered the term *koinonia* as the way to denote the divine unity, for the oneness of God, they declared, lies in the *koinonia* or communion of the three persons. According to Zizioulas, the genius of the Cappadocians lay in their insight into the ontological implications of this ecclesial reality. In his estimation, they devised an ontology of communion—a relational understanding of personhood—that points the way forward for both philosophical anthropology and trinitarian theology.

The Cappadocian transformation of the idea of person leads Zizioulas to a far-reaching, communal ontology of personhood. A person is not a static entity, he notes. A person is not the self-existent substance of Aristotelian philosophy determined by its inherent boundaries. Nor can a person be identified by appeal to a nature that is marked by certain qualities that all such beings supposedly share. As Nonna Verna Harrison points out, for Zizioulas, "the person is characterized by an absolute uniqueness that cannot be expressed in human language, which names qualities common to groups of things. . . . The person is a mystery transcending such measurable qualities, and its unique character is discerned only through the eyes of love."[113]

In an address to the eighth Orthodox Congress in Western Europe and subsequently published as "Communion and Otherness," Zizioulas elaborates a crucial aspect of his ontological proposal. He points out that the concept of "otherness" stands as perhaps the central existential concern in postmodern society. In this context, the Cappadocian doctrine of the Trinity provides the appropriate ontology of communion, he argues, for their understanding of persons-in-relationship takes otherness seriously and leads to the realization that rather than being merely a cause of division, difference is a vital element in true communion. In Zizioulas's estimation, this ontology takes its cue from the Christian conception of God as three persons in communal unity. Hence, insofar as "God is not first one and then three, but simultaneously One and Three" and because of the "unbreakable *koinonia*" existing among the three persons, otherness is not consequent upon unity but is constitutive and a sine qua non condition of unity. Moreover, the absolute difference among the three trinitarian persons suggests that "otherness is *absolute*." Furthermore, because we cannot declare "*what* each Person is," only "who He is," otherness is ontological. And finally, the realization that the terms "Father, Son and Spirit are all names indicating relationship" leads to the conclusion that "otherness is inconceivable apart from *relationship*."[114]

According to Zizioulas's ontological proposal, personhood is constituted by the interplay of *hypostasis* and *ekstasis*. A person is the result of the "ecstatic" drive toward transcending one's own boundaries (that is, the drive toward self-transcendence) as well as the desire to be an integrated unity. Personhood implies "the *ek-stasis* of being, i.e., a movement towards communion which leads to a transcendence of the boundaries of the 'self' and thus to *freedom*," while at the same time remaining "*hypostatic*, i.e., the bearer of its nature in its totality."[115] This leads Zizioulas to the constitutive role of communion in the ontology of personhood: "since 'hypostasis' is identical with Personhood and not with substance, it is not in its 'self-existence' but in *communion* that this being is *itself* and thus *is at all.*"[116] Such communion, he adds, establishes the uniqueness of each person, in that the person is an indispensable and irreplaceable part of a relational existence.[117]

As Zizioulas himself notes, this ontology of communion has far-reaching implications for anthropology and ecclesiology. His place in the story of trinitarian theology, however, is connected more directly to its significance for the understanding of the Trinity. To this end, he cites one additional innovation of the Cappadocians, their elevation of the idea of freedom and its implications for theology. This innovation, he declares, came by means of two "leavenings" which altered the focus on the necessity of being that dominated Greek philosophy. First, against the reigning philosophical schools of the day, the Greek theologians beginning with Athanasius argued that the existence of the world is a product of divine freedom, for creation is *ex nihilo.*[118] Although this doctrine secured God's freedom in relationship to creation, it needed to be augmented by a second leavening, which secured God's freedom in relationship to God's own being.[119] In this development, the Cappadocians played the leading role, for they identified the being of God with the person (more specifically, the person of the Father) rather than with the divine substance, as has been the typical approach of theologians in the Western tradition.

Zizioulas claims that this important move was evidenced by a historical detail often overlooked by historians of doctrine. Under the influence of the Cappadocians, the Council of Constantinople altered the statement of the Nicene Creed that the Son proceeds "from the substance of the Father" to read simply "from the Father." Zizioulas considers this to be "a clear expression of the Cappadocian interest in stressing that it is the person of the Father and not divine substance that is the source and cause of the Trinity."[120] Furthermore, Zizioulas adds, the Cappadocians came to attach the ontological idea of the one *arche* or source to the person of the Father, so that the one God was viewed as the Father.[121] By elevating the Father as the cause of both the generation of the Son and the procession of the Spirit, and hence of the being and life of God, the Cappadocians were able to speak of the triune God as the communion of the trinitarian persons. Rather than arising by necessity from the divine substance, this communion is the product of the personal freedom of the Father, who by begetting the Son and bringing forth the Spirit freely wills it.[122] Paul M. Collins explains Zizioulas's point: "The Father as a free person brings the divine communion and substance into being, *freely*. Neither communion nor substance are pre-existing categories which are imposed upon the deity by some external necessity. Both are freely chosen by the Father."[123] In this manner, the Cappadocians showed that the being of God arises out of freedom, that is, out of the personal freedom of God the Father.[124] Thereby, they provided an ontology in which the divine personhood precedes and provides the basis for the divine *ousia* and in which the being of the divine persons is constituted by the communion or relationality they enjoy.

Zizioulas believes that locating the cause of the divine existence in the person of the Father results in a monotheism that is both biblical and in keeping with trinitarian theology.[125] But this approach also suggests an ontology that moves in the opposite direction of Western thought, for it means that "particularity [that is, personhood] is . . . causative and not derivative in ontology,"[126] and hence that the nature of being—both divine and human—is communion. Furthermore, Zizioulas is convinced that only the Eastern approach with its focus on the person of the Father as the *arche* of the divine being can preserve freedom as well as love, understood as the ontological exercise of freedom. To advance this assertion, he returns to the idea of *ekstasis*, viewed as the aspect of personhood that is directed toward others or the act of breaking through boundaries "in a movement of communion."[127] According to Zizioulas, love is the expression of communion, for in love persons exist in *ekstatic* relationship. This is evident in the Johannine declaration, "God is love," from which text Zizioulas concludes that love does not emerge out of the divine substance, but constitutes that substance; love is what "makes God what he is, the one God."[128]

In this manner, Zizioulas elevates love to ontological status. He is convinced that full personal identity, whether in the case of the human person or the three trinitarian persons, is not ultimately connected to qualities associated with "essence" or "nature" but emerges only through a relationship that is so ontologically constitutive of personhood that it reflects the idea that relating is not appended to being but is being itself.[129] And this relationship is love. To summarize: the divine being is the *ekstasis* of the three trinitarian persons, which is grounded in the Father's "free event of love"[130] in begetting the Son and bringing forth the Spirit. In short, being is communion.

The Father-Caused Communion of the Three Persons

The Cappadocians developed their communal ontology of personhood in the context of theological dispute. Zizioulas's appropriation of this ontology, in contrast, is linked to his concern, born out of the conviction that "Trinitarian theology has profound existential consequences,"[131] that the church respond to contemporary currents in philosophical anthropology, including the "ontologizing of death" found in what he calls "humanistic existential philosophy."[132] He is convinced that the contemporary situation requires a radical philosophical shift not unlike that proposed by the Cappadocians in the context of ancient Greek philosophy. In his estimation, substance must give way to personhood "as the causing principle or *arche* in ontology";[133] a substance-focused ontology that elevates the self-existent, individual being must be replaced by an ontology of relationship that focuses on personhood. His importance to this discussion in contemporary Western philosophy has not been overlooked. David Fisher, for example, declares that Zizioulas has put forth "Christian ontology as formulated by the Fathers as a hopeful alternative to contemporary humanistic and existential philosophy."[134] John G. F. Wilks agrees, declaring that Zizioulas's work entails a "rigorous application of the doctrine of the Trinity to the contemporary problem of the dissolution of personhood in Western society"[135] and lauding him for having "demonstrated a way out of the existential despair concerning the nature of personhood" with which Western society has been saddled.[136]

Zizioulas's probing reaffirmation of the ontological primacy of personhood has likewise won him a place in the story of trinitarian theology. In the wake of the demise of the concept of "person" in Barth's and Rahner's proposals with their stated preference for such alternative linguistic expressions as "modes of being," he stands with a growing number of voices who are convinced that the language of "person" coined in the fourth century is of abiding importance to the doctrine of the Trinity.[137] Moreover, the Zizioulas Dictum, the assertion that "the one substance of God coincides with the communion of the three persons"[138]—that is, "being is communion"—has become a standard axiom in contemporary relational trinitarianism alongside Rahner's Rule and the Pannenberg

Principle. For good reason, therefore, Zizioulas has increasingly been looked to as providing a promising ontology that can facilitate the retention of the concept of "person" in trinitarian theology. Thus, Patricia Fox concludes that insofar as "God disclosed as 'persons in communion' reveals a totally shared personal life at the heart of the universe," Zizioulas has offered "a dynamic and thrilling vision of God."[139] Alan Torrance declares more specifically that Zizioulas's "revision of trinitarian expression by way of the category of 'person' stands to breathe new life into the Western debates by revising radically the traditionally static conceptualities that have done such damage to the doctrine of God."[140] Similarly, in the context of his appraisal of Zizioulas's contribution, Ted Peters notes, "Recent Trinity talk in both East and West affirms the need to speak about God in terms of personhood, to unite person and being, and to define a person not as an isolated individual but in relationship. . . . To understand the Trinity in terms of person-in-relationship has emerged as the aim of Trinity talking between East and West."[141]

Despite his widely recognized importance to the renaissance of trinitarian theology, even sympathetic readers express reservations about some dimensions of Zizioulas's proposal. Much of the discomfort centers on his treatment of the work of the Cappadocians. Criticisms arise already at the level of his rendition of their understanding of personhood. For example, Orthodox scholar Lucian Turcescu claims that Zizioulas "has not convincingly exegeted the Cappadocian theology of person." He argues, contra Zizioulas, that because the Greek fathers were not struggling with the ills of modern individualism, they did not distinguish "person" and "individual." Nor were they the personalists that the metropolitan of Pergamon makes them out to be. In the end, Turcescu fears that rather than importing the Cappadocian proposal directly, Zizioulas has in fact drawn his central insights from nineteenth- and twentieth-century sources "which he then foists on the Cappadocians."[142]

The theological question that critics almost invariably raise is connected to Zizioulas's supposition that the Cappadocians advanced the idea that the person of the Father, and not the divine substance, functions as the source and cause of the Trinity. As Ralph Del Colle points out, this theme marks the truly new aspect in Zizioulas's presentation, and it "captures the nub" of the "trinitarian foundation for his theological interests."[143]

Here again, historians of doctrine have called into question the accuracy of his historical treatment. In contrast to Zizioulas's suggestion that the causative role of the Father is the lynchpin of the entire Cappadocian proposal, John Wilks's historical research leads him to conclude that this idea actually played only a minor role in their scheme.[144] In fact, Wilks goes so far as to suggest that Zizioulas's account marks a clear departure from what the Cappadocians actually taught. Despite Zizioulas's claims to the contrary, Wilks maintains that the Greek fathers believed that the basis of the unity of the Godhead lay in the *ousia* rather than in the *hypostasis* or person of the Father.[145]

Some of Zizioulas's readers fear that his historical revisionism has opened the way to grave theological problems. Alan Torrance pinpoints what for many critics is the crucial difficulty: "Zizioulas' eagerness to explain the unity of God in a manner which obviates recourse to 'being' or *ousia* . . . involves projecting a causal ordering into the Godhead."[146] Torrance points out that this move possibly undercuts the ontologically primordial status of the Trinity insofar as the person of the Father becomes "*the* exclusively primordial reality,"[147] and it brings Zizioulas dangerously close to subordinating the Son to the Father.[148]

The charge of subordinationism is echoed by many detractors. Wilks concludes that Zizioulas has emphasized the Father as source and monarch to such a degree that he has confounded the person of the Father and the Godhead, and as a result he has slipped into the error of subordinating the Son and the Spirit to the first person of the Trinity.[149] Peter Leithart, in turn, notes that Zizioulas concedes that his elevation of the Father involves a kind of subordinationism but then argues that the church accepts this implication "as the price of securing the full personality of God." In Leithart's estimation, "this avoids one problem by creating another, equally serious one."[150]

This critique has not been voiced only by Western thinkers. Nonna Verna Harrison asserts that "Zizioulas emphasizes the primacy of the Father as cause so much that he has not thought through sufficiently the implications of the fact that the Son and Spirit are equally personal and thus ontologically free. Just as the Father as person bears within himself the whole of the divine essence, the Son bears within himself the whole of the divine essence, and the Holy Spirit likewise."[151] Harrison then counters what she perceives as Zizioulas's inattention to the importance of the *ousia* in the triune God. She writes:

While the three are directly related to each other as persons, they are also related to each other through the divine essence. It follows that nature or essence cannot be emptied of content as much as Zizioulas would like. The essence remains ontologically dependent on the persons, as he takes care to affirm, but it serves as a medium, so to speak, through which the persons actualize their relatedness and freely offer themselves to each other. . . . As common to the three, their essence is, as it were, a milieu in which they are related to each other within the intimate personal communion known only to themselves. . . . The common essence or nature is intrinsic to the relatedness which constitutes their existence, freedom and equality as persons.[152]

Despite the thoroughgoing character of criticisms such as these, they have not led to a wholesale dismissal of Zizioulas's proposal. On the contrary, even many of his sharpest detractors have built on his fundamental insights, while offering a kind of course correction to the direction he is pursuing. Paul Fiddes, to cite one helpful example, acknowledges the primacy of the Father, which lies at the heart of Zizioulas's proposal. But he draws this idea into his own preferred metaphor for the trinitarian life, the perichoretic image of the trinitarian dance: "The point in reserving the term 'source' *(arche)* to the Father is to affirm that woven in and through these to-and-fro movements that form the relationships there is a movement of 'sending out' that always flows one way, ultimately 'from the Father.'"[153] Yet Fiddes rejects Zizioulas's view that the asymmetry within the divine life is to be described as a distinction between the Father's "constituting" the Son and the Spirit and their mere "conditioning" of him. In Fiddes's estimation, the realization that the Son and Spirit in some way "make the Father what he is through their self-surrendering love" entails a mutual "constituting" among the three persons.[154]

Fiddes's corrective appears to reflect a trinitarian model that resembles aspects of the proposals of Moltmann and Pannenberg, who, like Zizioulas, acknowledge in some sense the primacy of the Father while arguing for a mutuality among the trinitarian persons. Other thinkers, in contrast, suggest that more drastic measures must be taken to salvage Zizioulas's overall program. Colin Gunton, for example, questions Zizioulas's attempt to ascribe preeminence to the Father on the basis of his being the cause of the communion within the triune God. The divine communion does not arise solely from the person of the Father, Gunton avers, for it is a constituent aspect of the nature of the Son and the Spirit as well.[155] Although T. F. Torrance's discussion partner is more directly the Cappadocian legacy rather than Zizioulas, he offers a similar corrective, the basis for which he finds present in one of the Cappadocians, Gregory of Nazianzus. In Torrance's estimation, Gregory provided "a rather more satisfactory view of the triunity of God than that of the other Cappadocians, for the *monarchia* is not limited to one person: it is a unity constituted by and in the trinity."[156]

The corrective proposed by Alan Torrance follows a somewhat similar tact, while pursuing further T. F. Torrance's counterproposal. He finds himself "agreeing strongly with Zizioulas that the West has everything to learn in these debates from the Greek Fathers."[157] Yet Alan Torrance suggests that Zizioulas has not followed his own ontological instincts regarding the status of the concept of communion. If communion does not refer to external relations involving preexisting persons but to the fellowship of persons who have their being in the *ekstasis* of that fellowship, Torrance wonders, then is "the intra-divine communion . . . not only a primordial concept but an eternal 'given,' that is, ontologically primitive and original?" Zizioulas claims that the Cappadocians introduced the concept of cause into the being of God so that the ultimate ontological category would not be some mere self-existing structure of communion. But, Torrance avers, insofar as the structure of communion is "nothing less than God," there is no reason why we should "*not* conceive of the intra-divine communion of the Triunity as the ground of all that is," that is, "as sufficient in itself and as indeed 'capable' of existing 'by itself.'"[158]

Having opened the possibility of a crucial revision of Zizioulas's proposal, Torrance then charts what he sees as the way forward. The kind of integrated articulation of the eternal communion of the Trinity that Zizioulas seeks, he declares, requires that he bring together the insights not only of Athanasius and Gregory of Nazianzus, but of Cyril of Alexandria as well. Following the lead of T. F. Torrance, whom he cites in this context, Alan Torrance draws from Cyril's idea of the procession of the Spirit from the Father through the Son, which in his estimation provides a richer doctrine of the mutual coinherence of the three trinitarian persons. This interpretation of the Trinity, he concludes, overcomes the difficulty he observed in Zizioulas's proposal, for it identifies the divine *monarchia* with the triunity of God and views it as denoting "God's external relations with the created order rather than (quasi-external!) relations internal to the Godhead."[159]

Communion and the Oikonomic Trinity:
Catherine Mowry LaCugna

The Greek patristic concept of interpersonal personhood, especially as it was retrieved by John Zizioulas, has become standard fare in much contemporary trinitarian theology. The renewed interest in the Cappadocians has, in turn, spawned a widespread questioning, and even a wholesale rejection, of Augustianian trinitarianism not only among Orthodox thinkers but more importantly among an increasing number of the heirs of the Western theological tradition as well. This is evident, for example, in the work of British theologian Colin Gunton, who concludes from his study of the patristic sources, "The achievement of the Cappadocians, an achievement which Augustine had failed adequately to understand, was to create a new conception of the being of God, in which God's being was seen to consist in personal communion."[160]

Perhaps no proposal among the growing list of offerings by those Western theologians who appropriate the Cappadocian program in general and the resultant ontology of being-as-communion in particular has been more widely hailed than that of the University of Notre Dame theologian Catherine Mowry LaCugna. Like Gunton, whose work she saw as paralleling her own in many respects,[161] LaCugna laid the greater responsibility for the current malaise of the doctrine of the Trinity at the feet of Augustine and the Western tradition, while looking to the Eastern heritage for the way forward. She announced the first aspect of her perspective as early as 1986. In her essay "Philosophers and Theologians on the Trinity," which previews the conclusion arising from the historical sketch that she would later offer in her book-length treatise on trinitarian theology, LaCugna wrote:

> The Augustinian approach certainly broke the back of Arianism once and for all. . . . But a heavy price was paid. More and more the doctrine of the trinity was detached from ordinary Christian life (liturgy, prayer) and came to be viewed *only* as a speculative and purely formal doctrine. . . . Small wonder, then, that not terribly long

after the western medieval tradition had accomplished the ultimate refinement of trinitarian metaphysics, Schleiermacher should find that he could make much better sense of Christianity (and of salvation) by relegating the doctrine to a brief appendix.[162]

Seven years later, in her contribution to *Freeing Theology* (1993), a collection of essays written by feminist theologians which she edited, LaCugna reaffirmed the other central dimension of her perspective, her preference for the Cappadocians: "In the effort to reunite doctrine and practice and restore the doctrine of the Trinity to its rightful place at the center of Christian faith and practice, great potential, I believe, lies in revitalizing the Cappadocian (rather than Augustinian) doctrine of the Trinity."[163]

LaCugna's retrieval of the Cappadocians traverses the pathway Zizioulas pioneered.[164] As a consequence, the Zizioulas Dictum—that the divine being is constituted by the communion of the three trinitarian persons—is readily evident in her proposal. At the same time, LaCugna is indebted to the work of other pioneers of the twentieth-century renaissance in trinitarian theology. As observers such as Michael Downey note, she "moves further along the path plowed by Barth and widened by Rahner."[165] Yet a more thorough account of the trajectory in which she stands might suggest that LaCugna combines impulses from Zizioulas with Barth's focus on the revelational significance of the divine self-disclosure in Christ, Rahner's linking of the immanent Trinity with the economic Trinity—which she revises and reformulates as *theologia* and *oikonomia*[166]—and the interest in viewing the divine life through the history of the trinitarian persons evident in Pannenberg, Moltmann, and Jenson.

Theologia as Oikonomia

LaCugna's place in the theological hall of fame is linked primarily to her award-winning book, *God for Us: The Trinity and Christian Life* (1991). The volume appeared as the culmination of an array of essays on trinitarian theology, published in various scholarly journals and books between 1984 and 1989. In the years immediately following the book's appearance until her death at the age of 44 on May 3, 1997,[167] she saw into print several additional essays that either recapitulated major themes in *God for Us* or sought to move the discussion forward. Despite the "magnum opus" status that the volume has attained since her death, LaCugna intended that *God for Us* serve merely as the prelude to a series of projects. Since her days as a graduate student, her desire had been to compose a work on the

Holy Spirit that was to be entitled *Living in the Spirit of God, the Spirit of Christ*. LaCugna wrote *God for Us* first, however, for she believed, as Elizabeth Groope notes, "that a theology of the Holy Spirit requires a solid trinitarian foundation."[168]

The overarching thesis LaCugna articulates in *God for Us* is that the doctrine of the Trinity, which entails the specifically Christian way of speaking about God, is a practical doctrine that shapes Christian life. In an essay aptly titled "The Practical Trinity," which appeared in the *Christian Century* soon after the publication of her treatise on trinitarian theology, she explains:

> The doctrine of the Trinity is in fact the most practical of all doctrines. Among other things, it helps us articulate our understanding of the gospel's demands; how personal conversion is related to social transformation; what constitutes "right relationship" within the Christian community and in society at large; how best to praise and worship God; and what it means to confess faith in and be baptized into the life of the God of Jesus Christ.[169]

Australian Roman Catholic theologian Patricia Fox characterizes the basic theological method she finds at work in *God for Us* (as well as in Elizabeth Johnson's *She Who Is*) as consisting of "analysis and critique, retrieval, and then amplification."[170] Although LaCugna's book may evidence this kind of a three-stage methodological procedure, it is structured more simply. *God for Us* is divided into two parts, evidencing the pattern of deconstruction and reconstruction.[171] The book begins with a historical survey tracing the trajectory that led to what LaCugna sees as the current sorry state of trinitarian theology. This is followed by LaCugna's delineation of her own prescription for the kind of theological approach that can move beyond the long-standing malaise.

The context: the "defeat" of the Trinity. LaCugna's jumping-off point in *God for Us* is her diagnosis of the current state of trinitarian theology. In her estimation, theology is beset by a misguided division between talk about the triune God *ad intra* and *ad extra*, between theology proper and soteriology, or to use her preferred terminology, between *theologia* and *oikonomia*. Reminiscent of Harnack,[172] LaCugna traces this unfortunate development to a type of "Constantinian fall" of theology that emerged at the time of the Arian controversy and the Council of Nicea, when the idea of divine impassibility came to be applied to the Logos, thereby opening the way for theologians to separate *theologia* from *oikonomia* and subsequently to concentrate on the former.[173]

LaCugna's narrative of this historical development occupies the first part of *God for Us*.[174] Her story begins with what might be seen as the pristine pre-Nicene era, a time when reflection on the triune divine life focused on *oikonomia*, understood as "the actualization in time and history of the eternal plan of redemption, the providential ordering of all things."[175] During this time, church thinkers devoted little energy to speculation regarding *theologia*, seen as the mystery of the eternal being of God. In fact, they viewed *theologia* and *oikonomia* as essentially one, LaCugna postulates, for the economy of salvation was deemed to be nothing less than the mystery of God manifested in history for the salvation of humankind. As becomes evident in part 2 of *God for Us*, the conjoining of *theologia* and *oikonomia* in the theologizing of the church prior to Nicea provides LaCugna with a central epistemic principle, namely, the rooting of all theological reflection in *oikonomia*.[176]

The watershed—or Waterloo—for theology, LaCugna continues, occurred at Nicea. The Arian controversy, which provided the impetus for the council, raised the question regarding the theological implications of the suffering of Christ narrated in the Bible, as well as the apparent subordination of the Son to the Father evident in the divine economy. Arius concluded that the subordination *kat' oikonomia* implied subordination *kata theologia*, but he then argued that because God cannot suffer, the suffering Logos must be a lesser God. The Nicene theologians, in contrast, correlated *theologia* and *oikonomia* in their insistence that Christ is the coming of God into the world but divorced the two by concluding that as true God, the Logos could not suffer.[177] In this manner, LaCugna notes, the commonly held principle that God could not suffer led both sides to distinguish between the ontology and the economy of God, albeit in different ways. Moreover, the Council of Nicea introduced the idea that the Son is of one nature *(homoousios)* with the Father with respect to his divinity, that is, at the level of *theologia*. But this created an incommensurability with *oikonomia*, which term was now linked specifically to the humanity of Christ.

The Nicenes bequeathed to fourth-century theologians the task of working out the details of the orthodox position. The solution to which they turned asserted that the subordination evident in the economy of salvation does not apply to the inner life of God. LaCugna draws out the trinitarian-theological implication: "This argument was defensible only on the presumption that speculation on God 'in Godself' was not only possible but in some sense distinct from reflection on God in Christ."[178]

What follows in *God for Us* is a narration of the deepening fissure between *oikonomia* and *theologia*—the increased attention given to God *in se* apart from God in salvation—that developed as this trajectory charted its course through theological history from the Cappadocians to the Middle Ages. LaCugna argues that the categories set by Nicea together with the elongated character of the struggle against Arianism and neo-Arianism led Christian theologians to focus their attention on the nature of *theologia* per se, that is, on the interrelationship among the divine persons and hence on God's self-relatedness or inner life. As this occurred, the centrality of a trinitarian theology of relation came to be replaced by an ontology of substance, and the emphasis on the threeness of persons yielded to the elevation of the oneness of God. Although she readily admits that their motive was soteriological, LaCugna observes that over time Christian theologians lost the sense that the economy of salvation was at all decisive in shaping conclusions about the intratrinitarian relations.[179] The result was "a drastic separation of the mystery of God and the mystery of salvation,"[180] leading to "a one-sided theology of God [that] had little to do with the economy of Christ and the Spirit, with the themes of Incarnation and grace, and therefore little to do with the Christian life."[181] This, LaCugna concludes, marked the "defeat" of the doctrine of the Trinity, an astounding judgment that she borrows from the patristic scholar Dorothea Wendebourg.[182]

Given how LaCugna has cast the historical problem, it comes as no surprise that Augustine and Aquinas figure prominently as villains in her narrative. The former, of course, stands at the head of the Latin approach and proposed, among other mistakes, a turn to the subject that looked for vestiges of the Trinity in the interior life of the human person. The latter, in turn, gave the Western approach to the Trinity its most complete medieval expression. Yet LaCugna's story offers surprises as well. In contrast to Zizioulas's recounting in which the Cappadocians emerge as unqualified heroes, she deems them to have been part of the problem, despite their importance in delineating an ontology of personhood. Even they were guilty of the practice of drawing conclusions "about the divine persons at the level of *theologia*" that are "different from those drawn about the persons revealed in *oikonomia*." Thereby they too contributed to the widening of "the gap between the mystery of God and the mystery of redemption."[183] Nor does the theological trajectory of the Eastern church emerge blameless in her recounting of the narrative. Rather, LaCugna finds a similar development at work in the Eastern tradition especially as it climaxes in the work of the fourteenth-century monk Gregory of Palamas, who, she notes, "has been criticized as leading to the same 'loss of the soteriological' that characterizes Latin theology after Augustine."[184]

The LaCugna corollary. In part 1 of *God for Us,* LaCugna offers the bold thesis that theologians in both the East and the West precipitated the "defeat" of the doctrine of the Trinity. Equally bold is her assertion, delineated in part 2, that the way out of this morass includes a retrieval of the connection between *theologia* and *oikonomia* that characterized trinitarian reflection in the era prior to Nicea. More accurately, she sees her work as "the effort to re-imagine the Christian doctrine of God along the lines of biblical, early creedal, and liturgical patterns, as well as to think through the full implications of Cappadocian theology minus the Nicene and post-Nicene breach between *oikonomia* and *theologia*."[185] To set forth the constructive proposal that she believes arises from this act of retrieval and reimaging, LaCugna introduces into the fluid lava of trinitarian theology a methodological axiom of such far-reaching significance that Ted Peters has denoted it "the LaCugna corollary."[186]

In a nutshell, the LaCugna corollary postulates that theology (proper) and soteriology are intertwined. As she declares in *God for Us,* "theology is inseparable from soteriology and *vice versa.*"[187] In her essay for the *Christian Century,* LaCugna offers a short explication of the idea: "The doctrine of the Trinity . . . is a doctrine about God. But because it is a doctrine about the God who shares life with us in an economy of redemption, it is also a doctrine about salvation."[188] To reformulate it in accordance with her preferred terminology, the LaCugna corollary means that *theologia* (theological reflection regarding the mystery of God[189]) is indivisible from *oikonomia* (the self-disclosure of and the experience of God in salvation, God *pro nobis*).

LaCugna cites Karl Rahner as the one who inaugurated the move in this direction. In fact, Rahner's Rule provides the point of departure for her own proposal. On the basis of his idea that God is by nature self-communicating, she reports, Rahner declared that no adequate distinction can be made between theology (proper) and soteriology.[190] As early as 1985, LaCugna hinted at the extent to which she would be indebted to Rahner. In an essay entitled "Re-conceiving the Trinity as the Mystery of Salvation," an elaboration on Rahner's contribution to trinitarian theology, she declared, "we shall argue that Rahner's *Grundaxiom* is the precondition for re-conceiving the trinitarian doctrine *as* the mystery of salvation."[191]

At the same time, however, Rahner's Rule remains *only* a point of departure for LaCugna, for she is convinced that her mentor's *Grundaxiom* stands in need of a radical revision. In her estimation, Rahner remains "caught in the stranglehold of the post-Nicene problematic," for he too views the distinctions of persons in the divine economy as a means to gain access to a supposedly eternal self-communication within the divine being.[192] According to LaCugna, theology must cut the Gordian knot. Theologians must realize that rather than continuing the older manner of drawing from the language of the economic Trinity and the immanent Trinity to speak about God *ad extra* and *ad intra*, they should focus solely on the *oikonomia*, understood as "the concrete realization of the mystery of *theologia* in time, space, history, and personality."[193] In short, LaCugna proposes a moratorium on the use of the language of immanent Trinity and economic Trinity "as one step toward greater precision."[194]

LaCugna's attempt to provide an alternative conceptual scheme to this reigning but, in her estimation, problematic language comprises perhaps the most difficult and most readily misunderstood aspect of her proposal. By *oikonomia* LaCugna does not mean the Trinity *ad extra* but "the comprehensive plan of God reaching from creation to consummation, in which God and all creatures are destined to exist together in the mystery of love and communion." Nor should *theologia* be equated with the Trinity *in se* but is to be understood "much more modestly and simply" as "the mystery of God," which, she adds, "as we know from the experience of being redeemed by God through Jesus Christ . . . is the mystery of God with us."[195]

This bold shift in terminology carries far-reaching implications for trinitarian theology. In what is possibly the most significant methodological declaration of her magnum opus, LaCugna asserts emphatically,

> *Theologia* is what is given in *oikonomia* and *oikonomia* expresses *theologia*. Since our only point of access to *theologia* is through *oikonomia*, then *an "immanent" trinitarian theology of God is nothing more than a theology of the economy of salvation*. An immanent theology of the Trinity therefore is not, properly speaking, a theology of an intradivine Trinity of persons unrelated to the world. An immanent theology of God is not concerned with a purely intradivine self-communication. As Rahner's theology shows, there is only *one* self-communication of God, one begetting of the Son, one breathing forth of the Spirit, with both eternal and temporal aspects. An immanent theology of the Trinity is thus ineluctably a theology of the "internal" structure of the economy of redemption.[196]

As this quotation indicates, the LaCugna corollary in effect redefines the idea of the immanent Trinity. But it also redefines theology. The maxim links trinitarian reflection indelibly to the divine work in salvation history, by means of which creatures are brought into communion with the Creator, a communion that LaCugna understands in terms of *theosis* ("divinization" or "deification").[197] Rather than being the science of the life of the eternal God apart from the world, therefore, Christian theology speaks about God and the world. As she puts it, "the doctrine of the Trinity is not ultimately a teaching about 'God' but a teaching about *God's life with us and our life with each other*. It is the life of communion and indwelling, God in us, we in God, all of us in each other."[198] For LaCugna, trinitarian theology is the exploration of the dynamic movement of God within the comprehensive divine plan from creation to consummation, a movement that is *a Patre ad Patrem*, that is, that begins and ends with the Father from whom everything originates and to whom everything returns.

LaCugna conceptualizes the ecstatic movement of the triune God in the *oikonomia* as following a parabolic trajectory, a model of the Trinity that Ted Peters lauds as having the potential for "guiding the flow of East-West conversation."[199] She envisages the divine dynamic as moving forward and downward from the Father, through the Son and the Spirit, to creation, and then traversing a pathway forward and upward from creation, through the Spirit and the Son, to the Father. In her essay "The Trinitarian Mystery of God," written for a multiauthored Roman Catholic systematic theology, she summarizes her proposal and draws out its methodological implications:

The parabolic model (*parabola*: to throw outward) expresses the one ecstatic movement of God whereby all things originate with God and are returned to God. The model admits neither a Neo-Palamite nor a Neo-Scholastic separation between "God" and "God-for-us." The subject matter of trinitarian theology is the one dynamic movement of God, *a Patre ad Patrem* (from the Father, to the Father), in the economy of incarnation and deification. There is no reason to single out one point as if it could be fixed or frozen in time. Christology is no more prominent than pneumatology; nor is the immanent Trinity conceived of as a reality separate from the economy of salvation. Rather, an immanent theology of God is a theology of the economy but from the point of view of its internal logic or its eternal ground.[200]

By redefining the idea of the immanent Trinity so as to tie it to the economy of salvation, LaCugna proposes a trinitarian theology of God that indeed is "ineluctably a theology of the economy."[201]

Personhood as communion. The LaCugna corollary leads to a theological method that builds from experience, more particularly, from "the experience of being saved by God through Christ in the power of the Holy Spirit."[202] As she remarks in her clarification of the distinction between mystery and doctrine in her essay "Philosophers and Theologians on the Trinity" (1986), "To be sure, doctrines intend to *refer to* holy mystery, or to the experience (collective or individual) of mystery, but no doctrine is itself the mystery. Strictly speaking, then, Christians do not 'believe in' doctrines but freely assent to them (Newman) insofar (and only insofar) as they elucidate and helpfully articulate *experience*."[203] LaCugna is convinced that the salvation experience reveals the mystery of God. Yet the mystery that is thereby revealed is the mystery of "persons in communion," and the communion effected by salvation entails our becoming by grace what God is by nature, namely, "persons in full communion with God and with every creature."[204]

As this statement suggests, driving LaCugna's *oikonomia*-focused trinitarianism is a thoroughgoing relational ontology of personhood, which Ted Peters deems to be "one of the most developed of the contemporary options."[205] In carving this out, LaCugna draws from contemporary currents such as John Macmurray, feminist and liberation theology, and Catholic moral thought. Yet the primary influence is John Zizioulas, through whom she appropriates (albeit not uncritically[206]) the Cappadocians. In her essay in *Freeing Theology*, LaCugna lauds the Greek patristic thinkers for what she sees as their greatest contribution, the elevation of person rather than substance as the primary ontological category:

> the radical move of the Cappadocians was to assert that divinity or Godhood originates with personhood (someone toward another), not with substance (something in and of itself). Love for and relationship with another is primary over autonomy, ecstasis over stasis, fecundity over self-sufficiency. Thus, personhood, being-in-relation-to-another, was secured as the ultimate originating principle of all reality.[207]

Although her approach differs somewhat from that of Zizioulas in that she moves from humans as persons to the divine persons, the end result is similar. Reminiscent of Zizioulas's language of *ekstasis* and *hypostasis*, LaCugna asserts that to be person means both to be open beyond oneself and to embody the totality of one's nature. Applying this principle to humans and the trinitarian persons, she declares, "each human person uniquely exemplifies what it means to be human just as each divine person uniquely exemplifies what it is to be divine."[208] To be a person, then, means to be "from and for another." Although LaCugna is willing to link the concept to both human and divine persons in this manner, she insists that the *oikonomia* remain the touchstone for the understanding of personhood set forth in any trinitarian theology. Hence, she declares, "While theology stands to learn a great deal from cultural, anthropological, philosophical, and psychological approaches to personhood, the doctrine of the Trinity ultimately must measure its reflections on personhood by the revelation of divine personhood in the face of Christ and the activity of the Holy Spirit."[209]

LaCugna readily admits that both the Greek and the Latin traditions affirm that communion is the nature of reality. The difference between them lies in how they apply this ontology to the divine reality. She characterizes the West as focusing on the communion of the three persons as an occurrence in the eternal divine reality, whereas the East situated the mystery of the communion of the three within the divine economy. The effect of the Western approach is to predicate God's attributes of the divine essence rather than of the three persons. It is precisely here that LaCugna (like so many other contemporary Western trinitarian theologians) sides with the Greek tradition.

Reframing the concept of God from an elevation of the divine substance to a person-centered ontology allows LaCugna to free the concept of divine incomprehensibility from its referential tie to a divine substance that supposedly lies beyond the limitations of the human mind. Viewed from the person perspective, the declaration "God is incomprehensible" means that as person God is "indefinable, unique, ineffable," just as all persons are. Understanding this reformulated attribute in connection with God's acts in the divine economy provides LaCugna with the key that unlocks the proper understanding of the theological concept of the divine mystery. What lies shrouded in mystery is not some purported transcendent reality that has not been revealed to humankind, as Western theologians have typically intimated. Rather, what is truly incomprehensible is the "unfathomable mystery of a God who comes to us through Christ in the Spirit."[210]

LaCugna likewise draws from the person-focused ontology to reconceptualize the nature of the divine monarchy. In her estimation, the Greek patristic trinitarianism with its focus on monarchy as the property of a person rather than of the divine substance opened the way to view it as communicable to, and shared by, more than one person. In this manner, the Greek thinkers came to see that God's *arche* is not a *mone arche* but a *triadike arche* (a threefold rule).[211] For LaCugna, this change carries far-reaching social implications. Reminiscent of the conclusions Moltmann and Boff derived from their understanding of the perichoretic model of the Trinity, LaCugna claims that the patristic insight regarding the shared monarchy of the trinitarian persons promotes mutuality and undermines every kind of hierarchy among humans. In her estimation, the vision of a nonhierarchical human society implied by the revival of a Cappadocian-inspired approach to the Trinity places it "on the same trajectory as the feminist concern for the equality of women and men."[212]

Above all, however, when added to the epistemic principle she derived from the pre-Nicene era, LaCugna's retrieval of the relational ontology of person leads back to her contention that the doctrine of the Trinity is not ultimately about the divine life *in se* but about God-for-us. As Mark Medley notes, "Following the Cappadocians, LaCugna argues that relationality and mutuality are at the heart of divine being. To say that person not substance is the cause, origin, and end of God and all that exists, means that the ultimate source of all reality is not a 'by-itself' or 'in-itself' but a 'toward-another.'"[213] Rather than finding its locus within a supposed self-enclosed, eternal intratrinitarian relationality, the divine "toward-another" includes creation to the extent that, to cite LaCugna's emphatic declaration, "*Trinitarian life is also our life.*"[214] This ontology of persons is ultimately what in LaCugna's estimation provides the basis for a theology that is truly practical. It is this relational ontology that leads to a trinitarian theology that "is inherently related to every facet of Christian life."[215]

The Uneasy Victory of Economic Relationality

Few twentieth-century treatises in trinitarian theology have been more loudly applauded by supporters and more roundly criticized by detractors than *God for Us*.

Typical of the accolades of LaCugna's fans is Michael Downey's declaration, "She makes her case persuasively, demonstrating a breath-stopping command of traditional sources as well as a comprehensive grasp of crucial practical issues facing those who seek to live in the Spirit of Christ in church and world today."[216] He then concludes his review of *God for Us* by claiming, "The importance of LaCugna's retrieval of the Trinitarian doctrine . . . simply cannot be overestimated."[217] Ted Peters is likewise uncharacteristically generous in his laudatory pronouncements. After lauding her work as "a spring of refreshing ideas"[218] and calling *God for Us* "a real jewel among the works of current Trinity talk," he waxes eloquent in his rapturous praise: "With lapidary precision, this University of Notre Dame theologian cuts through the roughly hewn doctrinal conversations through the centuries to polish the primary facets."[219] Nor have conservative Protestants absented themselves from the chorus. Writing in the *Journal of the Evangelical Theological Society* Roderick T. Leupp prophesies, "*God for Us* will be widely read, and deserves to be. It is that rare theology book with sophisticated reasoning *and* popular appeal."[220] Even ardent critics lavish high praise on LaCugna's work. Thus Roger Haight declares unequivocally, "*God for Us* is an extraordinary piece of theological scholarship."[221]

Detractors have been equally emphatic in their assessment of LaCugna's work. Paul Molnar, to cite one particularly vocal antagonist, declares unabashedly, "LaCugna's entire trinitarian theology is built upon a foundation of sand."[222]

Some critics have questioned several features of LaCugna's narrative, including what many sense is an oversimplified recounting of the story as a whole. Especially suspect is her claim that the focus in the pre-Nicene era was almost exclusively on the economic Trinity. Ben Leslie, for example, concludes, "While LaCugna cites numerous scholars in support of this contention, it remains a disputed point in the history of dogma." In support, he notes the findings of Leo Scheffczyk, which indicate the presence of a concern for the immanent Trinity among such theologians as Tertullian.[223] David Cunningham expands the point, citing such counter-examples to LaCugna's historical account as the strong affirmations of the inner life of God present in a variety of pre-Nicene sources as well as the attention given to the economy of salvation in Augustine's *De Trinitate*.[224] Duncan Reid, in turn, is not convinced that LaCugna—following Wendebourg—is correct in concluding that the (necessary) distinction between *theologia* and *oikonomia* evident in Gregory of Palamas contributed to the "defeat" of the doctrine of the Trinity.[225]

Detractors have also complained about several of the more explicitly theological dimensions of LaCugna's program, suggesting that it focuses on the personhood of the Father to the exclusion of the personhood of the Word and the Spirit,[226] that it embodies a subtle subordinationism,[227] or even that it harbors an implicit modalism.[228] More significant is the challenge articulated by Ted Peters, who would push LaCugna further in the direction of linking God with temporal history, thereby giving place to the temporality of God (as he believes Pannenberg and Jenson have done).[229] Peters writes, "If the internal relationality of the divine life is as tied to the course of world history as LaCugna seems to believe it is, then one would expect some investigation into the possible temporal dimensions of God's life."[230]

Yet the debate between LaCugna and her critics almost inevitably boils down to the validity of the LaCugna corollary, that is, her contention that *theologia* is *oikonomia* with its attendant rejection not only of the distinction between, but even of the language of, the immanent Trinity and the economic Trinity. Unfortunately, the discussion is sometimes hampered by the tendency of some readers to miss the manner in which LaCugna distinguishes the language of *theologia* and *oikonomia* from that of the immanent Trinity and the economic Trinity. For example, on the basis of his reading of the various essays LaCugna wrote on the topic over the years 1984 to 1995, Ben Leslie concludes, "While the basic shape of her argument remained consistent throughout her writings, there is a line of development in her thought which shifts from guarded caution regarding

the possibility of speaking of God *in se* to specific rejection of an immanent Trinity," a rejection that Leslie finds "fully articulated" in *God for
Us*.[231] Even as careful a reader as Ted Peters is guilty of simply identifying
the term *oikonomia* with the economic Trinity and of equating *theologia*
with "our knowledge of the eternal being of God."[232]

Many of those who understand the subtlety of LaCugna's terminological innovation nevertheless remain concerned that the LaCugna corollary
collapses God into the economy of salvation. This, critics add, risks losing
the divine freedom, reducing God to being merely a function of human
experience, and blurring the distinction between Creator and creature[233]
even to the point of harboring a latent pantheism.[234] The concern that
LaCugna has lost any conception of God beyond the economy of salvation
has been voiced by a wide variety of readers. For example, J. A. DiNoia cites
as a "serious difficulty" his sense that "the Father, Son and Holy Spirit as
the one God independent of their manifestation in the economy disappear
from view."[235] Similarly, Michael Hryniuk concludes his lengthy review of
God for Us by cautioning, "Theological re-conceptions of the doctrine of
the Trinity are obviously necessary, but they ought not be too quick to dis-
card the inner life of the Trinity with the bath water of sterile speculations
that may have historically surrounded it."[236] And Duncan Reid bemoans
what he sees as "the submersion of God's transcendence in God's *oikonomia*," which, he adds, citing Kathryn Tanner, "constitutes a revisionist violation of the 'rule for talk of God as transcendent.'"[237]

In the wake of such assertions, LaCugna's defenders have been quick to
clarify her intention. Elizabeth Groope avers that her point "is not that
theologians should speak only of the 'economic Trinity' and not the
'immanent Trinity' . . . but rather that contemporary trinitarian theology
would be enhanced by an alternative framework that prescinds from the
imprecise language of both."[238] Similarly, Ben Leslie explains, "While
LaCugna sometimes gives the impression that theology would do just fine
without the concept of God *in se*, a careful reading reveals that she never
actually surrenders the concept. What she surrenders is the possibility that
one may speak of God *in se* in abstraction from revelation."[239] Mark Medley is even more decisive in his rebuttal. "All these criticisms miss her
point," he declares confidently. Medley then clarifies the motivation he
sees at work in LaCugna's proposal: "Taking her cue from apophaticism,
LaCugna finds the language of 'in' God problematic because it gives the

impression that God has an inner life as if God were something into which something else could be placed, that we can have direct access to that inner life, and that trinitarian theology is mainly about that inner life of God."[240]

At first glance, LaCugna appears to confirm readings such as Leslie's and Medley's. Here and there she offers hints that she acknowledges the reality and even the knowability of God *in se*. For example, in her lengthy explication of the self-communication of God, she writes, "If God is truly *self*-communicating, then we do know the essence (personal existence) of God: we know God as God truly is, in the mediation of God's self-revelation in Christ and the Spirit." But lest the reader be tempted to conclude that the truly real God lies beyond the economy, she quickly adds, "The immanent Trinity is not transhistorical, transempirical, or transeconomic. Nor is the immanent Trinity a 'more real' God—more real because the mode of discourse used to describe it is ontological. Rather, to speak about God in immanent trinitarian terms is nothing more than to speak about God's life with us in the economy of Christ and the Spirit."[241] No wonder readers come away thinking that LaCugna wants to have it both ways.

Perhaps a clue to the heart of LaCugna's perspective is found in her 1985 essay, "Re-conceiving the Trinity as the Mystery of Salvation." In this extended engagement with Rahner's Rule, she notes that the terms "immanent Trinity" and "economic Trinity" are theological constructs that refer to a set of relations, one being internal to God and the other external. Rahner's Rule, in turn, declares that the one set is the other, and hence that "there is only one type of divine relationality with two distinct forms, one eternal, the other historical."[242] Had LaCugna stopped here, she might have invited the interpretation that she merely intends to tie as closely together what she fears can all too easily be separated by dualistic language such as "immanent Trinity" and "economic Trinity." LaCugna, however, takes the matter a step further. She asserts that not only the copula ("is") in Rahner's Rule but also the very idea of the Trinity itself are to be understood metaphorically. Consequently, she concludes that "the trinitarian model of God-in-relation, while not the equivalent of God's being, is nonetheless the appropriate framework for explicating the Christian's experience of salvation by God through Jesus in the Spirit."[243]

This takes us back to the point at which many of LaCugna's readers exit the train. They fear that in the end her trinitarian theology of God-for-us leaves us without a God who is inherently triune apart from us. Leslie speaks for many when he concludes, "There is a communal God *apart* from our communion with God who desires our communion. In LaCugna's framework, however, such an acknowledgment is extremely difficult to come to if at all."[244] In response to LaCugna's proposal, Joseph Bracken affirms the importance of the distinction between the immanent Trinity and the economic Trinity, which she appears to have left behind. He claims that this distinction is crucial, because it "guarantees that the reality of God will not be absorbed into the reality of human history even when the latter is presented as the progressive self-revelation of the triune God."[245]

In her laudatory remarks regarding LaCugna's theological contribution, Elizabeth Groope notes that in affirming "the inseparability of *oikonomia* (that is, the mystery of salvation) and *theologia* (that is, the mystery of God) as a viable framework for contemporary trinitarian theology," she "offered a constructive alternative to other contemporary approaches, specifically those that use the Trinity as a model for human relationships or those that employ the paradigm of the 'immanent Trinity' and the 'economic Trinity.'"[246] In so doing, LaCugna made a lasting contribution to the renaissance of trinitarian theology. Perhaps even more importantly, her work stands as a vivid indication that despite the ongoing influence of the focus on the divine subject championed by Hegel, Barth, and Rahner, apart from a few notable exceptions,[247] in contemporary trinitarian theology the psychological model has given way to variations on the theme of the divine relationality. And the relationality of the three trinitarian persons is first and foremost found in the *oikonomia*.

The Return of the Immanent Trinity

In the years following publication of their works on trinitarian thought, Leonardo Boff, John Zizioulas, and Catherine Mowry LaCugna have become standard names in theological circles. Their influence, coming on the heels of the work of such other luminaries as Wolfhart Pannenberg, Jürgen Moltmann, and Robert Jenson, solidified in the minds of most trinitarian theologians the basic appropriateness of seeing in the relationality of the three divine persons the key to understanding the triune dynamic.

Yet the triumph of relationality has by no means been complete. A few theologians have broken ranks with the proponents of the reigning consensus. Instead of following the trend toward relationality, they have launched a search for a more appropriate perspective from which to understand the connection between the diversity and unity of God. David Cunningham offers an especially promising perspective. In his estimation, what is to be emphasized "about the Three is not that they are *related* to one another . . . but that they *participate* in one another to such a degree that any attempt to understand them as independent existences is undermined."[1] A related development is the echo that LaCugna's reticence to continue approaching trinitarian theology on the basis of the categories inherent in Rahner's Rule has sounded in the work of others. Some thinkers not only have taken seriously her call for a "moratorium" on the language of the immanent Trinity and the economic Trinity but have traveled even farther down the road she charted. Thus, in a manner reminiscent of LaCugna, Philip Clayton eschews the language of the immanent Trinity. He is convinced that "success in specifying the transcendent divine nature is not best guaranteed by an immanent trinity of Father,

Son, and Holy Spirit, understood as the mirror image of the economic trinity, although now extrapolated into God's essence apart from any interaction with the world."[2] Clayton goes so far as to state categorically "there is no immanent trinity. The extrapolation from *deus pro nobis* to *deus in esse*, God *an sich*, is always arbitrary. Beyond God's actions in history, there is only the *potential structure* . . . the sort of structure accessible to pure reason."[3]

The loudest murmurings, however, have tended to move in a quite different direction. The waning years of the twentieth-century witnessed the emergence of a number of voices who were not yet ready to let go of all talk of God *ad intra*. Nor were they willing to concentrate solely on the relationality of the three trinitarian persons, at least not in a manner that entailed the elimination of any attempt to speak about the divine essence. Moreover, rather than believing that the day of the immanent Trinity had come to an end, these theologians sparked a renewed sense of the theological (and ethical) importance of explicating the concept of God *in se*. John G. F. Wilks voiced an aspect of this sentiment when he declared tersely, "The question of God's internal nature is not a puzzle needing to be solved but rather a doctrine in need of re-application to every culture and age of Christianity."[4]

The immanent Trinity reemerged in manifold ways and in the work of a variety of thinkers, who have not necessarily been sympathetic to one another's intentions. Despite the diverse and at times disparate character of the proposals that they offered, these theologians have provided pathways to speak about God *ad intra* without losing completely the focus on the divine relationality that had become such a widely held axiom of trinitarian theology.

The Trinity as Sophia:
Elizabeth Johnson

One year after the appearance of LaCugna's *God for Us*, another Roman Catholic theologian, Elizabeth A. Johnson, published an equally creative and challenging treatise in trinitarian theology bearing the provocative title *She Who Is: The Mystery of God in Feminist Theological Discourse*.[5] As the subtitle of her award-winning and widely acclaimed book suggests, Johnson's foremost passion is not trinitarian theology per se. Rather, she views herself primarily as a feminist theologian engaging—as her writings reveal—a variety of fronts. Hence, Johnson has attempted to breathe new life into classical doctrines, such as Christology,[6] pneumatology,[7] and even Mariology,[8] and she has tackled urgent contemporary concerns, including ecology[9] and ecclesiological renewal.[10] Johnson does so, however, always with a pastoral intent, believing that "nothing inspires a life of vital, active faith so powerfully as an occasional dose of good thinking about the faith, which we call theology," to cite the words from the preface to her 1990 publication, *Consider Jesus*.[11]

Johnson's commitment to the blending of theological reflection and the life of the church leads her inevitably to the doctrine of the Trinity. As she declares in the opening paragraphs of *She Who Is*, in the process of speaking to and about "the mystery that surrounds human lives and the universe itself," the designation "God" (which for Christians is the Trinity) "functions as the primary symbol of the whole religious system," and therefore it is "the ultimate point of reference for understanding experience, life and the world."[12] The literary gift that emerged from Johnson's engagement with the doctrine of the Trinity has been widely hailed as a significant, provocative, and potentially far-reaching contribution to the renaissance of trinitarian theology. Mary McClintock Fulkerson speaks for many when she observes that the volume marks "a constructive and quite successful first, namely, a feminist account of the trinitarian God of Christian faith."[13] In the process of setting forth this theological "first," Johnson retains the reigning focus on the divine relationality while attempting not to lose sight of the immanent Trinity.

Equivalent Imaging[14] of the Triune God

The title *She Who Is* puts the reader on notice that the book's point of departure is the story of Moses' encounter with God at the burning bush (Exod. 3:1-15) with its attendant question regarding the manner in which God is to be named. Insofar as it comprises Johnson's response to this crucial theological question,[15] *She Who Is* may be characterized as an exercise in the task of what its author, following Mary Daly and motivated by a sense of epistemological humility, prefers to describe as a "naming toward God."[16]

What's in a name? Naming as a theological problem. In Johnson's estimation, "naming" is a crucial endeavor. The reason is—simply stated—because words matter, and speech about God matters most. Such naming shapes both the speaking community and the believing individual. It forms the identity of the community and directs its praxis. It likewise provides the foundation for and gives direction to the believer's principles, values, relationships, and choices. In short, "the symbol of God functions," to cite the terse declaration that Johnson utters repeatedly in *She Who Is*.[17] Patricia Fox explains the significance of the repetitive presence of the assertion in the opening pages of the volume: "She uses this sentence like a flashing red light to alert the reader to the fact that this is a truth that would be dangerous to ignore."[18]

The importance of naming is not restricted to its molding influence. Johnson is convinced that at stake in this process is the very truth about God, which she believes is inseparable from both the human situation and the mission of the faith community.[19] Her interest, therefore, is epistemological. Nevertheless, the intended *telos* of her work is not simply epistemological, but concerns the epistemological insofar as it is related to the ethical. As a result, she articulates a far-reaching goal for her theological ruminations. Motivated by the belief that "right speech about God is inseparable from solicitude for all creatures, and in particular for human beings in the rightness of their personal, interpersonal, social and ecological relations,"[20] her intent is "to speak a good word about the mystery of God recognizable within the contours of Christian faith that will serve the emancipatory praxis of women and men, to the benefit of all creation, both human beings and the earth."[21] *She Who Is*, therefore, places its author in the growing company of thinkers who recognize the grave implications that speech about God carries not only for human theological knowledge but also for social relations and even for the future of life on earth.

Given her conviction that language and praxis are closely linked, it comes as no surprise that Johnson sees her work of "naming toward God" as a bridge-building project. Specifically, she desires to "braid a footbridge between the ledges of classical and feminist Christian wisdom."[22] She seeks to bring together the traditional manner of speaking about God and a commitment to feminist ideals. She does so, however, from a perspective that views the latter as a given and sees the former as up for grabs. Johnson explains: "*She Who Is* was written to explore the question of whether the Christian community can be converted to the equal and full humanity of women and still confess the richness of our core beliefs, especially about God."[23]

Johnson's intent is to provide a way for feminists to retain allegiance to the Christian heritage. She hopes that by "throwing a hermeneutical span from side to side," she might "enable some to cross over to the paradigm of women's coequal humanity without leaving behind all the riches of the tradition that has been their intellectual and spiritual home."[24] She is convinced that the way to bridge these two realms is by proposing a semantic field for speaking about God that, by emphasizing female images of the divine, can provide an alternative to the male-oriented, patriarchal language that dominated theological discourse throughout much of the history of the church.[25] Although her ultimate agenda is not the reformation of the doctrine of the Trinity per se, Johnson is convinced that the question regarding the way of speaking about the mystery of God as triune must be addressed, because this particular dimension of theological discourse has been an especially powerful tool in the patriarchal subordination of women. Viewed from this perspective, Johnson's book is an exercise in feminist theology, which she defines as "a reflection on God and all things in the light of God that stands consciously in the company of all the world's women, explicitly prizing their genuine humanity while uncovering and criticizing its persistent violation in sexism, itself an omnipresent paradigm of unjust relationships."[26] Yet even more significant for the story of the renaissance of trinitarian theology, *She Who Is* may be characterized as a treatise in "trinitarian feminism," to cite Harold Wells's description.[27]

The bridge between classical theology and feminist insight that Johnson seeks to build in *She Who Is* is constructed in four major sections. The first part provides the context and background for Johnson's program. Part 2 sets out the resources for her constructive proposal, which she finds in women's experiences, scripture, and classical theology. The heart of the book comes in the third part, in which she engages in the actual task of reimaging or renaming the triune God of the classical tradition in female terms, a process that includes testing "the capacity of female images to bear and disclose what Christian truth testifies to as the blessed action of God in the world," while calling "upon the language of classical theology to give these images density."[28] This is followed in part 4 by Johnson's reenvisioning of the relationship between God and creation in the light of her reimaged representation of God, that is, on the basis of her renaming God "She Who Is."

Yet the question remains: Why should trinitarian theology include female as well as male images? The obvious answer, and the one that forms the strongest motivation for Johnson's work, has already been mentioned. The program of renaming God is necessitated by the desire to promote the full humanity of women, a theological program that in her estimation carries far-reaching implications. At stake in the feminist agenda is not only "the freeing of both women and men from debilitating reality models and social roles," but also "the birthing of new forms of saving relationship to all of creation, and indeed the very viability of the Christian tradition for present and coming generations."[29] Viewed from this perspective, Johnson's proposal is a contextual theology born in response to the need of the contemporary world. She explains: "At this point in the living tradition I believe that we need a strong dose of explicitly female imagery to break the unconscious sway that male trinitarian imagery holds over the imaginations of even the most sophisticated thinkers."[30]

The proposal articulated in *She Who Is* arises out of a second and more explicitly theological motivation as well. Johnson is convinced that limiting speech about God to any one image risks leading the worshiping community to violate the First Commandment by confusing the image with the true God, who cannot be captured by any mere human construct. In her essay "The Incomprehensibility of God and the Image of God Male and Female," published in 1984, Johnson explains the charge of idolatry that feminist theologians have voiced: "Normative conceptualization of God in analogy with male reality alone is the equivalent of the graven image, a finite representation being taken for and worshiped as the whole. What is violated is both the creature's limitation and the unknowable transcendence of the true God."[31] She provides a related angle in *She Who Is*:

> any representation of the divine used in such a way that its symbolic and evocative character is lost from view partakes of the nature of an idol. Whenever one image or concept of God expands to the horizon thus shutting out others, and whenever this exclusive symbol becomes literalized so that the distance between it and divine reality is collapsed, there an idol comes into being. Then the comprehensible image, rather than disclosing mystery, is mistaken for the reality.[32]

In short, as Cynthia Rigby notes regarding Johnson's point, "to envision God as only male or only female is to idolize an image rather than to worship the mysterious, hidden God who lies behind that image."[33]

Johnson finds progress on both fronts to be stymied by the presence in the church of what she calls a "scotosis," a "hardening of the mind against unwanted wisdom."[34] By offering a new naming toward God that uses a thoroughly female image, *She Who Is* embodies her contribution to the process of overcoming this malaise.

Who does the naming? From women's experience to the divine Sophia. Johnson notes that recent years have netted two unsuccessful suggestions as to how God might be named in a more inclusive manner: by attributing feminine traits to God and by attempting to discover feminine dimensions in God. In her judgment, the current situation calls for a more radical strategy, namely, a program of "equivalent imaging" of God in both male and female symbols. Johnson admits that her work is only a partial contribution to this larger project. In fact, rather than presenting a complete picture of God (an enterprise that she would reject as impossible), her goal is much more modest. It is limited to that of providing a naming toward God that is cast in a female image appropriate to women's lived experience.

In keeping with her desire to connect theology with women's experience, Johnson launches her chasm-bridging proposal from the strong experiential basis that she sees as "an identifying mark of virtually all contemporary theology."[35] Elaine Farmer explains: "A fundamental basis of her work is that the naming of God ultimately cannot be separated from experience of, and relationship with, God. Our efforts to talk about the being of God arise from our experience of God's activity in history and in our own lives."[36] More specifically, as a "Christian feminist liberation theology" that reflects on "religious mystery from a stance which makes an a priori option for the human flourishing of women,"[37] her trinitarian theology has as its starting point "the pattern of women's religious experience in the structural margins."[38] Johnson likens this religious experience to conversion, in that women's awakening to their worth as human beings entails a new experience of God and even a new event in human religious history.[39] The result is the realization that because women share in the *imago dei* and therefore are "theomorphic," speech about God can be cast in female symbols. As Johnson states the point, "If women are created in the image of God, without qualification, then their human reality offers suitable, even excellent metaphor for speaking about divine mystery, who remains always ever greater."[40] Cognizant of this narrower experiential basis from which Johnson proceeds, Charles Marsh finds at work in *She Who Is* a three-step theological movement indicative of all experientially grounded theological proposals:

> The three steps of Johnson's argument, when formally construed, are constitutive of virtually all experiential theologies. First, she describes and justifies the experiential matrix, namely women's emancipation from patriarchy and their flourishing in creative and novel ways. Second, she criticizes the so-called traditional conception of the triune God from this feminist perspective. Third, she refigures the traditional conception through "the lens of women's flourishing."[41]

Her attempt to offer a theological interpretation of women's conversion experience leads Johnson, as a Christian theologian, to the Bible, viewed as "the literary precipitate of the founding religious experiences of the Jewish and Christian communities and a continuing resource for their life."[42] She finds in the pages of scripture three symbols that stand out as especially promising for the task of providing a naming toward God that moves from women's experience: spirit, wisdom, and mother. These themes are "enmeshed in an androcentric framework," however, and therefore they must be purified by "passing through the fire of critical feminist principles."[43] Entailed in this process is a contextualization that Harold Wells finds "comparable to what is commonly called 'the hermeneutical circle' in liberation theologies, i.e., contemporary knowledge and understanding was placed in conversation with the authoritative source, which remained essentially dominant, but which was in turn interpreted and critiqued by practical worldly wisdom and experience." Her efforts at contextualization, Wells adds, link Johnson to the ancient wisdom authors themselves.[44]

Johnson notes that repeatedly the biblical writers speak of the "spirit"—whom she describes as "the creative and freeing power of God let loose in the world"[45]—in ways that are analogous to women's historical reality. Yet "spirit" must give way to an even more important image: wisdom. Johnson concludes that Wisdom is not only "the most developed personification of God's presence and activity in the Hebrew Scriptures,"[46] it is also the one that is most consistently female in imagery. In her essay "The Incomprehensibility of God and the Image of God Male and Female," she offers a helpful summary of the connection between this symbol and the God of Israel: "Wisdom texts must be read within their historical religious context, which was (and remains) monotheism. Unless one thinks the Jewish community broke with its faith in one God when writing and receiving the wisdom literature, *Sophia's* functional equivalence with Yahweh requires that she be interpreted as a powerful female symbol of this one God."[47] The connection of Wisdom to Israel's God, together with its importance as a New Testament and early Christian christological title, mean that Sophia offers the most explicit manner of speaking about the divine mystery "in female symbol."[48] For this reason, the personification of God in the figure of Sophia emerges as the integrating motif within the trio of images standing at the heart of Johnson's proposal and the linguistic key for her naming toward God that can provide a female counterpoint to the dominant male image of Father-Son.

Johnson's choice of Wisdom as her central theological category is nothing short of masterful. The wealth of sources at her disposal means that she is able to argue with ease that Wisdom is prominent in the trajectory from the biblical texts to patristic trinitarian theology and that the concept also lies at the heart of contemporary feminist Christian spirituality.[49] As a consequence, Wisdom readily serves Johnson's goal of bridging the two seemingly disparate realms, and it thereby emerges as the winning candidate for her program of thoroughly reimaging God as triune in a manner in keeping with women's reality.

In addition to the female personifications of Israel's God that she finds in the biblical traditions, Johnson mines two important aspects of the Christian theological tradition: the consistent emphasis on the divine incomprehensibility and the methodological principle of analogy. She offers a succinct description of the former: "In essence, God's unlikeness to the corporal and spiritual finite world is total. Hence human beings simply cannot understand God. No human concept, word, or image, all of which originate in experience of created reality, can circumscribe divine reality, nor can any human construct express with any measure of adequacy the mystery of God who is ineffable."[50] According to Johnson, the divine incomprehensibility demands that the theologian follow the pathway of analogy in speaking about God.[51] This methodological approach, which she consciously borrows from Aquinas and Rahner, draws from the assumption that insofar as God is the cause of the world, creatures in some way resemble the Creator. A threefold epistemological movement follows from this ontological assumption: "Words predicated of God are affirmed, then negated in their creaturely connotations, and finally affirmed of God in a supereminent way transcending all our cognitive capabilities." In this dynamic of relational knowing, "God is darkly surmised, while remaining in essence conceptually inapprehensible."[52]

The divine incomprehensibility leads Johnson to a third methodological principle as well. She argues that the inapprehensible nature of God's essence not only opens the way for but even requires the use of many names in speaking about the divine mystery. In her 1984 essay on the topic she makes the point in the strongest terms possible: "The very incomprehensibility of God demands a proliferation of images and a variety of names, each of which acts as a corrective against the tendency of any one to become reified and literal."[53]

Johnson is convinced that these three resources lodged in the classical theological tradition facilitate an emancipation of speech about God. Not only do they move theology beyond the fixation on one or two "patriarchal symbols," they provide a place to stand that can lead to theological language that is not only sensitive to women's interpreted experience but also liberating for all creatures and even the earth itself.[54] What follows in *She Who Is* entails the constructive outworking of Johnson's appropriation of this classical legacy.

What is God's name? The triune Sophia. In recasting the Christian conception of the triune God, Johnson promises to follow the inductive method endemic to a theology "from below."[55] Moreover, in keeping with the approach pursued by many contributors to the renaissance in trinitarian theology, Johnson looks first at each of the three trinitarian persons and only then engages the unity of the triune God. Mary Rose D'Angelo applauds her explication of the work of the three persons as not only "far-ranging and luminous" but as one in which "insights and new vistas open on every page."[56]

In contrast to most of the contemporary proposals that have emerged in the wake of Barth, Johnson's declared starting point is not the divine self-disclosure in Jesus Christ but the experience of the Spirit as "God's livingness subtly and powerfully abroad in the world."[57] She offers the following characterization of this seemingly universal experience of the

Spirit: "Wherever we encounter the world and ourselves as held by, open to, gifted by, mourning for the absence of, or yearning for something ineffably more than immediately appears, whether that 'more' be mediated by beauty and joy or in contrast to powers that crush, there experience of the Spirit transpires."[58] This methodological shift to the Spirit as the starting point for the explication of trinitarian theology puts Johnson in the company of the various contemporary thinkers who—like she—are concerned to redress the neglect of pneumatology that they find in the Western theological tradition.[59]

According to Johnson's explication, the human experience of "being touched by a love that is not hostile (the 'third' person)" moves us "to inquire after a definitive historical manifestation of this love (the 'second' person)" and then to "point from there toward the mystery of the primordial source of all (the 'first' person)."[60] In this manner, the development of trinitarian theology explicated in *She Who Is*, flowing as it does from the Spirit through Jesus to the first person, reverses the pattern of Father—Son—Spirit that predominates in theological history.

Johnson came to this innovative approach only after attempting to follow the more traditional manner of theological construction. At first, she too sought to begin with the first person of the Trinity, the unoriginate origin of all things, whom she intended to interpret by means of a feminist analysis of motherhood as Mother-Sophia. Long hours of wrestling with her project led her to see the dissonance between the feminist approach, with its starting point in experience, and the older theological method.[61]

Johnson's redescribing of the three trinitarian persons begins with Spirit-Sophia. She presents the Spirit as God vivifying, renewing, liberating, and gracing all creation. More important than the specific manner in which Johnson casts the Spirit in female images is her conclusion that bringing the biblical and traditional theological materials in conversation with feminist insights leads to a presentation of the Spirit as being much more than merely the divine prototype for stereotypical patriarchal ways of viewing the feminine. She believes that her treatment of the Spirit facilitates her in subverting at the outset the patriarchal image of God that has been so detrimental to theology and the human community.

Even more radical than her treatment of the Spirit is Johnson's recasting of Jesus in a female image. In her reenvisioned Christology,[62] Jesus becomes Jesus-Sophia, the incarnation or embodied presence of Sophia within creation to heal, redeem, and liberate. In her 1993 essay "Wisdom Was Made Flesh and Pitched Her Tent among Us," which appeared in a collection that arose out of a symposium on feminist Christology, Johnson provides a concise summary of the biblical and classical basis for her perspective: "As the trajectory of wisdom Christology shows, Jesus was so closely associated with *Sophia* that by the end of the first century he is presented not only as a wisdom teacher, not only as a child and envoy of *Sophia,* but as an earthly appearance of Wisdom in person, the incarnation of *Sophia* herself."[63]

Recasting Jesus in this manner unavoidably leads to the question of the theological meaning of his existence as a male. In tackling this matter, Johnson is careful not to render Jesus' maleness as insignificant, but to critique the theological use to which this aspect of his existence is often put:

> Jesus' maleness is a constitutive element of his identity, part of the perfection and limitation of his historical contingency, and as such is to be respected. It is as intrinsic to his historical person as his familial, ethnic, religious, linguistic and cultural particularity, his Galilean village roots, and so forth. The difficulty arises, rather, from the way Jesus' maleness is construed in official androcentric theology and ecclesial praxis, a way that results in a christological view that effectively diminishes women.[64]

At the same time, Johnson finds herself constrained to press the highly controversial claim[65] that Jesus' maleness is "not theologically determinative of his identity as the Christ."[66] To this end, she draws from the biblical idea that Christ is a "pneumatological reality" who transcends the limitations posed by ethnicity, social status, and gender,[67] to which she adds the patristic emphasis on the inclusive character of Jesus' humanity. These impulses lead to a vision of "one human nature celebrated in an interdependence of multiple differences"[68] that can overcome the gender dualism that Johnson sees as haunting traditional Christology. In her contribution to *Freeing Theology* she summarizes what she sees as the far-reaching, liberating importance of the feminist perspective:

> Theology will have come of age when the particularity that is highlighted is not Jesus' historical sex but the scandal of his option for the poor and marginalized, including women, in the Spirit of his com-

passionate, liberating Sophia-God. That is the scandal of particularity that really matters, aimed as it is toward the creation of a new order of wholeness in justice. Toward that end, feminist theological speech about Jesus the Wisdom of God shifts the focus of reflection off maleness and onto the whole theological significance of what transpires in the Christ event.[69]

When filtered through the wisdom tradition, she finds that Jesus' significance resonates with the values associated with women's experience, and it contributes to the quest for justice for the poor, to the ideal of respectful encounter with other religious traditions, and to care for the earth.[70]

Johnson's reconceptualizing of the three persons in accordance with her central linguistic tool, Sophia, comes to completion in her attempt to recast the "unoriginate origin" as Mother-Sophia, an attempt that arises out of her concern to reclaim the power and vulnerability connected to women's life-giving experience of mothering.[71] Drawing from biblical and traditional materials, she sets forth the maternal compassionate power of God in mothering the universe as well as establishing what she calls the "mercy of justice."[72] The result is a way of speaking about God that overcomes the polarization between the divine immanence and transcendence by highlighting not only God's nearness in mystery but also the divine relationality. Indeed, "relationality" emerges as the key to Johnson's development of the doctrine of the Trinity itself, which follows in *She Who Is*.

Johnson claims that by unfolding the three trinitarian persons under the rubric of Wisdom and thereby setting forth "the vivifying ways of the Spirit, the compassionate, liberating story of Jesus Sophia, and the generative mystery of the Creator Mother,"[73] she has undermined all conceptions of God as an "isolated, static, ruling monarch" or a "self-enclosed absolute," in favor of a vision of God as "self-communicating mystery of relation," as a "relational, dynamic, tripersonal mystery of love."[74] Moreover, she finds transformational power in this symbol of the triune God as the Mystery of Relation, for it is able to evoke a "livingness in God."[75] Yet she cautions that this transformation can occur only when the symbol of the Trinity is freed from the tendency in theological history to take it literally instead of seeing it as a human construct that points indirectly to God's relationality.

Her elevation of the divine relationality places Johnson in the company of the large group of trinitarian theologians who are convinced that insofar as the three persons are constituted by their relationships to one another and are intelligible only as they are connected with one another, relationality—and not aloneness—lies at the heart of the Christian conception of God. Like many trinitarian thinkers, she draws from the language of *perichoresis* and *koinonia* to speak about the divine relationality. Yet in one crucial respect, Johnson stands out from the others. She proposes as the most helpful analogy to the divine relationality the human experience of friendship, a metaphor that she derives from feminist thought. Johnson explains her choice:

> Friendship is the most free, the least possessive, the most mutual of relationships, able to cross social barriers in genuine reciprocal regard. Like all good relations friendship is characterized by mutual trust in the reliability of the other(s), but what makes it unique is that friends are fundamentally side-by-side in common interests, common delights, shared responsibilities. Mature friendship is open to the inclusion of others in the circle, assuming an essential stance of hospitality.[76]

This experience leads to an image of Sophia-God as a trinity of friendship embracing the world with "befriending power," befriending the world, that is, "as unreachable Abyss, as self-expressive Word that joins history in the flesh, as overflowing Spirit that seeks out the darkest, deadest places to quicken them to new life."[77] Or, drawing from a geometric model, Johnson likens the triune God to a triple helix. In her estimation, this model "connotes the unfathomable richness of holy triune mystery, inwardly related as a unity of equal movements, each of whom is distinct and all of whom together are one source of life, new just order, and quickening surprise in an infinite mix." Moreover, the divine persons include human partners in the never-ending series of moves that mark the "twirling around" of the three-member helix they comprise.[78]

Johnson is convinced that theological models such as these portray the kind of mutual relationality, radical equality, and communal unity-in-diversity inherent in the symbol of Sophia-God. This radical vision of God, she adds, displaces patriarchal theological images. By presenting God as a "self-communicating mystery of relation, an unimaginable, open communion in herself that opens out freely to include even what is not herself . . . as a partner in the divine dance of life,"[79] one comes to view God and the world as related in a free, reciprocal manner. According to this paradigm, which Johnson (following others, such as Moltmann) denotes by the term *panentheism,*[80] God is seen as being in the world and the world in God, while each remains radically distinct from the other. Furthermore, Johnson finds that the panentheistic paradigm resonates well with the maternal and friendship metaphors that she gleans from women's experience. This connection, in turn, lends a final confirmation to the naming of God as "She Who Is."

Sophia's Theologian

Johnson's recasting of trinitarian theology in accordance with the Wisdom motif has gained her the appellation "Sophia's theologian."[81] Moreover, it has engendered applause from a wide variety of readers. Hence, in her review of *She Who Is,* Mary Hines extols what she sees as "Johnson's contribution to the effort to resymbolize and reimagine God in a post-modern world" as "a tour de force"[82] and "a remarkable achievement" that breaks open "the possibilities for language about God."[83] Mary Aquin O'Neill echoes this assessment. She writes, "It would be difficult to overestimate what Elizabeth Johnson has accomplished."[84] Mary C. Boys, in turn, finds in Johnson "a theologian with an ear for poetry."[85] So widespread and positive was the initial acceptance of *She Who Is* that barely a year after its appearance Susan Roll could begin her review by noting, "By now praise and further acclaim is almost superfluous for Johnson's thorough, well-grounded and profoundly visionary book which already . . . has won major awards and been well received by bishops, academic theologians and theologically articulate lay people alike."[86]

Yet the response to Johnson's work has not been uniformly laudatory. A surprising point of contention, given the academic nature of the book, is writing style. In her highly negative review of *She Who Is,* Janice Daurio complains that "the author is not articulate. The style is convoluted."[87] The indictment has even been voiced by those who embrace Johnson's proposal. For example, Jane Williams, who is generous in her praise of the volume, nevertheless declares, "Unfortunately, the enterprise is slightly marred by the author's extraordinarily turgid style. She never uses one word where she can say it in ten, and always prefers polysyllables to monosyllables."[88] Other reviewers, however, cite writing style as one of the outstanding aspects of the book. For example, Elaine Farmer declares, "Johnson's book is elegantly written in a refreshingly readable style. Her subject is profound and her scholarship prodigious but she nevertheless pursues her argument with a lightness that makes her work extremely accessible."[89] Mary Aquin O'Neill agrees: "Throughout, the author's prose is marked by clarity, grace and respectful attention to the audience, signified by explanation of technical terms and rigorous avoidance of jargon."[90] And Mary McClintock Fulkerson writes, "Johnson's facility with language is refreshing, and I find myself moved again and again by unsurprising and surprising images."[91]

More theologically substantial is the suggestion voiced by some critics that Johnson's proposal is not as pneumatologically oriented as it purports to be. These readers find lurking beneath the surface an implicit Christology that comprises a revelatory basis from which Johnson unknowingly draws in the process of determining if an encounter is truly an experience of the Spirit. Hence, Charles Marsh senses that Johnson's determination of the Spirit's presence "rests on a christological presupposition," so that for her "only on the basis of the God revealed in Jesus Christ does our experience of the divine have theological significance of depth."[92]

The feminist strand evident in Johnson's work has also raised the eyebrows of critics. John Carmody, who is otherwise quite sympathetic to her proposal, wonders if her "analysis of women's interpreted experience" is "sufficiently critical."[93] Mary McClintock Fulkerson remains unconvinced that Johnson has accomplished the goal that she set before herself. She asks rhetorically, "By posing 'She Who Is' do we really move beyond gender binaries? Or do we simply move beyond the obvious subordination of the feminine to the masculine, thereby creating two competing (binary) equals?"[94] Paul Molnar fears that Johnson has revised the symbol "God" for ideological reasons, but with disastrous results: "Indeed her basic argument is that '[t]he symbol God functions' and that we must make it function today so as not to exclude women. The suggestion clearly is that it is we who invest this symbol with meaning and it is we who thus must change the symbol in order to obtain the desired social result."[95] The upshot of this approach, he adds, is to "exchange the revelation of God for the experience of women and thus collapse theology into anthropology."[96] Mary Aquin O'Neill goes so far as to wonder if Johnson's feminist impulse has led her in the end to forsake the Christian God:

> By developing an image of God that has been neglected, and doing so with such poetic power, Johnson runs the risk of conjuring up

another God. By the end of the book Sophia seems to this reader to be not the female personification of the God known from Christian belief, but another God—one who sometimes complements, sometimes corrects, sometimes bests the traditional male God.[97]

Finally, Marsh determines that Johnson's feminist method is merely a variation of the discredited liberal program of constructing theology on the basis of human experience:

> In the end, her primary commitment to experience compromises her ability to explicate the Trinity as a mystery that patterns human social and moral experience. The very reverse is implied: human social and moral experience, that is, women's emancipation from patriarchy and their flourishing in full humanity, patterns our thinking about the Trinity. There is no inner logic or grammar in the triune mystery; or, stated differently, whatever inner logic or grammar we attribute to the Trinity is given through extrinsic sources, whether these be derived from liberation vocabularies, social ontologies or aesthetic categories. In this manner, Johnson's feminist revision is methodologically no less indebted to modern liberal theology than if she privileged morality, affectivity, thought, or some other mode of experience. While the content of her revision may be feminist, the form has its systematic origins in Hegel and Schleiermacher.[98]

As important as considerations such as these are, the most pertinent question that must be posed regarding Johnson's trinitarian theology lies elsewhere. In his engagement with her work, Carmody voices a query that is routinely asked of all relational theological proposals that begin "from below": "How do we best sustain, in relation to this divine relationality, the proper divine autonomy regarding the world?" Then in musing about her conclusion that "God . . . is never not related to the world,"[99] Carmody surmises,

> I suspect that, in addition to biblical warrants for the divine autonomy and transcendence . . . there are warrants in human experience for a desire that God be other not just generically but specifically in the mode of free of the world, complete unto the divine self, fully enjoying the perfection unique to God as God, a perfection we praise when we assert with the tradition that God plus the world is no addition to perfection.[100]

When placed in the context of the issues raised by other critics, Carmody's musings lead to what might at first glance seem to be a surprising question: Has Sophia's theologian lost the immanent Trinity?

This question is surprising in that Johnson's contribution to the renaissance of trinitarian theology lies above all in the attempt to foster a return of the immanent Trinity endemic to her recasting of the triune God according to the female image of Sophia. As several observers point out, Johnson does not march in lockstep with those who claim that proceeding "from below" leads inevitably to the conclusion that talk about the inner being of God is inappropriate or impossible.[101] On the contrary, she takes pains to point out that speaking about the immanent triune God remains possible, even though language for God is always analogical, symbolic, and inadequate. Drawing out the implications of Rahner's Rule, Johnson states in no uncertain terms that our experience of God as triune leads to talk about God *ad intra:* "The concrete ways that God is given to us in history point to three interrelated ways of existing within God's own being. God really corresponds to the way we have encountered divine mystery in time."[102]

Not only is such discourse possible and legitimate, in Johnson's estimation it is crucial. She is convinced that much would be lost if theologians ceased all talk of the immanent triune God. Johnson explains that trinitarian language

> is a pointer to holy mystery in trust that God really is the compassionate, liberating God encountered through Jesus in the Spirit. It is language which affirms that what is experienced in Christian faith really is of God; that what we are involved with is nothing other than saving divine mystery. At rock bottom it is the language of hope. No one has ever seen God, but thanks to the experience unleashed through Jesus in the Spirit we hope . . . that it is the livingness of *God* who is with us in the suffering of history, and so we affirm that God's relation to the world is grounded in God's own being capable of such relation.[103]

In short, speech about the inner divine dynamic is important because, as Mary Hines points out, it "is rooted in the firm hope that we can trust our experience of God acting in history."[104]

Despite Johnson's seemingly forthright desire to restore the immanent Trinity to theology, the close link that she—like LaCugna—forges between theological language and Christian (or women's) experience as "the generating matrix for language about God as triune" may in the end hinder her from attaining this lofty goal. In keeping with her conclusion that "the Trinity is a legitimate but secondary concept that synthesizes the concrete experience of salvation in a 'short formula,'"[105] Johnson declares that this symbol is "not a blueprint for the inner workings of the godhead." She then explains: "In no sense is it a literal description of God's being *in se*. As the outcome of theological reflection on the Christian experience of relationship to God, it is a symbol that indirectly points to God's relationality. . . . The Trinity is itself an analogy referring to divine livingness. Our speech about God as three and persons is a human construction that means to say that God is *like* a Trinity."[106] Statements such as this provide some credence to appraisals like that of Paul Molnar, who writes concerning Johnson's perspective, "What she says is that we do not know God in his inner essence as Father, Son and Holy Spirit. Rather, God is holy mystery, which can go by many other names."[107]

The apparent fuzziness that critics such as Molnar have perceived in Johnson's thinking has contributed to the mixed response that her proposal has engendered.[108] No wonder that Elaine Farmer concluded her review of Johnson's award-winning treatise with a prophecy: "The exercise of reading this book will frustrate many; others it will bring to God."[109] Although her book has been a frustration to some, Johnson's own desire is clearly to bring readers closer to the triune God.

Transcendental Trinitarianism: Hans Urs von Balthasar

Edward T. Oakes begins his study of Balthasar's[110] theology by noting, "When set against the wider background of twentieth-century theology, the figure of Hans Urs von Balthasar comes across as rather isolated, even lonely."[111] Balthasar's theological "loneliness" is evident in the only direct reference to him found in David Tracy's widely read sketch of the theological landscape written at the three-quarter point of the twentieth century, *Blessed Rage for Order* (1975). Tracy placed Balthasar among a small group of thinkers who were arguing for a reexamination of the role of the imagination in the study of religious texts "with a conviction and eloquence that seems matched only by the stunningly silent response of many of their fellow theologians."[112]

The theological isolation that dogged Balthasar throughout his life was due in part to the fact that he stood outside the academic guild. He pursued doctoral studies in German language and culture rather than theology, and he never held a university professorship. His estrangement may have been exacerbated by his claim, whether completely factual[113] or somewhat overdrawn,[114] that his theological work was closely linked to the mystical visions of Adrienne von Speyr, to whom he served as spiritual advisor. In any case, the "silent response" afforded to Balthasar throughout most of his life forms a striking contrast to the flurry of interest in his work that greeted the dawn of the new millennium. So significant has this shift been that in 2002, Kevin Mongrain could announce somewhat modestly that "a new, critical phase of von Balthasar studies is underway."[115]

Balthasar was one of the most prolific theologians of the twentieth century. The size of his scholarly output, which numbers eighty-five books and over five hundred essays,[116] led Peter Henrici to quip that he "wrote more books than a normal person can be expected to read in his lifetime."[117] The breadth of the Balthasar corpus evoked from Aidan Nichols the exclamation: "Any one area of his publications would constitute a decent life's work for a lesser [person]."[118] Drawing these two aspects together, Donald Keefe compared reading Balthasar to "wandering in a giant's castle."[119]

Despite the voluminous character of the Balthasar literary corpus, he did not understand his main vocation to be that of composing theological treatises. In reflecting on his life at the age of seventy and in keeping with a point he had made ten years earlier, he asserted, "the activity of being a writer remains and will always remain, in the working-out of my life, a secondary function, something *faute de mieux*."[120] The center of his life's work, to which he subordinated even his activities as a writer, was—in his words—"the task of renewing the Church through the formation of new communities that unite the radical Christian life of conformity to the evangelical counsels of Jesus with existence in the midst of the world, whether by practicing secular professions or through the ministerial priesthood to give new life to living communities."[121] Moreover, he described the radical Christian life that in his estimation formed "the true, undiminished program for the Church" as "the greatest possible radiance in the world by virtue of the closest possible following of Christ,"[122] a perspective that formed a central motif of his thought. To advance this cause, he sought to follow an approach that could bring theology and spirituality together. Jakob Laubach provides an illuminating report regarding this intention:

> Hans Urs von Balthasar, as he himself once put it, wants "a kneeling, not a sitting theology." Basically theology is "adoration and sanctity, or love of God and neighbor," even if "between these two poles of Christian dealings with the Word of God—poles which at once call for each other, fuse into one another—something is inserted that can be called a theoretical concern with the Word."[123]

Balthasar may have envisioned a kneeling theology. Yet, as the statement quoted above indicates, this vision did not preclude him from producing a theology of the Word. On the contrary, he was deeply concerned with the *deus dixit*, the divine Word that must judge all human speech about God, an orientation toward theology that he owed above all to Karl Barth.[124] Balthasar's desire to produce a robust, biblical theology of the Word resulted in the articulation of a proposal that was thoroughly trinitarian, even though he likely neither intended nor anticipated that he would be offering a unique contribution to the renaissance of trinitarian theology in the twentieth century.

The Trinity and the Transcendentals

In 1961, Balthasar began a sustained literary output that upon its completion twenty-six years later had developed into an oeuvre rivaling Barth's *Church Dogmatics* in length. The fruit of his labors was a trilogy consisting of a theological aesthetics, *The Glory of the Lord: A Theological Aesthetics*, which in the English translation stretches to seven volumes;[125] a five-volume theological dramatics, *Theo-Drama: Theological Dramatic Theory*;[126] and a theological logic, *Theo-Logic: Theological Logical Theory*, published in three installments.[127]

Balthasar devotes none of these fifteen volumes to the task of explicating the doctrine of the Trinity per se, even though he describes the concluding installment of his *Theo-Drama* as "trinitarian."[128] This is not surprising, given Balthasar's suspicion that the quest for a systematic synthesis is inconsistent with the transcendent, even paradoxical,[129] character of divine revelation,[130] and consequently his preference for a dialectical approach to theology.[131] Although his remarks about the divine triunity are scattered throughout the trilogy, the Trinity does not appear as an appendage to, but rather emerges as an integral dimension of, his entire proposal. As Werner Löser notes, his "whole theological work has trinitarian contours."[132] For this reason, Balthasar's contribution to trinitarian theology can only be understood within the context of the purposes that lie behind the composition of his multivolume trilogy.

The context: the theological trilogy. In the foreword to the inaugural volume of the theological aesthetics, Balthasar indicates that he envisioned such a project already at its inception, and this because he was convinced that a thoroughgoing theological articulation requires all three dimensions. In a concise statement that encapsulates the salient features of his entire project, Balthasar declares,

> In order to maintain a right balance, a 'theological aesthetics' should be followed by a 'theological dramatics' and a 'theological logic.' While the first of these has as its object primarily the perception of the divine self-manifestation, the 'dramatics' would have as primary object the content of this perception—which is God's dealings with man—and the 'logic' would define as its object the divine (or more exactly: the human-divine, and therefore already theological!) *manner of expressing* God's activity. Only then would the *pulchrum* appear in its rightful place within the total ordered structure, namely as the manner in which God's goodness *(bonum)* gives itself and is expressed by God and understood by man as the truth *(verum)*.[133]

Of the three works, commentators tend to laud *The Glory of the Lord*, which Karl Rahner considered to be the only theological aesthetics ever written,[134] as comprising Balthasar's most significant theological contribution. Louis Roberts claims that "aesthetics focuses all of Balthasar's writing."[135] Bede McGregor and Thomas Norris, in turn, go so far as to assert, "If Balthasar is to be seen as a genuinely great theologian—and that is a rare species—it will be in virtue of his appropriation of the treasures of the tradition and his recasting of them under the encompassing cipher—category of glory—beauty."[136] This widely followed tendency to elevate the theological aesthetics is not groundless. Its proponents can cite numerous statements from Balthasar himself that seem to support such a claim. Indeed, he repeatedly places the divine glory on center stage. For example, in this 1965 retrospective essay, he declares, "For the glory of God the world was created; through it and for its sake the world is also redeemed."[137] Similarly, in the preface to the fourth volume of the *Theo-*

Drama, he indicates the primacy of glory in his description of the "unity of 'glory' and the 'dramatic'": "God's glory, as it appears in the world—supremely in Christ—is not something static that could be observed by a neutral investigator. It manifests itself only through the personal involvement whereby God himself comes forth to do battle and is both victor and vanquished."[138]

Despite the primacy of "glory" in his theology, the foreword to *The Glory of the Lord* indicates that Balthasar did not intend that the theological aesthetics be viewed as his masterpiece. Rather, it forms the prelude to the whole and as such functions as a type of fundamental theology or apologetics. He explains his apologetical intention in the introduction to the opening volume of the final series in the trilogy. In reflecting on what motivated him to begin with the concept of glory, Balthasar declares, "Our idea was that today's positivistic, atheistic man, who has become blind not only to theology but even to philosophy, needed to be confronted with the phenomenon of Christ and, therein, to learn to 'see' again—which is to say, to experience the unclassifiable, total otherness of Christ as the outshining of God's sublimity and glory."[139] At the same time, the theological aesthetics sets the stage for what follows in the trilogy. In that sense, it is rightly to be granted a degree of preeminence within Balthasar's work.

Somewhat similar to Martin Heidegger, Balthasar viewed his intellectual task as that of grappling with the question of "being."[140] As John Riches notes, "His whole theological endeavor is directed towards learning to see things as they are in themselves, whole and entire, and in so seeing to perceive the reality of being in all its variety and concreteness."[141] In Balthasar's estimation, this task is best facilitated by a return to the classical and medieval concern for the "transcendentals" (those aspects of being that surpass all the classificatory categories and hence the terms that apply to all things regardless of their ontological classification[142]). Such a program of retrieval provides the way of countering what he sees as the misguided anthropological turn in modern theology that looks to the human subject for the starting point of theological reflection.[143]

Viewed from this perspective, Balthasar's trilogy may be seen as a response to German idealism, and especially the Hegelian synthesis, with its elevation of the idea that being is Spirit in the sense of self-consciousness or being-present-to-oneself. Balthasar is convinced that Christian revelation points in another direction, toward the idea that being is ecstatic love or, more specifically, the trinitarian love of the Father and the Son in the Holy Spirit that is likewise open to the world. In elevating this theme, Balthasar offers what Donald Keefe hails as "a third way of doing theology, the way of love,"[144] as the antidote to the "failed ways" of cosmology (followed by ancient and medieval theology) and anthropology (that marked modern theology).

Similar to such other twentieth-century luminaries as John Zizioulas, therefore, Balthasar offers an ontology of communion that in his case arises from this ontology of trinitarian love. Hence, in arguing for his controversial thesis that the inner life of God can be regarded as archetypal prayer, he writes, "We may say that each of the Divine Persons exists only in relation to the others, and that each desires and enhances the glory of the others. This means that God, regarded as the three Persons of the Trinity, is pure selflessness, pure devotion to the loved One."[145] Thomas Norris encapsulates Balthasar's perspective by declaring, "The revelation that Being at its summit is trinitarian love means that at the very heart of reality there is communion, the ecstasy of the exit from self."[146] In short, being is the mystery of love,[147] and this love is trinitarian.

As the statement from the foreword to *The Glory of the Lord* indicates, Balthasar elevates three transcendentals—the "true" *(verum)*, the "good" *(bonum)* and the "beautiful" *(pulcher)*—to which should be added a fourth, the "one" *(unum)* as denoting their unity. In keeping with what he termed "the circumincession of the transcendentals,"[148] he weaves all three together throughout the entire trilogy (adding the fourth in the *Theo-Logic*). This tactic leads to the seemingly circular character of his work, a feature that Balthasar considered unavoidable: "After all, there is simply no way to do theology except by repeatedly circling around what is, in fact, always the same totality looked at from different angles."[149] Despite the circularity of the whole, each part of his magnum opus focuses on one of the transcendentals. Furthermore, Balthasar's chosen order—beauty, good, and truth—represents a seemingly deliberate reversal of the flow of Immanuel Kant's trilogy, that is, reason, ethics, and aesthetics.

The trilogy, therefore, is to be read as a composite work that, although written in three parts, represents a unified approach to the theological task and forms a singular response to the question of being. In *The Glory of the Lord*, Balthasar draws from the Thomistic categories of "form" and "splendor" to develop a theological understanding of beauty. To this end he explicates the divine glory that is reflected above all in Christ's cross and resurrection, together with a delineation of the manner in which the Christian tradition has given expression to the aesthetic aspect of faith. The *Theo-Drama* shifts the accent to the good, as Balthasar presents the encounter of divine and human freedom as constituting the drama of salvation history. Then in the *Theo-Logic*, Balthasar responds to the question of the truth of being by engaging with the philosophical nature of truth, its relationship to Jesus' claim to be the truth and the role of the Holy Spirit in leading humans into the truth of Christ.

In the opening volume of *The Glory of the Lord*, Balthasar announces his beginning point: "Beauty is the word that shall be our first,"[150] and this because the beautiful "guards" and "sets the seal on" the other transcendentals.[151] His elevation of beauty lends a philosophical cast to his entire theological project. Louis Roberts explains:

> Balthasar's theological aesthetics begins with "beauty," an insight that is the heart of the classical world, its myths, philosophy, art, and literature. That which appears in the beauty of natural and created forms is the glory of being, *der Glanz des Seins*. It speaks of the mystery of that which transcends and yet inheres in all existents. Consequently, aesthetics is not just one department of knowledge, which in relative independence of others constitutes a relatively autonomous discipline. When one sees the beauty of a person, a work of art, or a sunset, one is confronted at the same time with the mystery of its otherness. This sense of the wonder of beauty, Balthasar believes, is at the root of all serious metaphysical endeavor.[152]

Despite the philosophical flavor that commentators rightly find in Balthasar's work, as an heir to the classical and medieval tradition, he can entertain no strict distinction between philosophy and theology. On the contrary, in his estimation, "In order to be a serious theologian, one must also, indeed, first, be a philosopher; one must—precisely also in the light of revelation—have immersed oneself in the mysterious structures of creaturely being."[153]

The content: glory, goodness, and truth—aesthetics, drama, and logic. Balthasar's understanding of the interconnection between the two disciplines leads him to posit a corresponding connection between the philosophical concept of beauty and the theological idea of glory: "The 'glorious' corresponds on the theological plane to what the transcendental 'beautiful' is on the philosophical plane."[154] According to Balthasar, the church fathers brought this classical perspective into Christian theology, but beginning in the late Middle Ages it began to wane and eventually was lost or even rejected—to the detriment of theology.

Despite the close attention Balthasar gives to beauty as a philosophical category, the ultimate topic of his theological aesthetics is the concept of glory. Hence, although *The Glory of the Lord* begins with the "teaching on seeing," in which aesthetics is understood in the Kantian sense of discourse about perception, it ends with the "teaching on rapture," that is, with the enrapturing power of the self-disclosure of the glory of God.[155] Balthasar's central purpose, therefore, is to indicate how in catching sight of or perceiving the glory of the selfless, divine, triune love disclosed in Jesus Christ, the human person is enraptured within that love.[156] In this manner, *The Glory of the Lord* becomes—to cite Roberts's characterization—"an interpretation of faith through the leitmotif of art," in which faith is compared to aesthetic contemplation.[157] Balthasar summarizes this perspective in his subsequent explanation of the choice of the title, *The Glory of the Lord* (German: *Herrlichkeit*). He declares that the work

> is concerned, first, with learning to see God's revelation and because God can be known only in his Lordliness and sublimity (*Herrheit* and *Hehr-heit*), in what Israel called *Kabod* and the New Testament *gloria*, something that can be recognized under all the incognitos of human nature and the Cross. This means that God does not come primarily as a teacher for us ("true"), as a useful "redeemer" for us ("good"), but to display and to radiate himself, the splendor of his eternal triune love in that "disinterestedness" that true love has in common with true beauty.[158]

Balthasar states quite clearly that his ultimate interest does not lie with beauty in the modern or even the transcendental sense but with the "surpassing of beauty in glory," that is, with the divine splendor as manifested in Jesus Christ and reflected, in turn, in Christians who "look upon their Lord." But even this manifestation of God is only the prelude to the central event, "the encounter, in creation and in history, between infinite divine freedom and finite human freedom."[159] Indeed, the God of revelation pours forth the divine goodness on humankind, an action that takes the form of a drama, the dramatic flow of God's history with humankind that has as its ultimate plot the reconciliation of the world in Christ.[160] The divine-human encounter comprises the topic of the second part of the trilogy, the *Theo-Drama*. It then becomes the basis for the task of setting forth what can be said about the activity of the Lord of glory—that is, the engagement with the question of truth—that follows in the *Theo-Logic*.

In many respects, the *Theo-Drama* forms the heart of Balthasar's trilogy. In fact, Oakes goes so far as to declare, "Balthasar has reached the apex of his theological achievement, for I regard the last three volumes of the Theodramatics as the culmination and capstone of his work, where all the themes of his theology converge and are fused into a synthesis of remarkable creativity and originality, an achievement that makes him one of the great theological minds of the twentieth century."[161] Above all, however, the *Theo-Drama* is central, because it mediates between the theological aesthetics and the theological logic. In these volumes, Balthasar puts the divine-human drama into image or form, so that in the *Theo-Logic*, in turn, it can be "transposed into human words and concepts for the purposes of comprehension, proclamation and contemplation,"[162] as he announced already in 1975.

Balthasar's goal in the *Theo-Drama* is to draw from dramatic categories to set forth a theology of history that is explicitly trinitarian. As a consequence, part two of the trilogy advances the trinitarian perspective announced in the theological aesthetics. As Balthasar explains,

> The Glory of the Lord (*Herrlichkeit*) took as its starting point that "form" (of the incarnate Word, Jesus Christ) which was true and radiant ("glorious") only insofar as it proclaimed its origin in the unity of the Father and returned thither in the Holy Spirit. But this "proclamation" and this "return" take place in a *Theo-drama (Theodramatik)* that, both in inner-worldly terms and in the economy of redemption, reveals an eternal Trinity in intense motion and interaction.[163]

The trinitarian drama of the ages that Balthasar narrates has the Father for its author (the one who is the ultimate source of the action), the Son as its chief actor (the one who enters the world to enact the script), and the Spirit as the director (the one who connects other actors to the chief actor and ensures the successful enactment of the script). Humans, in turn, take their rightful place in the drama as they fulfill their role or mission as those whom God calls to live in finite freedom. They do so above all as they come to be in Jesus Christ and as a consequence are drawn into the event of infinite freedom that comprises the eternal relationship between the Father and the Son.

At the heart of the *Theo-Drama* is the explication of the act of the triune God in dealing with the abuse of finite freedom. This act centers on the pascal mystery that forms the central narrative of the faith—the cross, the descent into hell, and the resurrection—each of which Balthasar presents as a trinitarian event affecting, but also arising out of, the inner life of God.

For Balthasar, the first of this trio of interrelated events—the cross— can be understood only in the context of the "primal divine drama" of the Father's generation of the Son, for this "implies such an incomprehensible and unique 'separation' of God from himself that it *includes* and grounds every other separation."[164] In this manner, he finds a basis in the triune God for the length to which God goes in sharing in the world's suffering, namely, to the point of taking on the godlessness of humankind.[165] Balthasar claims that he has thereby found a way to navigate his way between the twin mistakes that Aidan Nichols describes as "the Scylla of a Rahnerian formalism in speaking of the eternal divine self-communication . . . and the Charybdis of a Moltmann-esque submersion of the immanent Trinity in the world."[166] The resurrection, in turn, marks the overcoming, through the dynamism of the Spirit, of the separation of the Father and the Son in salvation history and hence their reunion "into a single (economic) principle of spiration—as the presupposition for the (economic) egress of the Spirit into the Church and the redeemed world."[167]

As important as Balthasar's proposal regarding the cross and resurrection is, in the eyes of many readers, his most significant contribution lies in his treatment of Holy Saturday.[168] Balthasar once claimed that the Son's *visio mortis* or descent into hell to experience the absolute Godforsakenness of the dead formed the center of all Christology.[169] According to readers such as John Riches and Ben Quash, his exposition of this theme "provides the core of Balthasar's most original theological reflection."[170]

Balthasar explains that the eternal Logos took upon himself not only the nature but also the condition of sinful humanity, not only of the pains of dying but of the actual state of being dead, and in so doing embraced that which is wholly opposed to God, while remaining God in the process. In his estimation, such a theological interpretation of the descent into hell is dependent on a trinitarian understanding of God. Not only does the presence of the divine in the Godforsakenness of hell require the distinction between the Father and the Son, it necessitates the reality of the Spirit as a third alongside the other two. As Balthasar explains in his *Elucidations,*

> This opposition between God, the creative origin (the "Father"), and the man who, faithful to the mission of the origin, ventures on into ultimate perdition (the "Son"), this bond stretched to the breaking point does not break because the same Spirit of absolute love (the "Spirit") informs both the one who sends and the one sent. God causes God to go into abandonment by God while accompanying him on the way with his Spirit.[171]

. Balthasar's explorations of the correspondence between creaturely beauty and divine glory and between human and divine freedom open the way for his inquiry into the third transcendental, and hence his investigation of the relationship between the structures of creaturely and divine truth. In keeping with the pathway he charts in the aesthetics and the dramatics, he frames the discussion of the resultant *Theo-Logic* in a trinitarian theological manner. The overarching question he poses is: "What role does 'truth' play in the event of God's self-revelation through the Incarnation of the Logos and the outpouring of the Holy Spirit?"[172] In Balthasar's estimation, the answer to this query lies in the truthfulness of revelation. He argues that the truth disclosed through the divine self-disclosure of revelation given in the Logos and set forth by the Spirit in the church is the ultimate norm of truth in the world. Revelation can claim this normative status, because it perfects worldly truth and elevates it above itself.

The Triune God of the Transcendentals

On May 10, 1988—a mere seven weeks before his death (June 26)—Balthasar presented a retrospective essay to a symposium on his theology held in Madrid, Spain. In his address, he declared that the Christian answer to the question posed by all human philosophy—that is, the problem of the Absolute Being—is contained in two central doctrines of the faith: the Trinity and the incarnation. "In the trinitarian dogma," he explained, "God is one, good, true and beautiful because he is essentially Love, and Love supposes the one, the other and their unity. And if it is necessary to suppose the Other, the Word, the Son, in God, then the otherness of the creation is not a fall, a disgrace, but an image of God, even as it is not God."[173] The incarnation is likewise crucial, Balthasar added, for "as the Son in God is the eternal icon of the Father, he can without contradiction assume in himself the image that is the creation, purify it and make it enter into the communion of the divine life without dissolving it (in a false mysticism)."[174]

The christological center. In these short sentences, Balthasar paints in broad strokes the general features of his trinitarian theological proposal and especially the christological orientation that lies at its heart. Already in 1955 in his book on prayer, he gave notice that his thought would be characterized by a christological focus. Balthasar wrote:

> Contemplation's object is God, and God is triune life. But as far as we are concerned, we only know of this triune life from the Son's incarnation. Consequently we must not abstract from the incarnation in our contemplation. We cannot contemplate God's triune life itself; if we did, we would sink into a vacuum, a world without substance, into conceptual mathematics or day-dreaming.[175]

He then reiterated the point a decade later in his reflective account of his writings: the "theological center, from which the world of creation and of history receives its structures, is occupied . . . by Christ."[176]

Declarations such as these have not gone unnoticed by his readers. In an early exposition of his work, published in 1964, Jakob Laubach expostulated, "The revelation of God's overflowing fullness in Jesus Christ! That is for Hans Urs von Balthasar the one central fact."[177] Six year later, Gerard Reedy echoed the theme. His awareness of this aspect of Balthasar's work led him to conclude, "If classical Christology was an attempt to fit Christ into the world of being, von Balthasar's is the opposite: to fit the world of being into Christ, the primary intelligible."[178] More recently, Thomas Norris offered a similar one-sentence characterization of Balthasar's perspective: "Christ is the *Gestalt* of Christianity: in his face the glory of God shines and from there radiates into the heart of Christians."[179] He then noted the foundational role that the christocentric orientation plays in the trilogy: "The event of Christ . . . is a divine aesthetic, a divine drama and a divine logic."[180]

In his christocentric approach to theology, Balthasar stands close to Karl Barth, whom he admired greatly. Indeed, in the introduction to the first volume of the trilogy, Balthasar acknowledged "the great service rendered to theology" by his older Protestant counterpart,[181] and in his book-length treatment of Barth's theology he even commended the Protestant thinker to Catholic theologians precisely because of the christocentric character of his thought.[182] Not only did Balthasar admire Barth, he set as his own goal the task of triggering a christocentric revolution in Roman Catholic theology after the pattern of Barth's contribution.[183] Being nearly two decades younger than his Protestant mentor placed him in a position to advance the cause that Barth had inaugurated and to bring Barth's christological orientation into conversation with newer impulses. Thus, John Thompson concludes, "Balthasar has been able, post-Barth, to carry the debate further in line with more recent Catholic and Protestant thinking on the relationship of the Trinity and the cross, the Trinity and the death of God and what this means for us."[184]

Like Barth, Balthasar believes that the basis for understanding God as triune lies in the divine self-disclosure in Jesus Christ. In the *Theo-Drama*, for example, he declares, "On the one side, we see Jesus pointing to the Father and on the other to the Spirit: and thus we discern the radiant reality of what will be formulated in terms of the divine Trinity," and then asserts simply and forthrightly, "We know about the divine 'Persons' only through the figure and disposition of Jesus Christ."[185] Balthasar reiterates the point in the second volume of the *Theo-Logic*: "Only from the conduct of Jesus toward his Father and toward the Holy Spirit do we experience anything about the inner-trinitarian life- and love-relations in the one and only God."[186]

According to Balthasar's characterization, Jesus steps onto the stage of the theo-drama as the Son who always defines himself as the one sent by the Father and whose mission is mediated by the Spirit.[187] So committed is Balthasar to the centrality of Jesus to the self-disclosure of the triune God that he offers the following pastoral admonition to his theological parishioners:

> We should never tire of reminding ourselves that, from a Christian standpoint, there is no possibility of distinguishing between God's act of revelation and the content of this revelation, for this revelation is inseparably both the interior life of God and the form of Jesus Christ. For the Word of God is *both* the divinity which expresses and reveals itself in the Trinity's eternity and in the economy of time *and* the man Jesus Christ, who is the Incarnation of that divinity.[188]

Yet Balthasar does not merely parrot his Protestant counterpart; he is not simply a Karl Barth in Roman Catholic guise. On the contrary, he self-consciously and deliberately places himself on the Catholic side of the great divide that Barth posited between those who continue to appeal to some sort of *analogia entis* and those, like Barth himself, who categorically reject such attempts as vestiges of a misguided medieval scholasticism.[189] Unlike Barth, Balthasar finds a profitable use for the idea of an *analogia entis*. In fact, his entire appeal to the transcendentals that drives the trilogy and constitutes his methodological contribution to theology[190] is closely connected to this methodological conviction. In keeping with this perspective, Balthasar declares, "Thus we see that the form of the revelation in Christ is in the first place characterized indirectly in its form-quality as the perfection of the form of the world."[191]

Despite his allegiance to the Roman Catholic theological tradition at this point, Balthasar does not bring the analogy of being into his theology unaltered. He draws not only from the patristic and medieval use of the transcendentals as a way of pressing the activities of creatures of all types into service in speaking about God, but also from the traditional acknowledgment of the dissimilarity between the creaturely and the Godly, a dissimilarity that Balthasar finds evident, for example, in all attempts to use the concept "person" to refer to both the human and the divine.[192] In poetic prose that rivals Balthasar's own, Nichols provides a graphic characterization of this seemingly two-sided relationship between the transcendentals and the divine self-disclosure evident in Balthasar's thinking:

> If the God of glory wished to show his beauty to the world in his incarnate Image he must at once take up forms within the world and shatter them so as to express the Glory beyond beauty. If the philanthropic God wished to show his goodness to the world in the protagonist of the saving drama that is the Lamb slain and victorious he must at once take up the dynamic pattern of human freedom and burst it from within so as to express the sovereign Love beyond all goodness. If the God of truth wished to make known his primordial truth to the world . . . then he must use, and in using take beyond their limits, laws of human thought and language so as to convey a revelation of truth beyond the heart of man in the incarnation of the Logos and the outpouring of the Holy Spirit.[193]

Perhaps even more significant is Balthasar's attempt, following the lead of Erich Przywara,[194] to transform the *analogia entis* into the basis for creaturely participation in the divine life, for he sees it as forming a reality present within the constitution of humans that presses them to go beyond themselves and move toward God. Nichols clarifies the implication of Balthasar's perspective: "That there is an analogy between our being and God's should not make us seek to domesticate God but, on the contrary, lead us to recognise an invitation—inscribed in the very nature of our being—to enter his mystery."[195]

Rather than finding it necessary to opt for a strict allegiance to either the medieval *analogia entis* or Barth's *analogia fidei*, Balthasar proposes a theological program that brings the two together under the rubric of the *kenosis* involved in the divine self-revelation disclosed in the incarnation. The result is an understanding that gives place to both an upward or "analogical" movement from the creaturely to the divine and a downward, "katalogical" movement from God to the world.[196] The double theological movement Balthasar proposes leads to the heart of his trinitarian theology.

Kenosis as an act within the immanent Trinity. In the fourth volume of the *Theo-Drama*, Balthasar offers a terse appraisal of the unfortunate state of trinitarian theology in the wake of Rahner's Rule: "Many theologians, in attempting to establish the relationship between immanent and economic Trinity, seem to lay such weight on the latter that the immanent Trinity, even if it is still distinguished from the other, becomes merely a kind of precondition for God's true, earnest self-revelation and self-giving."[197]

As his complaint suggests, Balthasar is quite unsympathetic to the widespread tendency among theologians to view the economy of salvation as definitive for the eternal divine reality. He would be especially uneasy about any attempt to elevate the economic Trinity as the "real" Trinity, thereby displacing the immanent Trinity entirely. At the same time, his conviction that only in Jesus Christ is the Trinity made accessible leads Balthasar to close ranks with the architects of such proposals in their desire to give proper place to the dynamic of the three trinitarian persons in the economy of salvation—that is, in the dramatic action of the theological persons.[198] On this basis, he voices agreement with the principle that "it is only on the basis of the economic Trinity that we can have knowledge of the immanent Trinity and dare to make statements about it."[199] Because he understands the concerns of advocates on both sides of the issue, Balthasar seeks to walk a fine line between the two perspectives by developing a trinitarian theological proposal—in a manner that typifies his dialectical approach to theology—in which God is seen to change in some sense, while preserving the idea that God always remains the same.[200] His attempt to do so opens the way for his unique understanding of the relationship between the immanent Trinity and the economic Trinity, which David Cunningham lauds as a reminder that "the missions and the processions are bound to one another, and that we *cannot even separate out* the categories of the 'immanent' and the 'economic' Trinity—let alone privilege one over the other."[201]

In a manner akin to Barth, Balthasar launches his attempt to walk the theological tightrope by appealing to the conception of God as "event," with the attendant idea that the eventfulness of God provides the basis for the becoming found in the world. He declares unhesitatingly, "All earthly becoming is a reflection of the eternal 'happening' in God, which . . . is per se identical with the eternal Being or essence."[202] In keeping with this outlook, Balthasar postulates that the entire theo-drama in the economy of salvation finds its basis in a theo-drama within the eternal divine dynamic. Hence, drawing from the medieval suggestion that the eternal processions within the dynamic of the triune God provide the condition for the very possibility of a creation,[203] he asserts that the world is the free extension of the otherness-in-love—the mystery of unity in diversity—that is present already within the divine life because of the generation of the Son from the Father and their union in the Spirit. Moreover, the *kenosis* inherent in the incarnation and the paschal events likewise finds its basis in the "supra-temporal yet ever actual event" of the divine processions,[204] so that the incarnation emerges as the extension into time and space of the Son's procession from the Father before all time.[205] Thus, in Balthasar's trinitarian theology, *missio* and *processio* are integrally connected, with the latter being the basis for the former but the former providing access to the latter. In short, the economic Trinity becomes the epistemological source of the immanent Trinity, but the immanent Trinity remains the ontological source of the economic Trinity.[206]

Central to this innovative theological move is a conception, which Balthasar sets forth in conversation with the Russian philosopher and theologian Sergei Bulgakov,[207] that an original or "super-*kenosis*" within the eternal divine life provides both the otherness and the unity that is required for the drama of redemption. Inherent in the procession of the Son from the Father is a kenotic movement of divine love—an "absolute renunciation"—that results in *kenosis* becoming not merely an act of the Son but more importantly a disposition of love within the eternal triune God.[208] Because the Father "will not be God for himself alone," Balthasar explains, he "strips himself, without remainder, of his Godhead and hands it over to the Son."[209] The Father's act constitutes the Son as the "Other" to stand in an I-Thou relationship to the Father. Taking the idea further, Balthasar declares that the Father's *kenosis* "involves the positing of an absolute, infinite 'distance' that can contain and embrace all the other distances that are possible within the world of finitude, including the distance of sin." Or stated in another manner, in letting go of his divinity, the Father "manifests a (divine) God-lessness (of love, of course)," that undergirds, renders possible, and goes beyond the godlessness found in the world. The *kenosis* of the Father opens the way, in turn, for the Son's act of responding to the "gift of Godhead" with selfless and unreserved eternal thanksgiving, and for the procession of the Spirit from both "as their subsistent 'We,'" as the one who "maintains the infinite difference between them, seals it and, since he is the one Spirit of them both, bridges it."[210] In this manner, Balthasar has traced a theological pathway from the salvation-historical drama into the inner life of the triune God, which is therefore seen to be characterized by separation and unity, and he has described the immanent Trinity as self-giving love, as the giving of oneself to the other.

In Balthasar's estimation, the concept of a *kenosis* within the eternal dynamic of the God who is inherently triune likewise suggests how the incarnation in general and the cross and resurrection in particular can mark some sort of change in God and thereby comprise our redemption. Were God merely an undifferentiated unity, the incarnation would unavoidably link the deity with the fate of the world in some mythological sense. However, because God is antecedently triune, the incarnation and the events of Holy Week serve to lift the world's fate into the economic Trinity and, by extension, into the immanent Trinity, without compromising the transcendent freedom of God. Balthasar readily admits that "the event of the Incarnation of the second Person does not leave the

inter-relationship of those Persons unaffected."[211] Yet he points out that
the incarnation can work such an effect only because the *kenosis* event is
already eternally present within the dynamic of the immanent Trinity.
With this in view, Balthasar can assert, "the Son's eternal, holy distance
from the Father, in the Spirit, forms the basis on which the unholy distance of the world's sin can be transposed into it, can be transcended and
overcome by it."[212]

The *kenosis* within the immanent Trinity likewise opens the way for
Balthasar to view the divine engagement with the world—in keeping with
his dialectical approach to theology—as somehow able to enrich God,
without thereby positing a change in or suggesting that something is lacking in the divine being.[213] Rather than consisting primarily of self-sacri-
fice, according to Balthasar, *kenosis* entails a movement of self-giving
toward the other so as thereby to receive the other. As such, it includes an
element of receptivity. As a consequence, Balthasar does not view personhood as a quality that is possessed, but as a unique identity that is received
in relations of love and freedom. Furthermore, these person-conferring
relations can only be labeled as kenotic.[214] Consequently, the love that
characterizes the relationality of the trinitarian persons bestows an "ever-
more" or "ever-greater" dimension to the divine life, a kind of "increase"
connected to the Spirit's identity as the "fruit" of the love of the Father
and the Son,[215] and an idea that leads Balthasar to invoke Gregory of
Nyssa's analogy of a fountain to understand the inner divine life.[216]
O'Hanlon offers a helpful description of the startling character of this
insight: "In this sense we may say that the Holy Spirit is constantly showing the Father and Son that their perfect love is more than they themselves had expected."[217]

The dynamic of kenotic mutual enrichment within the eternal life of
God in turn opens the way for creation to participate in the ever-more of
divine love as something that is "different from God" becoming more
itself within what is "different in God";[218] in so doing it contributes to the
divine love. In the concluding paragraph to the *Theo-Drama*, Balthasar
delineates what he sees this enrichment to be:

> What does God gain from the world? An additional gift, given to the
> Son by the Father, but equally a gift made by the Son to the Father,
> and by the Spirit to both. It is a gift because, through the distinct

operations of each of the three Persons, the world acquires an inward share in the divine exchange of life; as a result the world is able to take the divine things it has received from God, together with the gift of being created, and return them to God as a divine gift.[219]

Does the Future Belong to Balthasar?

In 1975, the well-known Roman Catholic theologian Henri de Lubac declared regarding Balthasar, "This man is perhaps the most cultivated of his time."[220] Twelve years later, Louis Roberts hailed Balthasar's theological aesthetics as constituting "a promising combination of the old and new for the future direction of theology."[221] This appraisal found echo in a 1984 review of the first volume of the aesthetics, in which Donald Keefe lauded Balthasar's work as "the most sustained and comprehensive theological enterprise by a Catholic scholar in his century, and one which must rank with the classic theological achievements of the Catholic past."[222] More recently, Norris lauded Balthasar's theological method for providing "a theologically sophisticated and a dramatically comprehensive vision of Christian faith, life and celebration."[223]

Despite the long parade of accolades he has garnered and the recent surge of treatises explicating his thought, theologians have been surprisingly slow to offer sustained critical engagement with Balthasar's theological proposal. Oakes pinpointed one crucial factor: "What makes assessing his theology particularly difficult at this time is his intention to undercut and undermine the fundamental foundations on which nearly all theology being done today rests."[224] Indeed, Mark McIntosh wonders whether Balthasar's "theological imagination could ever be comfortable within the standard norms of modern academic theology."[225]

Already in 1965, Karl Rahner forewarned that such might turn out to be the case. Regarding Balthasar's likely reception he prophesied, "Perhaps the effectiveness of such a theology inevitably takes longer than our impatience is ready to tolerate."[226] Gerard Reedy expressed similar sentiments five years later, when he mused that Balthasar's "full contribution will perhaps only be recognized in a more irenic age, when believers, freed from polemics, will have the leisure better to savor his rich oeuvre."[227]

There are signs that a change may be in the making. Balthasar's trinitarian proposal is beginning to engender scrutiny.[228] Even more telling is the trend among some theologians to draw explicit insights and themes from Balthasar's work en route to developing their own trinitarian theological perspectives.[229] Indicative of this development, the authors of a collection of essays entitled *Balthasar at the End of Modernity* noted in 1999, "Hans Urs von Balthasar is a theologian whose time appears to have come."[230] Other readers, especially those who have measured his work and found it wanting, are not sure. Mary Gerhart speaks for many of these critics when she writes, "Von Balthasar's three series will be remembered as one of the major theological achievements of modernism. However, I think it likely that he will prove to be more right in his critique of the overly abstract form of modernist theology than influential in his constructive attempts to replace that form."[231] Whatever his influence may turn out to be, Balthasar's work stands as a sustained and significant call for a return of the immanent Trinity in trinitarian theology that excels even that of Elizabeth Johnson. For this reason, subsequent trinitarian theologians overlook it only at their peril.

The Triune God of Scientific Theology:
Thomas F. Torrance

Elizabeth Johnson and Hans Urs von Balthasar represent two quite different attempts to rehabilitate the centrality of the immanent Trinity in the task of renewing trinitarian theology. Nevertheless, they share a singular methodological option, for both Johnson and Balthasar find ongoing theological value in the concept of the *analogia entis*, which has played such an important role in Roman Catholic theology since the Middle Ages. Other thinkers, however, remain unconvinced. Some find themselves on the Barthian side of the methodological line that he drew in the theological sand and as a consequence are looking once again to Barth for assistance in countering what they see as a grave danger precipitated by the erosion of the primacy of the immanent Trinity that has emerged in the wake of Rahner's Rule.

The Barthian-based revival of immanent trinitarianism is advanced by a variety of scholars. Paul Molnar, to cite one example, finds in Barth support for his contention, delineated in *Divine Freedom and the Doctrine of the Immanent Trinity* (2002), that a return to the immanent Trinity is crucial to the task of recognizing, upholding, and respecting God's freedom.[232] Barth's influence is likewise evident in the work of Alan Torrance, who nevertheless parts company with his German theological mentor at certain points. Thus, in *Persons in Communion* (1996),[233] Torrance appropriates anew the concept of person in the wake of Barth's displacement of it in favor of the language of modes of being, and he proposes that Barth's revelational approach to understanding the Trinity be replaced by a communion model in which the idea of indwelling takes precedence over the more cognitive concerns associated with interpretation, understanding, or communication.[234]

Yet the most influential Barth-oriented trinitarian theologian and the partisan to whom many others appeal[235] is Alan Torrance's uncle, Thomas F. Torrance. George M. Newlands, a fellow Scot, viewed Thomas Torrance's 1996 treatise on the Trinity, *The Christian Doctrine of God*[236] (together with the work of his nephew), as a solid indication that "a style of theological discourse which many had thought to be obsolescent has returned to the centre of theology and church in this country."[237] Already in 1984, the editors of *Reformed Review* acclaimed Torrance as not only "the leading Reformed theologian today in the Anglo-Saxon world" but also "one of the most brilliant and seminal thinkers of our time."[238]

Torrance is often lauded for his work on John Calvin and Karl Barth. This judgment arises largely from his diligent involvement in editing translations of their writings, especially Barth's monumental *Church Dogmatics*, as well as his engagement with the thought of his two theological predecessors.[239] As Daniel W. Hardy points out, however, Torrance is not interested in either Calvin or Barth as such. Rather, he is "attracted by the possibility for theology which their approaches exemplify, the possibility of a *scientific theology*."[240] Hardy's comment pinpoints what lies at the center of Torrance's agenda as a theologian. The most persistent theme of his work and the one for which he is most widely known[241] is the question of the proper interface of theology and science, which he explores in the context of his understanding of the scientific character of theology.[242] Torrance's contribution to the renaissance of trinitarian theology is inextricably bound up with this overarching program.

The Scientific Character of Theology

Like many other commentators, Alister McGrath underscores Torrance's importance to the theology-science discussion: "Thomas Forsyth Torrance is widely regarded, particularly outside Great Britain, as the most significant British academic theologian of the twentieth century, and is especially noted for his ground-breaking contribution to the study of the relationship of Christian theology and the natural sciences."[243] Similarly, Ted Peters describes Torrance's work as that of extending "the Barthian heritage into the theology-science interaction."[244] In an interview in 1984, Torrance confessed to a somewhat similar, albeit far more ambitious goal:

> My main interest has been to clear the ground for a dogmatics in the modern era, because the kind of dogmatics we have learned from Calvin and Barth needs to be thought out and expressed more succinctly within the rigorous scientific context in which we work and which will undoubtedly dominate the whole future. At the same time, this is my evangelistic interest, for I am concerned to evangelize the foundations, so to speak, of scientific culture, so that a dogmatics can take root in that kind of structure.[245]

Torrance's far-reaching objective, namely, that of evangelizing the foundations of scientific culture, gave rise to his involvement, under the auspices of the Templeton Foundation, in editing a series entitled Theology and Science at the Frontiers of Knowledge, for which he wrote the initial volume.[246] The stated purpose of the series—to foster "a reconstruction of the very foundations of modern thought and culture, similar to that which took place in the early centuries of the Christian era"[247]—reflects Torrance's desire that science and theology cooperate in the task of providing a grounding for and healing of Western culture in the midst of the current intellectual upheaval and fragmentation.[248] His efforts in promoting an interface of this magnitude were acknowledged already in 1978, when he was awarded the Templeton Foundation Prize for Progress in Religion.

The interplay of theology and science. Daniel Hardy declares, "the distinctive character of [Torrance's] work arises from the positive position which he adopts about what is proper to the content of Christian theology and that of science."[249] As Hardy suggests, Torrance's work is motivated by his conviction that theology and the natural sciences can be mutually enriching.[250] Not only is there "a hidden traffic between theological and scientific ideas of the most far-reaching significance for both theology and science," in his estimation the two disciplines "have deep mutual relations, and increasingly cry out for each other."[251] He is convinced that insofar as theology "has to do with the unlimited reality of God in his relations with the universe of all time and space,"[252] scientific exploration can shed light on the theological task of understanding the nature of God and the salvation found in Christ.[253] More importantly, however, theology provides the necessary fundamental attitude toward the universe as a whole that underlies the scientific enterprise itself,[254] an attitude that entails above all an awareness of both the order and contingency of the universe.

Yet the connection between the two disciplines runs deeper. Torrance maintains that theology is crucial to the scientific task of penetrating to the unitary logical basis of the relationships evident in the world.[255] At the same time, he acknowledges that the pursuit of the natural sciences is crucial to the essence of theology. The natural sciences raise theology's focus beyond the divine-human relationship to set it upon an understanding of humankind within the universe and as related to the God who is the creator of the universe.[256] Hence, the natural sciences assist theology in being concerned "not just with God/man relations, but with God/man/world or God/world/man relations," to cite Torrance's characterization.[257] He goes so far as to assert that without this interdisciplinary conversation "we are not really engaged in theology in the proper sense, and are not scientifically engaged with theology."[258]

In Torrance's estimation, theology and the natural sciences are intertwined both ontologically and epistemologically. They are united by the status they share as "science," which he describes as the process of grasping, or being conformed to, what is given or real, so that "every scientific pursuit" operates "with the correlation of the intelligible and the intelligent."[259] Viewed from this perspective, Torrance's approach could be termed a "realist" (or a "realistic"[260]) understanding of the nature of science. Yet he would not want his "critical realism"—to cite the designation he finds most attractive—to be viewed as simply a restatement of the medieval conception of the analogy of being. Instead, he theorizes that reality discloses itself in a manner that allows humans to come to understand it. Scientific knowledge, in turn, entails bringing "the inherent rationality of things to light and expression," which occurs, Torrance adds, "as we let the realities we investigate disclose themselves to us under our questioning and we on our part submit our minds to their intrinsic connections and order."[261]

As this statement suggests, Torrance posits a close relationship between the substance to be understood (ontology) and the means to understanding (epistemology), postulating that the latter must always be in accordance with the former.[262] Knowledge is possible, he theorizes, because the nature of the reality known prescribes the mode of rationality that facilitates this knowing. That is to say, a correspondence between reality and thought is possible insofar as the knower is conformed to the mode of rationality given by reality. Consequently, in the knowing process, a "logic of grace"[263] is at work. Reality actively presents itself to the knower in an act of "grace-giving" to which the knower in turn must respond in "gracefulness." Hardy provides a helpful explanation of Torrance's perspective, which indicates how close to the idea of an *analogia entis* he in fact comes: "Scientific knowledge might therefore be described as proceeding within a '*double activity*,' wherein reality actively gives itself, together with the appropriate mode of knowing it, and we actively respond by knowing it in the fashion it provides."[264]

In setting forth this particular understanding, Torrance is consciously reaching behind the advent of empirical science to the Hellenistic world, especially the thinking of Alexandria, which was so influential in the development of patristic theology.[265] Regarding the outlook prevalent in the ancient world, he writes, "Precise scientific knowledge was held to result from inquiry strictly in accordance with the nature of the reality being investigated, that is, knowledge of it reached under the constraint of what it actually and essentially is in itself, and not according to arbitrary convention." Such an approach, Torrance adds, "is the only way to reach real, exact or scientific knowledge in any field of inquiry."[266]

Seen in this light, theology is clearly a science. More specifically, it is "the science of God."[267] As such, theology is objective,[268] for it is "the positive science in which we think only in accordance with the nature of the given."[269] Thus, Torrance advises that in theological inquiry, "we must allow the divine realities to declare themselves to us, and so allow the basic forms of theological truth to come into view and impose themselves on our understanding."[270] He terms the discipline that seeks to clarify why this is so and how this occurs the "philosophy of theology" or the "philosophy of the science of theology."[271]

The link between theology and the natural sciences is made even stronger by Torrance's assertion that the human epistemological process is dependent on a fundamental stance that he calls belief or faith. *Belief,* as he uses it here, ought not to be confused with the modern sense of the term, which relegates it to the realm of the subjective. For Torrance, belief entails the kind of personal recognition of what is objective that is presupposed by and sustains the knowing process.[272] Belief is crucial, he argues, because such a stance is what allows the epistemological process to unfold. As Torrance puts it, "faith is the very mode of rationality adopted by the reason in its fidelity to what it seeks to understand, and as such faith constitutes the most basic form of knowledge upon which all subsequent rational inquiry proceeds."[273] In short, the stance of faith entails acknowledging certain beliefs that display a normative character or claim universal validity, even though they are not logically demonstrable.[274]

Understood in this manner, the stance of belief constitutes a point at which theology and the natural sciences converge, for ultimately faith comprises a response to God's self-giving action in creation and in Christ. Each branch of human inquiry explores its own particular dimension of the divine self-giving.[275] Natural science is directed to the contingent order of the universe, whereas theology seeks the source of this order in the self-presentation of the triune God. With a view toward the role of faith, Torrance summarizes his understanding of the epistemological process: "Faith entails the opening up of our subjectivity to the Subjectivity of God through His Objectivity. Faith is the relation of our minds to the Object who through His unconditional claims upon us established the centre of our knowing in Himself and not in us, so that the whole epistemological relation is turned round—we know in that we are known by Him."[276] This leads Torrance to propose what he calls a disclosure model of scientific thinking, "through which God's self-revelation impresses itself upon us, while discriminating itself from the creaturely representations necessarily employed by the model, and so bears upon our minds that its own inner relations are set up within them as the laws of our faithful understanding of God."[277]

Theological science and the triune God. Torrance's quest to determine the connection between science and theology leads him not only to acknowledge the scientific character of theology but also to assert the theological basis for science. In his estimation, the entire human epistemological project is dependent upon the self-disclosure of the God of the universe who is triune, for "as a unitary intelligible whole the universe must be thought of as ultimately integrated from above through the creative bearing upon it of the Trinitarian relations in God Himself."[278] What is true of human knowledge in general is even more explicitly the case in the process of theological knowing. Robert Palma places Torrance in the tradition of Athanasius, Calvin, and Barth, because of his concern to develop a theology that is "shaped at the outset by the reality of the triune God."[279] Indeed, Torrance himself speaks of the doctrine of the Trinity as "the *ultimate ground* of theological knowledge of God" and "the *basic grammar* of theology."[280]

At the heart of the trinitarian character of Torrance's theology is the crucial role he posits for the second trinitarian person in the dynamic of theological knowledge. In 1976, Torrance characterized his theology as being "deeply Nicene and doxological . . . with its immediate focus on Jesus Christ as Mediator, and its ultimate focus on the Holy Trinity."[281] Already in 1965, he offered his readers a preview as to just how christologically focused his theological proposal would be:

> Theology . . . is possible only because God has already condescended to come to us, and has indeed laid hold of our humanity, dwelt in it and adapted it to himself. In Jesus Christ he has translated his divine Word into human form and lifted up our human mind to understand himself. Hence, in theological inquiry we are driven back upon Jesus Christ as the proper ground for communion and speech with God. Because he is both the Word of God become Man and Man responding to that Word in utter faithfulness and truth, he is the Way that leads to the Father. It is in him and from him that we derive the basic forms of theological thinking that are appropriate both to divine revelation and human understanding.[282]

Statements such as these confirm Elmer Colyer's claim that "at the center of Torrance's theology is the whole incarnate life, death, and resurrection of Jesus Christ, who is none other than God the Son, the second Person of the Triune God, present to persons in astonishing closeness as a human being, Jesus of Nazareth."[283]

As Torrance's 1965 preview suggests, the christological focus of his trinitarian theology is closely connected to his understanding of the nature of the scientific enterprise as a whole. His rejection of the *analogia entis* leads Torrance to conclude that his general methodological principle—knowledge in any field of inquiry must proceed in accordance with "the nature of the reality being investigated"[284]—is even more crucial in theology. He writes,

> since there is no likeness between the eternal being of God and the being of created reality, God may be known only out of himself. Thus if we are to have any true and precise scientific knowledge of God, we must allow his own nature, as he becomes revealed to us, to determine how we are to know him, how we are to think of him, and what we are to say of him.[285]

Because God's self-disclosure is finally and uniquely given in Jesus Christ who is the incarnate Son, true knowledge of God, that is, knowledge that is "strictly in accordance with his divine nature,"[286] must arise from God. In this manner, the incarnation of the Word of God in Jesus Christ becomes the basis for human knowledge of God.

Torrance's rejection of the *analogia entis* likewise opens the way for the Spirit's role in the science of God. Reminiscent of Barth but drawing from Irenaeus, he argues that insofar as "only God can know himself," we can only come to know God by "sharing in some incredible way in the knowledge which God has of himself." Knowing God, therefore, occurs only as God brings us "into communion with him in the inner relations of his own being as Father, Son and Holy Spirit." For Torrance, this is the task of the Holy Spirit. He explains: "In Jesus Christ God has embodied in our human existence the mutual knowledge which the Father and the Son have of one another and in the Holy Spirit he gives us communion in the mutual relation of the Father and the Son and thus makes us share in the knowledge which the Father and the Son have of one another."[287] Torrance readily admits that knowledge of what the being of God is remains beyond our purview. Nevertheless, he is convinced that the doctrine of the Trinity encapsulates "knowledge of God that is directly and objectively grounded in his eternal being," so that we have "in some real measure . . . a conceptual grasp of God in his own internal relations."[288]

To understand why Christ and the Spirit play such crucial roles in the epistemological process, Torrance looks to the patristic concept of *homoousion*. According to McGrath, this idea provides Torrance with the ontological foundation for Christian theology, for by means of the concept "the entire Christian theological enterprise is . . . securely anchored in the ontological reality of the incarnation."[289] Tapio Luoma expresses substantial agreement with McGrath's assessment, while explaining the uniqueness of Torrance's perspective:

> What makes Torrance's point interesting is that, unlike many other theologians, he does not attach himself primarily to the doctrine of creation as the theological starting-point for interdisciplinary interaction but to Christology and especially to the doctrine of the Incarnation, involving the concept of *homoousion*, the Greek term with which the Early Church Fathers expressed their belief in the consubstantiality of the Son with the Father. For Torrance, the *homoousion* explicates the overlap in the common reality of God and human beings and the universe in which each of them is open toward others. Indeed, the *homoousion* is the substantial and structural principle of Torrance's theological thinking.[290]

Torrance argues that the conviction that God can be known only by a divine self-disclosure that occurs fully and ultimately only in Jesus Christ led the patristic thinkers to confess that Christ is consubstantial with the Father and then to apply the term to the Holy Spirit as well. In this manner, the term *homoousion* provided the church with the theological key that could unlock and bring to explicit formulation the implicit trinitarianism of the New Testament.[291] Because the incarnate Son and the Holy Spirit are of the very same being and nature as God the Father, Torrance argues, God has become truly knowable. More specifically, the concept of *homoousion* means that "Jesus Christ is . . . not a mere symbol, some representation of God detached from God, but God in his own Being and Act come among us, expressing in our human form the Word which he is eternally in himself, so that in our relations with Jesus Christ we have to do directly with the ultimate Reality of God."[292]

Like many architects of the renaissance of trinitarian theology, Torrance is convinced that the divine self-disclosure in Jesus Christ reveals a God who is inherently relational. Torrance is unique, however, in that he appeals not only to such themes as *perichoresis* but also to the concept of "onto-relation" to delineate the dynamic of the divine relationality and to explicate the significance of the designation "person." For Torrance, an onto-relation is basically "a being-constituting relation," and hence "the kind of relation subsisting between things which is an essential constituent of their being, and without which they would not be what they are."[293] He notes that the primary instance of an onto-relational reality in the history of thought is the person, for a person is what it is in relation.[294] This concept, he adds, emerged as a direct result of the development of Christian theology, especially Christology and the doctrine of the Trinity,[295] which depicts God as a dynamic, personal being-in-communion, or a communion of personal being, in which the ontic relations among the divine persons belong to the intrinsic identity of each trinitarian person. Torrance writes,

> The relations between the divine Persons are not just modes of existence but hypostatic interrelations which belong intrinsically to what Father, Son, and Holy Spirit are coinherently in themselves and in their mutual objective relations with and for one another. These relations subsisting between them are just as substantial as what they are unchangeably in themselves and by themselves. Thus the Father is Father precisely in his indivisible ontic relation to the Son and the Spirit, and the Son and the Spirit are what they are as Son and Spirit precisely in their indivisible ontic relations to the Father and to One Another. That is to say, the relations between the divine Persons belong to what they are as Persons—they are constitutive onto-relations.[296]

In the life of the triune God, Torrance notes, each person functions as the onto-relational source of qualities that characterize the one God. This perspective lies behind his insistence (in contrast to John Zizioulas's perspective) that the Council of Nicea was correct in postulating that the Son proceeds from the being rather than from the person of the Father, for "father" designates not only the first person of the Trinity but also the one being or *ousia* of the triune God.[297] The qualities contributed to the being of God by the three persons, in turn, come to the fore in the actions of the one God toward creation. Brad Kallenberg cites one example of this dynamic: "The Holy Spirit is the onto-relational source for the 'spiritness' of the Godhead by which God *as a whole* imbues creation with life, or spiritual power. God as a whole acts as spirit toward creation just as God as a whole acts as father toward creation. In this way God's activity outside the Godhead is not only indivisible . . . it is an important analogy to intra-trinitarian relations."[298] As Kallenberg's observation indicates, in making this connection Torrance draws from the idea of an *analogia relationis* between God's actions and the intratrinitarian relations, one that, he is careful to explain, is "freely posited by the Creator in the omnipotence of His Grace" and therefore retains the "utter difference between the creature and the Creator."[299] Above all, however, the *analogia relationis* leads Torrance to view the triune God not only as "a fullness of personal Being in himself," but also as a "person-constituting Being,"[300] the one who by entering into relationship with humans constitutes their personhood.

Scientific Theology and the Return of the Immanent Trinity

Publication of what many commentators hail as Torrance's most significant theological treatise, *The Christian Doctrine of God: One Being, Three Persons* (1996), catapulted him into the trinitarian theological limelight. Tapio Luoma, for example, considers it to be Torrance's "most significant book," insofar as in the volume "he draws together his theological understanding in concise form, repeating themes and viewpoints familiar to his readers from earlier writings and summing up the very heart of his mature theology."[301] Gerald Bray, in turn, finds that in the book Torrance "breaks new ground."[302] Similarly, Peter Somers Heslam lauds what he sees as the seminal character of the work: "The classical quality of the exposition promises to ensure that the book will remain a standard and serviceable volume for many years to come. It certainly represents the best of British theology from an orthodox, evangelical perspective."[303] Yet perhaps the strongest accolade offered to date comes from Elmer Colyer's pen: "In *The Christian Doctrine of God*, Thomas F. Torrance demonstrates, once again, that he has one of the most brilliant and fertile minds amongst Reformed theologians in the English-speaking world."[304] Above all, Colyer is impressed with Torrance's approach to the doctrine of the Trinity, for in his estimation, "No one in the Reformed tradition has developed a more rigorous account" of "how the doctrine of the Trinity actually arises out of the church's evangelical and doxological encounter with realities and events of God's self-revelation in the Gospel through the biblical witness."[305]

Despite what might be inferred from the subtitle, *One Being, Three Persons*, in *The Christian Doctrine of God* Torrance adds his voice to the growing chorus of thinkers who are calling for a move away from the older tendency to develop the doctrine of the Trinity by looking first to the one divine essence and only then speaking about the three persons.[306] As important as this feature may be, Torrance's significance in the story of the renaissance of trinitarian theology lies in another, more subtle feature of his thought. Colyer hints at this aspect when he notes that "the Trinity is the ultimate focus of Torrance's theology, for in the Trinity we find the ultimate ground of all knowledge and experience of God."[307] Torrance's central contribution emerges from the specific manner in which he sees the Trinity as providing the ultimate ground of theological knowledge, for this concern leads him to invest ultimate theological primacy in the immanent Trinity in the process of developing his scientific theology.[308]

The primacy of the immanent Trinity. Torrance's elevation of the immanent Trinity flows quite naturally out of a central feature of his scientific approach to theology, which arises, in turn, from his general epistemology. In his seminal work, *Reality and Scientific Theology* (1985), he delineates what he calls "the stratification of truth." Torrance's research into the scientific enterprise leads him to conclude that the human epistemological process proceeds by means of a process that leads into ever-deeper layers or ever-higher levels of the truth of reality. He writes,

> knowledge is gained not in the flat, as it were, by reading it off the surface of things, but in a multi-dimensional way in which we grapple with a range of intelligible structures that spread out far before us. In our theoretic constructions we rise through level after level of organised concepts and statements to their ultimate ontological ground, for our concepts and statements are true only as they rest in the last resort upon being itself.[309]

More specifically, following the lead of such theoreticians as Albert Einstein, Torrance sees scientific inquiry proceeding through three levels. It begins with ordinary experience, moves through the formulation of scientific theory, and finally arrives at the development of a higher logical unity.[310]

Torrance believes that theological reflection in general and knowledge of the Trinity in particular emerge in a similar manner. In the case of the latter, theological science moves from the experience of God in the gospel and in the life of the church ("the evangelical and doxological level"), through an analysis of God's self-disclosure in history but especially in Jesus Christ, which results in a delineation of the economic relations among the trinitarian persons, that is, the economic Trinity ("the theological level"), to conclusions regarding what the triune God is ontologically in all eternity, that is, the immanent Trinity (the "higher theological level").[311] Colyer offers a helpful summary of this aspect of Torrance's epistemological proposal: "Our Christian apprehension of God in the gospel moves *from* the evangelical level of our day-to-day relationship with God in the life of the church *through* what God is and has done for us in God's redemptive activity as Father, Son and Holy Spirit in history (God's *oikonomia* or the economic Trinity) *to* what God is antecedently and eternally in God's own being and life as Father, Son and Holy Spirit (the ontological Trinity)."[312]

Although this methodological understanding invests the economic Trinity with a kind of epistemological priority, it clearly views the immanent Trinity as possessing ontological primacy. Indeed, in Torrance's estimation, the immanent Trinity not only forms the goal of theological science but also comprises its "higher theological and scientific" or "controlling level."[313] In fact, he goes so far as to claim that theological knowledge is truly knowledge of *God* only if it is grounded ultimately "in the inviolable otherness" of God within the eternal divine being beyond the world.[314] If "knowledge of God toward us is not ontologically grounded in God," he declares unequivocally, it "is at the mercy of our knowledge of ourselves."[315] For this reason, Torrance concludes, "It is as our knowing of God passes from what is called the 'economic Trinity' to the 'ontological Trinity' that we have *theologia* in the supreme and proper sense, knowledge of God on the free ground of his own Being, knowledge of him in which our knowing is controlled and shaped by relations eternally immanent in God."[316]

The methodological commitment that elevates the immanent Trinity to ontological primacy brings to light what in Torrance's estimation is the chief significance of the patristic introduction of the concept of *homoousion*. As we have seen, for him, this concept, and hence the confession that Jesus Christ is one with the Father, provides the necessary connection that links the economic Trinity to the immanent Trinity. John Morrison puts his finger on the central importance that Torrance finds in this concept:

> To Torrance then the Nicene *homoousion* is both revolutionary and decisive for theo-logical thinking after the way of God for us because it clearly expresses the fact that in Jesus Christ what the eternal tri-

une God is "toward us" and "in the midst of us" in and through the Word made flesh he actually and truly is in himself from all eternity. To put that another way, the penetrating insight of the Nicene *homoousion* doctrine is found to be that God is in the transcendent internal relations of his own eternal being (the *perichoresis* or coinherence of the triune Persons) the very same Father, Son and Holy Spirit that he is in his self-revealing and redeeming activity in space-time for mankind.[317]

As Morrison's summary suggests, the close connection that Torrance sees between the economic Trinity and the immanent Trinity together with the primacy he sees in the immanent Trinity lead him to conclude that the relations evident in God's self-communication in history are not merely modes that God assumes in condescending to the transient conditions of creaturely existence. Nor do the designations Father, Son, and Spirit carry only metaphorical significance. Rather than merely designating the manner that God is in the divine economy of revelation and redemption, these terms also denote the manner in which God exists eternally, independent of both the divine self-disclosure and the act of human knowing.[318] Torrance is convinced that in this way his disclosure model of theological science has netted a trinitarian theology that can speak meaningfully, even if only partially, about the eternal reality of the triune God, that is, about the immanent Trinity, and that such speech—rather than mere metaphorical God-talk—is the final goal of the science of theology.

Yet the primacy of the immanent Trinity does not end here. Torrance is also convinced that such speech about God carries implications for human relationality, for the immanent Trinity provides the basis for human personhood and human communion. In his estimation, the loving, communion-establishing God who encounters humans in Christ is the one who is internally relational because of the eternal indwelling and communion of the three trinitarian persons within the inner dynamic of the triune God. This God brings humans to participate in the communion of love present throughout eternity within the perichoretic relations of the Father, Son, and Spirit. Thus, Torrance concludes,

> the communion of Love in God has interpenetrated our human existence in such a way as to generate within it a community of love which participates in and is sustained by God's own Communion of

Love in the consubstantial and interpenetrating relations of Father, Son and Holy Spirit. It is within this community of reciprocity with the Trinity that we come to realise not only that God himself eternally lives in and is a Communion of mutual Love in himself, but that the very core of personal being which we derive from him involves a movement of mutual love among us in the out-going and responding of persons to one another.[319]

A scientific theology for the contemporary church? Torrance's masterful attempt to set forth a scientific theology—to offer a theological approach and an explication of the Christian God that can speak within a scientific culture—has been greeted with enthusiasm by many thinkers. Not surprisingly, it has also engendered criticism.[320] Some critics have raised questions about the manner in which Torrance proposes that theology engage natural science,[321] whereas others cast a critical eye toward aspects of his trinitarian proposal,[322] including even his perspective on the immanent Trinity.[323] Perhaps the sharpest critique, however, questions the extent to which Torrance has offered a scientific trinitarian theology that gives sufficient seriousness to the communal character of Christian belief. Thus, Kallenberg concludes,

> Torrance may very well be correct that contemporary Western theology lacks the conceptual resources for correctly conceiving God. But it is not clear that such resources can be supplied by a meticulous explanation of ancient vocabulary that does not attend to the communal form of life which gave this vocabulary its original sense. In the end, Torrance may simply have invented a new language (using old words), the language of *onto-personality* and *perichoresis*, which is grounded in contemporary scientific culture rather than in the praxis of first-century faith.[324]

Torrance's writings consistently suggest, contra Kallenberg's appraisal, that he has always viewed the community of faith as providing the context for his theological program. For example, in 1969, he declared that insofar as it is only one aspect of our total response to God, theology "has its place within the whole complex of the Church's response in worship and obedience and mission."[325] Two years later, he acknowledged that theological statements "take place, so to speak, within historical conversation between God and His people," and so they "emerge out of the Church's obedient acknowledgment from age to age of the divine Self-revelation in Jesus Christ and are progressively deepened and clarified through the Church's worship and dialogue and repentant rethinking within the whole communion of saints."[326] Moreover, Torrance's application of the idea of the stratification of truth to theological method provides at least the procedural basis for fostering a trinitarian theology that arises explicitly out of the community of faith.

These considerations suggest that Kallenberg's critique may be slightly wide of the mark. Nevertheless, it does point in the direction of what might in the end be the crucial issue that Torrance's proposal poses. His quest for a scientific theology was largely motivated by what he called an "evangelistic interest," namely, his desire to foster a cooperation between theology and science in the task of providing a Christian theological grounding for Western, scientific culture. As worthy as this goal may appear to be, it raises the question as to the extent to which the program of cultural evangelization lies at the heart of the church's theological task. And even if such a program is central to the mission of the community of faith, the question remains: Does scientific society continue to be the primary context for theology's apologetic engagement?

Epilogue:

The Trinitarian Story in Retrospect

Leonard Hodgson began his Croall Lectures over sixty years ago by declaring in a somewhat matter-of-fact manner, "The subject of these lectures is to be the Christian doctrine of God, and in speaking to this audience I need not labour the point that this means the doctrine of the Trinity."[1] Hodgson's assessment may have been overly generous when he voiced it in January 1943. But today such an appraisal would likely be slighted as simply passé. The change in the reception that such a remark would engender is evidence of the fact that lying between Hodgson's visit to Edinburgh and the contemporary situation are six decades of trinitarian theological renewal.

The earliest stirring of renewal can be found in the brief treatment of the doctrine of the Trinity that concludes Schleiermacher's *The Christian Faith* and that, contrary to widely held prejudice, comprises more than merely an appendix to the work. The important yet admittedly meager attention that the celebrated Romantic theologian paid to the doctrine was almost immediately eclipsed by the thoroughgoing trinitarian intellectual project of his rival at the University of Berlin, Georg W. F. Hegel. More than any other nineteenth-century thinker, Hegel paved the way for the rediscovery of the doctrine of the Trinity by attempting to delineate a trinitarian account of the self-disclosure of the Absolute Spirit in the world process.

Despite these stirrings in the nineteenth century, the actual narrative of the rediscovery of the doctrine of the Trinity in theology does not begin until after the First World War. Standing at the headwaters of the trinitarian theological renaissance is the theologian who more than any other casts a long shadow over the entire history of twentieth-century theolog-

216

ical thought, Karl Barth. Barth observed that the trinitarian structure that Hegel found present in both thought and the unfolding process of history inheres in the revelatory act of God in Christ. By delineating a trinitarian understanding of the divine revelation—by showing that revelation is an event initiated by and disclosing the God who is eternally triune—Barth determined that any truly helpful Christian theology would need to be trinitarian in both method and content. Theologians who would follow in Barth's wake would find it necessary to busy themselves with the theme of the event character of the divine self-disclosure that he had announced. Moreover, they would need to pursue the question of the exact connection between revelation and the revealing God, that is, between God-in-revelation and God-in-eternity.

Like Barth, a generation later Karl Rahner was concerned to set forth the divine act of self-communication to human creatures as a trinitarian event that finds its basis in the eternal self-communication within the triune life. At the same time, he asserted against the Neoscholastics of his day that the doctrine of the Trinity, and hence statements about God in eternity, could only be developed by means of a consideration of the revelation of the triune God through the work of the three trinitarian members in salvation history. To bring these two concerns together, he articulated what quickly came to be viewed as the "classical" formulation of a far-reaching methodological principle now known as Rahner's Rule. This dictum ties together in the closest manner possible the self-revealing God (God-for-us or the economic Trinity) with the eternal God (God-in-eternity or the immanent Trinity). Rahner's Rule has been misunderstood, misappropriated, qualified, and recast since his day. Yet no principle has had a greater influence in shaping the trinitarian theological conversation in the twentieth century.

Although Barth viewed the focus of revelation in the Word of God, his work and that of Rahner left open the possibility that the divine self-disclosure and hence the identity of the triune God might be viewed as arising out of the interplay of the three trinitarian members within the flux of history and climaxing in the eschaton. Jürgen Moltmann, Wolfhart Pannenberg, and Robert Jenson led the expedition into this newly discovered theological territory. All three took seriously Rahner's Rule. All three built from Barth's idea that the doctrine of the Trinity must be grounded in the divine self-disclosure in Christ and hence in the economy of salvation.

Nevertheless, these three theologians changed the operative theological metaphor, for they drew from the idea that the eternity in which the triune God dwells lies at the end of history, rather than in some static realm above the temporal process. Convinced that history is the story of the three trinitarian persons, these "theologians of history" characterized the triune God as the God of history.

For his part, Moltmann tied the doctrine of the Trinity to the history of the perichoretic relationships among the three divine persons in effecting the divine program, which in his estimation comprises the history of God's love, liberation, and reconciliation of all creation. In this manner, he focused attention on the engagement of the triune God with the world, even to the point of concluding that God is in some sense affected by the world. Pannenberg offered a more comprehensive project, namely, that of setting forth a coherent statement of Christian truth as it centers on the self-disclosure of the triune God in history. On the basis of the idea that God is the power that determines everything, Pannenberg asserted that the deity of God is connected to the demonstration of the divine lordship over creation. This conclusion led, in turn, to what some have denoted as the Pannenberg Principle, that is, the dictum that God's being, which is likewise God's deity, is linked to the divine rulership over the world. For Pannenberg, this rulership is established through the historical working and mutual relations of the three trinitarian persons, but especially Jesus and the Spirit, a trinitarian working that climaxes in the eschaton. The doctrine of the Trinity, in turn, is the explication of the relationship of Jesus to the Father and to the Spirit as this relationship emerges in the historical movement of the trinitarian persons toward the eschaton. Jenson's chief contribution lies in his elevating of the importance of the narrative dimension of the history of salvation. In his estimation, God is identified both with and by the biblical narrative, which presents this God as three agents of one action. This divine narrative or drama, Jenson added, is radically temporal and eschatologically oriented.

Their sense of the importance of looking to the interplay of the three trinitarian persons in history led the "theologians of history" to follow a theological method similar to that proposed by Rahner. According to this methodological proposal, the doctrine of God must begin with the divine threeness and only then move to the exploration of the oneness of God. Unlike Rahner, however, Moltmann, Pannenberg, and Jenson highlighted the personhood of the three trinitarian members and viewed the relationality of the three divine persons as providing the key to the unity of the one God. In this sense, all three—but especially Moltmann—reformulated the social trinitarianism that had been proposed by several theologians earlier in the century. Yet the focus on relationality was most pronounced in the work of three other thinkers, Leonardo Boff, John Zizioulas, and Catherine Mowry LaCugna.

Unlike most twentieth-century theological trailblazers, Boff was less interested in offering a distinctive trinitarian proposal than in speaking to a social context characterized by oppression. Consequently, he sought to pursue the implications of the mystery of the divine triunity—and hence of a relational understanding of the Trinity—for human community and, by extension, to draw insights from the ideal human community for understanding the mystery of the Trinity. To accomplish this goal, Boff built his explication of trinitarian theology from the eternal communion, mutuality, or *perichoresis* of the three divine persons revealed in the historical actions of Jesus and the Spirit. For Boff, following Moltmann, this perichoretic mutuality characterizes God's relationship to the world as well.

In his approach to the divine relationality, Boff remained decidedly Western. Zizioulas did not. In keeping with his own loyalties to the Eastern tradition, he looked to the Cappadocian fathers for the key to the development of an ontology of relations to replace the substance ontology that has dominated most Western theological proposals. The result was the introduction of yet another methodological principle, the Zizioulas Dictum, into the fluid lava of the new trinitarianism. This axiom maintains that being is communion and consequently that the being of the triune God is constituted by the communion or relationality of the three trinitarian persons. Zizioulas's idea—that personhood, whether human or divine, is constituted by relationships—quickly came to be standard fare in trinitarian theology, both Eastern and Western.

LaCugna represents the many Western thinkers who took Zizioulas's point to heart and looked eastward for inspiration. She was not indebted solely to the Greek theologian, however. Rather, in a sense LaCugna drew together impulses from the various innovative thinkers who preceded her in a creative manner that allowed her to add her own distinctive cast to the whole. She set aside the language of immanent versus economic Trinity, and in keeping with what she saw as the pristine manner of theologizing that had characterized the pre-Nicene church, she called for a reconnecting of talk about the triune God *ad intra* and *ad extra*, between theology proper and soteriology, or between *theologia* and *oikonomia*. The result of her efforts was the inclusion of yet a fourth methodological principle to the theological mix, the LaCugna corollary. Although it can be variously formulated, this axiom, which builds from Rahner's Rule, stipulates that theology (proper) and soteriology (the experience of salvation) are intertwined. Or stated in another manner, theological reflection regarding the mystery of God is indivisible from reflection on the experience of God in salvation or God *pro nobis*.

In the eyes of many theologians standing near the end of the twentieth century, the line of development from the theologians of history to the relational trinitarians—and especially LaCugna's proposal—risked collapsing the eternal God into the economy of salvation, thereby compromising the divine freedom. In the context of this concern, several distinctive proposals that sought to preserve the importance of the immanent Trinity gained a wide hearing as the century began to fade. Three of these have been especially influential, those of Elizabeth Johnson, Hans Urs von Balthasar, and Thomas F. Torrance.

Johnson's feminist-inspired recasting of the Trinity by appeal to the category of wisdom or Sophia does not immediately come to mind as an attempt to preserve the immanent Trinity. Indeed, Johnson followed a thoroughgoing theology from below that begins with women's experience. Moreover, this method led her, in a way reminiscent of Moltmann, to develop a relational trinitarianism that included a panentheistic conception of the relationship between God and the world. Despite aspects such as these which point in the direction of a strong focus on the economic Trinity, Johnson's proposal did harbor a keen interest in preventing the immanent Trinity from collapsing into salvation history. She adamantly denied that the eternal God could be captured by any human linguistic conceptuality, claiming that all such constructs are in the end mere metaphors for the divine reality. Or, to restate the idea in a positive form, she argued that because God is incomprehensible, many names are needed to serve as pointers to the divine essence and to prevent the transformation of any one symbol into an idol.

Although Johnson gave significant place to the immanent Trinity, concern for the freedom of the eternal God was even more pronounced in

Hans Urs von Balthasar's work. The primacy of the immanent Trinity in his proposal arose out of his contention, paralleling that of Zizioulas, that being is communion, or, more specifically, it is trinitarian love. As a consequence, he was quite willing to speak about an inner life of God. According to Balthasar, the divine life consists of the pure devotion or love; it characterizes the three trinitarian persons, as each person desires and enhances the glory of the others. What is true eternally, Balthasar added, is likewise present within the created order, a connection that he found evident in each of the classical transcendentals: beauty, goodness, and truth. In keeping with this overarching perspective, Balthasar characterized salvation history as a divine drama involving all three persons of the Trinity. Moreover, drawing from Barth's christocentric trinitarianism, he saw at the heart of this drama the Jesus story, especially the kenotic events of Good Friday, Holy Saturday, and Resurrection Sunday, which, he added, arise out of a "super-*kenosis*" within the eternal divine life. Balthasar's relational conception of personhood opened the way for him to suggest that the events of the theo-drama likewise affect the life of the eternal God, albeit in a manner that is made possible by the super-*kenosis* that already characterizes the divine life in eternity.

As evident as it may be in Balthasar's work, the return of the immanent Trinity was most pronounced in Thomas F. Torrance's proposal, who also drew from Barth's christocentric focus, even if he put it to a quite different use than Balthasar did. Torrance's trinitarianism was closely connected to his interest in the construction of a scientific theology, which in his estimation arises in that the nature of the reality known (that is, God) prescribes the mode by which it is known. Torrance was convinced that human knowing, and especially theological knowledge, emerges out of God's self-disclosure. This divine revelation is found above all in Christ and is mediated by the Spirit, by means of whom humans come to participate in God's own eternal, trinitarian self-knowledge. His understanding of the epistemological dynamic led Torrance to conclude that knowledge of God begins with experience (more specifically, participation in the life of the church), it then rises to reflection on the economic Trinity, and it leads finally to conclusions about God in eternity (the immanent Trinity). According to Torrance, the relationality inherent in the eternal God provides the transcendent basis for speaking about human personhood and communion.

"Trinitarian thought is fluid," Ted Peters quipped in 1993.[2] At no time in history has this fluidity been more in evidence than in the decades that lie immediately behind us. Not content to stop with mere observation, however, Peters then went on to applaud the vibrant character of trinitarian theology: "It must remain ongoing," he explained. "It is *theologia viatorum*—that is, theology on the way—because it is aware that it points to, rather than possesses, the truth of a dynamic God. . . . The paradoxical nature of the initial problematic, combined with the ongoing work of the Holy Spirit, cannot leave us completely satisfied with past conceptualizations. . . . We need to feel free to return on occasion to the drawing board."[3] The spirit that Peters expressed was a major factor that sparked the twentieth-century rediscovery of the doctrine of the Trinity. Although the flurry of proposals seems to have begun to subside, as trinitarian thinkers turned their attention toward other endeavors, the work itself is not over.

As the preceding story indicates, the golden thread that weaves its way throughout a century of trinitarian theological renewal is the question as to how theology can conceptualize the relationship between God-in-eternity and God-in-salvation in a manner that both takes seriously the importance of the latter to the former and avoids collapsing the former into the latter or compromises the freedom of the eternal God. If the twentieth-century conversation reached any point of consensus regarding this issue, it is that any truly helpful explication of the doctrine of the Trinity must give epistemological priority to the presence of the trinitarian members in the divine economy but reserve ontological primacy for the dynamic of their relationality within the triune life. This apparent consensus raises, in turn, the deeper metaphysical question that has likewise reappeared sometimes explicitly and at other times merely implicitly throughout the previous century: What kind of ontology will facilitate this theological objective? And the provisional answer to which the story of the rediscovery of the triune God in the twentieth century points is: an ontology that is thoroughly eschatological and communal. James J. Buckley and David S. Yeago hinted at this latter aspect, when at the turn of the new millennium they declared, "Knowing the triune God is inseparable from participating in a particular community and its practices—a participation which is the work of God's Holy Spirit."[4] The development of just such an ontology remains an ongoing task that demands a continual returning to the drawing board.

Rather than a situation to be bemoaned, the never-ending character of theology that drives its practitioners back to the drawing board is actually a great strength of the discipline. In the end, it is the Holy Spirit who continually leads us, in order to spark in us new ways in which to imagine and to articulate the central aspects of the Christian understanding of God. As theologians return repeatedly to the drawing board and thereby commit themselves to participating in the task of understanding anew the great central hallmark of the Christian tradition—the triunity of the God we serve—trinitarian theology can continue to fulfill the practical intent that lies at its very heart. Thereby trinitarian theology can continue—in the words that Robert Wilken penned in 1982—to reach "to the deepest recesses of the soul" and help us "know the majesty of God's presence and the mystery of his love."[5]

Notes

Introduction: The Trinitarian Theological Story

1. Ted Peters, *God as Trinity: Relationality and Temporality in the Divine Life* (Louisville: Westminster John Knox, 1993), 7.

2. David S. Cunningham, *These Three Are One: The Practice of Trinitarian Theology* (Cambridge, Mass.: Blackwell, 1998), 19.

3. Claude Welch, *In This Name: The Doctrine of the Trinity in Contemporary Theology* (New York: Scribner's, 1952), viii–ix.

4. See, for example, several of the essays in *The Trinity in a Pluralistic Age: Theological Essays on Culture and Religion*, ed. Kevin J. Vanhoozer (Grand Rapids: Eerdmans, 1997).

5. See, for example, A. Okechukwu Ogbonnaya, *On Communitarian Divinity: An African Interpretation of the Trinity* (St. Paul: Paragon House, 1994).

6. Examples include Jung Young Lee, *The Trinity in Asian Perspective* (Nashville: Abingdon, 1996); Nozomu Miyahira, *Towards a Theology of the Concord of God: A Japanese Perspective on the Trinity* (Carlisle, U.K.: Paternoster, 2000).

7. Amy Plantinga Pauw, *The Supreme Harmony of All: The Trinitarian Theology of Jonathan Edwards* (Grand Rapids: Eerdmans, 2002), 192.

8. Robert W. Jenson, "Karl Barth," in *The Modern Theologians: An Introduction to Christian Theology in the Twentieth Century,* ed. David F. Ford, 2nd ed. (Cambridge, Mass.: Blackwell, 1997), 31.

9. See, for example, my own work on the topic of the *imago dei:* Stanley J. Grenz, *The Social God and the Relational Self: A Trinitarian Theology of the Imago Dei* (Louisville: Westminster John Knox, 2001).

10. An important example is Miroslav Volf, *After Our Likeness: The Church as the Image of the Trinity* (Grand Rapids: Eerdmans, 1998).

11. For a helpful example, see Samuel M. Powell, *Participating in God: Creation and Trinity* (Minneapolis: Fortress Press, 2003).

12. For one of the most creative offerings, see Cunningham, *These Three Are One.*

13. An example is Kevin Giles, *The Trinity and Subordinationism: The Doctrine of God and the Contemporary Gender Debate* (Downers Grove, Ill.: InterVarsity, 2002).

14. See, for example, Paul S. Fiddes, *Participating in God: A Pastoral Doctrine of the Trinity* (Louisville: Westminster John Knox, 2000).

15. Edmund J. Fortman, *The Triune God: A Historical Study of the Doctrine of the Trinity* (Philadelphia: Westminster, 1972), xv.

1. The Eclipse of Trinitarian Theology

1. John P. Whalen and Jaroslav Pelikan, "General Editors' Foreword," in Edmund J. Fortman, *The Triune God: A Historical Study of the Doctrine of the Trinity* (Philadelphia: Westminster, 1972), xiii.

2. Whalen and Pelikan, "General Editors' Foreword," xiii.

3. Fortman, *Triune God*, 35.

4. Paul Tillich, *A History of Christian Thought: From Its Judaic and Hellenistic Origins to Existentialism*, ed. Carl Braaten (New York: Simon & Schuster, 1968), 61–79.

5. See "The Creed of Nicaea," in *Documents of the Christian Church*, ed. Henry Bettenson, 2nd ed. (London: Oxford University Press, 1963), 24.

6. J. N. D. Kelly, *Early Christian Doctrines*, rev. ed. (San Francisco: Harper & Row, 1978), 259.

7. Kelly, *Early Christian Doctrines*, 256.

8. See "The Constantinopolitan Creed," in *Creeds of the Churches: A Reader in Christian Doctrine from the Bible to the Present*, ed. John H. Leith, 3rd ed. (Atlanta: John Knox, 1982), 33.

9. Kelly, *Early Christian Doctrines*, 258.

10. For a short discussion of this, see Millard J. Erikson, *Christian Theology*, 3 vols. (Grand Rapids: Baker, 1983–1985), 1:335–37.

11. Colin Gunton, *The Promise of Trinitarian Theology*, 2nd ed. (Edinburgh: T. & T. Clark, 1997), 39.

12. For a discussion of the development of the Trinity in Eastern thought, see Jaroslav Pelikan, *The Spirit of Eastern Christendom (600–1700)* (Chicago: University of Chicago Press, 1974).

13. For a discussion of these differences, see Kelly, *Early Christian Doctrines*, 3–28.

14. Cyril C. Richardson, "The Enigma of the Trinity," in *A Companion to the Study of St. Augustine*, ed. Roy Battenhouse (Oxford: Oxford University Press, 1955), 248–55.

15. Augustine, *On the Trinity* 8.10.14, trans. Arthur West Haddon, vol. 3, first series of *The Nicene and Post-Nicene Fathers* (hereafter *NPNF*), reprint ed. (Grand Rapids: Eerdmans, 1980), 124.

16. Augustine, *On the Trinity* 14.12.15 (*NPNF*, 191).

17. Augustine, *Confessions* 13.11.12, trans. R. S. Pine-Coffin (New York: Penguin, 1961), 318–19.

18. Fortman, *Triune God*, 141.

19. "The Nicaean-Constantinopolitan Creed," in Kelly, *Early Christian Doctrines*, 26.

20. The logic of Augustine's position is presented in Kelly, *Early Christian Doctrines*, 275.

21. For a discussion of the importance of these events, see Philip Schaff, *History of the Christian Church* (New York: Scribner's, 1899), 4:481–84.

22. Kenneth Scott Latourette, *A History of Christianity* (New York: Harper & Brothers, 1953), 304, 360.

23. Justo L. Gonzalez, *The Story of Christianity*, vol. 1: *The Early Church to the Dawn of the Reformation* (San Francisco: Harper & Row, 1984), 264–65.

24. For a similar characterization, see Fortman, *Triune God*, xx.

25. John R. Loeschen, *The Divine Community: Trinity, Church, and Ethics in Reformation Theologies* (Kirksville, Mo.: Sixteenth Century Journal, 1981), 17.

26. Roger E. Olson and Christopher A. Hall, *The Trinity*, Guides to Theology (Grand Rapids: Eerdmans, 2002), 55.

27. For a similar judgment, see Robert S. Franks, *The Doctrine of the Trinity* (London: Duckworth, 1953), 132.

28. Fortman, *Triune God*, 191. For a concise statement regarding Richard's influence in the twentieth century, see Gary D. Badcock, "Richard of St. Victor," in *The Dictionary of Historical Theology*, ed. Trevor A. Hart (Grand Rapids: Eerdmans, 2000), 488–89.

29. Grover A. Zinn, "Introduction," in *Richard of St. Victor*, ed. Grover A. Zinn, *The Classics of Western Spirituality* (New York: Paulist, 1979), 46.

30. Badcock, "Richard of St. Victor," 489; Olson and Hall, *Trinity*, 57.

31. Richard of St. Victor, *The Trinity* 3.2-3, 14-15, in *Richard of St. Victor*, 374–76, 387–89.

32. Gunton, *Promise of Trinitarian Theology*, 92.

33. Fortman, *Triune God*, 191.

34. Fortman, *Triune God*, 234.

35. Olson and Hall, *Trinity*, 64.

36. Thomas Aquinas, *Summa Theologica* 1a, 32, 1 ad 2, trans. The Fathers of the English Dominican Province, 5 vols. (1911; reprint, Westminster, Md.: Christian Classics, 1981), 1:168–70. In his *Summa Contra Gentiles* 1.3.2, Aquinas ranked the truth that God is triune among the theological truths that "exceed all the ability of the human reason." Thomas Aquinas, *On the Truth of the Catholic Faith: Summa Contra Gentiles, Book One: God*, trans. Anton C. Pegis (Garden City, N.Y.: Image, 1955), 63.

37. Thomas Aquinas, *Summa Theologica* 1a, 27 (1:147–51).

38. Thomas Aquinas, *Summa Theologica* 1a, 28, 4 (1:154–55). This characterization of Aquinas's argument is drawn from Catherine Mowry LaCugna, *God for Us: The Trinity and Christian Life* (San Francisco: HarperSanFrancisco, 1991), 154.

39. Fortman, *Triune God,* 206.

40. For a defense of Aquinas, see David S. Cunningham, *These Three Are One: The Practice of Trinitarian Theology* (Cambridge, Mass.: Blackwell, 1998), 33.

41. Karl Rahner, *The Trinity,* trans. Joseph Donceel (New York: Crossroad, 1997), 16–17. For a similar critique, see LaCugna, *God for Us,* 145.

42. In 1928 the Anglican theologian K. E. Kirk swam against the rising tide in declaring regarding Augustine's proposal, "So far from being 'unfortunate,' it was a flight of inspired genius" (reprinted as K. E. Kirk, "The Evolution of the Doctrine of the Trinity," in *Essays on the Trinity and the Incarnation,* ed. A. E. J. Rawlinson [London: Longman, Green, 1933], 237).

43. John B. Cobb Jr., "The Relativization of the Trinity," in *Trinity in Process: A Relational Theology of God,* ed. Joseph A. Bracken and Marjorie Hewitt Suchocki (New York: Continuum, 1997), 5.

44. See, for example, LaCugna, *God for Us,* 12.

45. Franks, *Doctrine of the Trinity,* 142.

46. Thomas à Kempis, *The Imitation of Christ* 1.1.3, ed. Harold C. Gardner, Image Books (New York: Doubleday, 1989), 31.

47. Philipp Melanchthon, introduction to the first edition of his *Loci Theologici* (1521). For a sympathetic appraisal of Melanchthon's omission of the doctrine of the Trinity in this work, see Samuel M. Powell, *The Trinity in German Thought* (Cambridge: Cambridge University Press, 2001), 17.

48. For this judgment, see Loeschen, *Divine Community,* 17–18.

49. For this judgment, see Claude Welch, *In This Name: The Doctrine of the Trinity in Contemporary Theology* (New York: Scribner's, 1952), viii.

50. Hence Holsten Fagerberg, *Die Theologie der lutherischen Bekenntnisschriften von 1529 bis 1537* (Göttingen: Vandenhoeck & Ruprecht, 1965), 116, 120; Regin Prenter, *Spiritus Creator,* trans. John M. Jensen (Philadelphia: Muhlenberg, 1953), 176, 180; Reiner Janson, *Studien zu Luthers Trinitätslehre,* Basler und Berner Studien zur historischen und systematischen Theologie 26, ed. Max Geigner and Andreas Lindt (Frankfurt: Peter Lang, 1976), 84–85, 223–24.

51. Faustus Socinus, *Racovian Catechism* qq. 21–23, as cited in Fortman, *Triune God,* 244.

52. For a summary of the discussion, see John Hunt, *Religious Thought in England from the Reformation to the End of the Last Century: A Contribution to the History of Theology,* 3 vols. (London: Strahan, 1873), 2:203–12.

53. For a similar judgment, see Powell, *Trinity in German Thought,* 61.

54. For this judgment, see, for example, Jaroslav Pelikan, *From Luther to Kierkegaard* (St. Louis: Concordia, 1950), 97.

55. Charles Hodge, for example, devoted a scant four pages to the doctrine in a magnum opus that runs three volumes and nearly 2,300 pages and that David Wells once hailed as "a summary of nineteenth-century evangelical faith" ("The Stout and Persistent 'Theology' of Charles Hodge," *Christianity Today* 18/23 [August 30, 1974]: 10). Hodge's treatment of the doctrine of the Trinity is slightly shorter than the chapter in which he refutes mysticism.

56. Stephen Sykes, *Friedrich Schleiermacher,* Makers of Contemporary Theology (Atlanta: John Knox, 1971), 49–51.

57. B. A. Gerrish, *A Prince of the Church: Schleiermacher and the Beginnings of Modern Theology* (Philadelphia: Fortress Press, 1984), 20.

58. Richard R. Niebuhr, *Schleiermacher on Christ and Religion* (London: SCM, 1965), 6.

59. For this common designation, see C. W. Christian, *Friedrich Schleiermacher,* Makers of the Modern Theological Mind (Waco, Tex.: Word, 1979), 11.

60. Robert R. Williams, *Schleiermacher the Theologian: The Construction of the Doctrine of God* (Philadelphia: Fortress Press, 1978), 1.

61. For an influential statement of this position originally published in 1937, see H. R. Mackintosh, *Types of Modern Theology: Schleiermacher to Barth* (New York: Scribner's, n.d.), 11. A more recent restatement of the critique is found in Roger E. Olson, *The Story of Christian Theology: Twenty Centuries of Tradition and Reform* (Downers Grove, Ill.: InterVarsity, 1999), 545. See also William J. Hill, *The Three-Personed God: The Trinity as a Mystery of Salvation* (Washington, D.C.: Catholic University of America Press, 1982), 84.

62. Karl Barth, *The Theology of Schleiermacher,* ed. Dietrich Ritschl, trans. Geoffrey W. Bromiley (Grand Rapids: Eerdmans, 1982), 192.

63. Welch, *In This Name,* 9. For a similar judgment, see Niebuhr, *Schleiermacher on Christ and Religion,* 155.

64. Ted Peters, *God as Trinity: Relationality and Temporality in Divine Life* (Louisville: Westminster John Knox, 1993), 85.

65. For this judgment, see, for example, Richard R. Niebuhr, *Schleiermacher on Christ and Religion* (London: SCM, 1964), 6–13. See also Powell, *Trinity in German Thought,* 88–90.

66. For the discussion that may well have set the tone for a more positive engagement with Schleiermacher's doctrine of the Trinity, see Robert R. Williams, *Schleiermacher the Theologian: The Construction of the Doctrine of God* (Philadelphia: Fortress Press, 1978), 139–59.

67. For a helpful discussion of Schleiermacher's relationship to early Romanticism and the "neo-Spinozism" associated with this movement, see Julia A. Lamm,

The Living God: Schleiermacher's Theological Appropriation of Spinoza (University Park: Pennsylvania State University Press, 1996).

68. Terrence N. Tice, "Introduction," in Friedrich Schleiermacher, *On Religion: Addresses in Response to its Cultured Critics*, trans. Terrence N. Tice (Richmond: John Knox, 1969), 12.

69. Tice, "Introduction," 24.

70. Schleiermacher, *On Religion*, 79.

71. Friedrich Schleiermacher, *The Christian Faith*, ed. H. R. Mackintosh and J. S. Stewart (Edinburgh: T. & T. Clark, n.d.), 12–18.

72. Tillich, *History of Christian Thought*, 392.

73. Martin Redeker, *Schleiermacher: Life and Thought*, trans. John Wallhausser (Philadelphia: Fortress Press, 1973), 39.

74. Schleiermacher's discussion of the "Essence of Religion" is found in *On Religion*, 67–176.

75. Keith W. Clements, *Friedrich Schleiermacher: A Pioneer of Modern Theology* (London: Collins, 1987), 24.

76. Tice, "Introduction," 12. See also Redeker, *Schleiermacher*, 48.

77. Schleiermacher, *Christian Faith*, 76.

78. Redeker, *Schleiermacher*, 102. For a similar judgment, see H. R. Mackintosh and J. S. Stewart, "Editors' Preface," in Schleiermacher, *Christian Faith*, v.

79. Schleiermacher, *Christian Faith*, 98.

80. See Schleiermacher, *Christian Faith*, 81, 92, 123–25.

81. Schleiermacher, *Christian Faith*, 194.

82. Schleiermacher, *Christian Faith*, 200.

83. Schleiermacher, *Christian Faith*, 751.

84. Schleiermacher, *Christian Faith*, 738.

85. Powell, *Trinity in German Thought*, 94.

86. Tillich, *History of Christian Thought*, 408.

87. Gerhard Spiegler, *The Eternal Covenant: Schleiermacher's Experiment in Cultural Theology*, ed. Jaroslav Pelikan, Makers of Modern Theology (New York: Harper & Row, 1967), 180.

88. Schleiermacher, *Christian Faith*, 739.

89. Franks, *Doctrine of the Trinity*, 168.

90. Friedrich Schleiermacher, *Die christliche Glaube* (1822), 190.2, as reprinted in *Friedrich Schleiermacher und die Trinitätslehre*, ed. Martin Tetz, *Texte zur Kirchen- und Theologiegeschichte* 11, ed. Gerhard Ruhhach (Gütersloh: Gütersloher Verlagshaus, 1969), 21. Translation mine.

91. Schleiermacher, *Christian Faith*, 738.

92. Friedrich Schleiermacher, "Über den Gegensatz zwischen der Sabellianischen und der Athanazianisched Vorstellung von der Trinität," in *Friedrich Schleiermacher und die Trinitätslehre*, 88. Translation mine.

93. Schleiermacher, *Christian Faith*, 739.

94. Williams, *Schleiermacher the Theologian*, 153.

95. For a somewhat similar conclusion, see Powell, *Trinity in German Thought*, 103.

96. Franks, *Doctrine of the Trinity*, 163.

97. For a similar judgment, see Spiegler, *Eternal Covenant*, 126.

98. Spiegler, *Eternal Covenant*, 183. For a rejection of Spiegler's critique, see Powell, *Trinity in German Thought*, 88–89.

99. Karl Barth, *The Word of God and the Word of Man*, trans. Douglas Horton (New York: Harper, 1957), 195–96. Although Barth later tempered his outlook toward Schleiermacher, he never abandoned his suspicion that his predecessor's theology was built on an anthropological starting point. See, for example, his "Concluding Unscientific Postscript on Schleiermacher," in Barth, *Theology of Schleiermacher*, 271–72.

100. For a similar judgment, see Walter Kasper, *The God of Jesus Christ*, trans. Matthew J. O'Connell (New York: Crossroad, 1984), 264.

101. Franks, *Doctrine of the Trinity*, 160.

102. For this opinion, see Claude Welch, *Protestant Thought in the Nineteenth Century*, volume 1, *1799–1870* (New Haven: Yale University Press, 1972), 90.

103. For this judgment, see Franks, *Doctrine of the Trinity*, 160.

104. See, for example, the helpful characterization in William Young, *Hegel's Dialectical Method: Its Origins and Religious Significance* (Nutley, N.J.: Craig, 1972), 9.

105. Georg Wilhelm Friedrich Hegel, *The Science of Logic*, 2 vols., trans. W. H. Johnston and L. G. Struthers (London: George Allen and Unwin, 1929), 2:477.

106. Horst Althaus, *Hegel: An Intellectual Biography*, trans. Michael Tarsh (Cambridge: Polity, 2000), 132.

107. Georg Wilhelm Friedrich Hegel, *Philosophy of Right*, trans. T. M. Knox (London: Oxford University Press, 1967), 10.

108. Althaus, *Hegel*, 127.

109. Emil L. Fackenheim, *The Religious Dimension in Hegel's Thought* (Chicago: University of Chicago Press, 1967), 98.

110. Fackenheim, *Religious Dimension in Hegel's Thought*, 98.

111. Fackenheim, *Religious Dimension in Hegel's Thought*, 20.

112. G. W. F. Hegel, *The Phenomenology of Mind*, trans. J. B. Baillie (New York: Harper & Row, 1967), 807–8. See also his poetic statement, p. 91.

113. George Lichtheim, "Introduction," in Hegel, *Phenomenology of Mind*, xxvi.

114. For a similar judgment, see Fackenheim, *Religious Dimension in Hegel's Thought*, 22.

115. Hans Küng, *The Incarnation of God: An Introduction to Hegel's Thought as Prolegomena to a Future Christology*, trans. J. R. Stephenson (New York: Crossroad, 1987), 362.

116. G. W. F. Hegel, *Lectures on the Philosophy of Religion*, ed. Peter C. Hodgson, trans. R. F. Brown, P. C. Hodgson, and J. M. Stewart, 3 vols. (Berkeley: University of California Press, 1984–1985), 3:247. Cf. G. W. F. Hegel, *Lectures on the Philosophy of Religion, Together with a Work on the Proofs of the Existence of God*, trans. E. B. Speirs and J. Burdon Sanderson, 3 vols. (London: Kegan Paul, Trench, Trübner, 1895), 3:151.

117. Hegel, *Lectures on the Philosophy of Religion* (Hodgson edition), 1:152–53. Cf. Hegel, *Lectures on the Philosophy of Religion* (Speirs and Sanderson translation), 1:19–20.

118. For a discussion of this point, see Tillich, *History of Christian Thought*, 424.

119. Powell, *Trinity in German Thought*, 108.

120. Hegel, *Lectures on the Philosophy of Religion* (Hodgson edition), 1:126–27.

121. For the suggestion of this language, see Küng, *Incarnation of God*, 277.

122. See, for example, Hegel's lecture manuscript on the philosophy of religion. Hegel, *Lectures on the Philosophy of Religion* (Hodgson edition), 3:125.

123. For a similar characterization, see Powell, *Trinity in German Thought*, 121–22.

124. John W. Burbidge, *Hegel on Logic and Religion: The Reasonableness of Christianity* (Albany: SUNY Press, 1992), 133. See also Hegel, *Encyclopedia of the Philosophical Sciences*, section 567. For an excerpt of the latter, see *G. W. F. Hegel: Theologian of the Spirit*, ed. Peter C. Hodgson (Minneapolis: Fortress Press, 1997).

125. Charles Taylor, *Hegel* (Cambridge: Cambridge University Press, 1975), 493.

126. For Hegel's understanding of the Trinity, see G. W. F. Hegel, *Philosophy of Mind: Being Part Three of the Encyclopedia of the Philosophical Sciences*, trans. William Wallace, together with the Zusätze in Boumann's Text, trans. A. V. Miller (London: Oxford University Press, 1971), Zusatz 381:12; 567:299.

127. Hegel, *Philosophy of Mind*, 564:298. Elsewhere he declares, "That Man knows God implies, in accordance with the essential idea of communion or fellowship, that there is a community of knowledge; that is to say, Man knows God only insofar as God Himself knows Himself in Man." Hegel, *Lectures on the Philosophy of Religion* (Speirs and Sanderson translation), 3:303.

128. Hegel, *Phenomenology of Mind*, 781.

129. Hegel, *Phenomenology of Mind*, 781.

130. Hegel, *Lectures on the Philosophy of Religion* (Hodgson edition), 3:220.

131. Franks, *Doctrine of the Trinity*, 161.

132. Taylor, *Hegel*, 506.

133. Welch, *In This Name*, 11.

134. Burbidge, *Hegel on Logic and Religion*, 149.

135. Fackenheim, *Religious Dimension in Hegel's Philosophy*, 8.

136. G. W. F. Hegel, *Enzyklopädie der philosophischen Wissenschaften im Grundrisse*, Vorrede zur zweiten Ausgabe [1827], in G. W. F. Hegel, *Werke in 20 Bänden* (Frankfurt am Main: Suhrkamp Verlag, 1970), 8:23. Translation mine. Online access to this volume is available at: http://www.hegel.de.

137. Powell, *Trinity in German Thought*, 140.

138. Kasper, *God of Jesus Christ*, 266.

139. For a negative expression of a similar idea, see Gerald O'Collins, *The Tripersonal God: Understanding and Interpreting the Trinity* (Mahwah, N.J.: Paulist, 1999), 154.

2. Restoring the Trinitarian Center to Theology

1. Samuel M. Powell, *The Trinity in German Thought* (Cambridge: Cambridge University Press, 2001), 174.

2. See, for example, Faye Ellen Schott, "God Is Love: The Contemporary Theological Movement of Interpreting the Trinity as God's Relational Being" (ThD diss., Lutheran School of Theology at Chicago, May, 1990), 38–65.

3. Gary Dorrien, *The Barthian Revolt in Modern Theology: Theology without Weapons* (Louisville: Westminster John Knox, 2000), 131.

4. For an example of such a judgment, see David L. Mueller, *Karl Barth*, Makers of the Modern Theological Mind (Waco, Tex.: Word, 1972), 13.

5. For a survey of recent appropriations of Barth's work, see William Stacy Johnson, "Barth and Beyond: Making Grace Real," *Christian Century* 118/14 (May 2, 2001): 16–20.

6. Representative examples of recent treatises include, in addition to Dorrien's *Barthian Revolt*, George Hunsinger, *How to Read Karl Barth: The Shape of His Theology* (New York: Oxford University Press, 1991); George Hunsinger, *Disruptive Grace: Studies in the Theology of Karl Barth* (Grand Rapids: Eerdmans, 2000); and Bruce L. McCormack, *Karl Barth's Critically Realistic Dialectical Theology: Its Genesis and Development 1909–1936* (New York: Oxford University Press, 1995). For an example of a more topic-specific treatment, see Daniel J. Price, *Karl Barth's Anthropology in Light of Modern Thought* (Grand Rapids: Eerdmans, 2002).

7. For example, Neil B. MacDonald, *Karl Barth and the Strange New World within the Bible* (Carlisle, U.K.: Paternoster, 2000).

8. Hence, William Stacy Johnson, *The Mystery of God: Karl Barth and the Postmodern Foundations of Theology* (Louisville: Westminster John Knox, 1997); and Graham Ward, *Barth, Derrida and the Language of Theology* (Cambridge: Cambridge University Press, 1995).

9. See the interesting judgment in Jenson, "Karl Barth," 25.

10. John Webster, "Introducing Barth," in *The Cambridge Companion to Karl Barth*, ed. John Webster (Cambridge: Cambridge University Press, 2000), 1.

11. Robert W. Jenson, "Karl Barth," in *The Modern Theologians: An Introduction to Christian Theology in the Twentieth Century*, ed. David F. Ford, 2 vols. (New York: Blackwell, 1989), 1:47.

12. Claude Welch, *In This Name: The Doctrine of the Trinity in Contemporary Theology* (New York: Scribner's, 1952), 46.

13. Helpful attempts to offer summaries of Barth's magnum opus include Otto Weber, *Karl Barth's Church Dogmatics: An Introductory Report on Volumes I:1 to III:4*, trans. Arthur C. Cochrane (Philadelphia: Westminster, 1953); and Geoffrey W. Bromiley, *An Introduction to the Theology of Karl Barth* (Grand Rapids: Eerdmans, 1979).

14. See, for example, Mueller, *Karl Barth*, 51.

15. For a helpful argument that Schleiermacher also started with revelation as an ongoing act of God and hence that Barth and Schleiermacher were not in fact as far apart as is generally supposed, see Bruce L. McCormack, "What Has Basel to Do with Berlin? Continuities in the Theologies of Barth and Schleiermacher," *Princeton Seminary Bulletin* 23/2 (2002): 146–73.

16. See, for example, Karl Barth, *Church Dogmatics* I/1, ed. G. W. Bromiley and T. F. Torrance, trans. G. W. Bromiley, 2nd ed. (Edinburgh: T. & T. Clark, 1975), 242.

17. McCormack, *Karl Barth's Critically Realistic Dialectical Theology*, 9. Here McCormack is summarizing the findings of Ingrid Spieckermann, *Gotteserkenntnis: Ein Beitrag zur Grundfrage der neuen Theologie Karl Barths*, Beiträge zur evangelischen Theologie 97 (Munich: Chr. Kaiser, 1985), 72–82.

18. Trevor Hart, "Revelation," in *The Cambridge Companion to Karl Barth*, 50.

19. Barth, *Church Dogmatics* I/1, 56, 70.

20. Barth, *Church Dogmatics* I/1, 4.

21. Barth, *Church Dogmatics* I/1, 250.

22. Karl Barth, *Church Dogmatics* I/2, *The Doctrine of the Word of God*, second half-volume, ed. G. W. Bromiley and T. F. Torrance, trans. G. T. Thomson and Harold Knight (Edinburgh: T. & T. Clark, 1956), 777.

23. Barth, *Church Dogmatics* I/1, 25.

24. Barth, *Church Dogmatics* I/1, 196.

25. Barth, *Church Dogmatics* I/1, 222.

26. For a nontechnical overview of Barth's concept of the Word of God written from a Roman Catholic perspective, see Jerome Hamer, *Karl Barth*, trans. Dominic M. Maruca (Westminster, Md.: Newman, 1962).

27. Barth, *Church Dogmatics* I/1, 120.

28. Barth, *Church Dogmatics* I/1, 264.

29. Barth, *Church Dogmatics* I/2.

30. Barth, *Church Dogmatics* I/1, 137.

31. Karl Barth, *Church Dogmatics* II/1, *The Doctrine of God*, ed. G. W. Bromiley and T. F. Torrance, trans. T. H. L. Parker, W. B. Johnson, Harold Knight, and J. L. M. Haire (Edinburgh: T. & T. Clark, 1957), 302–3.

32. Barth, *Church Dogmatics* I/1, 121.

33. Dorrien, *Barthian Revolt*, 78.

34. Barth, *Church Dogmatics* I/1, 291.

35. Barth, *Church Dogmatics* I/1, 306, 314.

36. Barth, *Church Dogmatics* I/1, 306.

37. See, for example, Barth, *Church Dogmatics* I/1, 299.

38. Barth, *Church Dogmatics* I/1, 296.

39. Barth, *Church Dogmatics* I/1, 315.

40. For this nomenclature, see Bromiley, *Introduction to the Theology of Karl Barth*, 14.

41. Barth, *Church Dogmatics* I/1, 353.

42. Barth, *Church Dogmatics* I/1, 363.

43. Eberhard Jüngel, *God's Being Is in Becoming: The Trinitarian Being of God in the Theology of Karl Barth, A Paraphrase*, trans. John Webster (Grand Rapids: Eerdmans, 2001), 27, 29.

44. G. W. Bromiley and T. F. Torrance, "Editors' Preface," in Barth, *Church Dogmatics* I/1, ix.

45. Peters, *God as Trinity*, 82.

46. Barth, *Church Dogmatics* I/2, 362.

47. Barth, *Church Dogmatics* I/2, 1.

48. Barth, *Church Dogmatics* I/2, 33.

49. Barth, *Church Dogmatics* I/1, 376.

50. Barth, *Church Dogmatics* I/1, 385.

51. Barth, *Church Dogmatics* II/1, 262.

52. Barth, *Church Dogmatics* I/1, 351–53.

53. Jüngel, *God's Being Is in Becoming*, 36.

54. Barth, *Church Dogmatics* I/1, 158; cf. Barth, *Church Dogmatics* II/1, 257, 260.

55. Barth, *Church Dogmatics* I/1, 158, 499.

56. Barth, *Church Dogmatics* I/1, 191.

57. Barth, *Church Dogmatics* I/1, 350–51.

58. Barth, *Church Dogmatics* II/1, 297.

59. Barth, *Church Dogmatics* I/1, 355.

60. Barth, *Church Dogmatics* I/1, 393.

61. Barth, *Church Dogmatics* I/1, 406.

62. Barth, *Church Dogmatics* I/1, 413.

63. Barth, *Church Dogmatics* I/1, 414.

64. Barth, *Church Dogmatics* I/1, 416.

65. Barth, *Church Dogmatics* I/1, 433.

66. Barth, *Church Dogmatics* I/1, 434.

67. Barth, *Church Dogmatics* I/1, 434.

68. Barth, *Church Dogmatics* I/1, 436.

69. Barth, *Church Dogmatics* I/1, 456.

70. Barth, *Church Dogmatics* I/1, 451.

71. Barth, *Church Dogmatics* I/1, 459.

72. Barth, *Church Dogmatics* I/1, 466.

73. Barth, *Church Dogmatics* I/1, 466, 467.

74. Barth, *Church Dogmatics* I/1, 479.

75. Barth, *Church Dogmatics* I/1, 480–81.

76. Barth, *Church Dogmatics* I/1, 483.

77. See, for example, Mueller, *Karl Barth*, 40.

78. That this view is commonplace is evident in the offhanded remark in James Brown, *Subject and Object in Modern Theology*, Croall Lectures of 1953 (London: SCM, 1955), 86.

79. See Hans Urs von Balthasar, *The Theology of Karl Barth: Exposition and Interpretation*, trans. Edward T. Oakes (San Francisco: Ignatius, 1992), 59–113.

80. McCormack, *Karl Barth's Critically Realistic Dialectical Theology*, 22.

81. McCormack, *Karl Barth's Critically Realistic Dialectical Theology*, 461–62.

82. Barth, *Church Dogmatics* II/1, 257.

83. See Barth, *Church Dogmatics* II/1, 299, 301, 321.

84. Barth, *Church Dogmatics* II/1, 262.

85. Barth, *Church Dogmatics* II/1, 264.

86. Eberhard Jüngel, *Karl Barth: A Theological Legacy*, trans. Garrett E. Paul (Philadelphia: Westminster, 1986), 19.

87. Barth, *Church Dogmatics* II/1, 179.

88. Barth, *Church Dogmatics* II/1, 49.

89. Barth, *Church Dogmatics* II/1, 49.

90. Barth, *Church Dogmatics* II/1, 214.

91. Barth, *Church Dogmatics* II/1, 229.

92. Johnson, *Mystery of God*, 52.

93. Barth, *Church Dogmatics* I/1, 383.

94. Webster, "Introducing Barth," 11.

95. Welch, *In This Name*, 165.

96. For this phrase as well as a response to the two central criticisms of Barth's proposal at this point, see Alan Torrance, "The Trinity," in *Cambridge Companion to Karl Barth*, 76–78.

97. Barth's purported debt to Hegel has been discussed by a variety of authors. See, for example, Horst George Pohlmann, *Analogia entis oder Analogia fidei? Die Frage der Analogie bei Karl Barth* (Göttingen: Vandenhoeck & Ruprecht, 1965).

See also Rowan D. Williams, "Barth on the Triune God," in *Karl Barth: Studies of His Theological Method,* ed. Stephen W. Sykes (Oxford: Clarendon, 1979), 188; Alan Torrance, *Persons in Communion: An Essay on Trinitarian Description and Human Participation* (Edinburgh: T. & T. Clark, 1996), 244–48.

98. Wolfhart Pannenberg, *Systematic Theology,* trans. Geoffrey W. Bromiley, 3 vols. (Grand Rapids: Eerdmans, 1991–1998), 1:296. For his sustained critique of Barth, see Wolfhart Pannenberg, *Grundfragen systematischer Theologie* (Göttingen: Vandenhoeck & Ruprecht, 1980), 2:96–111.

99. Catherine Mowry LaCugna, *God for Us: The Trinity and the Christian Life* (San Francisco: HarperCollins, 1992), 252.

100. See, for example, Barth, *Church Dogmatics* I/1, 355–60.

101. S. Paul Schilling, *Contemporary Continental Theologians* (Nashville: Abingdon, 1966), 36.

102. See, for example, Barth, *Church Dogmatics* I/1, 350.

103. Hunsinger, *Disruptive Grace,* 190–91.

104. Williams, "Barth on the Triune God," 165.

105. Barth, *Church Dogmatics* I/1, 320.

106. Barth, *Church Dogmatics* I/1, 324.

107. Hunsinger, *Disruptive Grace,* 191; see also Bromiley, *Introduction to the Theology of Karl Barth,* 16.

108. See, for example, Jürgen Moltmann, *Theology of Hope: On the Ground and the Implications of a Christian Eschatology,* trans. James W. Leith (Minneapolis: Fortress Press, 1993), 55–56.

109. Karl Barth, *Dogmatics in Outline,* trans. G. E. Thomson (1949; reprint, New York: Harper & Row, 1959), 134–35, as cited in Moltmann, *Theology of Hope,* 228.

110. Mueller, *Karl Barth,* 153.

111. Ward, *Barth, Derrida and the Language of Theology,* 14.

112. Barth, *Church Dogmatics* I/2, 878.

113. Barth, *Church Dogmatics* I/2, 879.

114. Jenson, "Karl Barth," 42.

115. For a fuller explication of this assertion that acknowledges the positive contribution of Barth, see Stanley J. Grenz and John R. Franke, *Beyond Foundationalism: Shaping Theology in a Postmodern Context* (Louisville: Westminster John Knox, 2001), 169–202.

116. Harvey D. Egan, *Karl Rahner: Mystic of Everyday Life* (New York: Crossroad, 1998), 19.

117. For this designation, see Karl-Heinz Weger, *Karl Rahner: An Introduction to His Theology,* trans. David Smith (New York: Seabury, 1980), 14.

118. For a helpful summary of Rahner's starting point and theological method, see William V. Dych, "Theology in a New Key," in *A World of Grace: An Introduc-*

tion to the Themes and Foundations of Karl Rahner's Theology, ed. Leo J. O'Dono-van (New York: Crossroad, 1981), 1–16. See also Anne E. Carr, "Starting with the Human," in *World of Grace*, 17–30.

119. Karl Rahner, "Some Problems in Contemporary Ecumenism," *Theological Investigations* 14, trans. David Bourke (New York: Seabury, 1976), 253.

120. *Karl Rahner in Dialogue: Conversations and Interviews, 1965–1982*, ed. Hubert Biallowons, Harvey D. Egan, and Paul Imhof (New York: Crossroad, 1986), 196.

121. Examples of one-volume overviews of Rahner's work that omit extended treatment of his understanding of the Trinity include Mary E. Hines, *The Transformation of Dogma: An Introduction to Karl Rahner on Doctrine* (Mahwah, N.J.: Paulist, 1989); Herbert Vorgrimler, *Understanding Karl Rahner: An Introduction to His Life and Thought*, trans. John Bowden (New York: Crossroad, 1986); Weger, *Karl Rahner*. Furthermore, Carr's short essay on Rahner's thought makes almost no mention of the doctrine of the Trinity. Anne Carr, "Karl Rahner," in *A New Handbook of Christian Theologians*, ed. Donald W. Musser and Joseph L. Price (Nashville: Abingdon, 1996), 375–86.

122. Egan, *Karl Rahner*, 10.

123. William V. Dych, *Karl Rahner* (Collegeville, Minn.: Liturgical, 1992), 148.

124. Yves M. J. Congar, *I Believe in the Holy Spirit*, trans. David Smith, 3 vols. (New York: Seabury, 1983), 3:11.

125. J. A. DiNoia, "Karl Rahner," in *Modern Theologians*, 1:197.

126. For this designation, see Ted Peters, "Trinity Talk," *Dialog* 26/1 (Winter 1987): 44–48 and 26/2 (Spring 1988): 133–38. Peters attributes the designation to Roger E. Olson. See Ted Peters, *God as Trinity: Relationality and Temporality in the Divine Life* (Louisville: Westminster John Knox, 1993), 213 n. 33.

127. Karl Rahner, *The Trinity*, trans. Joseph Donceel (New York: Crossroad, 1997), 22.

128. Walter Kasper, *The God of Jesus Christ*, trans. Matthew J. O'Connell (New York: Crossroad, 1984), 274.

129. Paul Fiddes, *Participating in God: A Pastoral Doctrine of the Trinity* (Louisville: Westminster John Knox, 2000), 6.

130. *Mysterium Salutis: Grundriss heilsgeschichtlicher Dogmatik*, ed. Johannes Feiner and Magnus Löhrer, 5 volumes in 7 (Einsiedeln, Germany: Benziger, 1965–1976).

131. Catherine Mowry LaCugna, "Introduction," in Karl Rahner, *Trinity*, viii.

132. Karl Rahner, "Oneness and Threefoldness of God in Discussion with Islam," *Theological Investigations* 18, trans. Edward Quinn (New York: Crossroad, 1983), 114.

133. F. A. Staudenmaier, *Die christliche Dogmatik* (Freiburg, 1844), 2:475, as cited in Kasper, *God of Jesus*, 274.

134. For the idea that Barth did not hold to Rahner's Rule, see Paul D. Molnar, "The Function of the Immanent Trinity in the Theology of Karl Barth: Implications for Today," *Scottish Journal of Theology* 42/3 (1989): 367–99.

135. Kasper, *God of Jesus Christ*, 273–74, citing Barth, *Church Dogmatics* I/1, 548.

136. For this judgment, see DiNoia, "Karl Rahner," 1:186.

137. Karl Rahner, *Foundations of Christian Faith. An Introduction to the Idea of Christianity*, trans. William V. Dych (New York: Seabury, 1978).

138. *Karl Rahner in Dialogue*, 147.

139. For an alternative, nonfoundationalist understanding of Rahner's theology, see Karen Kilby, "Philosophy, Theology and Foundationalism in the Thought of Karl Rahner," *Scottish Journal of Theology* 55/2 (2002): 127–40.

140. See, for example, DiNoia, "Karl Rahner," 185.

141. Carr, "Karl Rahner," 377.

142. DiNoia, "Karl Rahner," 191.

143. Joseph Donceel, "Translator's Preface," in Karl Rahner, *Hearer of the Word: Laying the Foundation for a Philosophy of Religion*, trans. Joseph Donceel, ed. Andrew Tallon (New York: Continuum, 1994), vi.

144. Rahner, *Hearer of the Word*, 66.

145. Rahner, *Hearer of the Word*, 142.

146. Rahner, *Foundations of Christian Faith*, 57–68.

147. Karl Rahner, "The Question of Meaning as a Question of God," *Theological Investigations* 21, trans. Hugh M. Riley (New York: Crossroad, 1988), 196–207. See also Karl Rahner, "The Human Question of Meaning in Face of the Absolute Mystery of God," *Theological Investigations* 18, trans. Edward Quinn (New York: Crossroad, 1983), 89–104.

148. Karl Rahner, "The Concept of Mystery in Catholic Theology," *Theological Investigations* 4, trans. Kevin Smith (New York: Crossroad, 1982), 48–60.

149. Rahner, *Foundations of Christian Faith*, 171.

150. Rahner, *Foundations of Christian Faith*, 174.

151. Rahner, *Foundations of Christian Faith*, 228.

152. Rahner, *Foundations of Christian Faith*, 224.

153. Rahner, *Foundations of Christian Faith*, 225.

154. Rahner, *Foundations of Christian Faith*, 136.

155. Rahner, "Concept of Mystery," 72–73.

156. Rahner, "Concept of Mystery," 70.

157. Karl Rahner, "Remarks on the Dogmatic Treatise 'De Trinitate,'" *Theological Investigations* 4, 97.

158. Rahner, "Remarks on the Dogmatic Treatise 'De Trinitate,'" 101.

159. Rahner, "Oneness and Threefoldness of God," 111.

160. Rahner, *Trinity*, 57.

161. Rahner, "Oneness and Threefoldness of God," 113.

162. Rahner, *Trinity*, 113.

163. Rahner, "Concept of Mystery," 70.

164. Rahner, *Trinity*, 39.

165. For a helpful summary of Rahner's engagement with Neoscholasticism, see LaCugna, "Introduction," vii–xxi.

166. For a similar judgment, see Kasper, *God of Jesus Christ*, 275.

167. Rahner, *Trinity*, 24.

168. Rahner, *Theological Investigations* 4, 69.

169. Rahner, *Trinity*, 86–87. Rahner offers a preliminary answer on pp. 87–99.

170. For his argument from the doctrine of grace, see Rahner, *Trinity*, 35–39.

171. Thomas Aquinas, *Summa Theologica* III.3.5, trans. Fathers of the English Dominican Province, 5 vols. (Westminster, Md.: Christian Classics, 1948), 4:2041–42.

172. Rahner, *Trinity*, 11. For his parallel statement regarding the Spirit, see *Trinity*, 85–86.

173. Rahner, *Trinity*, 11.

174. Rahner, *Trinity*, 28.

175. Rahner, *Trinity*, 99–101.

176. Rahner, *Theological Investigations* 4, 91–92. See also Rahner, *Trinity*, 30.

177. Rahner, *Foundations of Christian Faith*, 220.

178. Rahner, *Foundations*, 223.

179. Rahner, *Trinity*, 101–2.

180. Karl Rahner, "The Specific Character of the Christian Concept of God," *Theological Investigations* 21, 191.

181. Peters, *God as Trinity*, 96–97.

182. This is a paraphrase of the characterization offered in Egan, *Karl Rahner*, 35.

183. Peters, *God as Trinity*, 97.

184. LaCugna, "Introduction," xiv.

185. Kasper, *God of Jesus Christ*, 276.

186. Peters, *God as Trinity*, 96.

187. Eberhard Jüngel, *God as the Mystery of the World: On the Foundation of the Theology of the Crucified One in the Dispute between Theism and Atheism*, trans. Darrell L. Guder (Grand Rapids: Eerdmans, 1983), 369–70.

188. Karl Rahner, "The Theology of the Symbol," *Theological Investigations* 4, 236.

189. DiNoia, "Karl Rahner," 197–98.

190. John Thompson, *Modern Trinitarian Perspectives* (New York: Oxford University Press, 1994), 28.

191. Thompson, *Modern Trinitarian Perspectives*, 27.

192. Rahner, "Theology of the Symbol," 236–37.

193. Rahner, "Oneness and Threefoldness of God," 118.

194. Catherine Mowry LaCugna, *God for Us: The Trinity and Christian Life* (New York: HarperCollins, 1991), 213.

195. Congar, *I Believe in the Holy Spirit,* 3:13.

196. Helmut Thielicke, *The Evangelical Faith,* trans. Geoffrey W. Bromiley, 3 vols. (Grand Rapids: Eerdmans, 1974–1982), 2:181.

197. LaCugna, "Introduction," xv.

198. LaCugna, *God for Us,* 217.

199. Peters, *God as Trinity,* 102.

200. Rahner has been criticized for falling prey to several of the difficulties inherent in Hegel's proposal. See, for example, S. Paul Schilling, *Contemporary Continental Theologians* (Nashville: Abingdon, 1966), 225.

201. For an example of such an assertion made in the context of a discussion of Rahner's work, see T. F. Torrance, "Towards an Ecumenical Consensus on the Trinity," *Theologische Zeitschrift* 31/6 (1975): 347.

3. The Trinity as the Fullness of History

1. Ted Peters, *God as Trinity: Relationality and Temporality in Divine Life* (Louisville: Westminster John Knox, 1993), 82.

2. Bruno Forte, *The Trinity as History: Saga of the Christian God,* trans. Paul Rotondi (New York: Alba House, 1989).

3. In addition to his *God as Trinity,* see Ted Peters, *God—The World's Future: Systematic Theology for a Postmodern Era,* 2nd ed. (Minneapolis: Fortress Press, 2000).

4. M. Douglas Meeks, *Origins of the Theology of Hope* (Philadelphia: Fortress Press, 1974), xiii.

5. Thorward Lorenzen, "Jürgen Moltmann," in *A New Handbook of Christian Theologians,* ed. Donald W. Musser and Joseph L. Price (Nashville: Abingdon, 1996), 304.

6. Richard J. Bauckham, *Moltmann: Messianic Theology in the Making* (London: Marshall Pickering, 1987), 1.

7. Jürgen Moltmann, *Experiences in Theology: Ways and Forms of Christian Theology,* trans. Margaret Kohl (Minneapolis: Fortress Press, 2000).

8. Geiko Müller-Fahrenholz, *The Kingdom and the Power: The Theology of Jürgen Moltmann,* trans. John Bowden (Minneapolis: Fortress Press, 2000), 12.

9. Müller-Fahrenholz, *Kingdom and the Power,* 231.

10. For an acknowledgment of this criticism by a sympathetic reader of Moltmann, see Richard Bauckham, *The Theology of Jürgen Moltmann* (Edinburgh: T. & T. Clark, 1995), 25.

11. Müller-Fahrenholz, *Kingdom and the Power,* 12.

12. Jürgen Moltmann, "An Autobiographical Note," in A. J. Conyers, *God, Hope, and History: Jürgen Moltmann and the Christian Concept of History* (Macon, Ga.: Mercer University Press, 1988), 204.

13. Laurence W. Wood, "Editorial Note," *Asbury Theological Journal* 55/1 (Spring 2000): 5.

14. Bauckham, *Theology of Jürgen Moltmann*, 7.

15. This is the explicit starting point for Moltmann's central volume in trinitarian theology. See Jürgen Moltmann, *The Trinity and the Kingdom: The Doctrine of God*, trans. Margaret Kohl (Minneapolis: Fortress Press, 1993), 19.

16. Müller-Fahrenholz aptly titles his chapter on Moltmann's doctrine of the Trinity, "On Unification—The Theology of the Trinity as a Retelling of God's History of Love" (*Kingdom and the Power*, 137–52). See also Müller-Fahrenholz, *Kingdom and the Power*, 182; Meeks, *Origins of the Theology of Hope*, 37.

17. Moltmann, *Trinity and the Kingdom*, 19.

18. *Theology of Hope* was not Moltmann's first book. It was, however, the book that brought him to the attention of the wider theological world, and the volume in which he launched his theological program.

19. Jürgen Moltmann, *Theology of Hope: On the Ground and the Implications of a Christian Eschatology*, trans. James W. Leith (Minneapolis: Fortress Press, 1993).

20. For a helpful discussion of this difference between Pannenberg and Moltmann and their participation in the wider "revelation debate," see Meeks, *Origins of the Theology of Hope*, 64–80.

21. For an extended treatment of the role of promise in Moltmann's early writings, see Christopher Morse, *The Logic of Promise in Moltmann's Theology* (Philadelphia: Fortress Press, 1979).

22. Moltmann, *Theology of Hope*, 95–229.

23. Moltmann, *Theology of Hope*, 100.

24. Moltmann, *Theology of Hope*, 139–40, 203.

25. Moltmann, *Theology of Hope*, 227.

26. Jürgen Moltmann, "Theology as Eschatology," in *The Future of Hope; Theology as Eschatology*, ed. Frederick Herzog (New York: Herder and Herder, 1970), 10.

27. Ernst Bloch, *The Principle of Hope*, trans. Neville Plaice, Stephen Plaice, and Paul Knight, 3 vols. (Cambridge: MIT Press, 1986).

28. Jürgen Moltmann, *The Crucified God: The Cross of Christ as the Foundation and Criticism of Christian Theology*, trans. R. A. Wilson and John Bowden (Minneapolis: Fortress Press, 1993).

29. For a similar judgment regarding the significance of *The Crucified God* for the development of Moltmann's trinitarian theology, see Richard Bauckham, "Jürgen Moltmann," in *The Modern Theologians: An Introduction to Christian The-*

ology in the Twentieth Century, ed. David F. Ford, 2 vols. (New York: Blackwell, 1989), 1:296, 303.

30. Warren McWilliams, *The Passion of God: Divine Suffering in Contemporary Protestant Theology* (Macon, Ga.: Mercer University Press, 1985), 32.

31. Moltmann takes up the theme of the suffering God again in *Trinity and the Kingdom*, 20–60.

32. Moltmann, *Experiences in Theology*, 305.

33. Moltmann, *Crucified God*, 243.

34. Moltmann, *Crucified God*, 244.

35. Moltmann, *Crucified God*, 246.

36. For a succinct statement as to how Moltmann differs from process thought, see Laurence W. Wood, "From Barth's Trinitarian Christology to Moltmann's Trinitarian Pneumatology," *Asbury Theological Journal* 55/1 (Spring 2000): 60–61.

37. For a similar understanding of the significance of Moltmann's view, see Bauckham, *Moltmann*, 58.

38. Bauckham, *Moltmann*, 85.

39. Jürgen Moltmann, *The Church in the Power of the Spirit: A Contribution to Messianic Ecclesiology*, trans. Margaret Kohl (Minneapolis: Fortress Press, 1993). For a helpful summary of the contribution of this and several other lesser known writings to Moltmann's developing trinitarian theology, see Conyers, *God, Hope, and History*, 125–55.

40. Moltmann, *Trinity and the Kingdom*, 10–20.

41. Moltmann, *Trinity and the Kingdom*, 143–44.

42. Moltmann, *Trinity and the Kingdom*, 64.

43. This description stands in contrast to a similar yet quite different depiction found in Samuel M. Powell, *The Trinity in German Thought* (Cambridge: Cambridge University Press, 2000), 198.

44. Moltmann, *Trinity and the Kingdom*, 18–19, 144–48, 174–76.

45. Moltmann, *Trinity and the Kingdom*, 19.

46. Peters, *God as Trinity*, 103.

47. Moltmann, *Trinity and the Kingdom*, 161.

48. Moltmann, *Trinity and the Kingdom*, 161.

49. Moltmann, *Trinity and the Kingdom*, 90–96.

50. Moltmann, *Trinity and the Kingdom*, 126.

51. Jürgen Moltmann, *History and the Triune God: Contributions to Trinitarian Theology*, trans. John Bowden (New York: Crossroad, 1992), 86.

52. Moltmann, *History and the Triune God*, 86.

53. Moltmann, *Trinity and the Kingdom*, 175.

54. Moltmann, *Experiences in Theology*, 317.

55. For this description, see Bauckham, *Theology of Jürgen Moltmann*, 17.

56. Moltmann, *Church in the Power of the Spirit*, 60.

57. Moltmann, *Trinity and the Kingdom*, 19.

58. Bauckham, *Theology of Jürgen Moltmann*, 17.

59. For a similar characterization, as well as a critique of Moltmann's position, see John Thompson, *Modern Trinitarian Perspectives* (New York: Oxford University Press, 1994), 34.

60. Moltmann, *Crucified God*, 249.

61. Jürgen Moltmann, *God in Creation: A New Theology of Creation and the Spirit of God*, trans. Margaret Kohl (Minneapolis: Fortress Press, 1993), 98–103.

62. Moltmann, *God in Creation*, 86. See also Jürgen Moltmann, *The Coming of God: Christian Eschatology*, trans. Margaret Kohl (Minneapolis: Fortress Press, 1996), 297.

63. Moltmann, *Coming of God*, 281–82.

64. Moltmann, *Experiences in Theology*, 318–19.

65. Moltmann, *Experiences in Theology*, 323.

66. Moltmann, *Experiences in Theology*, 316, 322.

67. Moltmann, *God in Creation*, 91.

68. Müller-Fahrenholz, *Kingdom and the Power*, 148.

69. Moltmann, *Trinity and the Kingdom*, 17.

70. Moltmann, *Trinity and the Kingdom*, 17.

71. Moltmann, *God in Creation*, 279.

72. Moltmann, *Trinity and the Kingdom*, 221.

73. Hence Moltmann, *Coming of God*, 301.

74. Moltmann, *Coming of God*, 295, 307.

75. See Leonardo Boff, *Trinity and Society*, trans. Paul Burns (Maryknoll, N.Y.: Orbis, 1988).

76. Elizabeth A. Johnson, *She Who Is: The Mystery of God in Feminist Theological Discourse* (New York: Crossroad, 1992). For Johnson's appraisal of Moltmann, see *She Who Is*, 207–9.

77. Thomas F. Torrance, *The Christian Doctrine of God: One Being, Three Persons* (Edinburgh: T. & T. Clark, 1996), 247 n. 39.

78. Gerald O'Collins, *The Tripersonal God: Understanding and Interpreting the Trinity* (Mahwah, N.J.: Paulist, 1999), 158.

79. See, for example, George Hunsinger, "The Crucified God and the Political Theology of Violence," *Heythrop Journal* 14 (1973): 278.

80. Peters, *God as Trinity*, 109.

81. O'Collins, *Tripersonal God*, 158.

82. Thompson, *Modern Trinitarian Perspectives*, 51.

83. Bauckham, "Jürgen Moltmann," 304.

84. Powell, *Trinity in German Thought*, 201, 202.

85. Moltmann, *Trinity and the Kingdom*, 160.

86. Moltmann, *Trinity and the Kingdom,* 151.

87. Moltmann, *Trinity and the Kingdom,* 151–52. See also Moltmann, *Coming of God,* 325.

88. Jürgen Moltmann, "The Trinitarian History of God," *Theology* 78 (December 1975): 644. See also Moltmann, *Coming of God,* 330–32.

89. Moltmann, *Trinity and the Kingdom,* 152.

90. Moltmann, *Trinity and the Kingdom,* 153.

91. For a somewhat different characterization of Moltmann's point, see Powell, *Trinity in German Thought,* 199–200.

92. Moltmann, *Trinity and the Kingdom,* 161.

93. Moltmann, *Trinity and the Kingdom,* 160.

94. Powell, *Trinity in German Thought,* 201, 202.

95. For a concise defense of Moltmann against charges of Hegelianism, see Wood, "From Barth's Trinitarian Christology to Moltmann's Trinitarian Pneumatology," 60–61.

96. For a helpful engagement with Pannenberg's contribution, see *Beginning with the End: God, Science, and Wolfhart Pannenberg,* ed. Carol Rausch Albright and Joel Haugen (Chicago: Open Court, 1997). For a critical engagement with this volume, see Stanley J. Grenz, "'Scientific' Theology/'Theological' Science: Pannenberg and the Dialogue between Theology and Science," *Zygon* 34/1 (March 1999): 159–66.

97. Jacqui A. Stewart, *Reconstructing Science and Theology in Postmodernity: Pannenberg, Ethics and the Human Sciences* (Aldershot, U.K.: Ashgate, 2000), 2.

98. For a discussion of the theme of the unity of all reality in Pannenberg's theology and especially in his doctrine of creation, see Cornelius A. Buller, *The Unity of Nature and History in Pannenberg's Theology* (Lanham, Md.: Littlefield, 1996).

99. Mark William Worthing, *Foundations and Functions of Theology as a Universal Science: Theological Method and Apologetic Praxis in Wolfhart Pannenberg and Karl Rahner* (Frankfurt: Peter Lang, 1996), 3.

100. John B. Cobb Jr., "Foreword," in David P. Polk, *On the Way to God: An Exploration into the Theology of Wolfhart Pannenberg* (Lanham, Md.: University Press of America, 1989), xi–xii.

101. Ted Peters, "Wolfhart Pannenberg," in *A New Handbook of Christian Theologians,* ed. Donald W. Musser and Joseph L. Price (Nashville: Abingdon, 1996), 363.

102. For my lengthier overview of Pannenberg's project, see Stanley J. Grenz, *Reason for Hope: The Systematic Theology of Wolfhart Pannenberg* (New York: Oxford University Press, 1990).

103. For a helpful, albeit now dated, comparison of the ontologies of Barth and Pannenberg interpreted in the context of the idealist tradition, see Timothy Bradshaw, *Trinity and Ontology: A Comparative Study of the Theologies of Karl Barth and Wolfhart Pannenberg* (Edinburgh: Rutherford House, 1988).

104. Wolfhart Pannenberg, *Basic Questions in Theology*, trans. George H. Kehm, 2 vols. (Philadelphia: Fortress Press, 1971), 1:15.

105. E. Frank Tupper, *The Theology of Wolfhart Pannenberg* (Philadelphia: Westminster, 1973), 20.

106. Wolfhart Pannenberg, *Systematic Theology*, trans. Geoffrey W. Bromiley, 3 vols. (Grand Rapids: Eerdmans, 1991–1998). For a concise summary of this work, see Christoph Schwöbel, "Rational Theology in Trinitarian Perspective: Wolfhart Pannenberg's *Systematic Theology*," *Journal of Theological Studies* NS 47/2 (October 1996): 498–527.

107. Shults demurs from this widely held interpretation of Pannenberg's thought, suggesting instead that the basic principle is "the attempt to understand and explain all things *sub ratione Dei*." F. LeRon Shults, *The Postfoundationalist Task of Theology: Wolfhart Pannenberg and the New Theological Rationality* (Grand Rapids: Eerdmans, 1999), 92–110. Shults has thereby underscored an important dimension of Pannenberg's theological method. Yet, as Shults himself admits, Pannenberg does not himself use this phrase in his treatments of anthropology and history (p. 95). Moreover, the centrality of this concern to Pannenberg's understanding of the theological task does not indicate the manner in which he sets out to accomplish this goal, which is via a focus on history as the locus of the unfolding of the divine relationality.

108. See "The Crisis of the Scripture Principle," in Pannenberg, *Basic Questions in Theology*, 1:1–14.

109. For an engagement with Pannenberg's doctrine of scripture, see Frank Hasel, *Scripture in the Theologies of W. Pannenberg and D. G. Bloesch: An Investigation and Assessment of Its Origin, Nature, and Use* (Frankfurt: Peter Lang, 1996).

110. See, for example, Wolfhart Pannenberg, *Anthropology in Theological Perspective*, trans. Matthew J. O'Connell (Philadelphia: Westminster, 1985), 71–73.

111. See "On Historical and Theological Hermeneutic" and "What Is a Dogmatic Statement," in Pannenberg, *Basic Questions in Theology*, 1:137–210.

112. Pannenberg, *Basic Questions in Theology*, 2:1–27.

113. See Pannenberg, "Faith and Reason," *Basic Questions in Theology*, 2:52–53.

114. Pannenberg, *Systematic Theology*, 1:59–61. See also Pannenberg, *Basic Questions in Theology*, 2:1–27.

115. Wolfhart Pannenberg, *An Introduction to Systematic Theology* (Grand Rapids: Eerdmans, 1991), 8.

116. Wolfhart Pannenberg, *Theology and the Kingdom of God*, ed. Richard John Neuhaus (Philadelphia: Westminster, 1969), 55–56.

117. Pannenberg, *Theology and the Kingdom of God*, 55–56.

118. See the essay "What Is Truth?" in Pannenberg, *Basic Questions in Theology*, 2:1–27.

119. Pannenberg, *Introduction to Systematic Theology*, 12.

120. Pannenberg, *Systematic Theology*, 1:107–18.

121. See, for example, the conclusion reached in Pannenberg, *Systematic Theology*, 1:256–57.

122. Wolfhart Pannenberg, "God's Presence in History," *Christian Century* 98 (March 11, 1981): 263.

123. For a methodological preview of his doctrine of the Trinity, see Wolfhart Pannenberg, "The God of History," *Cumberland Seminarian* 19 (Winter/Spring 1981): 28–41. Pannenberg's doctrine of the Trinity is discussed in Roger E. Olson, "Trinity and Eschatology: The Historical Being of God in Jürgen Moltmann and Wolfhart Pannenberg," *Scottish Journal of Theology* 36 (1983): 213–27; and Roger E. Olson, "Wolfhart Pannenberg's Doctrine of the Trinity," *Scottish Journal of Theology* 43 (1990): 175–206.

124. Pannenberg, *Systematic Theology*, 1:299.

125. Pannenberg, *Systematic Theology*, 1:327.

126. Pannenberg, *Systematic Theology*, 1:298.

127. In volume one of his *Systematic Theology*, Pannenberg treats "The Trinitarian God" in chapter 5 and then "The Unity and Attributes of the Divine Essence" in chapter 6.

128. Pannenberg, *Systematic Theology*, 1:296.

129. Pannenberg, *Systematic Theology*, 1:304.

130. For his development of this concept in the context of Christology, see Wolfhart Pannenberg, *Jesus—God and Man*, trans. Lewis L. Wilkins and Duane A. Priebe, 2nd ed. (Philadelphia: Westminster, 1977), 181–83, 340.

131. Wolfhart Pannenberg, *Grundfragen systematischer Theologie: Gesammelte Aufsätze*, vol. 2 (Göttingen: Vandenhoeck & Ruprecht, 1980), 109.

132. Pannenberg, *Systematic Theology*, 1:308–19.

· 133. Olson, "Wolfhart Pannenberg's Doctrine of the Trinity," 199.

134. Pannenberg, *Theology and the Kingdom of God*, 55–56; Pannenberg, *Basic Questions in Theology*, 2:240–42.

135. Pannenberg, *Systematic Theology*, 1:311–13.

136. Peters, *God as Trinity*, 137.

137. Pannenberg, *Systematic Theology*, 1:313.

138. Pannenberg, *Systematic Theology*, 1:313.

139. Pannenberg, *Systematic Theology*, 1:315.

140. For this term, see Peters, *God as Trinity*, 138.

141. See Pannenberg, *Grundfragen systematischer Theologie*, 2:110.

142. Wolfhart Pannenberg, "Problems of a Trinitarian Doctrine of God," *Dialog* 26/4 (Fall 1987): 251.

143. Pannenberg, *Systematic Theology*, 1:317–19. See also Pannenberg, *Jesus—God and Man*, 183.

144. Pannenberg, *Systematic Theology*, 1:327. See also Pannenberg, *Grundfragen systematischer Theologie*, 2:112–28.

145. Pannenberg, *Systematic Theology*, 1:325.

146. Pannenberg, *Systematic Theology*, 1:334.

147. For this judgment, see Christoph Schwöbel, "Wolfhart Pannenberg," in *Modern Theologians*, 1:280.

148. Shults, *Postfoundationalist Task of Theology*, 92.

149. Tupper, *Theology of Wolfhart Pannenberg*, 19.

150. Peters, *God as Trinity*, 135.

151. Bradshaw, *Trinity and Ontology*, 343.

152. Moltmann, *Theology of Hope*, 79.

153. Schwöbel, "Wolfhart Pannenberg," 282.

154. Paul Molnar, "Some Problems with Pannenberg's Solution to Barth's 'Faith Subjectivism,'" *Scottish Journal of Theology* 48 (1995): 322.

155. J. A. Colombo, *An Essay on Theology and History: Studies in Pannenberg, Metz, and the Frankfurt School* (Atlanta: Scholars Press, 1990), 46.

156. Colombo, *An Essay on Theology and History*, 46.

157. Schwöbel, "Wolfhart Pannenberg," 286–87.

158. Paul S. Fiddes, *Participating in God: A Pastoral Doctrine of the Trinity* (Louisville: Westminster John Knox, 2000), 268.

159. Pannenberg, *Systematic Theology*, 1:319.

160. See, for example, Henri Blocher, "Immanence and Transcendence in Trinitarian Theology," in *The Trinity in a Pluralistic Age: Theological Essays on Culture and Religion*, ed. Kevin J. Vanhoozer (Grand Rapids: Eerdmans, 1997), 113–14.

161. Molnar, "Some Problems with Pannenberg's Solution," 318.

162. Tupper, *Theology of Wolfhart Pannenberg*, 19.

163. For an example of this pressing criticism, see Polk, *On the Way to God*, 290–91.

164. Thompson, *Modern Trinitarian Perspectives*, 36. For the related issue as to the implications of Pannenberg's position for the nature of eternity, see Bradshaw, *Trinitarian Ontology*, 339–42.

165. See, for example, Worthing, *Foundations and Functions of Theology as Universal Science*, 223–33.

166. See also Powell, *Trinity in German Thought*, 207–8.

167. Pannenberg, *Systematic Theology*, 1:328.

168. Powell, *Trinity in German Thought*, 238.

169. Pannenberg, *Systematic Theology*, 1:328–29; 2:392–93.

170. Pannenberg, *Systematic Theology*, 2:393.

171. For a similar judgment, see Bradshaw, *Trinitarian Ontology*, 343.

172. Pannenberg, *Systematic Theology*, 1:331.

173. Pannenberg, *Systematic Theology*, 1:331.

174. Pannenberg, *Systematic Theology*, 401–10.

175. For example, Pannenberg, *Introduction to Systematic Theology*, 48.

176. Pannenberg, *Introduction to Systematic Theology*, 49.

177. Pannenberg, *Introduction to Systematic Theology*, 49.

178. Examples include Robert W. Jenson, "The Triune God," in *Christian Dogmatics*, ed. Carl E. Braaten and Robert W. Jenson, 2 vols. (Philadelphia: Fortress Press, 1984), 1:79–191; Robert W. Jenson, "The Logic of the Doctrine of the Trinity," *Dialog* 26/4 (1987): 245–49; Robert W. Jenson, *Essays in Theology of Culture* (Grand Rapids: Eerdmans, 1995), 84–94, 190–201; Robert W. Jenson, "The Point of Trinitarian Theology," in *Trinitarian Theology Today*, ed. Christoph Schwöbel (Edinburgh: T. & T. Clark, 1995), 31–43.

179. Robert W. Jenson, *The Triune Identity: God according to the Gospel* (Philadelphia: Fortress Press, 1982).

180. Robert W. Jenson, *Systematic Theology*, 2 vols. (New York: Oxford University Press, 1997–1999).

181. Carl E. Braaten, "God and the Gospel: Pluralism and Apostasy in American Theology," *Lutheran Theological Journal* 25/1 (May 1991): 47.

182. R. Kendall Soulen, "YHWH the Triune God," *Modern Theology* 15/1 (January 1999): 35.

183. Mark C. Mattes, "An Analysis and Assessment of Robert Jenson's *Systematic Theology*," *Lutheran Quarterly* 14/4 (Winter 2000): 463.

184. See, for example, Robert W. Jenson, *The Knowledge of Things Hoped For: The Sense of Theological Discourse* (New York: Oxford University Press, 1969).

185. See, for example, Robert W. Jenson, *God after God: The God of the Past and the God of the Future Seen in the Work of Karl Barth* (Indianapolis: Bobbs-Merrill, 1968). See also Robert W. Jenson, "Proclamation without Metaphysics," *Dialog* 1 (Autumn 1962): 27; Robert W. Jenson, "A Call to Faithfulness," *Dialog* 30 (Winter 1991): 91.

186. For this description as well as a helpful sketch of the continuity of Jenson's thought, see David S. Yeago, "Catholicity, Nihilism, and the God of the Gospel: Reflections on the Theology of Robert W. Jenson," *Dialog* 31/1 (Winter 1992): 18–23.

187. Robert W. Jenson, "A Reply" [to Paul Molnar], *Scottish Journal of Theology* 52/1 (1999): 132.

188. Carl E. Braaten, "Robert William Jenson—A Personal Memoir," in *Trinity, Time, and Church: A Response to the Theology of Robert W. Jenson*, ed. Colin E. Gunton (Grand Rapids: Eerdmans, 2000), 4.

189. James J. Buckley, "Intimacy: The Character of Robert Jenson's Theology," in *Trinity, Time, and Church*, 12.

190. Jenson, *Essays in Theology of Culture*, 88.

191. Jenson, *Systematic Theology,* 1:108.

192. Jenson, *Triune Identity,* ix–x, 114.

193. Paul D. Molnar, "Robert W. Jenson's *Systematic Theology,* Volume 1: *The Triune God,*" *Scottish Journal of Theology* 52/1 (1999): 118. This essay appears in a slightly altered form in Molnar, *Divine Freedom,* 68–81.

194. Jenson, *Systematic Theology,* 1:46.

195. Jenson, *Systematic Theology,* 1:59.

196. For this judgment, see John R. Albright, "The Story of the Triune God: Time and Eternity in Robert Jenson's Theology," *Christian Scholar's Review* 26/1 (1996): 40 n. 12.

197. Buckley, "Intimacy," 14.

198. Jenson, *Essays in Theology of Culture,* 192. See also Jenson, "What Is the Point of Trinitarian Theology?" 38.

199. Jenson, "What Is the Point of Trinitarian Theology?" 37.

200. Jenson, *Systematic Theology,* 1:57.

201. Jenson, *Systematic Theology,* 1:57.

202. See, for example, Robert W. Jenson, "The Religious Power of Scripture," *Scottish Journal of Theology* 52/1 (1999): 89–105. For a sketch of Jenson's doctrine of scripture, see Scott A. Dunham, "From Modernism to Postmodernism: The Development of Biblical Authority in the Theology of Robert W. Jenson," in *Full of the Holy Spirit and Faith: Essays Presented in Honour of Dr. Allison A. Trites, Pastor, Teacher, Scholar,* ed. Scott A. Dunham (Wolfville, N.S.: Gaspereau, 1997), 89–106.

203. Jenson, *Systematic Theology,* 1:58.

204. Jenson, *Systematic Theology,* 1:42.

205. Jenson, *Systematic Theology,* 1:75.

206. For a recent essay that uses "spiritual exegesis" to uncover the presence of the Trinity in several biblical texts, see Robert W. Jenson, "The Bible and the Trinity," *Pro Ecclesia* 11/3 (Summer 2002): 329–39.

207. Jenson, *Systematic Theology,* 1:154–56.

208. Jenson, *Systematic Theology,* 1:153.

209. Jenson, *Systematic Theology,* 1:59.

210. Jenson, *Systematic Theology,* 1:59.

211. Jenson, *Systematic Theology,* 1:60.

212. Jenson, *Systematic Theology,* 1:126.

213. Jenson, *Systematic Theology,* 1:133.

214. Jenson, *Systematic Theology,* 1:125.

215. Jenson, *Systematic Theology,* 1:145.

216. Jenson, *Systematic Theology,* 1:137.

217. Jenson, *Systematic Theology,* 1:138.

218. Jenson, *Systematic Theology,* 1:66.

219. Jenson, *Systematic Theology*, 1:159.

220. Jenson, *Systematic Theology*, 1:66; cf. 1:159.

221. Jenson, *Systematic Theology*, 1:67.

222. Jenson, *Systematic Theology*, 1:157.

223. Jenson, *Systematic Theology*, 1:157.

224. Ted Peters, "Trinity Talk: Part II," *Dialog* 26/2 (Spring 1987): 135.

225. Philip Cary, review of Robert W. Jenson, *Systematic Theology*, volume 1: *The Triune God, Scottish Journal of Theology* 52/1 (1999): 135.

226. For appraisals of this aspect of Jenson's proposal, see Albright, "Story of the Triune God"; and Peters, *God as Trinity*, 128–34.

227. Jenson, *Essays in Theology of Culture*, 199.

228. Cary, review of Jenson, *Systematic Theology*, volume 1, 135.

229. Mary M. Solberg, "Concerning God's Proper Name: Some Comments on Robert Jenson's Discussion of 'The Masculinity of "Father,"'" *Dialog* 30/4 (Autumn 1991): 325. The specific target of Solberg's attack was Jenson's treatment of the doctrine of God in *Christian Dogmatics*, 87–96. For a summary of the spectrum of opinion on the question, see Ted Peters, "The Battle over Trinitarian Language," *Dialog* 30/1 (Winter 1991): 44–49.

230. See, for example, Molnar, "Robert W. Jenson's *Systematic Theology*, Volume 1," 125–27. See also Douglas Farrow, David Demson, and J. Augustine DiNoia, "Robert Jenson's *Systematic Theology:* Three Responses," *International Journal of Systematic Theology* 1/1 (March 1999): 93.

231. For this critique, see Christoph Schwöbel, "Once Again, Christ and Culture: Remarks on the Christological Bases of a Theology of Culture," in *Trinity, Time, and Church*, 124.

232. Susan K. Wood, "Robert Jenson's Ecclesiology from a Roman Catholic Perspective," in *Trinity, Time, and Church*, 182.

233. Wolfhart Pannenberg, "Eternity, Time, and the Triune God," in *Trinity, Time, and Church*, 70.

234. Pannenberg, "Eternity, Time, and the Triune God," 70.

235. See Farrow's section in Farrow, Demson, and DiNoia, "Robert Jenson's *Systematic Theology*," 90.

236. Jenson, *Triune Identity*, 139–41.

237. Buckley, "Intimacy," 12.

238. DiNoia's section in Farrow, Demson, and DiNoia, "Robert Jenson's *Systematic Theology*," 103.

239. Molnar, "Robert W. Jenson's *Systematic Theology*, Volume 1," 120, 121, 122, 124, 130.

240. Jeremy Ive, "Robert W. Jenson's Theology of History," in *Trinity, Time, and Church*, 157.

241. Cary, review of Jenson, *Systematic Theology*, volume 1, 134.

242. Robert W. Jenson, *America's Theologian: A Recommendation of Jonathan Edwards* (New York: Oxford University Press, 1988).

243. Jenson, *Systematic Theology*, 1:234.

244. Jenson, *Systematic Theology*, 1:226.

245. Jenson, *Systematic Theology*, 1:236.

246. See, for example, Jenson, *Systematic Theology*, 2:130.

247. Jenson, *Systematic Theology*, 2:369.

4. The Triumph of Relationality

1. Douglas Farrow, David Demson, and J. Augustine DiNoia, "Robert Jenson's *Systematic Theology*: Three Responses," *International Journal of Systematic Theology* 1/1 (March 1999): 94–95.

2. David S. Cunningham, *These Three Are One: The Practice of Trinitarian Theology* (Cambridge, Mass.: Blackwell, 1998), 26.

3. Marjorie Hewett Suchocki, "Introduction," in *Trinity in Process: A Relational Theology of God*, ed. Joseph A. Bracken and Marjorie Hewitt Suchocki (New York: Continuum, 1997), x–xi.

4. Joseph Bracken, *The Triune Symbol: Persons, Process and Community* (Lanham, Md.: University Press of America, 1985), 7.

5. Leonardo Boff, *Jesus Christ Liberator: A Critical Christology for Our Time*, trans. Patrick Hughes (Maryknoll, N.Y.: Orbis, 1978).

6. Leonardo Boff, *Trinity and Society*, trans. Paul Burns (Maryknoll, N.Y.: Orbis, 1988).

7. Leonardo Boff, *Holy Trinity, Perfect Community*, trans. Phillip Berryman (Maryknoll, N.Y.: Orbis, 2000).

8. Boff, *Trinity and Society*, v.

9. Boff, *Trinity and Society*, v.

10. See, for example, the accolades offered by the following reviewers: Tod Swanson, *Journal of Religion* 70 (1990): 651; John Bolt, *Christian Scholar's Review* 21 (1992): 326; and Robert T. Sears, *Theological Studies* 51 (1990): 143.

11. John W. Cooper, review of *Trinity and Society*, *Calvin Theological Journal* 26 (April 1991): 170.

12. Leonardo Boff, *Faith on the Edge: Religion and Marginalized Existence*, trans. Robert R. Barr (San Francisco: Harper & Row, 1989), 98.

13. Otto Maduro, "Leonardo Boff," in *A New Handbook of Christian Theologians*, ed. Donald W. Musser and Joseph L. Price (Nashville: Abingdon, 1996), 77.

14. Boff, *Trinity and Society*, 1.

15. Boff, *Trinity and Society*, 2.

16. Boff, *Trinity and Society*, 27.

17. Boff, *Trinity and Society*, 3.

18. Boff, *Trinity and Society,* 6–7.

19. Boff, *Trinity and Society,* 119.

20. Leonardo Boff, *Liberating Grace,* trans. John Drury (Maryknoll, N.Y.: Orbis, 1979), 211.

21. Boff, *Trinity and Society,* 13.

22. Boff, *Trinity and Society,* 13.

23. Boff, *Trinity and Society,* 13.

24. Boff, *Trinity and Society,* 11, 151.

25. Boff, *Trinity and Society,* 20–23.

26. Boff, *Trinity and Society,* 148–51.

27. Boff, *Trinity and Society,* 163.

28. Boff, *Trinity and Society,* 28–35.

29. Boff, *Liberating Grace,* 208.

30. Leonardo Boff, *Passion of Christ, Passion of the World: The Facts, Their Interpretation, and Their Meaning Yesterday and Today,* trans. Robert R. Barr (Maryknoll, N.Y.: Orbis, 1987), 24.

31. Delineating this heritage comprises chapters 3, 4, and 5 of his treatise on the Trinity. Boff, *Trinity and Society,* 43–122.

32. Boff, *Trinity and Society,* 123.

33. Boff, *Trinity and Society,* 97–99.

34. Boff, *Trinity and Society,* 119–20.

35. Boff, *Trinity and Society,* 123.

36. Boff, *Trinity and Society,* 5.

37. Boff, *Trinity and Society,* 5.

38. Boff, *Trinity and Society,* 136.

39. Boff, *Trinity and Society,* 172.

40. Boff, *Trinity and Society,* 173.

41. Paul S. Fiddes, *Participating in God: A Pastoral Doctrine of the Trinity* (Louisville: Westminster John Knox, 2001), 77.

42. This has been noted by several reviewers of Boff's work. See, for example, Shirley C. Guthrie, review of *Trinity and Society, Theology Today* 46 (1989): 205.

43. Boff, *Trinity and Society,* 146, 147.

44. Boff, *Trinity and Society,* 147.

45. Boff, *Trinity and Society,* 147.

46. Leonardo Boff, *When Theology Listens to the Poor,* trans. Robert R. Barr (San Francisco: Harper & Row, 1988), x.

47. Boff, *Trinity and Society,* 95.

48. Boff, *Trinity and Society,* 215.

49. Boff, *Trinity and Society,* 215.

50. Boff, *Trinity and Society,* 96.

51. Boff, *Trinity and Society,* 215.

52. Boff, *Trinity and Society*, 163.

53. Boff, *Trinity and Society*, 142.

54. For his more focused treatment of Mariology, see Leonardo Boff, *The Maternal Face of God: The Feminine and Its Religious Expressions*, trans. Robert R. Barr and John W. Diercksmeier (San Francisco: Harper & Row, 1987).

55. Boff, *Trinity and Society*, 210.

56. Boff, *Trinity and Society*, 210–11.

57. Boff, *Faith on the Edge*, 105.

58. Boff, *Trinity and Society*, 212.

59. Boff, *Trinity and Society*, 113.

60. Boff, *Trinity and Society*, 183.

61. Boff, *Trinity and Society*, 211.

62. Boff, *Trinity and Society*, 183.

63. See, for example, Boff, *Trinity and Society*, 95.

64. Although Boff uses this designation repeatedly in *Trinity and Society;* see especially 170–71.

65. Boff, *Trinity and Society*, 122.

66. Maduro, "Leonardo Boff," 78.

67. Maduro, "Leonardo Boff," 79.

68. See, for example, Todd H. Speidell, "A Trinitarian Ontology of Persons in Society," *Scottish Journal of Theology* 47/3 (1994): 289–91.

69. See, for example, Michael G. Lawler, "*Perichoresis:* New Theological Wine in an Old Theological Wineskin," *Horizons* 22/1 (1995): 49–66.

70. Boff, *Trinity and Society*, 211.

71. See, for example, Charles Talbert's review, *Perspectives in Religious Studies* 17 (Summer 1990): 192.

72. Boff, *Trinity and Society*, 139.

73. Guthrie, review of *Trinity and Society*, 206.

74. Cunningham, *These Three Are One*, 181.

75. Cunningham, *These Three Are One*, 52–53.

76. Cunningham, *These Three Are One*, 51.

77. Cunningham, *These Three Are One*, 51 n. 101.

78. Peters, *God as Trinity*, 114.

79. Peters, *God as Trinity*, 113.

80. Boff, *Trinity and Society*, 89.

81. For a helpful engagement with several criticisms of the social model, see John L. Gresham Jr., "The Social Model of the Trinity and Its Critics," *Scottish Journal of Theology* 46/3 (1993): 325–43.

82. For a helpful summary of this development, see Claude Welch, *In This Name: The Doctrine of the Trinity in Contemporary Theology* (New York: Scribner's, 1952), 29–34.

83. Wilfred Richmond, *Essay on Personality as a Philosophical Principle* (London: Edward Arnold, 1900), 17.

84. A. M. Fairbairn, *The Place of Christ in Modern Theology* (New York: Scribner's, 1893), 394.

85. J. R. Illingworth, *The Doctrine of the Trinity* (London: Macmillan, 1907), 142–43.

86. See, for example, George A. Gordon, *Ultimate Conceptions of the Faith* (Boston: Houghton & Mifflin, 1903), 374, 382–83.

87. Charles F. D'Arcy, "Trinity," in *Dictionary of Christ and the Gospels,* ed. J. Hastings, 2 vols. (New York: Scribner's, 1908), 2:762, 765–66. See also D'Arcy, *Idealism and Theology: A Study of Presuppositions* (London: Hodder and Stoughton, 1899), 212–14.

88. William Adams Brown, *Christian Theology in Outline* (New York: Scribner's, 1906), 154–55.

89. Nicholas Lash, *Believing Three Ways in One God: A Reading of the Apostles' Creed* (London: SCM, 1992), 32.

90. Lash, *Believing Three Ways in One God,* 31–32.

91. David A. Fisher, "Byzantine Ontology: Reflections on the Thought of John Zizioulas," *Diakonia* 29/1 (1996): 57.

92. Yves Congar, "Bulletin d'ecclésiologie," *Revue des sciences philosophiques et théologiques* 66 (1982): 88. For the English language translation of the quotation cited here, see Patricia Fox, *God as Communion: John Zizioulas, Elizabeth Johnson, and the Retrieval of the Symbol of the Triune God* (Collegeville, Minn.: Liturgical, 2001), 6.

93. John D. Zizioulas, *Being as Communion: Studies in Personhood and the Church,* Contemporary Greek Theologians 4 (Crestwood, N.Y.: St. Vladimir's Seminary Press, 1985).

94. For a short biographical summary of Zizioulas's academic career, see Fox, *God as Communion,* 3–10.

95. John D. Zizioulas, "Human Capacity and Human Incapacity: A Theological Exploration of Personhood," *Scottish Journal of Theology* 28/5 (October 1975): 401–48.

96. Two of these are especially noteworthy: Metropolitan John (Zizioulas) of Pergamon, "The Church as Communion," *St. Vladimir's Theological Quarterly* 38/1 (1994): 3–16; "Communion and Otherness," *St. Vladimir's Theological Quarterly* 38/4 (1994): 347–61.

97. The three most significant essays are: John D. Zizioulas, "On Being a Person: Towards an Ontology of Personhood," in *Persons, Divine and Human,* ed. Christoph Schwöbel and Colin E. Gunton (Edinburgh: T. & T. Clark, 1991), 33–46; "The Doctrine of God the Trinity Today: Suggestions for an Ecumenical Study," in *The Forgotten Trinity: A Selection of Papers Presented to the BCC Study*

Commission on Trinitarian Doctrine Today, ed. Alisdair I. C. Heron (London: British Council of Churches, 1991), 19-31; "The Doctrine of the Holy Trinity: The Significance of the Cappadocian Contribution," in *Trinitarian Theology Today: Essays on Divine Being and Act*, ed. Christoph Schwöbel (Edinburgh: T. & T. Clark, 1995), 44–60.

98. Zizioulas, *Being as Communion*, 24.

99. For this judgment, placed within the context of a helpful survey of recent Orthodox theology, see T. Allan Smith, "A Century of Eastern Orthodox Theology in the West," *Religious Studies and Theology* 16/1 (June 1997): 72.

100. Zizioulas, *Being as Communion*, 26; cf. 20.

101. Zizioulas, *Being as Communion*, 15.

102. Zizioulas, "Communion and Otherness," 352.

103. Zizioulas, "Doctrine of the Holy Trinity," 44, 45.

104. For a summary of his understanding of the Cappadocian contribution, see Zizioulas, "Doctrine of the Holy Trinity," 52–55.

105. Zizioulas, *Being as Communion*, 35.

106. Zizioulas, *Being as Communion*, 35.

107. Zizioulas, "Doctrine of the Holy Trinity," 45–47; *Being as Communion*, 27–39.

108. Zizioulas, *Being as Communion*, 88.

109. Zizioulas, "Doctrine of the Holy Trinity," 49.

110. Zizioulas, "Doctrine of the Holy Trinity," 50.

111. John G. F. Wilks, "The Trinitarian Ontology of John Zizioulas," *Vox Evangelica* 25 (1995): 76.

112. Zizioulas, *Being as Communion*, 16–17.

113. Nonna Verna Wilks, "Zizioulas on Communion and Otherness," *St. Vladimir's Theological Quarterly* 42/3-4 (1998): 274–75.

114. Zizioulas, "Communion and Otherness," 353.

115. Zizioulas, "Human Capacity," 408; cf. *Being as Communion*, 46–47.

116. Zizioulas, "Human Capacity," 409.

117. Zizioulas, "Human Capacity," 410.

118. Zizioulas, *Being as Communion*, 39; cf. 83–89.

119. For this interpretation, see C. Paul Schroeder, "Suffering towards Personhood: John Zizioulas and Fyodor Dostoevsky in Conversation on Freedom and the Human Person," *St. Vladimir's Theological Quarterly* 45/3 (2001): 245.

120. Zizioulas, "Doctrine of the Holy Trinity," 52.

121. Zizioulas, "Doctrine of the Holy Trinity," 52.

122. Zizioulas, *Being as Communion*, 39–44.

123. Paul M. Collins, *Trinitarian Theology, West and East: Karl Barth, the Cappadocian Fathers, and John Zizioulas* (Oxford: Oxford University Press, 2001), 179.

124. Zizioulas, *Being as Communion,* 40–41.

125. Zizioulas, "Doctrine of the Holy Trinity," 52.

126. Zizioulas, "On Being a Person," 38.

127. Zizioulas, "Human Capacity and Human Incapacity," 409.

128. Zizioulas, *Being as Communion,* 46.

129. Zizioulas, "On Being a Person," 46.

130. Zizioulas, "Doctrine of the Holy Trinity," 59.

131. Zizioulas, "Doctrine of God the Trinity Today," 19.

132. See, for example, Zizioulas, *Being as Communion,* 47–49.

133. Zizioulas, "Doctrine of the Holy Trinity," 52.

134. Fisher, "Byzantine Ontology," 63.

135. Wilks, "Trinitarian Ontology of John Zizioulas," 63.

136. Wilks, "Trinitarian Ontology of John Zizioulas," 84.

137. See, for example, Lawrence B. Potter, "On Keeping 'Persons' in the Trinity: A Linguistic Approach to Trinitarian Thought," *Theological Studies* 41 (1980): 530–48; William J. Hill, *The Three-Personed God: Trinity as a Mystery of Salvation* (Washington, D.C.: Catholic University of America Press, 1982), 255; Walter Kasper, *The God of Jesus Christ,* trans. Matthew J. O'Connell (New York: Crossroad, 1984), 154–56, 286–89; Christopher Kiesling, "On Relating to the Persons of the Trinity," *Theological Studies* 47 (1986): 599–616; Anthony Kelly, *The Trinity of Love: A Theology of the Christian God,* New Theology Series 4, ed. Peter C. Phan (Wilmington, Del.: Michael Glazier, 1989), 185–87.

138. Zizioulas, *Being as Communion,* 134.

139. Fox, *God as Communion,* 51.

140. Alan J. Torrance, *Persons in Communion: An Essay on Trinitarian Description and Human Participation* (Edinburgh: T. & T. Clark, 1996), 290.

141. Peters, *God as Trinity,* 71.

142. Lucian Turcescu, "'Person' Versus 'Individual,' and Other Modern Misreadings of Gregory of Nyssa," *Modern Theology* 18/4 (October 2002): 536.

143. Ralph Del Colle, "'Person' and 'Being' in John Zizioulas' Trinitarian Theology: Conversations with Thomas Torrance and Thomas Aquinas," *Scottish Journal of Theology* 54/1 (2001): 70.

144. Wilks, "Trinitarian Ontology of John Zizioulas," 77.

145. Wilks, "Trinitarian Ontology of John Zizioulas," 78, 82.

146. Torrance, *Persons in Communion,* 289.

147. Torrance, *Persons in Communion,* 292.

148. Torrance, *Persons in Communion,* 293.

149. Wilks, "Trinitarian Ontology of John Zizioulas," 79.

150. Peter J. Leithart, "'Framing' Sacramental Theology: Trinity and Symbol," *Westminster Theological Journal* 62/1 (Spring 2000): 12.

151. Harrison, "Trinitarian Ontology of John Zizioulas," 279.

152. Harrison, "Trinitarian Ontology of John Zizioulas," 279–80.

153. Fiddes, *Participating in God,* 79–80.

154. Fiddes, *Participating in God,* 79.

155. Colin Gunton, *The Promise of Trinitarian Theology* (Edinburgh: T. & T. Clark, 1991), 165–67.

156. Thomas F. Torrance, *The Trinitarian Faith* (Edinburgh: T. & T. Clark, 1988), 231.

157. Torrance, *Persons in Communion,* 293.

158. Torrance, *Persons in Communion,* 293.

159. Torrance, *Persons in Communion,* 294.

160. Gunton, *The Promise of Trinitarian Theology,* 53.

161. See Catherine Mowry LaCugna, review of *The Promise of Trinitarian Theology, Modern Theology* 9/1 (January 1993): 307.

162. Catherine M. LaCugna, "Philosophers and Theologians on the Trinity," *Modern Theology* 2/3 (April 1986): 174.

163. Catherine Mowry LaCugna, "God in Communion with Us: The Trinity," in *Freeing Theology: The Essentials of Theology in Feminist Perspective,* ed. Catherine Mowry LaCugna (San Francisco: HarperSanFrancisco, 1993), 90.

164. For a statement of her indebtedness to Zizioulas, see LaCugna, review of *The Promise of Trinitarian Theology,* 307.

165. Michael Downey, review of *God for Us, Modern Theology* 28/1 (Spring 1993): 73. For a similar conclusion using almost the exact terminology, see Peters, *God as Trinity,* 127.

166. Catherine Mowry LaCugna, *God for Us: The Trinity and Christian Life* (San Francisco: HarperSanFrancisco, 1991), 13, 209–24.

167. For a short memorial essay written by one of her doctoral students, see Nancy A. Dallavalle, "In Memory of Catherine Mowry LaCugna (1952–1997)," *Horizons* 24/2 (1997): 265–66.

168. Elizabeth Groope, "From *God for Us* to *Living in the Spirit of God, the Spirit of Christ*: Catherine LaCugna's Trinitarian Theology as a Foundation for Her Theology of the Holy Spirit," *Horizons* 27/2 (2000): 343.

169. Catherine Mowry LaCugna, "The Practical Trinity," *Christian Century* 109/22 (July 15–22, 1992): 679.

170. Patricia Fox, "The Trinity as Transforming Symbol: Exploring the Trinitarian Theology of Two Roman Catholic Feminist Theologians," *Pacifica* 7/3 (October 1994): 276.

171. For the use of this more postmodern way of characterizing *God for Us,* see Mark S. Medley, *Imago Trinitatis: Toward a Relational Understanding of Becoming Human* (Lanham, Md.: University Press of America, 2002), 27.

172. For a similar observation, see Gunton, *Promise of Trinitarian Theology,* xviii; Paul D. Molnar, *Divine Freedom and the Doctrine of the Immanent Trinity: In*

Dialogue with Karl Barth and Contemporary Theology (London: T. & T. Clark, 2002), 273.

173. For her discussion of this development, see LaCugna, *God for Us*, 21–44.

174. For a synopsis of the longer narrative, see Catherine Mowry LaCugna, "The Trinitarian Mystery of God," in *Systematic Theology: Roman Catholic Perspectives*, ed. Francis Schüssler Fiorenza and John P. Galvin, 2 vols. (Minneapolis: Fortress Press, 1991), 1:165–74.

175. LaCugna, *God for Us*, 25.

176. For a somewhat similar judgment, see Medley, *Imago Trinitatis*, 23, 27.

177. LaCugna, *God for Us*, 35.

178. LaCugna, *God for Us*, 37.

179. LaCugna, *God for Us*, 209–10.

180. LaCugna, *God for Us*, 37.

181. LaCugna, *God for Us*, 210.

182. See LaCugna, *God for Us*, 8, 196.

183. LaCugna, *God for Us*, 70.

184. LaCugna, "Trinitarian Mystery of God," 173.

185. Catherine Mowry LaCugna, "Author's Response," *Horizons* 20/1 (Spring 1993): 137.

186. Peters, *God as Trinity*, 124.

187. LaCugna, *God for Us*, 211.

188. LaCugna, "Practical Trinity," 681.

189. LaCugna, *God for Us*, 223.

190. LaCugna, *God for Us*, 211. LaCugna here cites Rahner, *The Trinity* (New York: Herder and Herder, 1970), 24.

191. C. M. LaCugna, "Re-conceiving the Trinity as the Mystery of Salvation," *Scottish Journal of Theology* 38/1 (1985): 3.

192. LaCugna, *God for Us*, 222.

193. LaCugna, *God for Us*, 223.

194. LaCugna, "Author's Response," 131.

195. LaCugna, *God for Us*, 223–24.

196. LaCugna, *God for Us*, 224.

197. LaCugna, *God for Us*, 228.

198. LaCugna, *God for Us*, 228.

199. Peters, *God as Trinity*, 71.

200. LaCugna, "Trinitarian Mystery of God," 177.

201. LaCugna, "Trinitarian Mystery of God," 178.

202. LaCugna, *God for Us*, 3.

203. LaCugna, "Philosophers and Theologians on the Trinity," 175.

204. LaCugna, *God for Us*, 1.

205. Peters, *God as Trinity*, 126.

206. For her critique of the Cappadocian acceptance of the divine impassibility, see LaCugna, *God for Us*, 300.

207. LaCugna, "God in Communion with Us," 86–87.

208. LaCugna, *God for Us*, 290.

209. LaCugna, *God for Us*, 292–93.

210. LaCugna, *God for Us*, 302–3.

211. LaCugna, *God for Us*, 390–91.

212. LaCugna, "God in Communion with Us," 91.

213. Medley, *Imago Trinitatis*, 40.

214. LaCugna, *God for Us*, 228.

215. LaCugna, *God for Us*, 250.

216. Downey, review of *God for Us*, 73.

217. Downey, review of *God for Us*, 75.

218. Peters, *God as Trinity*, 71.

219. Peters, *God as Trinity*, 122.

220. Roderick T. Leupp, review of *God for Us*, *Journal of the Evangelical Theological Society* 39/2 (June 1996): 318.

221. Roger Haight, "Review Symposium: *God for Us*," *Horizons* 20/1 (Spring 1993): 129.

222. Molnar, *Divine Freedom*, 4.

223. Ben Leslie, "Does God Have a Life?: Barth and LaCugna on the Immanent Trinity," *Perspectives in Religious Studies* 24/4 (Winter 1997): 385 n. 32.

224. Cunningham, *These Three Are One*, 37.

225. Duncan Reid, "The Defeat of Trinitarian Theology: An Alternative View," *Pacifica* 9/3 (October 1996): 289–300.

226. Robrecht Michiels, review of *God for Us*, *Louvain Studies* 20/1 (Spring 1995): 91.

227. See, for example, J. A. DiNoia, review of *God for Us*, *Modern Theology* 9/2 (April 1993): 215–16. See also Medley, *Imitatio Trinitatis*, 55–56.

228. See, for example, Paul Molnar, "Toward a Contemporary Doctrine of the Immanent Trinity: Karl Barth and the Present Discussion," *Scottish Journal of Theology* 49 (1996): 320. See also Earl Miller, "The Science of Theology: A Review of Catherine LaCugna's *God for Us*," *Gregorianum* 75 (1994): 331–35; Robert Davis Hughes III, review of *God for Us*, *Sewanee Theological Review* 35 (1992): 306.

229. Peters, *God as Trinity*, 143.

230. Peters, *God as Trinity*, 128.

231. Leslie, "Does God Have a Life?" 384.

232. Peters, *God as Trinity*, 123.

233. Barbara A. Finan, "Review Symposium: *God for Us*," *Horizons* 20/1 (1993): 134–35.

234. Molnar, "Toward a Contemporary Doctrine of the Trinity," 314–15; Colin Gunton, review of *God for Us, Scottish Journal of Theology* 47 (1994): 136–37. See also Molnar, *Divine Freedom*, 128.

235. DiNoia, review of *God for Us*, 216.

236. Michael Hryniuk, "Triumph or Defeat of the Trinity? An Eastern Christian Response to Catherine LaCugna," *Diakonia* 33/1 (2000): 25–26.

237. Reid, "Defeat of Trinitarian Theology," 292.

238. Groope, "From *God for Us* to *Living in the Spirit of God*," 344 n. 2.

239. Leslie, "Does God Have a Life?" 394.

240. Medley, *Imago Trinitatis*, 36.

241. LaCugna, *God for Us*, 229.

242. LaCugna, "Re-conceiving the Trinity," 10–11.

243. LaCugna, "Re-conceiving the Trinity," 14.

244. Leslie, "Does God Have a Life?" 396.

245. Joseph A. Bracken, review of *God for Us, Theological Studies* 53/3 (September 1992): 559.

246. Groope, "From *God for Us* to *Living in the Spirit of God*," 344.

247. One such exception is Kelly's attempt to begin with the church's experience as the people of God who have an identity in God as Love. Kelly, *Trinity of Love*, 3.

5. The Return of the Immanent Trinity

1. David Cunningham, "Participation as a Trinitarian Virtue: Challenging the Current 'Relational' Consensus," *Toronto Journal of Theology* 14/1 (1998): 10.

2. Philip Clayton, "Pluralism, Idealism, Romanticism: Untapped Resources for a Trinity in Process," in *Trinity in Process: A Relational Theology of God*, ed. Joseph A. Bracken and Marjorie Hewitt Suchocki (New York: Continuum, 1997), 123.

3. Philip Clayton, "Pluralism, Idealism, Romanticism," 139.

4. John G. F. Wilks, "The Trinitarian Ontology of John Zizioulas," *Vox Evangelica* 25 (1995): 63.

5. Elizabeth A. Johnson, *She Who Is: The Mystery of God in Feminist Theological Discourse* (New York: Crossroad, 1992).

6. See Elizabeth A. Johnson, *Consider Jesus: Waves of Renewal in Christology* (New York: Crossroad, 1990).

7. See, for example, Elizabeth A. Johnson, "God Poured Out: Recovering the Holy Spirit," *Praying* 60 (May–June 1994): 4–8, 41.

8. See, for example, Elizabeth A. Johnson, "The Marian Tradition and the Reality of Women," *Horizons* 12/1 (1985): 116–35; "The Symbolic Character of Theological Statements about Mary," *Journal of Ecumenical Studies* 22/2 (Spring 1985): 312–35; "Mary and the Female Face of God," *Theological Studies* 50 (1989): 500–526; "Saints and Mary," in *Systematic Theology: Roman Catholic Perspectives*,

ed. Francis Schüssler Fiorenza and John P. Galvin, 2 vols. (Minneapolis: Fortress Press, 1991), 2:143–76; "Mary as Mediatrix," in *The One Mediator, the Saints and Mary*, ed. H. Anderson (Minneapolis: Augsburg, 1992), 311–26.

9. For an example of her engagement with this topic, see Elizabeth A. Johnson, *Women, Earth, and Creator Spirit* (New York: Paulist, 1993). See also Elizabeth A. Johnson, "Heaven and Earth Are Filled with Your Glory: Atheism and Ecological Spirituality," in *Finding God in All Things: Essays in Honor of Michael J. Buckley, S.J.*, ed. Michael J. Himes and Stephen J. Pope (New York: Crossroad, 1996), 84–101.

10. For an example of her engagement with this concern, see Elizabeth A. Johnson, *Friends of God and Prophets: A Feminist Theological Reading of the Communion of Saints* (New York: Continuum, 1999). See also *The Church Women Want: Catholic Women in Dialogue*, ed. Elizabeth A. Johnson (New York: Herder and Herder, 2002).

11. Johnson, *Consider Jesus*, ix.

12. Johnson, *She Who Is*, 3–4.

13. Mary McClintock Fulkerson, review of *She Who Is, Religious Studies Review* 21 (January 1995): 21.

14. For this designation see Elizabeth A. Johnson, "The Incomprehensibility of God and the Image of God Male and Female," *Theological Studies* 45/3 (September 1984): 454.

15. Johnson, *She Who Is*, 5.

16. Johnson, *She Who Is*, 5.

17. See, for example, Johnson, *She Who Is*, 4, 5, 38.

18. Patricia Fox, *God as Communion: John Zizioulas, Elizabeth Johnson, and the Retrieval of the Symbol of the Triune God* (Collegeville, Minn.: Liturgical, 2001), 102.

19. Johnson, *She Who Is*, 4.

20. Johnson, *She Who Is*, 14.

21. Johnson, *She Who Is*, 8.

22. Johnson, *She Who Is*, 12.

23. Elizabeth A. Johnson, author's response to the *She Who Is* Review Symposium, *Horizons* 20/2 (Fall 1993): 339.

24. Johnson, *She Who Is*, 12.

25. For a similar interpretation, see Mary C. Boys, "Wisdom Restored," *Cross Currents* 43 (Summer 1993): 269.

26. Johnson, *She Who Is*, 8.

27. Harold Wells, review of *She Who Is, Touchstone* 13/1 (January 1995): 37.

28. Johnson, *She Who Is*, 13.

29. Johnson, *She Who Is*, 15.

30. Johnson, *She Who Is*, 212.

31. Johnson, "Incomprehensibility of God," 443.

32. Johnson, *She Who Is*, 39.

33. Cynthia L. Rigby, review of *She Who Is*, *Insights* 111 (Spring 1996): 44.

34. Johnson, *She Who Is*, 13.

35. Johnson, *She Who Is*, 61.

36. Elaine Farmer, review of *She Who Is*, *St. Mark's Review* 159 (Spring 1994): 37.

37. Johnson, *She Who Is*, 17.

38. Johnson, *She Who Is*, 122.

39. Johnson, *She Who Is*, 62.

40. Johnson, *She Who Is*, 71.

41. Charles Marsh, "Two Models of Trinitarian Theology: A Way Beyond the Impasse?" *Perspectives in Religious Studies* 21 (Spring 1994): 61.

42. Johnson, *She Who Is*, 76.

43. Johnson, *She Who Is*, 82, 103.

44. Harold Wells, review of *She Who Is*, *Touchstone* 13/1 (January 1995): 38–39.

45. Johnson, *She Who Is*, 83.

46. Johnson, *She Who Is*, 86–87.

47. Elizabeth A. Johnson, "Wisdom Was Made Flesh and Pitched Her Tent among Us," in *Reconstructing the Christ Symbol: Essays in Feminist Christology*, ed. Maryanne Stevens (Mahwah, N.J.: Paulist, 1993), 99.

48. Johnson, *She Who Is*, 86.

49. This point is noted in Mary R. D'Angelo, "Review Symposium: *She Who Is*," *Horizons* 20/2 (Fall 1993): 332.

50. Johnson, *She Who Is*, 105.

51. For a synopsis of Johnson's analogical method, see Gloria L. Schaab, "Of Models and Metaphors: The Trinitarian Proposals of Sallie McFague and Elizabeth A. Johnson," *Theoforum* 33/2 (2002): 230.

52. Johnson, "Incomprehensibility of God," 452. See also *She Who Is*, 113–17.

53. Johnson, "Incomprehensibility of God," 444.

54. Johnson, *She Who Is*, 120.

55. See her explicit characterization of her theological method, Johnson, *She Who Is*, 123.

56. D'Angelo, "Review Symposium: *She Who Is*," 333.

57. Johnson, *She Who Is*, 122.

58. Johnson, *She Who Is*, 124–25.

59. For her appraisal of the situation, see Johnson, *Women, Earth, and Creator Spirit*, 129–31, 294 nn. 14–17.

60. Johnson, *She Who Is*, 122–23.

61. Johnson, author's response to the Review Symposium, 340.

62. For a sympathetic engagement with Johnson's Christology set forth in the context of feminist thought, see Shannon Schrein, *Quilting and Braiding: The Feminist Christologies of Sallie McFague and Elizabeth A. Johnson in Conversation* (Collegeville, Minn.: Liturgical, 1998).

63. Johnson, "Wisdom Was Made Flesh," 103.

64. Johnson, *She Who Is*, 152.

65. For a questioning of this claim by a sympathetic reader, see Mary Aquin O'Neill, review of *She Who Is*, *Religious Studies Review* 21 (January 1995): 21.

66. Johnson, *She Who Is*, 156.

67. Johnson, *She Who Is*, 162.

68. Johnson, *She Who Is*, 155.

69. Elizabeth A. Johnson, "Redeeming the Name of Christ," in *Freeing Theology: The Essentials of Theology in Feminist Perspective*, ed. Catherine Mowry LaCugna (San Francisco: HarperSanFrancisco, 1993), 131.

70. Johnson, "Redeeming the Name of Christ," 131–34.

71. Johnson, *She Who Is*, 175.

72. Johnson, *She Who Is*, 183.

73. Johnson, *She Who Is*, 191

74. Johnson, *She Who Is*, 192, 222.

75. Johnson, *She Who Is*, 192.

76. Johnson, *She Who Is*, 217.

77. Johnson, *She Who Is*, 218.

78. Johnson, *She Who Is*, 221.

79. Johnson, *She Who Is*, 222.

80. Johnson, *She Who Is*, 231.

81. Mary Aquin O'Neill, review of *She Who Is*, *Religious Studies Review* 21 (January 1995): 21.

82. Mary E. Hines, "Review Symposium: *She Who Is*," 324.

83. Hines, "Review Symposium: *She Who Is*," 331.

84. O'Neill, review of *She Who Is*, 19.

85. Mary C. Boys, "Wisdom Restored," *Cross Currents* 43 (Summer 1993): 269.

86. Susan K. Roll, review of *She Who Is*, *Louvain Studies* 18 (Winter 1993): 374.

87. Janice Daurio, review of *She Who Is*, *New Oxford Review* 61/28 (April 1994): 28.

88. Jane Williams, review of *She Who Is*, *Modern Theology* 10 (January 1994): 114.

89. Elaine Farmer, review of *She Who Is*, *St. Mark's Review* 159 (Spring 1994): 38.

90. O'Neill, review of *She Who Is*, 19.

91. Fulkerson, review of *She Who Is,* 22.

92. Charles Marsh, "Two Models of Trinitarian Theology: A Way beyond the Impasse?" *Perspectives in Religious Studies* 21 (Spring 1994): 62.

93. John Carmody, "Review Symposium: *She Who Is,*" 336.

94. Fulkerson, review of *She Who Is,* 23.

95. Paul D. Molnar, *Divine Freedom and the Doctrine of the Immanent Trinity: In Dialogue with Karl Barth and Contemporary Theology* (London: T. & T. Clark, 2002), 9.

96. Molnar, *Divine Freedom and the Doctrine of the Immanent Trinity,* 10.

97. Mary Aquin O'Neill, review of *She Who Is, Religious Studies Review* 21 (January 1995): 21.

98. Charles Marsh, "Two Models of Trinitarian Theology: A Way beyond the Impasse?" *Perspectives in Religious Studies* 21 (Spring 1994): 63.

99. Johnson, *She Who Is,* 236.

100. Carmody, "Review Symposium: *She Who Is,*" 337.

101. For an example of this judgment, see Fox, *God as Communion,* 136.

102. Johnson, *She Who Is,* 200.

103. Johnson, *She Who Is,* 201.

104. Hines, "Review Symposium: *She Who Is,*" 329.

105. Johnson, *She Who Is,* 198.

106. Johnson, *She Who Is,* 204–5.

107. Molnar, *Divine Freedom and the Doctrine of the Immanent Trinity,* 23–24.

108. In one of the most caustic reviews of *She Who Is* published to date, Janice Daurio writes, "The theological world sorely needs articulate feminist theologians who know how to write, who can get past all the rhetoric, and, above all, who can provide satisfying solutions to important theological problems raised by women. But this book does not do that." She then advises, "This is not the book feminists who are faithfully Christian have been waiting for." Janice Daurio, review of *She Who Is, New Oxford Review* 61/28 (April 1994): 28.

109. Farmer, review of *She Who Is,* 38.

110. The secondary literature reveals three ways of designating the surname of the Swiss theologian: "von Balthasar" (for example, Kevin Mongrain, *The Systematic Thought of Hans Urs von Balthasar: An Irenaean Retrieval* [New York: Crossroad, 2002]), "Urs von Balthasar" (for example, John Macquarrie, "Foreword," in Hans Urs von Balthasar, *The God Question and Modern Man,* trans. Hilda Gräf [New York: Seabury, 1967]), and "Balthasar" (for example, Edward T. Oakes, *Pattern of Redemption: The Theology of Hans Urs von Balthasar* [New York: Continuum, 1994]). In this book, I use this third, simpler designation.

111. Oakes, *Pattern of Redemption,* 1.

112. David Tracy, *Blessed Rage for Order: The New Pluralism in Theology* (New York: Seabury, 1975), 79.

113. Oakes, *Pattern of Redemption*, 3–4.

114. Mongrain, *Systematic Thought of Hans Urs von Balthasar*, 11–12.

115. Mongrain, *Systematic Thought of Hans Urs von Balthasar*, 14.

116. For these figures, see Peter Henrici, "Hans Urs von Balthasar: A Sketch of His Life," in *Hans Urs von Balthasar: His Life and Work*, ed. David Schindler (San Francisco: Ignatius, 1991), 31.

117. Henrici, "Hans Urs von Balthasar: A Sketch of His Life," 7. For a similar statement, see Raymond Gawronski, *Word and Silence: Hans Urs von Balthasar and the Spiritual Encounter between East and West* (Grand Rapids: Eerdmans, 1995), xiii.

118. Aidan Nichols, "Introduction," in Hans Urs von Balthasar, *Mysterium Paschale: The Mystery of Easter*, trans. Aidan Nichols, 2nd ed. (Grand Rapids: Eerdmans, 1993), 3.

119. Donald J. Keefe, "A Methodological Critique of von Balthasar's Theological Aesthetics," *Communio* 5/1 (Spring 1978): 23.

120. Hans Urs von Balthasar, *My Work: In Retrospect* (San Francisco: Ignatius, 1993), 95.

121. Balthasar, *My Work*, 95.

122. Balthasar, *My Work*, 58.

123. Jakob Laubach, "Hans Urs von Balthasar," in *Theologians of Our Time*, ed. Leonhard Reinisch (Notre Dame, Ind.: University of Notre Dame Press, 1964), 146–47.

124. John Riches, "Hans Urs von Balthasar," in *The Modern Theologians: An Introduction to Christian Theology in the Twentieth Century*, ed. David F. Ford, 2 vols. (New York: Blackwell, 1989), 1:243.

125. Hans Urs von Balthasar, *The Glory of the Lord: A Theological Aesthetics*, ed. Joseph Fessio and John Riches, 7 vols. (San Francisco: Ignatius, 1982–1989).

126. Hans Urs von Balthasar, *Theo-Drama: Theological Dramatic Theory*, trans. Graham Harrison, 5 vols. (San Francisco: Ignatius, 1988–1998).

127. Hans Urs von Balthasar, *Theo-Logic: Theological Logical Theory*, trans. Adrian J. Walker, 3 vols. (San Francisco: Ignatius, 2000–). Currently, only volume 1 is available in English.

128. Hans Urs von Balthasar, *Theo-Drama: Theological Dramatic Theory*, vol. 5: *The Last Act*, trans. Graham Harrison (San Francisco: Ignatius, 1998), 13, 57.

129. Balthasar declares, "Alas, we see God's glory only in reflections and riddles, even unto the greatest paradox, the abandonment of Christ by God on the cross." Hans Urs von Balthasar, "Theology and Aesthetic," *Communio* 8 (Spring 1981): 67.

130. See Hans Urs von Balthasar, *The Theology of Karl Barth*, trans. Edward T. Oakes (San Francisco: Ignatius, 1992), 309–11; *Truth Is Symphonic*, trans. Graham Harrison (San Francisco: Ignatius, 1987), 53–55; *Love Alone: The Way of*

Revelation, trans. Alexander Dru (New York: Herder and Herder, 1969), 25, 58–59.

131. For a discussion of this characterization of his theological approach, see Keefe, "Methodological Critique," 23–27.

132. Werner Löser, "Trinitätstheologie Heute: Ansätze und Entwürfe," in *Trinität: Actuelle Perspektiven der Theologie,* ed. Wilhelm Breuning (Freiberg: Herder, 1984), 22.

133. Hans Urs von Balthasar, *The Glory of the Lord: A Theological Aesthetics,* vol. 1: *Seeing the Form,* ed. Joseph Fessio and John Riches, trans. Erasmo Leiva-Merikakis (San Francisco: Ignatius, 1982), 11.

134. Karl Rahner, "Hans Urs von Balthasar," *Civitas* 20 (1964/65): 602.

135. Louis Roberts, *The Theological Aesthetics of Hans Urs von Balthasar* (Washington, D.C.: Catholic University of America Press, 1987), 189.

136. Bede McGregor and Thomas Norris, "Introduction," in *The Beauty of Christ: An Introduction to the Theology of Hans Urs von Balthasar,* ed. Bede McGregor and Thomas Norris (Edinburgh: T. & T. Clark, 1994), 3.

137. Balthasar, *My Work,* 80.

138. Hans Urs von Balthasar, *Theo-Drama: Theological Dramatic Theory,* vol. 4: *The Action,* trans. Graham Harrison (San Francisco: Ignatius, 1994), 12.

139. Hans Urs von Balthasar, *Theo-Logic,* vol. 1: *Truth of the World,* trans. Adrian J. Walker (San Francisco: Ignatius, 2000), 20.

140. For a helpful discussion of this point, see John O'Donnell, *Hans Urs von Balthasar* (London: Continuum, 1991), 6.

141. Riches, "Hans Urs von Balthasar," in *Modern Theologians,* 1:240.

142. For a helpful explanation of this medieval concept, see Scott MacDonald, "Transcendentals," in the *Cambridge Dictionary of Philosophy,* ed. Robert Audi, 2nd ed. (Cambridge: Cambridge University Press, 1999), 926–27.

143. Gerard O'Hanlon, "Theological Dramatics," in *Beauty of Christ,* 93.

144. Keefe, "Methodological Critique," 26.

145. Hans Urs von Balthasar, "Christian Prayer," *Communio* 5/1 (Spring 1978): 20.

146. Thomas Norris, "The Symphonic Unity of His Theology: An Overview," in *Beauty of Christ,* 251.

147. For the observation that this thesis is the theme of the first two volumes of the *Theo-Logic,* see John R. Sachs, review of *Theologik 1: Wahrheit der Welt; 2: Wahrheit Gottes, Theological Studies* 49 (June 1988): 356.

148. Balthasar, *Theo-Logic,* 1:8.

149. Balthasar, *Theo-Logic,* 1:8.

150. Balthasar, *Glory of the Lord,* 1:18.

151. Balthasar, *Glory of the Lord,* 1:38–39.

152. Roberts, *The Theological Aesthetics of Hans Urs von Balthasar,* 122.

153. Balthasar, *Theo-Logic*, 1:8.

154. Balthasar, *My Work*, 80.

155. Hans Urs von Balthasar, *The Glory of the Lord: A Theological Aesthetics*, vol. 7: *Theology: The New Covenant*, ed. John Riches, trans. Brian McNeil (San Francisco: Ignatius, 1989), 28.

156. For a similar characterization, see Brendan Leahy, "Theological Aesthetics," in *Beauty of Christ*, 29.

157. Roberts, *Theological Aesthetics of Hans Urs von Balthasar*, 3–4, 25.

158. Balthasar, *My Work*, 80.

159. Balthasar, *My Work*, 96–97.

160. See, for example, Hans Urs von Balthasar, *Theo-Drama: Theological Dramatic Theory*, vol. 1: *Prolegomena*, trans. Graham Harrison (San Francisco: Ignatius, 1988), 18–19.

161. Oakes, *Pattern of Redemption*, 230.

162. Balthasar, *My Work*, 99.

163. Balthasar, *Theo-Drama*, 5:72.

164. Balthasar, *Theo-Drama*, 4:325.

165. Balthasar, *Theo-Drama*, 4:324.

166. Aidan Nichols, *No Bloodless Myth: A Guide through Balthasar's Dramatics* (Washington, D.C.: Catholic University of America Press, 2000), 166. See also Balthasar, *Theo-Drama*, 4:319–23.

167. Balthasar, *Mysterium Paschale*, 210.

168. For the most complete treatment of this theme, see Balthasar, *Mysterium Paschale*, 148–88.

169. Balthasar, *Love Alone*, 57.

170. John Riches and Ben Quash, "Hans Urs von Balthasar," in *The Modern Theologians: An Introduction to Christian Theology in the Twentieth Century*, ed. David Ford, rev. ed. (Cambridge, Mass.: Blackwell, 1997), 143.

171. Hans Urs von Balthasar, *Elucidations*, trans. John Riches (San Francisco: Ignatius, 1975), 82.

172. Balthasar, *Theo-Logic*, 1:7.

173. Balthasar, *My Work*, 118.

174. Balthasar, *My Work*, 118.

175. Hans Urs von Balthasar, *Prayer*, trans. Graham Harrison (San Francisco: Ignatius, 1986), 193.

176. Balthasar, *My Work*, 60.

177. Laubach, "Hans Urs von Balthasar," 155.

178. Gerard Reedy, "The Christology of Hans Urs von Balthasar," *Thought* 45 (1970): 409.

179. Norris, "Symphonic Unity of His Theology," 216.

180. Norris, "Symphonic Unity of His Theology," 250.

181. Balthasar, *Glory of the Lord*, 1:53.

182. Balthasar, *Theology of Karl Barth*, 383–84.

183. For this judgment, see Nichols, "Introduction," in Balthasar, *Mysterium Paschale*, 4.

184. John Thompson, "Barth and Balthasar: An Ecumenical Dialogue," in *Beauty of Christ*, 186.

185. Balthasar, *Theo-Drama*, 3:507–8.

186. Hans Urs von Balthasar, *Theologik*, vol. 2: *Wahrheit Gottes* (Einsiedeln: Johannes Verlag, 1985), 117. Translation mine.

187. See Hans Urs von Balthasar, *Theo-Drama: Theological Dramatic Theory*, vol. 3: *The Dramatis Personae: The Person in Christ*, trans. Graham Harrison (San Francisco: Ignatius, 1992), 510–11.

188. Balthasar, *Glory of the Lord*, 1:182.

189. For his critique of Barth's characterization of the Roman Catholic perspective, see Balthasar, *Theology of Karl Barth*, 382. For a helpful appraisal of Balthasar's response to the Protestant attack on the analogy of being, see Steffen Lösel, "Love Divine, All Loves Excelling: Balthasar's Negative Theology of Revelation," *Journal of Religion* 82/4 (October 2002): 586–616.

190. For this judgment, see Angelo Scola, *Hans Urs von Balthasar: A Theological Style* (Grand Rapids: Eerdmans, 1995), 30–31.

191. Balthasar, *Glory of the Lord*, 1:432.

192. Balthasar, *Glory of the Lord*, 1:195.

193. Aidan Nichols, *The Word Has Been Abroad: A Guide through Balthasar's Aesthetics* (Washington, D.C.: Catholic University of America Press, 1998), xix.

194. Przywara's influence on Balthasar is described in Francesca Murphy, "The Sound of the *Analogia Entis*: An Essay on the Ontological Difference as the Context of von Balthasar's Theology," *New Blackfriars* 74/11 (November 1993): 516–19.

195. Nichols, *Word Has Been Abroad*, xiii–xiv.

196. Balthasar, *Theologik*, 2:33.

197. Balthasar, *Theo-Drama*, 4:320.

198. See, for example, Balthasar, *Theo-Drama*, 3:508.

199. See, for example, Balthasar, *Theo-Drama*, 3:508.

200. For a helpful discussion of this aspect of his thought, see Gerard O'Hanlon, *The Immutability of God in the Theology of Hans Urs von Balthasar* (Cambridge: Cambridge University Press, 1990), 112.

201. David S. Cunningham, *These Three Are One: The Practice of Trinitarian Theology* (Cambridge, Mass.: Blackwell, 1998), 79.

202. Balthasar, *Theo-Drama*, 5:67.

203. Balthasar, *Mysterium Paschale*, viii.

204. Balthasar, *Mysterium Paschale*, viii.

205. For a similar characterization, see Norris, "Symphonic Unity of His Theology," 221.

206. For a similar conclusion, see Mongrain, *Systematic Thought of Hans Urs von Balthasar*, 213.

207. For this connection, see Aidan Nichols, *Say It Is Pentecost: A Guide through Balthasar's Logic* (Washington, D.C.: Catholic University of America Press, 2001), 92. See also Gawronski, *Word and Silence*, 96.

208. For a similar observation, see Graham Ward, "Kenosis: Death, Discourse and Resurrection," in Lucy Gardner, David Moss, Ben Quash, and Graham Ward, *Balthasar at the End of Modernity* (Edinburgh: T. & T. Clark, 1999), 45.

209. Balthasar, *Theo-Drama*, 4:323–24.

210. Balthasar, *Theo-Drama*, 4:323–24.

211. Balthasar, *Mysterium Paschale*, 30.

212. Balthasar, *Theo-Drama*, 4:362.

213. Balthasar, *Theo-Drama*, 5:514. For a helpful engagement with this aspect of Balthasar's thought, see Thomas G. Dalzell, "The Enrichment of God in Balthasar's Trinitarian Eschatology," *Irish Theological Quarterly* 66/1 (Spring 2001): 3–18.

214. For a similar understanding of Balthasar's position, see Aristotle Papanikolou, "Person, *Kenosis* and Abuse: Hans Urs von Balthasar and Feminist Theologies in Conversation," *Modern Theology* 19/1 (January 2003): 42.

215. Balthasar, *Theo-Drama*, 3:287.

216. Balthasar, *Theo-Drama*, 4:371–72.

217. O'Hanlon, *Immutability of God*, 114.

218. Balthasar, *Theo-Drama*, 4:78.

219. Balthasar, *Theo-Drama*, 5:521.

220. Henri de Lubac, "A Witness of Christ in the Church," *Communio* 2/3 (Fall 1975): 230.

221. Louis Roberts, *The Theological Aesthetics of Hans Urs von Balthasar* (Washington, D.C.: Catholic University of America Press, 1987), 1.

222. Donald J. Keefe, review of *The Glory of the Lord*, vol. 1, *Thomist* 48 (1984): 663.

223. Norris, "Symphonic Unity of His Theology," 225.

224. Oakes, *Pattern of Redemption*, 305.

225. Mark A. McIntosh, review of *Theo-Drama: Theological Dramatic Theory*, vol. 4, *The Action, Journal of Religion* 76 (July 1996): 491.

226. Karl Rahner, "Hans Urs von Balthasar," *Civitas* 20 (1965): 604.

227. Gerard Reedy, "The Christology of Hans Urs von Balthasar," *Thought* 45 (1970): 419.

228. One promising, albeit minimal, engagement is that of David Coffey, who bemoans that after acknowledging a distinction between the "procession"

model and the "return" model of the Trinity, Balthasar lapses back into the former, thereby showing "no appreciation of the fact that the new order (or taxis) in the economic Trinity calls for a new trinitarian model." David Coffey, *Deus Trinitas: The Doctrine of the Triune God* (New York: Oxford University Press, 1999), 144.

229. See, for example, Cunningham, *These Three Are One*, 78–79, 294–95; Paul S. Fiddes, *Participating in God: A Pastoral Doctrine of the Trinity* (Louisville: Westminster John Knox), 184–85.

230. Lucy Gardner, David Moss, Ben Quash, and Graham Ward, "Preface and Acknowledgements," in Gardner et al., *Balthasar at the End of Modernity*, vii.

231. Mary Gerhart, review of *The Glory of the Lord*, vols. 4–7, and *Theo-Drama*, vols. 1–2, *Religion and Literature* 25 (Spring 1993): 74.

232. Molnar, *Divine Freedom and the Doctrine of the Immanent Trinity*, x.

233. Alan Torrance, *Persons in Communion: An Essay on Trinitarian Description and Human Participation* (Edinburgh: T. & T. Clark, 1996).

234. This shift is noted by Tony Gray, review of *Persons in Communion*, *Themelios* 22/2 (January 1997): 71; George M. Newlands, review of *The Christian Doctrine of God* and *Persons in Communion*, *Scottish Journal of Religious Studies* 17/2 (Autumn 1996): 161.

235. See, for example, Molnar's explicit acknowledgment of his dependence on Torrance in Molnar, *Doctrine of the Immanent Trinity*, 1, 317.

236. Thomas F. Torrance, *The Christian Doctrine of God: One Being, Three Persons* (Edinburgh: T. & T. Clark, 1996).

237. George M. Newlands, review of *The Christian Doctrine of God* and *Persons in Communion*, *Scottish Journal of Religious Studies* 17/2 (Autumn 1996): 159.

238. "Preface," *Reformed Review* 38/1 (1984): 47.

239. See Thomas F. Torrance, *Calvin's Doctrine of Man* (London: Lutterworth, 1952); *The Hermeneutics of John Calvin* (Edinburgh: Scottish Academic Press, 1988); *Karl Barth: An Introduction to His Early Theology: 1910–1913* (London: SCM, 1962); *Karl Barth: Biblical and Evangelical Theologian* (Edinburgh: T. & T. Clark, 1990).

240. Daniel W. Hardy, "Thomas F. Torrance," in *Modern Theologians* (1st ed.), 74.

241. See, for example, the comment of the editors who commend Torrance above all for "making a unique contribution to the important question of the relation of theological science to the natural sciences." "Preface," *Reformed Review* 38/1 (1984): 47.

242. Hence Thomas F. Torrance, *The Christian Frame of Mind* (Edinburgh: Handsel, 1985); *Christian Theology and Scientific Culture* (New York: Oxford University Press, 1981); *Divine and Contingent Order* (New York: Oxford University Press, 1981); *God and Rationality* (New York: Oxford University Press, 1971); *The Ground and Grammar of Theology* (Charlottesville: University Press of Virginia,

1980); *Reality and Evangelical Theology* (Philadelphia: Westminster, 1982); *Reality and Scientific Theology* (Edinburgh: Scottish Academic Press, 1985); *Space, Time, and Incarnation* (New York: Oxford University Press, 1969); *Space, Time, and Resurrection* (Grand Rapids: Eerdmans, 1976); *Theological Science* (New York: Oxford University Press, 1969); *Transformation and Convergence in the Frame of Knowledge: Explorations in the Interrelations of Scientific and Theological Enterprise* (Grand Rapids: Eerdmans, 1982).

243. Alister E. McGrath, *Thomas F. Torrance: An Intellectual Biography* (Edinburgh: T. & T. Clark, 1999), xi.

244. Ted Peters, "Theology and Natural Science," in *Modern Theologians* (2nd ed.), 657. It should be added that Peters knows full well that Torrance did not follow Barth in thinking that theology could be isolated methodologically from other disciplines. See Peters, "Theology and Natural Science," 659.

245. I. John Hesselink, "A Pilgrimage in the School of Christ—An Interview with T. F. Torrance," *Reformed Review* 38/1 (Autumn 1984): 59.

246. See Torrance, *Reality and Scientific Theology*.

247. Torrance, *Reality and Scientific Theology*, x. For his rendition of the perspective of the patristic theologians, see Torrance, *Christian Frame of Mind*, 5–15.

248. For this point, see Elmer M. Colyer, "Thomas F. Torrance," in *A New Handbook of Christian Theologians*, ed. Donald W. Musser and Joseph L. Price (Nashville: Abingdon, 1996), 462. Torrance voices this basic theme repeatedly. See, for example, Torrance, *Reality and Scientific Theology*, x; *Space, Time, and Incarnation*, ix; *Reality and Evangelical Theology*, 47.

249. Hardy, "Thomas F. Torrance," 71.

250. See, for example, Torrance, *Christian Frame of Mind*, 3.

251. Torrance, *Reality and Scientific Theology*, x.

252. Torrance, *Reality and Scientific Theology*, 67.

253. See, for example, Torrance, *Space, Time, and Incarnation*, viii.

254. Torrance, *Divine and Contingent Order*, 1.

255. Torrance, *God and Rationality*, 11.

256. Torrance, *Divine and Contingent Order*, 1.

257. Torrance, *Ground and Grammar of Theology*, 45.

258. Torrance, *Reality and Evangelical Theology*, 27. See also Torrance, *Divine and Contingent Order*, 1–2.

259. Torrance, *Reality and Scientific Theology*, xiii.

260. For this judgment, see Hardy, "Thomas F. Torrance," 76.

261. Torrance, *Theological Science*, xi.

262. Note his statement to this effect regarding theology in Torrance, *Theological Science*, 281.

263. For a use of the idea in a somewhat different context, see Torrance, *Theological Science*, 128.

264. Hardy, "Thomas F. Torrance," 77.

265. Already in his postgraduate studies with Karl Barth, he showed a keen interest in patristic thought, especially Athanasius. See Thomas F. Torrance, *The Doctrine of Grace in the Apostolic Fathers* (Edinburgh: Oliver and Boyd, 1948). This volume formed his dissertation under the direction of Karl Barth. See also Thomas F. Torrance, *Theology in Reconciliation: Essays towards Evangelical and Catholic Unity in East and West* (Grand Rapids: Eerdmans, 1975). This interest is evident as well in his important engagement with the theology of the Niceno-Constantinopolitan Creed: Thomas F. Torrance, *The Trinitarian Faith: The Evangelical Theology of the Ancient Catholic Church* (Edinburgh: T. & T. Clark, 1988).

266. Torrance, *Trinitarian Faith*, 52.

267. Note the appearance of this designation as a chapter title in Torrance, *Reality and Scientific Theology*, 64.

268. For this judgment, see Peters, "Theology and Natural Science," 657.

269. Thomas F. Torrance, *Theology in Reconstruction* (Grand Rapids: Eerdmans, 1965), 9.

270. Torrance, *Theology in Reconstruction*, 9.

271. See, for example, Torrance's use of this term in Hesselink, "A Pilgrimage in the School of Christ," 58, 59. For the former term, see Torrance, *Theological Science*, viii–ix.

272. For a helpful explication of Torrance's perspective, see Daniel W. Hardy, "Theology through Philosophy," in *Modern Theologians*, 2nd ed., 258.

273. Torrance, *Transformation and Convergence*, 194.

274. Torrance, *Transformation and Convergence*, 196.

275. Torrance, *Christian Theology and Scientific Culture*, 8.

276. Torrance, *Theological Science*, 132.

277. Torrance, *Reality and Scientific Theology*, 162.

278. Torrance, *Christian Theology and Scientific Culture*, 38.

279. Robert J. Palma, "Thomas F. Torrance's Reformed Theology," *Reformed Review* 38/1 (Autumn 1984): 13.

280. Torrance, *Ground and Grammar of Theology*, 158–59.

281. R. D. Kernoha, "Tom Torrance: The Man and the Reputation," *Life and Work* 32/5 (May 1976): 14.

282. Torrance, *Theology in Reconstruction*, 10; cf. 128.

283. Colyer, "Thomas F. Torrance," 463.

284. Torrance, *Trinitarian Faith*, 52.

285. Torrance, *Trinitarian Faith*, 52.

286. Torrance, *Trinitarian Faith*, 3.

287. Torrance, *Trinitarian Faith*, 54–55.

288. Torrance, *Trinitarian Faith*, 67.

289. Alister E. McGrath, *Thomas F. Torrance: An Intellectual Biography* (Edinburgh: T. & T. Clark, 1999), 158.

290. Tapio Luoma, *Incarnation and Physics: Natural Science in the Theology of Thomas F. Torrance* (Oxford: Oxford University Press, 2002), 7.

291. Torrance, *Christian Doctrine of God*, 81.

292. Torrance, *Ground and Grammar of Theology*, 160.

293. Torrance, *Reality and Evangelical Theology*, 42–43.

294. In his engagement with this aspect of Torrance's trinitarian theology, Nozomu Miyahira notes that the idea, although perhaps new to Westerners, is quite familiar to thinkers from Asian nations. Review of *The Christian Doctrine of the Trinity*, *Themelios* 22/2 (January 1997): 70.

295. Torrance, *Reality and Evangelical Theology*, 43.

296. Torrance, *Christian Doctrine of God*, 157.

297. Torrance, *Christian Doctrine of God*, 140–41.

298. Brad J. Kallenberg, review of *The Christian Doctrine of God*, *Andrews University Seminary Studies* 36 (Autumn 1998): 314.

299. Torrance, *Christian Doctrine of God*, 220.

300. Torrance, *Reality and Evangelical Theology*, 43; cf. 139–40.

301. Luoma, *Incarnation and Physics*, 8.

302. Gerald Bray, review of *The Christian Doctrine of God*, *Churchman* 111/4 (1997): 378.

303. Peter Somers Heslam, review of *The Christian Doctrine of God*, *Theology* 100 (March–April 1997): 128.

304. Elmer Colyer, review of *The Christian Doctrine of God*, *Scottish Journal of Theology* 50/3 (1997): 389.

305. Colyer, review of *The Christian Doctrine of God*, 390.

306. Torrance, *Christian Doctrine of God*, 112. See also Torrance, *Ground and Grammar of Theology*, 147.

307. Colyer, "Thomas F. Torrance," 464.

308. See, for example, Torrance, *Christian Doctrine of God*, 133. For an extended comparison of Rahner and Torrance regarding the connection between the immanent Trinity and the economic Trinity, see Molnar, *Doctrine of the Immanent Trinity*, 167–96.

309. Torrance, *Reality and Scientific Theology*, 136.

310. Torrance, *Ground and Grammar of Theology*, 168–71.

311. For the fullest explication of this, see Torrance, *Christian Doctrine of God*, 88–107.

312. Elmer M. Colyer, *How to Read T. F. Torrance: Understanding His Trinitarian and Scientific Theology* (Downers Grove, Ill.: InterVarsity, 2001), 292.

313. Torrance, *Reality and Evangelical Theology*, 36. For his fuller explication of this theological movement, see Torrance, *Ground and Grammar of Theology*, 156–59.

314. Torrance, *Reality and Evangelical Theology*, 21.

315. Torrance, *Reality and Evangelical Theology*, 23–24.

316. Torrance, *Reality and Evangelical Theology*, 23–24.

317. John Douglas Morrison, *Knowledge of the Self-Revealing God in the Thought of Thomas Forsyth Torrance* (New York: Peter Lang, 1997), 208.

318. Torrance, *Ground and Grammar of Theology*, 158.

319. Torrance, *Reality and Scientific Theology*, 182.

320. For a synopsis of the critical response to Torrance's success in devising a scientific theology, see Morrison, *Knowledge of the Self-Revealing God*, 241–84.

321. See, for example, Peters, "Theology and Natural Science," 659.

322. See, for example, Kallenberg, review of *The Christian Doctrine of God*, 315. See also the series of essays published in *The Promise of Trinitarian Theology: Theologians in Dialogue with T. F. Torrance*, ed. Elmer M. Colyer (Lanham, Md.: Rowman and Littlefield, 2001).

323. For a detailed response to Colin Gunton's critique of this aspect of Torrance's proposal, see Molnar, *Divine Freedom and the Doctrine of the Immanent Trinity*, 317–30.

324. Kallenberg, review of *The Christian Doctrine of God*, 316.

325. Torrance, *Theological Science*, 55.

326. Torrance, *God and Rationality*, 190.

Epilogue: The Trinitarian Story in Retrospect

1. Leonard Hodgson, *The Doctrine of the Trinity* (New York: Scribner's, 1944), 15.

2. Ted Peters, *God as Trinity: Relationality and Temporality in Divine Life* (Louisville: Westminster John Knox, 1993), 26.

3. Peters, *God as Trinity*, 26.

4. James J. Buckley and David S. Yeago, "Introduction," in *Knowing the Triune God: The Work of the Spirit in the Practices of the Church*, ed. James J. Buckley and David S. Yeago (Grand Rapids: Eerdmans, 2001), 1.

5. Robert Wilken, "The Resurrection of Jesus and the Doctrine of the Trinity," *Word and World* 2/1 (Winter 1982): 28.

Index